Human Rights in Turmoil

International Studies in Human Rights

Volume 92

The titles in this series are listed at the end of this volume.

# Human Rights in Turmoil

## Facing Threats, Consolidating Achievements

by

**Stéphanie Lagoutte, Hans-Otto Sano and Peter Scharff Smith**

MARTINUS NIJHOFF PUBLISHERS
LEIDEN • BOSTON

A C.I.P. record for this book is available from the Library of Congress.

*Printed on acid-free paper.*

ISBN 10 90 04 15432 9
ISBN 13 978 90 04 15432 2



http://www.brill.nl



Typeset by jules guldenmund layout & text, The Hague.

Printed and bound in The Netherlands.

# Table of Contents

# Introduction

## Human Rights in Turmoil: Facing Threats, Consolidating Achievements

*Stéphanie Lagoutte, Hans-Otto Sano and Peter Scharff Smith*

### 1 Introduction

Are human rights gaining or losing ground? This question has become relevant after two decades of unprecedented progress in developing human rights standards and institutions. The political climate during the Cold War created many obstacles, but the fall of the Berlin Wall in 1989 and its aftermath during the following decade created a sense of promise and progress among human rights scholars and actors. The World Conference on Human Rights in 1993 was instrumental in creating this atmosphere. The international community reaffirmed its commitment to human rights by signing a programme of action which made the promotion and the protection of all human rights a priority objective of the United Nations.[1]

So why, a little more than a decade later, do we find ourselves wondering whether human rights are currently losing rather than gaining ground? What has happened to the promise and commitment of the international community?

A number of alarming signs are clouding the sky. Actions, statements and initiatives questioning the legitimacy and validity of human rights, or even threatening their very existence, have become a regular part of current political realities, even in states traditionally dedicated to the rule of law. This would have been inconceivable ten or twenty years ago. The world's leading democracy, the United States of America, for example, seems to be disregarding commonly accepted standards of international law and human rights in its current war on terrorism. The leader of the free world is, paradoxically, also the globally leading incarcerator, the number one prison nation in the world. Human rights are also challenged in several other old democracies, apparently irrespective of the political orientations – right or left – of their governments. One important observer, for example, has addressed what she calls "the retreat from human rights" in the United Kingdom

1 World Conference on Human Rights, The Vienna Declaration and Programme of Action, 1993.

*S. Lagoutte, H-O. Sano and P. Scharff Smith (eds.),* Human Rights in Turmoil, *pp. 1-6.*
 *ISBN 90 04 15432 9.*

under the Labour government.[2] In Denmark, ambiguous political views on human rights also seem to have taken root during the last decade, originally motivated by a toughening of attitudes towards immigration, but now reinforced by security and nationalist agendas. This political ambiguity is supported by some Danish scholars who are attacking the working methods and legitimacy of the European Court of Human Rights.[3] One cannot help asking whether human rights are simply not "in" at the moment.

At the same time, there are tendencies and developments which tell the precisely opposite story of the undeniable consolidation of human rights. Human rights conventions and case law are now influencing legal norms and practice everywhere in the world. In Europe, for example, the European Court of Human Rights has become a fundamental institution for the protection of human rights and today has a significant impact on domestic parliaments and courts in 46 countries. The language of human rights has become mainstream in legal circles and among NGOs and government organisations all over the world. Globally, democratisation is continuing to spread, a fact which increases the demand for the institutionalisation of rights regimes and for enhancing the scope of treaty body monitoring across the world.

So where does this leave us? One thing seems certain: human rights are in turmoil and are being challenged, weakened and strengthened in important and groundbreaking ways in different areas and settings. This calls for closer analysis.

## 2 Human Rights under Attack

In the past five years, human rights have increasingly come under attack as a result of efforts to combat terrorism. The situation is worrying and it is pertinent to consider how democratic nations can make decisions that seem to disregard some of the most basic human rights, little more than half a century after the horrors of the Second World War. The practices adopted in the detention facility at Guantanamo Bay are well known, but other reports have appeared of detainee abuse in American detention facilities in Iraq and Afghanistan.[4]

---

2 Helena Kennedy, *Just Law: The Changing Face of Justice – and Why it Matters to Us All*, Vintage 2005, p. 301.

3 There was a long debate in the Danish press during spring 2005 initiated by an article by Professor Mads Bryde Andersen (*Berlingske Tidende*, 13 March 2005), and followed by a number of replies from various Danish scholars.

4 This is covered in an extensive literature. See, for example, report on the "Situation of detainees at Guantánamo Bay", Economic and Social Council, E/CN.4/2006/120, 15 February 2006. Concerning Iraq, see, for example, "Article 15-6 Investigation of the 800th Military Police Brigade" – the so-called "Taguba report". Available at http://www.humanrightsfirst.org/us_law/800th_MP_Brigade_MASTER14_Mar_04-dc.pdf (assessed 14 December 2005). See also Leonard Rubenstein et al. "Coercive US Interrogation Policies. A Challenge to Medical Ethics" in *Journal of American Medical Association*, Vol. 294, Sept. 28. 2005.

Even though similar examples still seem unthinkable in Europe, it is an open question to what extent the European states have been involved, directly or indirectly, in handing over citizens to foreign intelligence services for special interrogation in secret places of detention. In a similar vein, legislation permitting increased surveillance, enforced secret police powers, special measures for police detention of suspected terrorists etc. is a common source of worry for human rights experts and organisations in Europe.

These tendencies indicate a faltering in the support for human rights respect among dominant Western powers. This is all the more worrying because such trends may serve to undermine the legitimacy of human rights in a situation where threats and challenges are still imminent in parts of the world where human rights violations prevail and where secular and religious values are contentious.

Generally, apart from the problems created by the war against terrorism, three current challenges to human rights consolidation can be identified, namely

- The threats of nationalist and particularistic values.
- The threats emanating from insufficient response to poverty and its consequences.
- The threats posed by weak performance of the human rights enforcement system.

The threat from trends in the development of nationalist and particularistic values is expressed in religious as well as in neo-nationalist discourses. From within the Western world restricted access to citizenship and the tightening of asylum legislation are examples of nationalist agendas. Outside the West, religious fanatics, and governments sometimes focus on religious issues in a manner which makes it difficult to imagine that consensus can be established on future human rights reinforcement.

These trends are exacerbated by inadequate responses to poverty, corruption, and migration flows. It can be argued that actors pushing to strengthen human rights should do more to bridge human rights and development agendas, but the reality is also that the political will in developing as well as developed states to deal with these issues has been undermined by security, nationalist and ideological agendas.

Finally, while the UN system is under reform, weak or inadequate systems of human rights monitoring, dispute handling and enforcement are still prevailing. There is a need for a heightened focus on implementation, but this has been the call for the last 10 years. It remains therefore to be seen whether the current UN reform process will spur enhanced effectiveness in terms of treaty body monitoring and in increased state respect for the conventions ratified.

## 3 Consolidation of Human Rights Law and Practices

It is also true, however, that the human rights regime gained significant ground during the last part of the twentieth century. Human rights have become accepted norms in international politics and regulation, being endorsed by states, international institutions and civil societies. This is expressed in the ratification of conventions[5] and the impressive growth of national human rights institutions,[6] as well in the establishment of the International Criminal Court and in the special tribunals that have been set up to deal with human rights abuses in Yugoslavia, Rwanda and Sierra Leone. Human rights are also increasingly used by local civil societies in the South and in the East in actions focused on awareness-raising, advocacy and litigation.

It can be argued that human rights have become a reference point and sometimes even an integral part of the agenda in international organisations dealing with justice, peace and development. It has become a global public good in interstate relations and local and global interactions. A very important indicator of the growing significance of human rights in international politics is the integration of human rights concerns in the Resolutions of the UN Security Council justifying humanitarian interventions, such as those in Somalia, northern Iraq, Rwanda and East Timor in the 1990s. Human rights values, principles and efforts for their protection, as well as the remedies and guarantees of their implementation, have therefore become aspects of many spheres and vital policy areas, not least in religious affairs. In that sense, it seems fair to conclude that the human rights agenda carries much more legal, social and political weight today than it did even a few decades ago.

The consolidation of the legal protection of human rights that has taken place during the past fifty years also has positive consequences in the turbulent situation the world is in currently. The reaction of the human rights community has been strong and immediate against attacks on human rights in the name of the fight against terrorism. In the same way, an enormous amount of work is being done, in the United Nations and the Council of Europe, for example, aimed at consolidating the human rights protection mechanisms that are being jeopardized by political attacks. The tremendous demand for human rights protection is evident in the growing number of cases that the European Court of Human Rights is having to deal with, a success story that has burdened the Court way beyond its capacity.

## 4 Human Rights in Turmoil

The following chapters show that human rights concerns are at the centre of many vigorous debates and discussions today: debates about secularism and religious norms, about minimum social standards and social security, about the future regulation of citizenship, about prison reform and the use of less inhumane methods

---

5 Between 1985 and 2006, 70 states ratified the International Covenant on Economic, Social and Cultural Rights, meaning that 152 states have ratified the Covenant, and 77 states ratified the International Covenant on Civil and Political Rights, yielding a total of 155 states having ratified. See www.ohchr.org.

6 In 1990 there were eight national human rights institutions, while in 2005 there were 60 certified institutions, plus 40 waiting to be certified according to the Paris Principles (see Morten Kjærum's chapter in this book).

of detention. Still, mainstreaming human rights is not the same as ensuring their effective protection. Weak implementation is exacerbated by the current threats and turmoil surrounding human rights.

First, systemic problems have appeared and need to be solved. Weaknesses in supra-national human rights protection systems have emerged over the last twenty years. It is now clear that human rights mechanisms are not well adapted to the handling of the ever-increasing number of complaints or to the effective implementation of human rights. These tendencies are discussed in the chapters by Morten Kjærum and Stéphanie Lagoutte, who deal respectively with the reform of the UN system and the challenges facing the now overburdened European Court of Human Rights.

Secondly, at the political level human rights are gaining as well as losing ground. A significant change during the 1990s was the evolving practices of the UN Security Council concerning humanitarian intervention where concern for gross human rights violations prevailed over considerations of sovereignty. Of crucial importance also is the institutionalisation of human rights regulation in bilateral and multilateral donor policies, in peace-keeping operations, and not least in civil society advocacy. However, attacks on the consolidation of human rights resulting from the Western war against terrorism also demonstrate that the alliance of old democracies which contributed to the promotion of human rights during the previous decade is far from stable at the present time. These trends are discussed in the chapters by Helle Malmvig, Hans-Otto Sano, John Cerone and Peter Vedel Kessing.

Thirdly, the question of the adequacy, legitimacy and scope of human rights is still a live one. Sten Schaumburg-Müller's chapter deals in a general manner with the uneasy balance between individual rights and the interests of communities. Similarly, Eva Maria Lassen's chapter relates to the dialogue between human rights and religion. Hatla Thelle's chapter on social rights shows that while these are considered legitimate in principle, the legitimacy of their actual and concrete implementation is much more uncertain in practice. The problem of establishing effective human rights protection is also evident in the context of prisons, as is shown in Peter Scharff Smith's historical analysis concerning the use of solitary confinement in Denmark and the US. Finally, Eva Ersbøll shows that the European Convention on Human Rights may acquire increased importance in nationality matters in the future, despite the fact that the Convention does not refer explicitly to a right to nationality.

Looking back over his career, Professor Isi Foighel, formerly a judge at the European Court of Human Rights, refers in the final contribution to a "judicial revolution" concerning the tremendous advances that have taken place in the field of human rights. Perhaps the turmoil we are witnessing today is a natural reaction to this revolution. As human rights become more significant and continue to strengthen the individual, they also become more disturbing for certain interest groups and states. The extension of human rights is being challenged by contrary ideological and political responses, and states are reacting to the limitations that human rights impose on their actions, especially where they feel threatened and vulnerable. Today, there can be no doubt that we are experiencing a time of tension, in which a forceful response from the human rights community is essential.

# 1. The UN Reform Process in an Implementation Perspective

*Morten Kjærum*

## 1 The UN Reform Process

In 2005, the UN Secretary-General launched a major reform process of the UN in the report "In larger freedom: towards development, security and human rights for all."[1] In his report, the Secretary-General states:

> While purposes should be firm and principles constant, practice and organisation need to move with the times. If the United Nations is to be a useful instrument for its Member States and for the world's peoples...it must be fully adapted to the needs and circumstances of the twenty-first century.

This is an ambitious and necessary task, which includes the creation of new mechanisms like the "Peace Building Commission", as well as reforming older institutions such as the Security Council and the Human Rights Commission. The basic structure of the UN was modelled in the aftermath of the Second World War and structured according to a Cold War political rationale. In the twenty-first century, the world is dramatically different: the Cold War is over, many new democracies want to play an active part in global policy-making, old alliances have vanished and new ones emerged, issues such as religion have regained a strong momentum, and human rights have become integrated into global politics.

In her 2005 Plan of Action,[2] an addendum to the report *In larger freedom*, the UN High Commissioner for Human Rights specifies the needs for reforms in the human rights machinery. In the introduction she writes:

> The historic legacy of the United Nations human rights programme is found especially in the wide-ranging body of human rights norms and standards produced in the past 60 years. But putting new resources and capacities to work in response to the human

1 A/59/2005.
2 A/59/2005/add.3.

*S. Lagoutte, H-O. Sano and P. Scharff Smith (eds.),* Human Rights in Turmoil, *pp. 7-23.*
 *ISBN 90 04 15432 9.*

> rights problems posed today by poverty, discrimination, conflict, impunity, democratic deficits and institutional weaknesses will necessitate a heightened focus on implementation.

Her plan concerns the strengthening of the UN human rights machinery in order to boost the implementation process. Her report represents an important cornerstone in building *a comprehensive human rights protection regime* by stressing the link between what happens in the international human rights machinery with reality on the ground. For decades, these two worlds have had a very rudimentary relationship, which has often been characterised by a mutual lack of respect and lack of understanding of the different roles and functions of the actors on the ground and at the international level. This is slowly changing, and the plan of action provides inspiration in considering the approaches that ought to be adopted.

This chapter will focus on two dimensions of human rights reform, namely reform of the UN Human Rights Commission and the UN Treaty Bodies. These instruments are particularly important because they have great potential for strengthening the implementation process. By the time this chapter is printed,[3] the reform process will have moved many steps beyond from where it is currently. Therefore I shall not focus on the details of the suggestions tabled at this stage but rather outline some general principles and possibilities in the interaction between domestic and international bodies.

## 2 The Implementation of Human Rights

The UN World Conference on Human Rights in 1993 represents an international milestone for the new human rights agenda, its main focus being on implementation. An international programme of action was adopted,[4] providing guidance and inspiration on how to move ahead with the implementation of human rights within the domestic legal order in all spheres of legislation and practice. The programme of action focused in particular on the protection of the most vulnerable groups in society. The World Conference stimulated and pressed for a shift to local domestic problems being discussed in human rights terms, which was not the case in most countries during the Cold War.

A strong indicator of this development is the emergence of national human rights institutions. In 1990 there were eight such institutions worldwide; in 2005 the number had grown to approximately sixty.[5] These institutions play a key role in monitoring human rights domestically, training officials at all levels in society and informing the general public about their rights. National institutions have con-

3 The chapter was finalised 15 March 2006.

4 Vienna Declaration and Programme of Action, World Conference on Human Rights, Vienna, 1993.

5 Morten Kjærum, 'National Human Rights Institutions Implementing Human Rights', in Morten Bergsmo (ed.), *Human Rights and Criminal Justice for the Downtrodden*, Martinus Nijhoff Publishers, 2003.

tributed to demystify human rights as remote and vague international norms and thus made them accessible to the organs of the state that are responsible for their implementation, as well as to people in general.

Another indicator of the extent of national implementation is the increased application of international human rights standards in domestic courts. In Denmark up to 1990, the Supreme Court had directly applied the European Convention on Human Rights in one case only. Since then, the Court has referred to the European Convention or, to a lesser extent, UN conventions in approximately thirty cases annually.[6] Denmark may be a particularly extreme case due to the weak protection offered by the constitution, though similar trends are being detected in countries in all parts of the world. As a spill-over effect of the increased number of cases addressing human rights issues in domestic courts, the number of cases brought to the European Court of Human Rights and the Inter-American Court of Human Rights has increased in the last decade, most dramatically in Europe where the backlog at the European Court of Human Rights was approximately 75,000 by the end of 2005.[7]

A third indicator is the degree to which human rights advocacy has been adopted by local NGOs as part of their strategies of seeking to improve the conditions of vulnerable groups. Apart from drawing inspiration from rights-based strategies of development, local NGOs have also taken advantage of the freedom offered by new democratic constitutions and have thus become increasingly vocal on the domestic scene, often with considerable success. They have linked a poverty agenda to human rights and have often skillfully used cooperation opportunities offered by the presence of international NGOs and by UN organisations to advance their objectives.[8]

A last indicator of the strengthened impact of human rights domestically is the fact that the corporate sector is increasingly taking compliance with international human rights standards into account. More and more companies realise that, in order to accommodate the demands not only of consumers but also from a general public, they need to take human rights into account in developing their corporate strategies. Numerically only a small number of companies are actively doing this as part of their current activities. However, influential companies are involved in establishing an international agenda which is stimulated and supported by institutions such as the UN Global Compact, the Business Leaders Initiative on Human Rights, the Danish Institute for Human Rights and other key actors internationally, regionally and domestically. In short, it can be said that, in an important number of companies, support for human rights has moved from the public relations department – human rights prizes, financial support to NGOs etc. – into the boardrooms of CEOs.

6 See Human Rights in Denmark, Status 1999, 2000, 2001, 2002, 2003, 2004 and 2005, The Danish Institute for Human Rights.

7 See the chapter by Stephanie Lagoutte in this volume.

8 See the chapter by Hans-Otto Sano in this volume.

These and other developments added together have created a broader understanding of human rights domestically. Human rights have moved from the negotiation tables of the UN and the Council of Europe to the local level and acquired a different flavour from the communities in which they operate. This has in many cases added important weight to the respect and protection of the rights of the individual. Whether this is a good or a bad development is up to the individual to decide, but a rough assessment is that in most parts of the world the rights of the individual are respected more today than a decade ago. There is no single indicator of this, but a number of different indicators support this impression. First of all, the number of democracies has risen from 50 in 1990 to 88 in 2005,[9] and it is generally perceived that human rights are better protected in democracies than in authoritarian regimes. This should be linked to the findings of Gurr and his colleagues that the number of governments actively discriminating against ethnic minorities went down from 45% in 1950 to 25% in 2003.[10] Finally, the number of international wars and civil wars has also gone down since the end of the Cold War.[11] The latter indicator is relevant since human rights violations most often increase in the lead up to a conflict and may also be grossly and systematically violated during it.

These changes have come about due to a wide array of developments, but key factors are undoubtedly 1) increased respect for the individual human being, and 2) the anti-violence norms which have shaped human thinking for the past couple of centuries. Within the most recent decades, these norms have acquired both the opportunity and the maturity to be transformed into domestic policies, laws and institutions. A number of countries can be mentioned where the human rights situation has improved considerably in recent years, such as the Baltic States, South Africa, Chile, Morocco, Serbia and Indonesia. Each of these countries and regions and many more tell their own stories about how gross and systematic human rights violations are decreasing if not completely disappearing.

A third factor which has been indispensable in this process is the role played by regional and international institutions, both intergovernmental and non-governmental. With the end of the Cold War, a number of intergovernmental organisations received a unique opportunity to play a more active role in peace building, supporting democratisation processes, intervening to prevent gross and systematic human rights violations, and entering into a constructive dialogue with governments on human rights capacity-building, etc. The role of the UN, OSCE, OAS and other such organs should not be underestimated in adding weight to the creation of a *culture of human rights* and non-violence. A particularly important process was the establishment of the ad hoc tribunals for the war crimes committed during the conflict in the former Yugoslavia and during the genocide in Rwanda, which eventually led to the creation of the International Criminal Court (ICC). Parallel to this, a number of governments prosecuted agents of former regimes for grave

9 Monthy G. Marshall and Ted Robert Gurr, *Peace and Conflict*, Center for International Development & Conflict Management, University of Maryland, College Park, 2005.

10 *Ibid.*

11 *Human Security Report 2005.*

human rights abuses. These steps represented a direct attack on the *culture of impunity* and sent an unmistakeable message to those next in line to become torturers or give orders for the commission of other forms of gross and systematic human rights violations.

These positive developments should not overshadow the fact that still more than half of the countries in the world are non-democratic, that by the end of 2005 there were more than twenty active armed conflicts globally and there has been an eightfold increase in "significant international terrorist attacks" over the last two decades.[12] In all regions, racial and religious tensions are on the rise, and there are still far too many human rights violations, which need to be addressed with the same vigour as previously. Therefore, the question is how the human rights machinery can be strengthened based on the lessons learned during the previous decade in order to create a *comprehensive protection regime* which embraces both local and global actors. Previous experience indicates that it will pay off.

## 3 The UN and Its Human Rights Mechanisms

The human rights mechanisms of the UN have had their share in these developments. UN institutions developed considerably in the aftermath of the Cold War and actively supported the creation of a culture of human rights. They have played this role despite dramatic underfunding. In 2006, the human rights budget was increased as part of the UN reform package. Until then, however, only 1.8% of the overall UN budget was allocated to human rights work. In the years to come, the budget will be doubled to 3.6%. Thus the human rights structure of the UN cannot be described as being strong. With more resources, a lot more could have been achieved and can be achieved in the future.

The key institutions are the Commission on Human Rights, including the mechanisms and special procedures established by the Commission, the Treaty Bodies established by the seven UN conventions on human rights,[13] the High Commissioner for Human Rights, and the Office of the High Commissioner for Human Rights (OHCHR).

### *3.1 The High Commissioner for Human Rights and the OHCHR*

Establishing a High Commissioner for Human Rights was for many years a strong desire of key NGOs. It was, however, only decided in 1993 at the World Conference on Human Rights. The mandate of the High Commissioner became a man-

12 *Human Security Report 2005.*

13 Convention on the Elimination of All Forms of Racial Discrimination (1965), Covenant on Civil and Political Rights (1966), Covenant on Economic, Social and Cultural Rights (1966), Convention on the Elimination of All Forms of Discrimination Against Women (1979), Convention Against Torture (1984), Convention on the Rights of the Child (1989), Convention on the Rights of All Migrant Workers and Members of their Families (1990).

date focusing strongly on the implementation of human rights. Thus, the High Commissioner was at the same time to be the international beacon and ultimate spokesperson for human rights and a resource for governments in their attempts to implement international commitments under the conventions they had ratified. It is not always easy to strike a balance here. To support the High Commissioner, the UN Centre for Human Rights was transformed into the Office of the High Commissioner for Human Rights (OHCHR).

Apart from servicing the High Commissioner for Human Rights, the core function of the OHCHR is to support the Commission on Human Rights, the special mechanisms and the Treaty Bodies. It is a core function because, if the OHCHR does not provide these services, no-one else will. Apart from these core functions, the Office is also involved in technical assistance to support governments in building a culture of human rights by, for example, offering assistance in establishing national human rights institutions.

The office has always been underfunded, creating severe limitations in its ability to carry out its mandate fully. At times, the funding has been so desperate that meetings in Treaty Bodies had to be cancelled due to a lack of funds to pay for the travel of Treaty Body members. One of the issues in the UN reform that most states seem to agree on is an increase in the regular budget of the OHCHR. This will be an important contribution to the realisation of the mandate of the Office.

### *3.2 The Human Rights Commission and Council*

The decision of world leaders at the summit held in New York in September 2005 to establish a Human Rights Council to replace the discredited Commission on Human Rights was important in principle. However, the lack of any decisions regarding its status, mandate, size, composition or membership leaves many open questions and uncertainties at the time of writing.[14]

The Human Rights Commission, established as a subsidiary body to ECOSOC in 1946, has achieved a great deal and developed interesting procedures. Just to mention a few of the successes, the Commission drafted the Universal Declaration of Human Rights and several of the Conventions elaborating on the Declaration. Thematic special rapporteurs and working groups established by the Commission have played a crucial role in monitoring and reporting on torture, involuntary disappearances, racism etc. The special procedures have also provided protection and redress for victims of human rights violations. However, in recent years, more and more thematic rapporteurs have been appointed on issues which, although important, are only remotely related to human rights, for example on environmental issues. They have added to the OHCHR's burdens, drained its scarce resources and thus slowly undermined the credibility of the Commission, since its performance in this regard could not meet the standards expected of it.

14 With draft Resolution A/60/L. 48 the UN General Assembly established the Human Rights Council on 15. March 2006. 170 Member States voted in favour, 4 against and 3 abstained.

The Commission has also addressed country specific issues in both closed and open meetings. This has provided governments with an international arena for discussing specific gross and systematic human rights violations. In an integrated world, it is important for a forum to exist in which states can discuss serious human rights violations or incidents which may lead to such violations. However, the ways in which states have dealt with country-specific discussions have been highly biased, with groups of countries defending themselves against supposedly unfriendly attacks from other groups. Alliances have been made to shield even those countries that have committed the most heinous violations.[15]

Despite all its weaknesses, the Commission on Human Rights demonstrates the importance of having an international focal point and meeting place, where governments and others can discuss key human rights issues of both a general and specific nature. However, there is no doubt that a reform of the Commission is needed in order to satisfy the implementation agenda. The new structure should develop methodologies to create a more fruitful and constructive dialogue. Too often, the distance from the meeting rooms in Geneva to the vulnerable groups in the field has been too great.

In this regard, the so-called Cardoso Report of 2004 on the relationship between the United Nations and civil society, written by a panel of eminent persons set up by the UN Secretary-General, is of great interest.[16] The gist of the report is that global governance is no longer the sole domain of governments. Instead, the "growing participation and influence of non-State actors is enhancing democracy and reshaping multilateralism. Civil society organizations are also the prime movers of some of the most innovative initiatives to deal with emerging global threats."[17] The panel put forward a number of interesting suggestions as to how the UN in general can interact more constructively with NGOs, the corporate sector, parliamentarians and other relevant stakeholders. In the report, this is perceived as not an option but a necessity, and it is also stated that opening up the United Nations to a plurality of constituencies and actors should not be seen as a threat to governments, but as a powerful way of reinvigorating the intergovernmental process itself.[18]

One positive achievement of the Human Rights Commission is the unique degree of participation by NGOs in its debates. The arrangements made for NGOs under ECOSOC must be maintained and strengthened to ensure that they play a more active role in the deliberations of the Human Rights Council. This will be particularly relevant since the Human Rights Council is established as a subsidiary body of the General Assembly which does not have a practice of close engagement

15 For a systematic and valuable examination of the track record of the CHR in respect of country situations, see Miko Lempinen, *The United Nations Commission on Human Rights and the Different Treatment of Governments: An Inseparable Part of Promoting and Encouraging Respect for Human Rights?*, Åbo Akademi University Press, 2005.

16 A/58/817 (11. June 2004).

17 *Ibid.*

18 *Ibid.*

with NGOs. Furthermore, the decision of the Commission at its 61st session[19] to grant speaking rights to national human rights institutions under all agenda items should be carried over to the Council. The role of NGOs, national institutions and other civil society actors could be enhanced through regular dialogues with states on thematic and country-specific issues in the context of the meetings of the Human Rights Council. As underlined in the Cardoso Report, civil society representatives from all parts of the world should be given the capacity to engage in such processes. A stronger and more focused interaction between states and non-state actors may help create a new and more constructive dynamic in the global human rights dialogue.

The question of country-specific resolutions has divided the Human Rights Commission for many years. It has been suggested that the Human Rights Council would undertake a periodic review of human rights implementation in all countries. This would help strengthen human rights protection and could assist in filling an obvious gap in the existing UN human rights program. This would be in line with the strategic assessment that the program is now moving from setting standards to national enforcement and implementation, as well as to international monitoring on the basis of existing legal obligations. The review should be implementation-oriented, based on the findings made in respect of each state by the Treaty Bodies and through the special procedures of the Council. It should therefore seek to reinforce the work of the special procedures and Treaty Bodies.

Thus, the focus of the review would be first on the institutional arrangements in place in a particular state, such as independent courts, national human rights institutions, legal framework guaranteeing an independent press etc. Secondly, the review would focus on the practical implementation of the findings by Treaty Bodies and special procedures. It would thus provide encouragement to develop and strengthen domestic mechanisms and would also provide political backing for the monitoring bodies by exerting political pressure on governments that ignore or challenge the findings of Treaty Bodies or special procedures.

The debate over the formation of the Human Rights Council has the potential to strengthen further the international agenda regarding implementation. At the time of writing, however, the negotiations seem to be stuck in familiar rhetoric and antiquated positions, which to a large extent stem from the Cold War era. In many cases, there seems to be very little interaction between substantial and focused domestic implementation strategies and what is being said in the negotiating rooms in New York or Geneva. A reason for this lack of coherence may be that in many countries very little attention is paid to what are perceived as foreign-policy issues, with civil servants at negotiating tables being left to lead a life of their own, which is partly also a life in the past. Civil society actors must therefore be more alert to the positions being taken by their governments on foreign-policy issues. They must realise that what is agreed in New York or Geneva in terms of general human rights policies may return to civil society as something which in the end either strengthens or weakens their ability to increase human rights protection domesti-

19 E/CN.4/RES/2005/74.

cally. In the area of human rights it is difficult to separate national and international policies, which are closely intertwined. Until there is a certain level of domestic interest and pressure in relation to the broader issues, it will be difficult to move the international human rights agenda into the present millennium.

### 3.3 Treaty Bodies

The United Nations human rights treaty system provides the backbone of the international human rights machinery. The work of the Treaty Bodies has developed gradually from the late 1960s till today. The Committee on the Elimination of All Forms of Racial Discrimination commenced its work in 1970 as the first Treaty Body. The most recent Treaty Body is the Committee on the Rights of Migrant Workers and their Families, which held its first session in 2004. By establishing the Treaty Bodies, state parties to the conventions request independent experts to monitor progress in implementation and provide authoritative guidance on the meaning of treaty provisions and the measures needed to protect rights at the national level. The work of the Treaty Bodies has had a direct impact in countries in all parts of the world, leading to changes in national law, policy and practice, and bringing redress to individual victims.[20] All states are parties to at least one of the seven treaties, and more than 75% of states are parties to four or more, including the two covenants.[21]

In his 2002 reform report, *Strengthening the United Nations: An agenda for further change*,[22] the Secretary-General called for a more coordinated approach to reporting, and the adoption by Treaty Bodies of streamlined working methods and procedures and harmonised reporting guidelines. He also suggested that states should be allowed to submit a single report outlining implementation of those treaties to which they were parties. Progress has been made in harmonizing Treaty-Body working methods and procedures, and Treaty Bodies are adopting these on a best practice basis. Work in this area is continuing, as is work to streamline reporting requirements using an expanded core document and targeted treaty-specific reports.

In his report *In Larger Freedom: Towards development, security and human rights for all*,[23] the Secretary-General emphasised the need "to streamline and strengthen the Treaty Body system" and called for "implementation of harmonized guidelines on reporting to all treaty bodies, so that they can operate as a unified system". In her Plan of Action,[24] the High Commissioner reiterated this call. However, she also made it clear that, "in the long term, the work of the treaty bodies

20 *Final Report on the Impact of Findings of the United Nations Human Rights Treaty Bodies*, pp.e 621-88, International Law Association Report of the Seventy-First Conference, Berlin 2004.

21 A/59/2005/ Add. 3.

22 A/57/387.

23 A/59/2005

24 A/59/2005/add.3.

should be further consolidated, including through the creation of a Unified Treaty Body."

The repeated demands to reform the treaty body system are provoked by two sets of problems.[25] A *first cluster* of issues is linked directly to the work of the Treaty Bodies. Some states find it burdensome to report separately to different Treaty Bodies, often on similar or overlapping issues. Reports are delayed or, when submitted, are often inadequate, and in some cases there is insufficient time to consider them. Moreover, the concluding observations adopted by the Treaty Bodies do not always carry sufficient precision to guide reform efforts.[26] The *second cluster* of issues relates to the weak implementation by a number of state parties of both obligations under the conventions and, in particular, of recommendations put forward by the Treaty Bodies. These problems are closely linked to a lack of knowledge of how to implement treaty obligations, as well as an insufficient capacity to translate recommendations from paper into local realities. Finally, there is in some countries a lack of sincere commitment to human rights.

These particular concerns need to be taken seriously, since the problems raised lead to the Treaty Body system being considered irrelevant to the improvement of the human rights situation in a number of states. However, the concerns need to be addressed and solved in a way which does not work to the detriment of the many States which do meet their reporting obligations and are seriously working on implementing the recommendations. Thus, the question is how these problems can best be solved.

The High Commissioner for Human Rights has tabled a proposal for the creation of a Unified Treaty Body as a single mechanism mandated to deal with all seven conventions. In relation to the *first cluster* of issues, there are a number of advantages linked to having one Unified Treaty Body rather than seven different ones as now. States parties will only have to submit one report every four years (or so), instead of seven reports that partly overlap. The pressure on state parties will then be greater since the burden is less demanding, and better reports can be expected. A single body will also meet the demand to achieve greater coherence and consistency of interpretations and working methods. It may also offer the ability to undertake the country examination over a longer period of time, thus creating a platform for a more profound dialogue. Finally, this may make it easier for NGOs and national institutions to relate to one single body and deliver high-quality supplementary reports.

It must be realised, however, that amending all the treaties will in itself be a major legal undertaking, which may take years to finalise.[27] Thus, in the light of

25 Anne F. Bayefsky, *The UN Human Rights Treaty System: Universality at the Crossroads*, Transnational Publishers, Inc., 2001; Philip Alston and James Crawford (eds.), *The Future of UN Human Rights Treaty Monitoring*, Cambridge University Press, 2000.

26 See unpublished paper, 'Assessment of the Usefulness of the Concluding Observations of the Committee on the Rights of the Child', UNICEF, Global Policy Section, 2006.

27 Martin Scheinin, 'The Proposed Optional Protocol to the Covenant on Economic, Social and Cultural Rights: A Blueprint for UN Human Rights Treaty Body Reform

this, consideration should be given to whether some of the positive dimensions of a Unified Treaty Body in relation to the first cluster of issues can be accommodated in a different manner. Within the legal framework of the treaties, there is space for improvement of the procedures and approaches of most existing Treaty Bodies.

The burden of reporting is being discussed in the inter-committee meetings and the meetings of chairpersons. One realistic way forward would be to produce a unified report, combined with specific questions or a listing of issues related to the conventions being considered. The advantage for governments would be that they would only have to make one general report. The listing of issues could be prepared well in advance of the examination and would make it easier for the state party to prepare the latter. Furthermore, it could help avoid duplication since the list of issues would be prepared on the basis of previous examinations under the specific Treaty Body, as well as on relevant issues brought up under other Treaty Bodies.

In relation to the concluding observations, the criticism of the present system is that, in some cases, the recommendations are not sufficiently precise and thus difficult to implement by state parties. The Committees on the Elimination of Racial Discrimination and the Rights of the Child[28] have taken note of this criticism and have in recent years expanded the concluding observations and recommendations in order to make them more relevant and accessible for implementing agencies at the domestic level. There is a risk that, in a Unified Treaty Body, the concluding observations and recommendations would lose specificity because the committee would have to deal with all issues under all seven conventions.

Linked to the issue of specificity, by its very nature a Unified Treaty Body will not be able to attract the same number of experts as the present Treaty Body system. The present system is unique in the way that a great number of experts, with a wide variety of expertise from all over the world, make themselves available to the international community free of charge. This is a tremendous resource that will be undermined if, as envisaged, the members of the Unified Treaty Body are full-time experts in Geneva in the future. The number of experts will be smaller, and after a time, as full-time Treaty Body experts, they will lose their links with local developments.

In relation to some of the other issues, solutions could be found on the basis of greater coordination between the existing Treaty Bodies. The inter-committee meetings and meetings of chairpersons could be held more regularly, even as a standing body, in order to harmonise further the work on both substantial and procedural issues. The meetings of chairpersons could create a joint "genocide alert function" as well as early-warning and urgent-action procedures. These meetings could also develop joint general recommendations between two or more Treaty Bodies. For example, the Committee on the Elimination of Racial Discrimination, the Committee on the Elimination of Discrimination against Women, the Human

– Without Amending the Existing Treaties'. Forthcoming in *Human Rights Law Review* 2006:1.

28 See unpublished paper, 'Assessment of the Usefulness of the Concluding Observations of the Committee on the Rights of the Child', UNICEF, Global Policy Section, 2006.

Rights Committee and the Committee on Economic, Social and Cultural Rights could produce a joint general recommendation on the rights and non-discrimination of indigenous women.

Establishing a joint follow-up mechanism should also be considered. The Human Rights Committee, the Committee against Torture and the Committee on the Elimination of Racial Discrimination already have such mechanisms in place. Follow-up mechanisms offer a particular opportunity to enter into a more continuous dialogue with the state party. At the same time the state party, NGOs and national human rights institutions acquire a focal point in the Treaty Body to which they can turn for advice on the implementation of particular recommendations. Finally, a joint follow-up mechanism could develop policies for in-country visits.

Greater coherence in jurisprudence would be of profound benefit for the establishment of a Unified Treaty Body. It is in particular through individual communications that Treaty Bodies develop jurisprudence.[29] Thus the demand for coherence is highly relevant in this regard. Creating a Unified Treaty Body dealing only with communications could be a model helping to ensure coherence and ease the backlogs of the existing Treaty Bodies. Furthermore, certain legal procedures could be elaborated in order to raise the level of professionalism in dealing with individual cases. Such a Unified Treaty Body for communications could be the forerunner of a global human rights court. Valuable experiences from the various regional systems, such as the African, European and Inter-American systems, should be harnessed.

The *second cluster* of issues relates to the implementation of Treaty Body recommendations. It is through their implementation that human rights become relevant for the most vulnerable persons in society, who are the actual target of human rights protection. One advantage of a Unified Treaty Body in relation to the second cluster of issues is that it will be likely to enjoy a higher degree of visibility at the national level, because of both its uniqueness and the simplicity of the structure (one single Treaty Body, not seven). In preparing reports, which will be more comprehensive and definitive, it will be possible to create a genuine national dialogue involving all key stakeholders. After the examination the media will be more interested in reporting on the concluding observations and recommendations, as the report will only be issued every four years. The recommendations may enjoy greater authority and thus increase the likelihood of recommendations being implemented. With increased media interest and greater authority, NGOs and national institutions may also put more pressure on governments to ensure implementation. Furthermore, it will be easier for remoter stakeholders, such as development agencies, to relate to one set of recommendations rather than seven and thus be instrumental in building capacity to ensure their implementation.

However, it is relevant to ask whether the Treaty Bodies really need a high profile, or whether they should rather be providers of sound analyses and strong

29 *Final Report on the Impact of Findings of the United Nations Human Rights Treaty Bodies*, pp. 621-88, International Law Association Report of the Seventy-First Conference, Berlin 2004.

recommendations on how the state party can improve the human rights situation in its country. To some extent, this represents a choice between the classic blaming and shaming approach, which is dependent on a high level of media awareness, and following an implementation agenda.[30] Treaty Bodies should have a high profile among the stakeholders in the implementation process.

If the main focus is to be on implementation, then the real challenge lies in shifting the burden of reporting into something relevant and meaningful for those civil servants and others who are dealing with the issues under consideration. This has not been explored fully as yet. One option is to link national human rights plans of action to the recommendations of the Treaty Bodies. As a result of the World Conference on Human Rights (1993), the Fourth World Conference on Women (1995), and the World Conference on Racism, Racial Discrimination, Xenophobia and Related Intolerance (2001), more and more countries are developing strategies and plans of action in order to address the issues raised at these conferences. Concluding observations from Treaty Body examinations can easily provide inspiration for the concrete plans, and the recommendations can take on the role of indicators or benchmarks for the latter.

The civil servant is thus given inspiration and ideas for the formulation of the plan of action. In his or her capacity as a rapporteur to the government or parliament on the indicators, the civil servant is at the same time gathering information for the next periodic report to be given to the relevant committee. Thus the *reporting cycle* to Treaty Bodies are unified with national implementation strategies and the two can provide mutual inspiration. Reporting to international mechanisms moves from being a burden carried out mainly to satisfy a group of experts in Geneva to becoming of direct relevance to the work of those institutions that are safeguarding human rights protection at the domestic level.

Since many of these issues are raised in relation to developing countries, it is equally relevant that organisations such as the UNDP, bilateral donors and others are aware of the richness of recommendations in the concluding observations of the Treaty Bodies. Today only very few development workers are familiar with the Treaty Body system, although they are increasingly addressing human rights issues with the recipient states within the framework of a rights-based approach to development. It is surprising that recommendations from the Treaty Body system is not being used to a greater extent, since it could provide a strong platform for dialogue with governments. In recent years, however, this has happened more often, turning feedback to the Treaty Bodies into a highly valuable tool for experts to adjust how recommendations are being structured.

Finally, national human rights institutions and NGOs could interact with Treaty Bodies to a much greater extent, not least in the implementation phase.

30 Philip Alston, 'Beyond 'them' and 'us': putting treaty body reform into perspective', in Philip Alston and James Crawford (eds.), *The Future of UN Human Rights Treaty Monitoring*, Cambridge University Press, 2000; Patrick Thornberry, 'Confronting Racial Discrimination: A CERD Perspective', *Human Rights Law Review* 5:2, pp. 266-7, Oxford University Press, 2005.

Some national institutions integrate Treaty Body recommendations into their national strategies and plans of action, thus helping to create a more comprehensive protection regime by linking international concerns to domestic strategies. However, there is still a long way to go before all national institutions fully use Treaty Body recommendations in their domestic work. The OHCHR and other organizations have been running a number of workshops in order to provide tools for national institutions and NGOs on how to interact with Treaty Bodies. Altogether, there is much greater awareness and recognition of the importance of the work of Treaty Bodies among national institutions and NGOs today than was the case just a few years ago.

The implementation agenda is still very young, and until recently little had been done in order to redirect the work of Treaty Bodies from being primarily part of a blaming and shaming approach to including implementation thinking too. We are slowly witnessing an increasing level of attention in Treaty Bodies, the OHCHR and elsewhere on how the examination can be made relevant for all actors, including those working on the ground who will ultimately be safeguarding the protection of the rights of those vulnerable groups of people who are of specific concern to the individual Treaty Bodies. Before making major changes in the present system, it may be useful to see how far this work can bring the implementation process. Based on these experiences, relevant changes can be made subsequently.

## 4 Conclusion

In entering the 21st century, the international human rights community was able to look into the future on a platform of tremendous success in the past decade. There was optimism for the future based on the global democratization process, which has deepened respect for human rights on all continents since the end of the Cold War. What started in southern Europe in the 1970s, with the reform of dictatorial regimes in Spain, Portugal and Greece as fully fledged democracies, continued in several Central and Latin American countries in the 1980s and stimulated changes in the communist countries of eastern and central Europe, in South Africa and in a number of Asian countries in the 1990s. This was a tremendous success for those who had fought for decades for human rights at the domestic and international levels.

In his book *Humanity*, Jonathan Glover recalls our forefathers, who, on the threshold of the twentieth century, had a similar optimism, when he writes:

> At the start of the century there was an optimism, coming from the Enlightenment, that the spread of a humane and scientific outlook would lead to the fading away, not only of war, but also of other forms of cruelty and barbarism. They would fill the chamber of horrors in the museum of our primitive past. In the light of these expectations, the century of Hitler, Stalin, Pol Pot and Saddam Hussein was likely to be a surprise. Volcanoes thought to be extinct turned out not to be.[31]

31 Jonathan Glover, *Humanity: A moral history of the twentieth century*, Pimlico, 2001.

Although human rights have obtained an unprecedented status in domestic legal orders within the last decade, there is still a long way to go in most countries before they are satisfactorily protected, respected and fulfilled. The optimism of just a few years ago that this is a linear progressive development has been replaced with a more cautious attitude as outlined by the High Commissioner for Human Rights in her 2005 Plan of Action.[32] The sharp increase in terrorism has considerably increased fear and anxiety in communities all over the world. This fear and anxiety were already developing as by-products of the escalating globalization, with many people around the world experiencing difficulties in orienting themselves within the new international regime, where market orientation is the dominant feature influencing all spheres of life.[33]

Governments are being pushed to address these anxieties in a way which makes it seem that they are in control, resulting in drastic measures targeting terrorism and organised crime, which often challenge vital human rights norms and standards. At the same time, "us and them" dichotomies are used to divert attention and create a feeling of belonging to a certain group demarcated in relation to other groups. Thus, nationalism, xenophobia and racism are blooming in the new century. These divisions were dramatically illustrated at the beginning of 2006 by the uproar in the Muslim world against the west provoked by a set of cartoons that were felt to insult the Muslim community.

Furthermore, globalisation is also leading to increasing gaps between rich and poor in the world. Poverty has not been sufficiently addressed in the new world order. Whereas in many parts of the world destitute communities have benefited from the increase in globalization, it is obvious that others have not gained anything or rather have been disadvantaged and marginalized in terms of international finance and information flows. Vast communities, particularly in Africa, have witnessed a deepening of poverty structures and the collapse of traditional infrastructures which might have created some kind of safety net. Thus not even the most fundamental human rights are respected or protected in these areas.

In the light of these developments, the international human rights machinery must be reformed and modernized in order to meet the challenges that confront human dignity in all parts of the world. The implementation agenda is still very new, and until recently little had been done in order to redirect the work of the UN human rights machinery, in particular the Human Rights Commission and Treaty Bodies, from being primarily part of a blaming and shaming approach to include implementation thinking too.

This chapter has argued that a precondition for developing the implementation agenda is that a broader range of key actors must be closely involved in UN mechanisms. This is regarded not as an option, but as a necessity. Moreover, the opening up of the United Nations to a plurality of constituencies and actors should

32 See p. 1.

33 Zygmunt Bauman, *Globalization: The Human Consequences*, Polity Press 1999; Anthony Giddens, *Runaway world: How globalisation is reshaping our lives*, Profile Books, 1999; Thomas Friedman, *The Lexus and the olive tree*, Financial Times, 2000.

not be seen as a threat to governments, but as a powerful way to reinvigorate the intergovernmental process itself. A positive achievement of the Human Rights Commission is the unique degree of participation of NGOs in its debates. The role of NGOs, national institutions and other civil society actors could, however, be enhanced in a new Human Rights Council through regular dialogues with states on thematic and country-specific issues in the context of the meetings of the Council. The Treaty Bodies could take inspiration from this to ensure much greater interaction with national human rights institutions and NGOs.

If a future Human Rights Council does venture into conducting a review process of states, the review should be implementation-oriented and should be based on the findings made in respect of each state by the Treaty Bodies and through the special procedures of the Council. It should therefore reinforce the work of the special procedures and the Treaty Bodies. This would be an additional reason to strengthen the work of the Treaty Bodies, which can be done either within the existing legal framework of the treaties or through a more comprehensive reform involving new protocols or amendments to the treaties. Within the existing system, a number of initiatives can be taken to strengthen the work of the Treaty Bodies, including creating a greater degree of coordination between them. One option could be to create a permanent presidency comprising all the chairpersons, who could coordinate joint general recommendations, joint follow-up missions, joint urgent-action procedures etc. Another option of great potential benefit would be to create a Unified Treaty Body dealing only with communications, which would help provide greater coherence. This could be an important first step towards a global human rights court.

A major challenge and precondition for the Treaty Body system to survive in the long term is that it be perceived as relevant to domestic actors. The task is simply to turn the reporting obligations from being a burden carried out mainly to satisfy a group of experts in Geneva becoming of direct relevance to the work of those institutions that safeguard human rights protection at the domestic level. The only way in which this can happen is if the key actors working domestically incorporate the recommendations of Treaty Bodies into their strategies, plans of action, human rights dialogues, etc.

In the words of the UN Secretary General:

> The United Nations exists not as a static memorial to the aspirations of an earlier age, but as a work in progress – imperfect, as all human endeavours must be, but capable of adaptation and improvement.[34]

In previous decades, human rights work was largely about developing international norms and subsequently getting governments to sign up to the norms and standards. While this has been achieved, broadly speaking, the challenges today are to transform these standards into local realities by creating a culture of human rights and to underpin a rights-based approach to development. In the light of the on-

34 A/57/387.

going reform process in the UN, this chapter has explored how the interaction between international and regional monitoring mechanisms and national levels can create a stronger and more dynamic protection regime. In a spirit of cautious optimism, the potential for deepening the emerging cultures of human rights is within reach.

# 2. The Future of the European Human Rights Control System: Fighting with Its Back to the Wall

*Stéphanie Lagoutte*

## 1 Introduction

Human rights are in turmoil, and the control mechanisms put in place to protect them cannot escape being affected too. The human rights system set up under the United Nations needs to be rethought,[1] and the control mechanism of the European Convention of Human Rights, generally considered the most efficient and developed regional human rights system, is arousing more and more concern. Since the mid-1990s, the general tone and discourse surrounding the European Court of Human rights has been anything but cheerful. The Court seems to be losing some of its credibility, among other things because the cases being brought before it are taking too long to resolve. Judges, experts and scholars are telling a depressing story of the European human rights system no longer playing its role, and they are questioning both the efficiency and the quality of the system, which has existed (with some modifications) since the 1950s. They are also raising the issue of the legitimacy and necessity of a system that is no longer functioning as intended.[2] The risk is that the European states may cease to see any reason why they should support and maintain such cumbersome and slow legal machinery. The Court itself has identified the greatest danger as being that "the inexorable accumulation of cases, both inadmissible and substantial cases, will increasingly asphyxiate the sys-

1 See, *inter alia*, the report of the Secretary-General of the United Nations, Kofi Annan, *In larger freedom: Towards development, security and human rights for all*, 21 March 2005 (A/59/2005), and especially: pp. 153-219: 'Strengthening the United Nations'. See also Chapter by Morten Kjærum in this book.

2 See the references in this chapter, in particular the texts and speeches of L. Wildhaber, as well as the new publication by Gérard Cohen-Jonathan and Jean-Francois Flauss, op. cit., note 5.

*S. Lagoutte, H-O. Sano and P. Scharff Smith (eds.),* Human Rights in Turmoil, *pp. 25-47.*
 *ISBN 90 04 15432 9.*

tem so as to deprive the great majority of incoming cases of any possibility of being heard within a reasonable time and therefore of any practical effect".[3]

Of course an inherent difficulty exists with an organisation – the Council of Europe – that joins together 46 states, each with its own very distinct history and legal tradition. Nevertheless, the member states of the Council of Europe have consistently shown their determination and formal commitment to adapt the European human rights system to the enlargement of the Council of Europe. A large-scale reform of the Court was carried out at the end of the 1990s, and a new Protocol 14 will enter into force in the coming year or two. However, these reforms may well be outdated already by the time they enter into force. This gives the impression of a Court that is perpetually fighting against a huge backlog of applications with its back to the wall. As a consequence, it is imperative to find a solution in order to maintain a sustainable system and improve it. As the President of the European Court of Human Rights expressed the matter, there is a need for the European human rights system to survive in a meaningful manner. In other words, a system is required which is efficient, irreproachable and exemplary in all respects.[4]

This "reforming the reforms" inevitably touches on some very basic aspects of the European regional human rights protection system. With regard to the role played by the states, their lamenting the fact that too many applications actually reach the Court is duplicitous. Indeed, it is the responsibility of the states parties to guarantee the proper implementation of the Convention in their domestic legal order, ensure better training for the legal profession, and provide more information on the case law of the Court. As regards the European Court of Human Rights specifically, the tricky question is whether Europe just needs a more efficient Court of Human Rights, or whether it needs another type of Court. In other words, is it the nature of the system itself which has to be rethought, or can we cope by throwing more money at the human rights mechanism and "reviving" the commitment of the states parties to the European Convention?

The aim of this chapter is first to analyse the present situation of the European Court of Human Rights and to attempt to unravel the different problems that are raised year after year. Secondly the current situation will be investigated in respect of the accuracy of these very pessimistic views on the future of the Court and its actual problems. Possible remedies will also be examined, in terms of their relevance and their shortcomings, particularly those that are being put forward by the states parties and the Court itself. It is crucial to try and determine what kind of future can be expected for the Court. The chapter therefore also investigates how to find or restore some points of balance within the European human rights system: the balance between efficiency, legitimacy and equity on the one hand, and the balance between the Court and the states, which have created the Court, on the other.

---

3 Speech by Luzius Wildhaber, President of the European Court of Human Rights, at the Solemn hearing of the European Court of Human Rights on the occasion of the opening of the judicial year, 22 January 2004.

4 Speech by Wildhaber, 2004, *supra,* note 3.

In seeking to fulfil its aims, the chapter is built around three main standpoints. First, there is a need to increase the judicial efficiency of the European Court of Human Rights in such a way as it should not undermine the level of protection afforded to all individuals. Secondly, there is a need to find a balance between the Court's independence, which is crucial to the legitimacy of the system, and the role that the states are bound to play in a system that they have created themselves. Finally, the member states of the Council of Europe can only obtain the human rights mechanism that they agree to build, develop and pay for, and it is only their commitment, both political and financial, that can make the system function.

As this chapter discusses some rather new developments in the control mechanism of the European Convention of Human Rights, its main source is a number of documents and transcriptions of speeches produced by a variety of actors connected with the European human rights system. In addition, some of the viewpoints presented in this chapter concern the internal functioning of the European Court of Human Rights, sources for which are rather scarce. All in all, scholarly contributions to the issues being dealt with in the chapter are very few.[5]

After first envisaging what is actually the situation of the European Court of Human Rights today **(2)**, the chapter proceeds with an in-depth analysis of some of the problems faced by the Court and the solutions adopted by the reform process, as well as their shortcomings **(3)**. Finally, the chapter will draw some preliminary conclusions as to the kind of European Court of Human Rights Europe desires for the future **(4)**.

## 2 A Never Ending Nightmare: Perpetually Reforming the Reforms?

In 1998, the old system established in 1950 by the European Convention on Human Rights was replaced by a full-time single Court.[6] At that time it was common to say that the Court was a victim of its own success. Therefore one of the main purposes of the reform set out in Protocol 11 was to simplify the system in order to reduce the length of proceedings in Strasbourg, which had already become a problem. In addition, the reform was based on a reinforcement of the judicial character of the proceedings.[7] The European human rights protection system became entirely judicial, as the right of individual application and the jurisdiction of the Court became compulsory, and the role of the Committee of Ministers in the proceedings was brought to an end.[8] However, ten years after Protocol 11, an urgent need reappeared

5 See, however, a new publication, Gérard Cohen-Jonathan and Jean-Francois Flauss, 'La Réforme du système de contrôle contentieux de la Convention européenne des droits de l'homme', *Droit et Justice*, Vol. 61. Bruxelles: Bruylant, 2005.

6 Protocol No. 11 of 11 May 1994, which entered into force on 1 November 1998.

7 For example, Yvonne Klerk, 'Protocol No 11 to the European Convention: A Drastic Revision of the Supervisory Mechanism under the ECHR', *Netherlands Quarterly of Human Rights*, Vol.14, no.1, 1996, 35-46.

8 However, the Committee of Ministers remains in charge of the supervision of the execution of the judgements by the states concerned (ECHR, Art. 46).

which called for a revision of the mechanisms set out in the European Convention on Human Rights, which would guarantee its pre-eminent role in protecting human rights in Europe.

### *2.1 The Figures Speak for Themselves*[9]

The statistics produced by the European Court of Human Rights are shocking. Since Protocol 11 took effect in 1998, the Court has rendered about 61,600 decisions and judgements; this figure should be compared with the approximately 38,400 decisions and judgements rendered by the European Commission and Court in the 44 years up to 1998.[10] Since the enlargement of the Council of Europe since the beginning of the 1990s,[11] the number of individual applications has risen significantly and continuously.[12] In 2004, approximately 41,000 new applications were lodged before the Court, and by 1st of September 2004, approximately 75,800 applications were actually pending before it.[13]

It is obvious that applications and cases are basically arriving, piling up and accumulating in Strasbourg. There is no way the system can process all applications, and as a consequence the backlog is simply increasing continually. In addition, the situation will clearly not improve on its own. On the contrary, it is very likely that the annual number of applications brought before the Court could in the future far exceed the figures that we have seen the past years.[14]

An analysis of the statistics produced by the Court's registry shows that the system is facing two major problems. First of all, about 90% of all (individual) applications are terminated without a ruling on their merits, mostly because they are declared inadmissible according to Article 35 of the Convention. Secondly, among the applications which actually reach the stage of an examination of their merits, more than half concern violations of the European Convention on Human Rights which derive from the same structural cause as an earlier application which has

9 Luzius Wildhaber, 'Consequences for the European Court of Human Rights of Protocol 14 and the Resolution on judgments revealing an underlying systemic problem: practical steps and challenges', in *Reform of the European human rights system: proceedings of the high-level seminar*, Oslo, 18 October 2004. Council of Europe, 2004, 31.

10 The figures given in this article can be found in the '2004 Survey', published by the European Court of Human Rights, which rendered 205 judgments between 1955 and 1989, 30 in 1990, 56 in 1995, 695 in 2000 and 889 in 2001.

11 In 2004, the European Convention applied to approximately 800 million individuals.

12 From 5,279 in 1990 to 10,335 in 1994 (+96%), 18,164 in 1998 (+76%) and 34,546 in 2002 (+90%).

13 Of these, 49,000 were pending before a decision body, while the others were awaiting preliminary examination and/or allocation to a decision body (see *Reform of the European human rights system: Proceedings of the high-level seminar*, Oslo, 18 October 2004, Council of Europe, 2004, 44).

14 Stéphanie Lagoutte, 'Reaching beyond the horizon: how to preserve an efficient protection of human rights in Europe?', in *Festskrift om Menneskerettigheder til C.A. Nørgaard*. Copenhagen: Jurist- og Økonomforbundets Forlag, 2004, 241-2.

led to a judgement finding a breach of the Convention; these are called "repetitive cases". In 2003, 96% of cases examined were disposed of at the admissibility stage (17,270 declared inadmissible). Of the remaining 753 applications that were declared admissible, the Court rendered 703 judgements, of which about 60% were repetitive cases.[15]

## 2.2 *The New Reform: Protocol 14*

Since Protocol 11 entered into force, there has been a renewed concern within the Council of Europe with the increasing volume of individual applications and its consequences for the effectiveness of the Convention system.[16] Consequently, the Committee of Ministers of the Council of Europe instructed the Steering Committee for Human Rights (CDDH)[17] to prepare a draft amending the Protocol to the Convention, an explanatory report, a draft declaration, three draft recommendations and a draft resolution. This last reform ended in the middle of May 2004, when, with few modifications, the Committee of Ministers adopted almost all the draft texts.[18]

The new reform has two aspects: a re-affirmation of the principle of subsidiarity, and the increased efficiency of the functioning of the Court. It is clear that measures must be taken at both the regional level (i.e. the level of the Council of Europe, and more specifically at the level of the Court) and the national level in order to prevent violations, improve domestic remedies and the domestic implementation of the Convention, and enhance and expedite execution of the Court's judgements. Therefore some measures are aimed directly at the states parties to the Convention and at the Committee of Ministers.

15 *Reform of the European human rights system: proceedings of the high-level seminar*, Oslo, 18 October 2004, Council of Europe, 2004, 44.

16 In 2000, Resolution 1 on 'Institutional and functional arrangements for the protection of human rights at national and European level', European Ministerial Conference on Human Rights, Rome, November 2000 (H-Conf(2001)001, Resolution I).

17 The CDDH is composed of government experts from the member states of the Council of Europe. Various other institutions and authorities are consulted by the CDDH and/or participate in its meetings, e.g. the office of the Council of Europe Commissioner for Human Rights, NGOs or national human rights institutions.

18 Protocol 14 to the Convention for the protection of human rights and fundamental freedoms, amending the control system of the Convention, CETS No.194, and Explanatory Report as adopted by the Committee of Ministers at its 114th Session on 12 May 2004. See also Resolution Res(2004)3 of the Committee of Ministers on judgements revealing an underlying systemic problem; Recommendation Rec(2004)4 of the Committee of Ministers to member states on the European Convention on Human Rights in university education and professional training; Recommendation Rec(2004)5 of the Committee of Ministers to member states on the verification of the compatibility of draft laws, existing laws and administrative practice with the standards laid down in the European Convention on Human Rights; and Recommendation Rec(2004)6 of the Committee of Ministers to member states on the improvement of domestic remedies. All were adopted by the Committee of Ministers on 12 May 2004, at its 114th Session.

It is important to stress that Protocol 14 does not make any radical changes to the control system established by the Convention; rather, its purpose is to change some aspects of the functioning of the system by improving it and by giving the Court the procedural means and flexibility necessary to increase its efficiency. Thus the Court will be able to concentrate on the most important cases, which require more time and more in-depth examination.

Even before the entry into force of Protocol 14, the Court had argued that this reform would not be sufficient. On the one hand, the states parties to the Convention have to fulfil the obligations that they have agreed to under the Convention by ensuring its effective implementation at the national level and the redressing of all violations of the Convention, as well as actively guaranteeing to supervise the execution of the Court's judgements within the Committee of Ministers. On the other hand, the Court also pointed out recently the need for a long-term strategy and reflection on the *nature* of the system:

> The potentially substantial increases in judicial productivity which may ultimately be achieved by protocol 14 will not on their own be sufficient to close the gap between the level of incoming cases and the Court's output capacity. [...] It is necessary to start reflecting on the long term options available for further action capable of ensuring a stable, practicable system providing the highest possible effective protection, while preserving the basic philosophy underlying the ECHR. Ultimately the Governments are faced with a choice about the nature of the international protection machinery which must be provided to individuals in the Europe of the 21st century. This in depth discussion and reflection will have to take into account the new challenges resulting from the pan-European dimension which the system has now acquired.[19]

This shows that there is no way to escape a debate on the very nature of the European human rights system. Some voices are already advocating a transformation of the European Court of Human Rights into a type of quasi-constitutional court that would only deal with major human rights issues.[20]

### *2.3 Restoring the Balance*

The major problems that the European Court of Human Rights has faced in the past ten years cannot be solved only by reforming the Court itself: the flow of applications must be stemmed at the national level. The Court has stressed many times that there is a "need to restore the balance between national and international jurisdiction in implementing the Convention".[21] According to the President of the Court, in recent years this balance has been upset to the detriment of the

19 Memorandum by the European Court of Human Rights, contribution to the third summit of the Council of Europe, 27 April 2005, points 5 and 6.

20 See *infra* at the end of this article, paragraph 4.3 on the evolution of the role of the Court.

21 Speech by Wildhaber, *supra*, note 3.

international component, i.e. the European Court, which is now forced to bear a disproportionate burden in enforcing the Convention.[22] The principle of subsidiarity is a pre-condition for the establishment of any supra-national human rights control mechanism and is – or should still be one of the foundations of the European system.

In concrete terms, this implies that the implementation of measures to facilitate and support information and education regarding the European human rights system at the domestic level will reduce the number of manifestly unfounded applications that are sent to the Court. Legal professionals must make themselves better acquainted with the system and its potentialities in order to participate, directly or indirectly, in a more effective implementation of the Convention at the domestic level.[23] Clearly, implementation of the Convention in domestic legal systems must be improved, particularly the judgements of the Court, so as to prevent repetitive violations in similar cases.[24]

Undoubtedly, none of these issues concern directly the functioning of the Court itself: it is for the states parties to improve their legislation, practices and domestic remedies in order to put an end to this flow of both inadmissible applications and repetitive cases. Concerning the Court itself, however, a number of problems also need to be solved to ensure the safeguarding of the European human rights system.

## 3 Critical Points in the New Reform Initiatives

The long-term strategy requested by the European Court of Human Rights will have to cover two intertwined crucial points in order to ensure its optimal functioning: efficiency and credibility. The constant search for a higher degree of efficiency might reduce the level of protection afforded to individuals. It is therefore paramount for the survival of the system to establish a sustainable reform that will increase the Court's efficiency without damaging its functioning **(3.1)**. The standing of the institution is also crucial to its survival. In a general sense, the Court enjoys immense prestige, though this is coming under scrutiny. This chapter therefore analyses some of the more severe criticisms that have been voiced against it. **(3.2)**.

22 Wildhaber, 2004, *supra*, note 9, 24-5.

23 See Recommendation Rec(2004)4 of the Committee of Ministers to member states on the European Convention on Human Rights in university education and professional training, 12 May 2004.

24 See Recommendation Rec(2004)6 of the Committee of Ministers to member states on the improvement of domestic remedies, 12 May 2004.

### 3.1 The Efficiency of the Court[25]

This part of the chapter scrutinises the measures and proposals discussed during the reform process, as well as some of the initiatives taken by the Court on its own: new admissibility criteria, the filtering of applications, repetitive cases and pilot judgements, redress and compensation, as well as some of its working methods. These various measures, proposals, initiatives and new practices can all play a role in safeguarding the efficiency of the European Court of Human Rights, but some of them need to be reconsidered or improved.

The figures and analysis previously presented show that the Court is now continually fighting with its back to the wall. The flow of incoming applications seems unstoppable, and the Court still has to deal with it in a manner that is not detrimental to the quality of its work. Since the Court has to deal with a huge number of inadmissible applications and repetitive cases, the time left to it to examine the merits of the other cases is limited. In addition, some inadmissibility decisions require a considerable amount of work by the Court: as all scholars and legal professionals who are familiar with the Court's case law know, such decisions are very complex.[26]

#### 3.1.1 Choosing Cases

The Court itself has pointed out that "always trying to increase judicial productivity has its limits".[27] While the system strives for higher productivity, the more complex cases are being put on hold by the Registrar, in order to enable the Court to deal with as many cases as possible.[28] For this reason, the president of the Court announced at the beginning of 2005 that "the Court has decided to devote more attention to adjudicating on the meritorious cases, i.e. cases in which the applicant often has a serious claim of being the victim of a human rights violation".[29] In making such choices, the Court can prioritise its work in a manner that is not directly contrary to the Convention. Interestingly some judges urged the authors of Protocol 14 to consider giving the Court the ability to sort out and select the cases it would examine and thus to refuse to adjudicate cases that it considered less important or meritorious. This position has been defended especially by the President of the Court, but its judges have not been able to agree on the merits of allocating such discretionary power to it. Accordingly, this possibility is not covered by Pro-

25 This part of the chapter is built upon and elaborates further on a previous article, see: Lagoutte, 2004, *op. cit.*, note 14, 237-259.

26 From 1 January to 1 September 2005, the European Court of Human Rights rendered or struck off 18,766 inadmissibility decisions. The figure for the same period in 2004 was 13,542.

27 Speech by L. Wildhaber, 2005, *supra*, note 21.

28 Peer Lorenzen, 'Fem år med den nye menneskerettighedsdomstol: reform af en reform', in *Festskrift om Menneskerettigheder til Carl Aage Nørgaard*, Copenhagen: Jurist- og Økonomforbundets forlag, 2004, 270.

29 Speech by L. Wildhaber, 2005, *supra*, note 21.

tocol 14, though it does set out a new and rather controversial –criterion of admissibility, which is a first step in this direction.

### 3.1.2 The New Criterion of Admissibility

Protocol 14's new admissibility criterion has been added to Article 35 of the Convention (new Article 35 paragraph 3-b). Individual petitions can now be declared inadmissible "if the applicant has not suffered a significant disadvantage". This new criterion is followed by a safeguard clause containing two conditions. First, even if the applicant has not suffered a significant disadvantage, his or her application will not be declared inadmissible "if respect for human rights as defined in the Convention and the Protocols thereto requires an examination of the application on the merits". Secondly, the Committee of Ministers added another safeguard, to apply simultaneously: an application, even if trivial, will not be rejected if the case "has not been duly considered by a domestic tribunal". The point of this new Article is to provide the Court with an additional tool to help the judges focus on those cases which deserve an examination on their merits. It is, of course, for the Court alone to interpret the new admissibility requirement and decide on its application. This creates some flexibility in the system, in that the Court can avoid examining cases that are trivial or that do not require an examination on their merits, as well as those cases that have already been duly examined at the national level. It is evidently going to take some time for the Court, the Chambers and the Grand Chamber to interpret this new criterion and its two safeguard components.[30]

The main concern pertaining to the new criterion is that it seems rather disproportionate. Certainly 90% of individual applications are inadmissible under the current criteria. Furthermore, as already mentioned, 60% of admissible cases are repetitive ones, which means that they are similar to cases where the Court has previously found a violation; they therefore need redress before the Court. Consequently, only a very small number of existing cases will be dealt with under this new criterion. It may, of course, be necessary to deal with them by simply declaring them inadmissible, but the consequences for the whole system seem rather out of proportion.

First of all, this will present the Court with the huge task of interpreting the new criterion (what constitutes a "significant disadvantage"?) and its two safeguards. Secondly, it will have the consequence that some violations, which have not been redressed in the domestic legal system, will not be redressed at the regional level either. This sends out a disastrous signal that some human rights violations are minor (raising the question, "in comparison to what"?). Obviously, the new criterion places the question of the intensity of damage at the heart of the system,

---

30 In this connection, the Committee of Ministers has also added to the original draft of the CDDH a transitional provision that states: 'In the two years following the entry into force of this Protocol, the new admissibility criterion may only be applied by Chambers and the Grand Chamber of the Court'; see Protocol 14, Article 20 paragraph 2 *in fine*. The same article also specifies that this criterion will not apply to applications declared admissible before the entry into force of Protocol 14.

instead of continuing to focus on whether or not there has been a violation of human rights. In addition, there may be an apprehension that the level of protection afforded by the Court will vary from one member state of the Council of Europe to another. In other words, what might be a significant disadvantage in one country might appear totally insignificant in another.

The new criterion is therefore not the most appropriate solution. A more recommendable path is to alleviate the burden created by inadmissible applications and repetitive cases in order to release time for the Court to hear all meritorious cases. In this respect, the problem that needs an urgent and efficient solution is that of how to filter applications.

### 3.1.3 Filtering Applications

The only way actually to deal with the huge mass of *unmeritorious* applications is to reinforce the Court's filtering capacity. Consequently, Protocol 14 allows for the filtering capacity of the Court to be increased by empowering a single judge with the necessary competence to declare cases inadmissible or strike out individual applications, "where such a decision can be taken without further examination" (new Article 27, paragraph 1). In this case, the decision is final; if the judge does not declare an application inadmissible, the application is forwarded to a Committee or a Chamber for further examination (new Article 27, paragraphs 2 and 3). The words "where such a decision can be taken without further examination" need to be clarified by the Court. However, the Explanatory Report indicates that the competence of the single judge would only concern clear-cut cases, "where the inadmissibility of the application is manifest from the outset".[31] As some non-governmental organisations have proposed, it might be worth considering whether the competence of the single judge should be limited to admissibility criteria that do not require the exercise of a wide degree of discretion by the single judge (requirements relating to persons, place, subject matter or time, such as the six-months' time limit, or the requirement for all domestic remedies to have been exhausted).[32]

The European Court of Human Rights itself suggested the creation of a separate filtering body composed of persons other than the judges of the Court.[33] This idea was rejected by the drafters of Protocol 14, which was based on two fundamental premises: first, the filtering work must be carried out within the judicial framework of the Court; and secondly, the same body should not have different categories of *judges*. It is difficult to understand the reasons for the second premise: there could easily be two categories of *judicial personnel*, for example. As the Court stated in its response to the CDDH, the "separation of the filtering function (for

31 Explanatory Report to Protocol 14.

32 For example, Amnesty International's Comments on the Interim Activity Report: Guaranteeing the Long-Term Effectiveness of the European Court of Human Rights, February 2004, §48 (AI Index: IOR 61/005/2004).

33 Response of the European Court of Human Rights to the CDDH Interim Activity Report prepared following the 46$^{th}$ Plenary Administrative Session on 2 February 2004, CDDH-GDR(2004)001, 10 February 2004.

both the Registry and the Court) and that of the adjudication of substantial cases will prove essential for the long-term capacity of the system both to produce in good time high-quality and well-reasoned decisions in substantial cases and to dispose of manifestly inadmissible cases with sufficient expedition".[34]

In fact, the problem seems to be primarily that the creation of a separate filtering body requires the appointment of new judges and therefore additional financial resources. Anyhow, whatever the circumstances, an increase in the human and financial resources of the Registry is unavoidable if Protocol 14 is to be implemented and the capacity of the Court developed.[35]

### 3.1.4 Dealing with Repetitive Cases

Protocol 14 deals very deliberately with repetitive cases. In order to accelerate their adjudication, the competence of the committees of three judges is extended: committees are empowered to rule, using a simplified procedure, not only on the admissibility but also on the merits of an application, "if the underlying question in the case is already the subject of well-established case law of the Court" (new Article 28). Here too, it will be necessary for the Court to define "well-established case law". The drafters have given some indications regarding this matter (case law consistently applied by a Chamber or a judgement from the Grand Chamber), but it will be up to the Court to interpret this new article, since both parties will be able to contest the applicability of this accelerated procedure. Again, the drafters have specified that the adversarial character of the proceedings and the principle of judicial and collegial decision-making on the merits will be preserved. The purpose of the new Article 28 is to increase the work capacity of the Court and thus its efficiency, since only three judges (the Committee) will be required to examine these repetitive cases instead of seven judges (the Chamber) today.

In addition, the Court (i.e. the Chambers) has also been given greater latitude to rule simultaneously on the admissibility and merits of individual applications. In fact, joint decisions on the admissibility and merits of individual cases are not only encouraged, but will become the norm. However, the Court will be free to choose to take separate decisions on admissibility on a case-to-case basis (new Article 29).[36]

---

34 Response of the European Court of Human Rights to the CDDH Interim Activity, 2004, *supra*, note 33.

35 In a recent publication, Professor Cohen-Jonathan advocates a different model, according to which the present European Court of Human Rights would be transformed into a tribunal of first instance, and a new human rights court with a limited number of judges (like the International Court of Justice or the Inter-American Human Rights Court) would take care of the more important or serious cases. He stresses that this rethinking of the system would only require the appointment of eleven judges, an increase in the financing of the Registry being a sine qua non for any efforts to increase the efficiency of the European Court of Human Rights. Gérard Cohen-Jonathan, 'Propos introductifs', in Cohen-Jonathan and Flauss, 2005, *op. cit.*, note 5, 46-51.

36 As a result of the implementation of the new Articles 28 and 29, there should be fewer separate decisions on admissibility. As a consequence, the Court is now free to place

### 3.1.5 The Court's Attempt to Find a Solution: The Pilot Judgements

During the drafting of the last reform of the control mechanism of the European Convention on Human Rights, the question of establishing a special procedure for pilot judgments was discussed several times, among both judges[37] and government experts.[38]

In the case of a violation originating from a structural or systemic problem in the domestic legal order, the Court proposed to create a formal possibility within the Convention to impose an accelerated execution process on member states. This would include an obligation for the member state to create retroactive domestic remedies to deal with all repetitive cases. This would therefore also allow the Court to decline to examine these cases until they had been through the new domestic remedy procedure. In the end, it was decided that the Court could establish such a procedure for pilot judgements without any amendment of the Convention.

Following this line of thought, in the *Broniowski* judgment, the Court took upon itself the responsibility for designing such a procedure.[39] After finding that there had been a violation of Article 1, Protocol 1, in the case of the applicant, the Court decided to look more closely at the obligation of the defendant state as far as the execution of the judgment was concerned, i.e. under Article 46 of the Convention.

First of all the Court stressed that:

> the violation of the applicant's right guaranteed by Article 1 of Protocol no. 1 originated in a *widespread problem* which resulted from a malfunctioning of Polish legislation and administrative practice and which has affected and remains capable of affecting a large number of persons. The unjustified hindrance on the applicant's "peaceful enjoyment of his possessions" was neither prompted by an isolated incident nor attributable to the particular turn of events in his case, but was rather the consequence of administrative and regulatory conduct on the part of the authorities towards an identifiable class of citizens, namely the Bug River claimants.[40]

---

itself at the parties' disposal with a view to securing a friendly settlement at any stage in the proceedings, and not only after an application had been declared admissible; see new Article 39, paragraph 1.

37 Response of the European Court of Human Rights to the CDDH Interim Activity Report, 2004, *supra*, note 33, §24, and the Court's position paper of 12 September 2003, §§43-46, where the Court urged the introduction of a Convention provision formally establishing a pilot judgment procedure.

38 Among others, the Interim Activity report of 26 November 2003 (CDDH (2003) 026 Addendum I Final, §20-21.

39 *Broniowski v. Poland* [GC], app. no. 31443/96, ECtHR 22 June 2004. This case concerns Poland's failure to implement the applicant's entitlement to compensatory property; the applicant's family had been repatriated from the 'territories beyond the Bug River' after the Second World War and had to abandon their property (see historical background at §§10-12).

40 *Broniowski*, §189.

The Court also stressed that the Polish judicial authorities also considered that a systemic dysfunction existed. In addition, the *Broniowski* judgment provided for a definition of systemic violation where there exists in the legal order of the State concerned "a shortcoming as a consequence of which a whole class of individuals have been or are still denied the peaceful enjoyment of their possessions."[41]

The Court stated explicitly that the deficiencies in national law and practice identified in the applicant's individual case might give rise to numerous subsequent well-founded applications. Indeed the Court underlined that

> the violation which it has found in the present case has as its cause a situation concerning large numbers of people. The failure to implement in a manner compatible with Article 1 of Protocol no. 1 the chosen mechanism for settling the Bug River claims has affected nearly 80,000 people. There are moreover already 167 applications pending before the Court brought by Bug River claimants.[42]

In principle, it is not for the Court to determine what measures (remedies) may be appropriate to satisfy the respondent state's obligations (subsidiarity principle). According to the jurisprudence of the Court, the respondent state remains free to choose the means by which it will fulfil its obligations under Article 46 of the Convention, provided that such means are compatible with the conclusions set out in the Court's judgment and subject to monitoring by the Committee of Ministers.[43] It is therefore only because of the identified systemic situation that the Court considered general measures at the national level to be necessary for the concrete and effective execution of this judgment. Such measures should take into account the many people affected by the situation and should remedy the systemic defect underlying the Court's finding of a violation. In this case the Court stated explicitly that the purpose of this "intervention" by the Court is "not to overburden the Convention system with large numbers of applications deriving from the same cause".[44] Very pedagogically, the Court explained that:

> Such measures should therefore include a scheme which offers to those affected redress for the Convention violation identified in the instant judgment in relation to the present applicant. In this context the Court's concern is to facilitate the most speedy and effective resolution of a dysfunction established in national human rights protection. Once such a defect has been identified, it falls to the national authorities, under the supervision of the Committee of Ministers, to take, retroactively if appropriate, the necessary remedial measures in accordance with the subsidiary character of the Convention, so that the Court does not have to repeat its finding in a lengthy series of comparable cases.[45]

41 *Broniowski*, §189.
42 *Broniowski*, §193.
43 *Broniowski*, §192.
44 *Broniowski*, §193.
45 *Broniowski*, §193.

Concerning all the remaining cases pending before the Court which deal with exactly the same situation, also called "Bug River cases", the Court concluded that their substantive examination was linked to the execution of the *Broniowski* judgment and the implementation of the measures indicated by the Court to the Polish Government. Consequently, on 6 July 2004 the Court decided that all similar applications, including future ones, should be adjourned pending the outcome of the leading case and the adoption of the measures to be taken at the national level.

According to the President of the European Court of Human Rights, the *Broniowski* case represents a groundbreaking judgment and an attempt from the Court to spell out very clearly its judicial policy. In his view, this new approach is wholly justified, both in terms of the philosophy of restoring the balance, and on a practical level, by reducing the number of well-founded cases that the Court and its registry will have to process through to a judgment on their merits. In addition, this new trend may result in a solution being found at the domestic level, which will mean that "a greater number of individual applicants will be secured redress more rapidly than if the Court were to attempt to process each and every application in turn".[46]

Similarly, in January 2005, the Court decided to adjourn approximately eight hundred Italian cases pending its decision in a test case concerning the application of the "Pinto Law" in Italy.[47] In its judgment in the case of *Scordino v. Italy*,[48] the Court found that the compensation awarded to the applicants under the Pinto Law could not be considered adequate and that a violation of the Convention had therefore taken place.[49] Soon afterwards, the Italian Government requested that the case be referred to the Grand Chamber of the Court, where the request is currently pending before a Grand Chamber panel. At the same time, the Italian Government also asked that all cases raising the same issues as *Scordino* be suspended pending the panel's decision, and, should the panel accept the referral request, the Grand Chamber judgment. In December 2004 the Court agreed to adjourn all "clone cases" prior to the panel's decision, which is expected early in 2005.[50]

46 Wildhaber, 2004, *op. cit.* (note 9), 26.

47 These eight hundred applications concerned the excessive duration of legal proceedings in Italy. The Pinto Law of 2001 introduced a legal remedy in such cases before the Italian courts, in cases in which applicants claim that they have received insufficient compensation, although, in applying the Pinto Law, the Italian courts found that the length of the civil, criminal or administrative proceedings to which they were parties had been excessive. These cases are all relying on Article 6 § 1 (right to a fair hearing within a reasonable time) and, in some cases, on Article 13 (right to an effective remedy) of the European Convention on Human Rights.

48 *Scordino v. Italy*, app. no. 36813/97, ECtHR decision of 27 March 2003, and judgment of 29 July 2004.

49 Article 6 § 1 and Article 1 of Protocol No. 1.

50 A Chamber of the Court has also decided to relinquish jurisdiction to the Grand Chamber in another case concerning the level of compensation awarded by the Italian courts in the Pinto decisions, namely *Cagnoni v. Italy*, app. no. 48156/99, ECtHR 7 November 2000).

Pilot judgements are not a solution to all the problems of the European human rights protection system. This jurisprudence needs to be developed and refined in order to be fully accepted by the member states. For example, the *Broniowski* judgment has been mildly criticised for addressing not a structural problem but a specific problem concerning a large number of individuals.[51] Professor Lambert-Abdelgawad has also briefly identified two other aspects needing further development by the Court: the actual monitoring of the conformity of the measures taken by member states to implement pilot judgements, and the risk inherent to such a solution, namely that individuals who have previously presented their cases in Strasbourg will have to go back to the domestic courts, where they cannot be assured of finding effective redress. If this happens, they will have to go back to the European Court of Human Rights once again, thus extending considerably the length of the proceedings in their cases and threatening their rights to an effective remedy.[52] However, the jurisprudence of pilot judgements is also the result of a constructive dialogue between the member states of the Council of Europe and the European Court of Human Rights. Significant here is the face that, in the *Broniowski* judgment, the Court refers directly to Recommendation 2004(6) on the improvement of domestic remedies, which, in paragraph 14, deals with the methods used by the Court in this case.

### 3.1.6 Dealing With Redress and Compensation

According to the judge elected in respect of Denmark, Peer Lorenzen, the case law of the Court can in itself be a contributory factor in the increase in the number of cases being presented to the European Court. He refers here to the case law concerning reparation under Article 41 in connection with the finding of a violation of Article 6 §1 (duration of civil proceedings) and to the practice to which these cases almost always lead, namely the state being condemned to pay quite significant reparations for non-pecuniary damages. According to Lorenzen, the fact that more than 50% of the judgments pronounced by the Court in 2001-2003 and 20% of the 17,000 applications pending before a Chamber by 1st of April 2004 concern allegations of a violation of Article 6 §1, duration of civil trial, is linked to the possibility of obtaining reparation.[53] By making use of pilot judgements, part of the case law to which Lorenzen refers could be avoided. However, the concern he has raised shows that there is a need for a further development of the Court's compensation policy. In many well-founded cases, the most complex issue is the determination of compensation, an issue which the Court is singularly ill-equipped to deal with: "We simply lack the expertise in Strasbourg to carry out sophisticated property valuations, for example, even if we had the time to devote to such exercises. We must

51 On this distinction, see the presentation by Pierre Lambert at the Oslo high-level seminar in *op. cit.*, note 9, 2004, 33-43.

52 Elisabeth Lambert-Abdelgawad, 'Le protocole 14 et l'exécution des arrêts de la Cour européenne des droits de l'homme', in : Cohen-Jonathan and Flauss, 2005, *op. cit.*, note 5, 102.

53 Lorenzen, 2004, *op .cit.*, note 28, 273-5.

therefore look for ways to transfer that task to other bodies, preferably domestic bodies or possibly to special Claims Commissions."[54]

From a broader perspective, the Court has strengthened its jurisprudence concerning redress during the past two years. As mentioned above, every respondent state remains free to choose the means by which it will fulfil its obligation to execute the Court's judgment (under the Convention's subsidiarity principle). However, in the case of *Maestri v. Italy*,[55] which concerned the disciplinary action taken against a career judge because of his membership of a Masonic lodge, the Court stipulated more clearly the terms of the Italian Government's obligation. First, hand, the respondent state has to remove any obstacles in its domestic system that might prevent the applicant's grievance from being adequately redressed. Secondly, the Italian authorities should take appropriate measures to redress the effects of any past or future damage to the applicant's career resulting from the disciplinary action against him, which the Court found to be in breach of the Convention.[56]

On the one hand, the complicated issue of compensation shows that the European Court of Human Rights might itself be partly responsible for the influx of applications that is flooding it. On the other hand, the strengthening of the Court's jurisprudence concerning redress illustrates that solutions can be found by the Strasbourg judges themselves.

#### 3.1.7 Reforming the Working Methods of the Court

On a more practical level, the Court is also adapting to the situation through working methods to increase its efficiency. It is difficult for researchers and scholars to document this evolution, because they have to rely either on informal sources or on the few written contributions by the Court's judges. In a recent Danish article, Judge Peer Lorenzen has described some of the internal reforms of the working methods of the Court,[57] mentioning three improvements in particular:

First of all, the Court has aimed at significantly reducing the number of hearings. They still take place before the Grand Chamber, but have become the exception before the Chambers.

Secondly, on the basis of Article 29, §3, the Court has tried internally to introduce a joint examination of the admissibility and merits of an application (see Rules 54 and 54A in the Rules of the Court). This effort has been approved by the Committee of Ministers in its acceptance of the formalisation of this internal policy of the Court in Protocol 14. According to the new Article 29, the Court has greater latitude to rule jointly on the admissibility and merits of the case.

---

54 Wildhaber, 2004, *op. cit.*, note 9, 27.

55 *Maestri v. Italy*, app. no. 39748/98, ECtHR 17 February 2004 [GC], violation of Article 11.

56 *Maestri*, §47.

57 Lorenzen, 2004, *op .cit.*, note 28, 273-5.

Finally, the Chambers have decided in the most "obvious" cases to rule on both the admissibility and the merits of an application at the same time. This possibility has also been formalised in the new Article 29 (Protocol 14).

To sum up on the efforts made to increase the efficiency of the European human rights protection system, the previous developments show that various initiatives are now being put into practice. These initiatives take place at the different levels (domestic level, European Court of Human Rights or Committee of Ministers). We have shown that the sum of these efforts and concrete initiatives should without doubt *improve* the situation. It is not sure, however, that they can actually *solve* the problems that the Court is facing and will be facing in the coming years.

### 3.2 Credibility of the System: The Independence of the Judges

The credibility of the European human rights system has been evoked during the debates over the reform of the European Court of Human Rights, mostly in connection with the discussion on efficiency. However, more specific concerns have also been raised and have led to the adoption of provisions reinforcing the independence of the judges of the European Court of Human Rights.

The question of the independence (and impartiality) of the judges is crucial, because it is at the heart of the principle of the rule of law. Besides, and more generally, the independence and appearance of independence of the judiciary plays a major role in securing its legitimacy and authority. The elements at the foundation of the independence of the judiciary can be summed up as follows: transparent appointment procedures, appropriate status and remuneration, security of tenure, appropriate social protection and retirement benefits, etc. As a consequence, the judges must be protected not only during their tenure, but also thereafter. In other words, they should not be dependent on any other income when they leave the Court.

Very critical comments have been expressed concerning some of the key elements linked to the independence or appearance of independence of the judges of the European Court of Human Rights. For example, the question of the appointment of judges, that is, both their nomination at the national level and their election at the international level, has raised quite a number of concerns.[58] Similarly, issues such as the appointment of the "national" judge as judge-rapporteur, the appointment procedures for *ad hoc* judges and the risk of pressure being exerted on judges in relation to their re-election can be seen as rather challenging. More generally, there was an obvious need in Strasbourg to strengthen the Court's ability to act "without fear or favour"[59] and to ensure, both in reality and in appearance, that it was absolutely free from any outside pressure or interference.

58 Interrights: *Judicial Independence: Law and Practice of Appointment to the European Court of Human Rights*. London, May 2003, 84 pp.

59 For instance, Recommendation 1649 (2004) on Candidates for the European Court of Human Rights, adopted by the Parliamentary Assembly, 30 January 2004.

Protocol 14 addresses two issues relating to the independence or appearance of independence of the Court's judges: their terms of office, and the appointment of *ad hoc* judges. Other issues still remain to be dealt with, such as the role of the national judge and the function of the judge-rapporteur.

### 3.2.1 Terms of Office

In order to avoid any pressure which might be exercised on judges in connection with their re-election, Protocol 14 states that they may not be re-elected. As a corollary of this, their terms of office have also been changed and increased to nine years (new Article 23, paragraph 1) from six, so as to guarantee that they serve the Court for a significant period of time. This innovation mostly has some organisational implications in helping to avoid the simultaneous departure of large numbers of judges and arrival of a large number of new ones. The indications in the Explanatory Report concerning the renewal of the Court and the set of transitional provisions set forth in the Protocol should permit the regular renewal of the Court's composition over time.

### 3.2.2 Appointment of *ad hoc* Judges

Prior to Protocol 14, the appointment of *ad hoc* judges was briefly mentioned in the Rules of the Court: "If the judge elected in respect of a Contracting Party concerned is unable to sit in the Chamber, withdraws, or is exempted, or if there is none, the President of the Chamber shall invite that Party to indicate whether it wishes to appoint to sit as judge either another elected judge or an ad hoc judge and, if so, to state at the same time the name of the person appointed."[60] This procedure lacked legitimacy and allowed the state party to choose an *ad hoc* judge after the beginning of proceedings, which was prejudicial to at least the *appearance* of the Court's independence.

Protocol 14 partially remedies this unsatisfactory situation by making provisions for a new system of appointment for *ad hoc* judges. The new Article 26, paragraph 4, provides for a judge's replacement by a person – the *ad hoc* judge – chosen by the President of the Court from a list submitted in advance by the state party. Under this new rule, therefore, state parties are required to draw up a list of *ad hoc* judges from which the President of the Court can appoint an *ad hoc* judge when necessary.

Obviously, the appointment of *ad hoc* judges still lacks the democratic legitimacy of election by the Parliamentary Assembly.[61] However, the appearance of the Court's independence is strengthened by this new system, since a state party will no longer play a crucial role in the appointment of a judge if it is the respondent state.

60 Rule 29, paragraph 1(a).

61 Report of the Committee on Legal Affairs and Human Rights of the Parliamentary Assembly (Doc. 10147, 23 April 2004) on Draft Protocol 14.

### 3.2.3 The Role of the National Judge

In order to alleviate the burden of work which rests on some judges (i.e. those elected for states parties where a structural problem is leading to repetitive cases before the Court), it is not mandatory for this judge to be a member of the Committee. However, Article 28, paragraph 3, specifies that he or she can be invited to take the place of one of the members of the Committee at any stage of the proceedings *"if that State has contested the application of the expedited procedure."* During the debates on Protocol 14, representatives from civil society expressed their concerns that such an explicit reference in the Convention raises serious issues concerning the appearance of the Court's independence. Indeed, this very explicit reference in paragraph 3 seems rather unnecessary for two reasons. First of all, the active presence of the "national" judge in these cases, or in all cases – i.e. as part of the bench and not as a mere expert – is highly questionable. The appointment of competent lawyers from all the member states of the Council of Europe to the Registry should be sufficient in providing all the necessary information to the Court on the various domestic systems. In addition, they would also help solve the huge hurdles created by the fact that the documentation submitted with applications is often not translated into a working language of the Court. This is often seen as the main issue justifying the appointment of the national judge as judge-rapporteur. With regard to repetitive cases, it is not obvious that the presence of the national judge can benefit the situation, but only create a problem with regard to the appearance of the Court's independence. Secondly, if the expertise of the national judge be deemed indispensable, then it is important to mention it in the new text, but without referring to the specific situation where the state party does not agree with the Court: it is, and must remain, the discretionary power of the Committee of three judges to ask the national judge to be present. In this way, Article 28 seems to be an illustrative and unfortunate example of the balance that still has to be maintained within the European human rights system between the concessions made by state parties and the few means of "control" that still remain or seem to remain.

### 3.2.4 The Role of the Judge Rapporteur

Protocol 14 specifies that, when sitting as a single judge, a judge shall never examine an application against the state party in respect of which he or she has been elected (new Article 26, paragraph 3). This explicit prohibition is very important in order to ensure the Court's independence and appearance of independence. In this connection, it is extremely important for the Court to reconsider the appointment of the "national" judge as judge-rapporteur in the Committees and Chambers. Even if this practice is very convenient in terms of knowledge of the language or the domestic law of the state concerned, it is not compatible with the principle of the independence of the judiciary. Indeed, the strengthening of the Registry of the Court is a determinant in bringing an end to this practice: the Registry's staff (and among it, the lawyers from the state concerned) would prepare the case for the judge-rapporteur, who would then present his or her preliminary conclusions for discussion with the other judges. The national judge would participate in both the discussion and the vote, but would not be the one presenting preliminary conclusions on the case to the other judges. Thus there would be no reason to retain the current system, which is far from being exemplary of the requirement of appearance of independence of the European Court of Human Rights.

As shown above, some areas touching on the independence and/or the appearance of independence of the European Court of Human Rights might still prove problematic. As shown by the question of the appointment of a judge-rapporteur, it may even appear that the issue of the Court's efficiency has overcome all other concerns. All measures that increase the Court's independence or appearance of independence help reinforce its prestige. Ultimately, another way to reinforce the Court's standing would be to modify its role and the nature of its function.

## 4 Which European Court of Human Rights for Tomorrow?

The European Court of Human Rights is the result of an on-going consensus between the Member States of the Council of Europe, and all its reforms are the results of negotiations between these states. Hence, the fate of the Court is primarily in the hands of the state parties to the Convention and of the legal experts who will design the future Court. The judges will also play a role in this design, as they possess both the moral authority and the concrete experience to do so. Consequently it is important to listen to the various criticisms emanating from the judges, as well as to those from scholars and experts, regarding the Court and the reform of its procedures, in order to be able to reflect more broadly on the Court's future.

This chapter has argued that different kinds of solutions can be found in order to ameliorate the functioning of the European human rights protection system if two main concerns are kept in mind: the efficiency of the Court, and the restoration of a balance between it and the role of the states. Yet the solutions that have been provided do not seem to be able to stop the dramatic increase in the number of applications being sent to Strasbourg. Therefore, one crucial question remains: should experts and governmental representatives now come up with yet more radical changes to the protection system? The last part of this chapter attempts to situate the reform in a broader perspective in order to show that the present system can evolve and be improved if the member states of the Council of Europe are ready to renew their commitment to the European human rights system.

### 4.1 *Pragmatism*

Certain current, well-known problems can be dealt with by the Court in a pragmatic way. For example, the consequences of the recent enlargement of the Council of Europe eventually need to be taken seriously into consideration. Most of the serious structural or systemic problems stem from joining of the newer contracting states from central and eastern Europe. It would be hypocritical to refuse to see the impact of the adhesion of these new member states on the Court's work in terms of an increase in the number of applications, the arrival of new judges, new staff and new types of cases, as well as the reactions of new state parties to their losing a case, etc. It has been argued that the new members were not granted a reasonable period of time after their adhesion to the Council of Europe to sign and ratify the Convention, since they should have been given an adequate period of adjustment in order to bring their legal systems into conformity with the Convention.[62] The positive aspect of this reality is that most problems will be solved as time goes by. In the meantime, the Court has emphasised that the development of the jurisprudence of pilot judgments must be understood in this context, namely the identification and resolution of problems that should have been dealt with before the ratification of the Convention.[63]

Pragmatic solutions are not incapable of giving rise to concerns, as the pilot judgement solution shows.[64] However, this is also the result of an implicit agreement between the European Court of Human Rights and the member states of the Council of Europe. This shows that the Court should be encouraged to make the necessary technical adjustments to enhance its efficiency. This also requires the states to trust the Court to be able to cope by itself with some of its organisational problems. A similar strategy could be followed in order to increase the Court's filtering capacity.[65]

### 4.2 Commitment

There is a need for political adjustments and a revival of the commitment of state parties to the European human rights protection system. It is hardly fair to allow the system to go downhill and then accuse it of no longer being efficient. In this respect, the states that created the Court are responsible for its functioning. They must also accept that the system can only function with the strong commitment and support from the member states of the Council of Europe, as well as the increased influence of these states through the Committee of Ministers. As shown in the case of the pilot judgement, the European Court of Human Rights is in effect saying to the respondent state and the Committee of Ministers that they too must play their roles and assume their responsibilities. More radically, the new infringement proceedings (new Article 46) confronts the states with their international responsibilities, both as defendant states and as committed members of the Council of Europe.[66] It is, however, quite clear that a procedure that empowers the Committee of Ministers to bring infringement proceedings against one of its member

62 Jean-François Flauss, 'Propos conclusifs sous forme d'opinion séparée', in Cohen-Jonathan and Flauss, 2005, *op. cit.*, note 5, 182. The President of the European Court talks about this lack of time to adjust as an 'historical mistake': Wildhaber, 2004, *supra*, note 9, 27.

63 Wildhaber, 2004, *supra*, note 9, 27.

64 See *supra* paragraph (3.1) on the efficiency of the Court.

65 See also the recommendations made in a new report conducted at the invitation of the Secretary General of the Council of Europe and the President of the European Court of Human Rights, *Review of the Working Methods of the European Court of Human Rights*, December 2005, by the Right Honourable The Lord Woolf.

66 For a description of this new procedure and its implications, see Lagoutte, 2004, *op. cit.*, note 13, 253-4.

states before the Court requires political courage and commitment on the part of the member states of the Council of Europe.[67]

In addition, regardless of the form the measures will take, it is crucial to the success of any reform that the European Court of Human Rights receives *financial* support from the state parties. The figures are well known, but it is worth repeating here that the Court's funding represents only one quarter of that provided for the European Court of Justice.[68] Maintaining a European human rights protection system is expensive and is a question of the commitment of the individual member states, as well as being a priority for the Secretary General of the Council of Europe. If the European Court of Human Rights has to be able to process cases within a reasonable time, the Registry of the Court will have to continue to grow. Similarly, the possible appointment of a number of judges – if a filtering section or a tribunal of first instance are eventually set up – will require increased financial support.

### 4.3 The Evolution of the Role of the Court

The European Court of Human Rights plays two intertwined roles in the European legal system. First, it deals with individual and concrete applications and offers redress for human rights violations. Secondly, and in the course of its work, it creates European human rights standards, also called the "European human rights public order". Some voices are pushing for a transformation of the Court towards a type of "constitutional" Court, which would only adjudicate cases concerning major human rights issues, that is, very serious or more systematic violations of human rights.[69] As the French professor and specialist in the European Convention of Human Rights, Jean-François Flauss, has shown in a recent article, an evolution is already taking place in Strasbourg towards the "objectivation" of the case law developed in European Court of Human Rights.

In his article, Flauss points out various trends in the case law of the Court and in the configuration of the European human rights protection system, which is moving towards a new role for the Court, namely to find generally applicable solutions to specific and concrete problems. Hence, while examining a concrete case in conformity with its mandate, it tends to accept "*privilégier le traitement du droit à celui des droits*" (to privilege dealing with the law instead of with rights). Flauss naturally calls attention to the case law relating to pilot judgments, but also to other phenomena, as, for instance, the fact that the Court has agreed to control *in ab-*

67 The Explanatory Report to Protocol 14 already specifies that this new procedure should be only used in exceptional circumstances (§100).

68 See, for example, Gérard Cohen-Jonathan, 'Propos introductifs', in Cohen-Jonathan and Flauss, 2005, *op. cit.*, note 5, 51.

69 The leading voice here seems to be that of the President of the European Court of Human Rights, who, while supporting the reforms which are taking place today, has repeatedly insisted on the necessity of envisaging more radical avenues: Wildhaber, 2004, *supra*, note 9, 31. See also the rather critical views of Jean-François Flauss, 'Propos conclusifs sous forme d'opinion séparée', in Cohen-Jonathan and Flauss, 2005, *op. cit.*, note 5, 169.

*stracto* the conformity of a law to the European Convention of Human Rights[70] or the refusal of the Court to strike out of its rules a case in which the applicant had died leaving no successor to pursue his case. In this particular case, the Court recalled that, "although the primary purpose of the Convention system is to provide individual relief, its mission is also to determine issues on public-policy grounds in the common interest, thereby raising the general standards of protection of human rights and extending human rights jurisprudence throughout the community of Convention States".[71] These three examples show that the European Court of Human Rights is itself actively participating in a transformation of its own role, while proclaiming its attachment to its role as a Court for all individual applicants.

To conclude this chapter, it must be reiterated that the European Court of Human Rights is a subsidiary mechanism. Today it sometimes seems as if only the European Court itself is aware of this fundamental element for the survival of the whole European human rights protection system. The Court has developed a complicated and very rich case law based upon the principle of subsidiarity. Now it is the turn of the member states, and especially the newcomers, to return to the original idea that is the foundation of the whole system. By offering effective redress to human rights violations at the domestic level, they will be participating actively in the ongoing formation and development of European human rights standards, as well as ensuring the preservation of a system that has been the pillar of human rights protection in Europe for more than half a century.

---

70 *Thlimmenos v. Greece*, app. no. 34369/97, ECtHR 6 April 2000.

71 *Karner v. Austria*, app. no. 40016/98, ECtHR 24 October 2003, §§25-26. In the present application, the Court considered that the difference in treatment of homosexuals as regards succession to tenancies under Austrian law involved an important question of general interest, not only for Austria, but also for other state parties to the Convention. It decided, therefore, that continuing the examination of the present application would contribute to elucidating, safeguarding and developing the standards of protection under the Convention.

# 3. Human Rights Reinforcement and Globalisation: Reflections about Global Governance

*Hans-Otto Sano*

## 1 Introduction

This chapter seeks to map out some of the important changes which have occurred globally over the last two decades and to analyse how and where these processes impact on human rights reinforcement. However, the chapter also seeks to identify shortcomings and negative human rights change. At the general level, the chapter is motivated by an interest in the processes by which human rights are realised as rights which are actually enjoyed by people. The objective of the chapter is therefore to capture some of the structural and institutional changes which are taking place globally and to reflect on how these changes may contribute to human rights reinforcement and setbacks.

Human rights reinforcement takes place through the international monitoring of human rights compliance, international adjudication of human rights, constitutional processes, and domestic adjudication. This is the legal track of human rights reinforcement and implementation. However, the chapter focuses on an alternative and broader track of human rights implementation: consolidation through non-legal means, i.e. the institutionalisation of human rights through political and administrative decision-making, for instance, with respect to resource allocation or through the broader processes of dialogue and value change in society and between social actors in different societies.[1]

Post-Cold War processes of globalisation are not only marked by political developments that serve to strengthen human rights. During this period, human rights enforcement has been threatened partly by conservative forces from within the constellation of powers that have contributed to the spread of the international rule of law and human rights, but also by the existence of criminal states and in-

1 See Habermas, Jürgen, 2004: Transition of International Law from a National to a Post-national Constellation. Translated into Danish from a presentation held in Istanbul 2003: 'Folkeretten i overgangen til den post-nationale konstellation' in *Distinktion. Scandinavian Journal of Social Theory*, no. 8.

*S. Lagoutte, H-O. Sano and P. Scharff Smith (eds.),* Human Rights in Turmoil, *pp. 49-70.*
 *ISBN 90 04 15432 9.*

ternational terrorism,[2] as well as by economic globalisation in weak states. These issues are discussed further below.

The chapter asks three specific questions:

1. In what way does human rights reinforcement relate to processes of globalisation? Is it possible to delineate a conceptual framework that can be used to describe such processes?
2. How do local and international forces interact to create processes of human rights reinforcement?
3. In what areas and under what conditions are globalisation processes bringing about adverse changes to human rights?

The chapter proceeds with an outline of the current processes of globalisation and their conceptualisation in section 2. Human rights reinforcement and their undermining from above is addressed in section 3, and from below in section 4. Section 5 concludes the chapter.

## 2 Globalisation from Above and Below

Scholte defines globalisation as

> The processes whereby many social relations become relatively delinked from territorial geography, so that human lives are increasingly played out in the world as a single place.[3]

This definition stresses the growing interdependence across continents, but also the relative unevenness of the process of globalisation. It is expressed with a certain vagueness, with changing territorial geography and social interdependence being the main features. Nothing is said about political or institutional interaction, although these features may be implicit in the concept of social relations.

An interesting question is how old the process of globalisation is. Some would argue that processes of globalisation were already taking place from about 500 BC, reflecting the argument of Fernand Braudel, the historian, that there have always been "world economies". Others would link globalisation to post-Cold War developments, while arguing that there are also certainly continuities with the Cold War period, including as far as human rights are concerned.[4]

John Donnelly, however, argues that processes of globalisation are fundamentally new: "whatever parallels or antecedents, the pace of change is accelerating,

2 Habermas, 2004, p. 13.

3 Jan Aart Scholte, 2001. 'The Globalization of World Politics.' In Baylis, John and Steve Smith (eds.). *The Globalization of World Politics: An Introduction to International Relations.* Oxford, 2nd edn., pp. 14-15.

4 Clark, Ian, 2001. 'Globalization and the Post-Cold War Order.' In Baylis, John and Steve Smith (eds.). *The Globalization of World Politics: An Introduction to International Relations*, pp. 634-647.

with important qualitative differences". Donnelly therefore argues that globalisation is characteristic of the decades on either side of the year 2000. He emphasises that globalisation is connected with the recent interpenetration of national labour markets and the communication-mediated creation of a single global capital market. The "third wave" of electoral democracy and the spread of human rights ideals are also related to globalisation, according to Donnelly.[5]

The line of argument pursued in the present chapter agrees with Donnelly that the post-Cold War period gave rise to qualitative changes, which are sometimes epitomised as a new order, i.e. a change in the configuration of values, the roles of international organisations, institutional structures and political cleavages. It would be wrong to argue that processes of globalisation in terms of market penetration, trans-national investments and changing techniques of communication were not present before the end of the Cold War. What *is* new, however, justifying Donnelly's claim of qualitative change, is the enhancement of institutional initiatives with global reach, that is, the enhanced importance of international institutions with roles in regulating trade (WTO), finance (IMF and World Bank), security and peace (UN Security Council), and human rights and international law (ICC, Office of the High Commissioner for Human Rights). The scholarly and practical political debate on global public goods that has emerged since the late 1990s is part of this development.[6]

Also both new to and inherent to the processes of post-Cold War globalisation are new dimensions of accountability. In a recent book, Goetz and Jenkins argue that a new accountability agenda is in the making, with four key elements: "1. a more direct role for ordinary people and their associations in demanding accountability, across 2. a more diverse set of jurisdictions, using 3. an expanded repertoire of methods, and on the basis of 4. a more exacting standard of social justice".[7]

Globalisation is therefore not only about "flows" of commodities, capital and people. These tendencies are obvious, but the post-Cold War order is also characterised by the growth of international organisations and institutions[8] and the interactions between the various actors and institutions at different levels, including new opportunities for interaction from below. This phenomenon is important to capture, not least with respect to changes to human rights in the current process of globalisation.

5 See John Donnelly: 'Human Rights, Globalization Flows, and State Power.' In Brysk, Alison (eds.), 2002. *Globalization and Human Rights*, pp. 226-27.

6 *See* Kaul, Inge et al., 2003. *Providing Global Public Goods: Managing Globalization.* UNDP, Oxford University Press. *See also* Sano, Hans-Otto, 2005: 'Er god regeringsførelse et globalt offentligt gode?' I: Andersen, Erik André, Birgit Lindsnæs og Stig Rée. *På vej mod nye globale strategier: Offentlige goder og Menneskerettigheder.* Djøf-forlaget 2005.

7 Goetz, Anne Marie and Rob Jenkins, 2005. *Reinventing Accountability: Making Democracy Work for Human Development.* Palgrave, p. 4.

8 *See* Ruggie, John Gerard, 1998. *Constructing the World Polity: Essays on International Institutionalization,* quoted in Brysk, 2002, *Introduction.* In Brysk, Alison (eds.), 2002. *Globalization and Human Rights*, p. 6.

What does globalisation mean for human rights? This is not a small question, and its answer must come from a conceptual framework that seeks to identify the levels and processes of interactions between states, institutions and actors. Some scholars have attempted to address this question, but they have done so with a point of departure either in case studies[9] or in outlines based on particular aspects of the subject.[10] This means that the present chapter must be explorative, especially as limitations of space rule out a more exhaustive discussion.

## 2.1 Global Governance

The concept and model used in this chapter to discuss the human rights implications of globalisation is *global governance*. As a concept, this has been used by scholars[11] during the last decade to conceptualise the changing international relations after the cold war and to define processes of democratisation and accountability, not only within states, but also between both states and citizens. The concept can be used as part of a theoretical framework of cosmopolitanism[12] which defines power and accountability as the result of complex interactions from local communities to international organisations. Global governance relates to substantive processes of democratisation at the international level as important, complementary dimensions of formalised access to international institutions through governments, and to the importance of value dimensions in shaping interactions among international institutions.[13]

Global governance has been defined by Held and McGrew as the layered and interlocking complex structure of decision-making and authority formation under which political management and global regulation takes place.[14]

An alternate, more descriptive definition is that of Clark, who defines global governance as:

> the loose framework of global regulation, both institutional and normative, that constrains conduct. It has many elements: international organizations and law; trans-na-

9 See Alison Brysk (eds.). 2002, *Globalization and Human Rights.*

10 See Paul Gready's article, 2004: 'Conceptualizing Globalisation and Human Rights: Boomerangs and Borders' in *International Journal of Human Rights*, vol. 8, no. 3.

11 For reference, see e.g., the journal *Global Governance.* For a discussion about the distinctions between *global* and *international governance*, see Ngaire Woods: 'Good Governance in International Organizations', *Global Governance*, 5, 1999.

12 For elaboration of cosmopolitanism as a theoretical concept, see Eva Erman, 2005. *Human Rights and Democracy. Discourse Theory and Global Rights Institutions.* Ashgate.

13 *See* Halliday, Fred. 2003. 'Global Governance. Prospects and Problems.' In: Held, David and Anthony McGrew (eds.). *The Global Transformations Reader*, 2nd ed.. Polity Press.

14 David Held, 2002. *Introduction.* Held, David and Anthony McGrew (eds.). *The Global Transformation Reader.*

tional organizations and frameworks; elements of global civil society; and shared normative principles.[15]

*Figure 1. A Model of Global Governance*

A model of global governance has been incorporated above as Figure 1. The model indicates three levels of interaction: local (represented by civil society), state and international. One central feature of global governance is the important role of mutual interaction and networks, between civil societies, between international agencies and civil society groups, and between states and non-state actors. Ultimately individual action (agency) is also possible. A central element in the conceptualisation of global governance is the importance of values in constituting actors and in influencing interaction. Seven cosmopolitan principles have been defined by one of the central scholars in the texts about global governance:

- Equal worth and dignity
- Active agency

15 Ian Clark, op. cit., 2001, p. 637.

- Personal responsibility and accountability
- Consent
- Reflexive deliberation and collective decision-making through voting procedures
- Inclusiveness and subsidiarity.
- Avoidance of serious harm and the amelioration of urgent need.[16]

The model of global governance indicates that globalisation processes are engendered from below as well as from above. For human rights, since they are part of globalisation processes, this implies that a reinforcement as well as a weakening and undermining of the human rights regime may take place either from above or below.

What do "from above" and "from below" mean? These concepts are linked to an understanding of social hierarchies and also to distinctions between formalised institutions and corporations and social actors operating in local networks, often on a less formalised basis. Globalisation from above relates to the processes set in motion by trans-national corporations, market forces, international organisations, governments and members of parliamentary assemblies in states and regional organisations, the result of which are, for example, the de-linking of social relations from territorial geography. Globalisation from below is described by Falk as a subaltern agenda and discourse, while other scholars equate advocacy networks and trans-national civil society networks (and their interaction with international institutions) with the processes of globalisation from below.[17]

## 3 Human Rights Reinforcement and Threats from Above

The perspective from above is one where state, inter-state and market forces are seen to contribute to the reinforcement as well as the erosion of human rights. Forsythe argues that the analysis of human rights reinforcement in international relations since World War II must be analysed from a perspective of competing realist and liberal interpretations, the latter reinforcing international law and human rights, the former emphasizing national interest and power relations. The enormous gap between legal theory and political behaviour must be taken into consideration in any explanation of why public authorities simultaneously endorse and

16 *See* David Held and Anthony McGrew (eds.), 2002. *The Global Transformation Reader. An Introduction to the Globalization Debate.*

17 See Richard Falk, 2002. 'Interpreting the Interaction of Global Markets and Human Rights' In Brysk, Alison (eds.), 2002. *Globalization and Human Rights*, pp. 61-76. *See also* Richard A. Falk, 2004. *The Declining World Order. America's Imperial Geopolitics.* Routledge, pp. 87-94. For an example of how the interplay between international institutions and trans-national networks has been working to create better solutions to the debt situation of poor countries, *see* Callaghy, Thomas M., 2001. 'Networks and Governance in Africa: Innovation in the Debt Regime.' In: Callaghy, Thomas, Ronald Kassimir and Robert Latham (eds.): *Intervention and Transnationalism in Africa. Global-Local Networks of Power*. Cambridge University Press, pp. 115-48.

violate human rights.[18] Economic globalisation (the intensified trans-continental flow of commodities, labour, people and financial capital) provides asymmetries of development and of the concentration of power that threaten to undermine not only human dignity, but in particular the efforts to restore dignity where it has long been in deficit.

The analysis below presents two contrasting perspectives of the reinforcement and undermining of human rights respectively. The focus is on reinforcement or its opposite through either political and economic development or socio-cultural change, rather than on legal processes of human rights reinforcement.

## *3.1 Human Rights Reinforcement from Above*

Human rights have become objects and standards of bilateral foreign policy and development assistance to an unprecedented degree during the last two decades.[19] This development is coupled with significant changes in international institutional development as regards human rights reinforcement, such as the establishment of the High Commissioner for Human Rights and the expansion of national human rights institutions.[20] The emerging practice of humanitarian intervention based on norms to protect victims of gross human rights violations represents one such development, while in the legal sphere the strengthening of international human rights jurisdictions represented by the regional human rights courts and by the establishment of the International Criminal Court is another.

### 3.1.1 Human Rights in Foreign Policy and Development Assistance

Human rights have become an issue in foreign policy since the late 1980s and early 1990s. In Danish foreign policy and development assistance, human rights emerged on to the agenda in the wake of the processes of democratisation in Africa and in Eastern Europe during the early 1990s, an agenda that was expressed in the so-called democracy package of 1993.[21]

---

18 Forsythe, David P., 2000. *Human Rights in International Relations.* Cambridge University Press, p. 6.

19 *See* Liang-Fenton, Debra (ed.), 2004. *Implementing US Human Rights Policy. Agendas, Policies, and Practices.* United States Institute of Peace Process, p. 445. *See also* Forsythe, 2000, op.cit., chapter 6, and Dunér, 2002, chapter 5. *See also* Brandtner, Barbara and Allan Rosas, 1998: 'Human Rights and the External Relations of the European Community. An Analysis of Doctrine and Practice.' *European Journal of International Law*, 9, p. 468-490. *See also* Youngs, Richard, 2002, 'The European Union and Democracy Promotion in the Mediterranean: A New Disingenuous Strategy' In: Gillespie, Richard and Richard Youngs (eds.). *The European Union and Democracy Promotion. The Case of North Africa.* Frank Cass, pp. 40-62.

20 *See* Morten Kjærum, 2003, 'National Human Rights Institutions Implementing Human Rights', In: Bergsmo, Morten (ed.): *Human Rights and Criminal Justice for the Down-Trodden: Essays in Honour of Asbjørn Eide.* Martinus Nijhoff.

21 *See* Sano, Hans-Otto, 2000, 'Development and Human Rights: The Necessary, but Partial Integration of Human Rights and Development.' *Human Rights Quarterly*, vol. 22, 3

In the US, disputes between Congress and the executive over Chile and South Africa served to make human rights an issue during the 1970s and 1980s. Constructive engagement policies, that is, engaging rights-abusive regimes in dialogues in order to increase leverage, resulted from disputes over how to deal with apartheid in South Africa and the oppressive regime in El Salvador. The situation in China after the student rebellion of Tiananmen Square created a situation where human rights issues took prominence in the US's dialogue with China on a par with economic agendas. However, what spurred the US governments to support humanitarian intervention was the experiences of human rights violations in Somalia and of massive atrocities in Rwanda and later in Bosnia.[22]

Human rights have thus entered the foreign policy agenda as an important issue during the last decades. Within the EU, human rights conditionality has figured as an important element in the Copenhagen Criteria established in 1993 regulating access to the Union of new candidate countries, and currently in deciding whether negotiations should be opened with Turkey concerning membership in the Union.

Danish development assistance to democracy and human rights was evaluated in 1999. It was estimated that support for human rights and democracy (HR&D) had increased from approximately 0.4% of development assistance in 1991 to 5.8% during 1998. Danish HR&D assistance is channelled through both multilateral and bilateral flows, as well as via Danish and international NGOs. Local NGOs are often supported through the discrete facilities Danish embassies command to support civil society work, up to a certain level. About half of Danish support for democracy and human rights is provided through Danish NGOs. In terms of allocation, the biggest share of HR&D assistance was given for capacity-building, technical advisory services and training.[23]

Two outcomes become prominent when assessing the importance of the integration of human rights concerns into foreign policy and development assistance.

First, the integration of human rights into foreign policy has contributed to the emergence of a new order based on modified sovereignty.[24] Secondly, the integration of human rights into foreign policy has also implied a stronger institutionalisation of human rights in international relations; like good governance, human rights standards have emerged among the principles and issues that are regulating part of the interaction between states. Human rights, like good governance stand-

August.

22 Donnelly, Jack and Debra Liang-Fenton, 2004. 'Introduction', In: Liang-Fenton, Debra (ed.): *Implementing US Human Rights Policy. Agendas, Policies, and Practices.* United States Institute of Peace Process.

23 *Udenrigsministeriet* [Foreign Ministry], Danida, 2000. *Evaluering. Menneskerettigheder og demokrati. Et sammendrag.* København, Udenrigsministeriet.

24 The subject is treated in Helle Malmvig's article in this volume and is not discussed in detail here.

ards, are among the issues that are debated as a global public good,[25] that is, as one of the key institutional developments of the emerging world order.

The partial integration of human rights into development assistance has implied an institutionalisation of human rights values, principles and specific rights as part of the domestic development of democratising and developing states. It would be misleading to argue that human rights have become fully mainstreamed in Western development assistance, or that donors pursue rights-based approaches in their assistance policies,[26] or even that human rights assistance has had a strong impact on the human rights accountability of governments. It would be more correct to argue that the growth in human rights development assistance and support within OSCE and other bodies working outside the sphere of development has had two important implications in recipient countries:

- A strengthening of human rights institutionalisation within states
- A growing level of interaction between human rights NGOs, donors and international organisations

Human rights principles and specific rights have thus become an issue not only in the courtrooms and jurisprudence of recipient states, but also in institutions dealing with such diverse issues as governance and transparency generally, as well as in matters of tax payment, policing, prison reform, educational reforms, health policies (including policies on HIV/Aids) and media legislation. The importance of a rights dimension is not just an occasional reference to values, but the concrete regulation of procedures according to human rights and human rights principles.[27]

In addition, the growing support for local human rights NGOs implies that public debates, advocacy campaigns and political development at large are developing with considerable inspiration from the human rights framework. As argued above, it cannot be taken for granted that these developments entail strong advances in the actual enjoyment of rights; at least it cannot be presumed that there is a mechanical line of causation between the integration of norms, principles, and rights-induced institutional change and actual human rights protection. However, the mere institutionalisation of a rights-based philosophy can be seen as a precondition for actual protection to reach even the poorest sections of communities. The changes described are therefore not insignificant, but they must also be seen in the light of countervailing forces in order to arrive at a more tempered balance.

---

25 *See* Kaul et al, 2003. *See also* Sano, 2005: 'Er god regeringsførelse et globalt offentligt gode?' in Andersen, Erik André, Birgit Lindsnæs og Stig Rée. *På vej mod nye globale strategier. Offentlige goder og Menneskerettigheder.* Djøf-forlaget 2005.

26 *See* Kirkemann Hansen, Jakob and Hans-Otto Sano, 2005, forthcoming. 'The Implication and Value Added of a Rights-based Approach' in Andreassen, Bård Anders and Stephen P. Marks: *Development as a Human Right.* A Nobel Symposium Book.

27 According to Wilson, human rights must be considered one of the most globalised political values of our age. Richard A. Wilson, 1997. *Human Rights, Culture and Context.* Introduction.

### 3.2 *Threatening Human Rights*

> What happened in Bosnia must give pause to anyone who believes in the virtues of cosmopolitanism. It is only too apparent that cosmopolitanism is the privilege of those who can take a secure nation for granted ... we are not in a post-nationalist age, and I cannot see how we will ever [be]. The cosmopolitan order...depends critically on the rule-enforcing capacities of the nation-state .... In this sense, therefore, cosmopolitans like me are not beyond the nation; and a cosmopolitan, post-nationalist spirit will always depend, in the end, on the capacity of nation states to provide security and civility for their citizens. In that sense alone I am a civic nationalist, someone who believes in the necessity of nations and in the duty of citizens to defend the capacity of nations to provide the security and rights we all need in order to live cosmopolitan lives. At the very least, cosmopolitan disdain and astonishment at the ferocity with which people will fight to win a nation state of their own is misplaced. They are, after all, only fighting for a privilege cosmopolitans have long taken for granted.[28]

Michael Ignatieff points in the quote above to the key protective role of nation states, even in a system based on a rapid spread of international institutions and with stronger notions of non-state human rights accountability than before. Ignatieff is also warning that an all too ready belief in the advances in the role of international institutions must be tempered by a realism born of an appreciation of the factors that threaten human rights protection.

In reflecting on such factors, a number of observations can be made:

- Threats derive from weak system performance. The international human rights regime has yet to adapt to its growing (political) importance. Although initiatives have been taken recently to reform the system, the outcome is far from clear; yet reform remains urgent, as system ineffectiveness – in terms of weak enforcement and the processes and effectiveness of monitoring – is instrumental in undermining the credibility of the human rights system.[29]
- Countervailing forces from inside the Western world are threatening to undermine some of the gains made in the promotion of an international rule of law. Such countervailing forces are based not only on notions of nationalist protectionism,[30] but also on objections to the consolidation of a broader human rights agenda founded on economic, social and cultural rights. An important and unresolved controversy remains concerning the relinquishing of

---

28 Quote from Michael Ignatieff, 1994, *Blood and Belonging. Journeys into the New Nationalism.* Quoted in Paul Gready, 2004. *International Journal of Human Rights*, vol. 8, no 3, p. 351.

29 See Dunér 2002, op.cit., p. 27 passim. See also the article by Stéphanie Lagoutte in the present volume.

30 Protection against refugee flows and migration are important factors, though. See Maher, Kristen Hill, 2002. 'Who has a Right to Rights? Citizenship's Exclusion in an Age of Migration,' in Brysk, Alison (ed.).: *Globalization and Human Rights.* University of California Press.

power to regional courts, supra-national bodies and international institutions generally.[31] Specific interest groups are thus contributing to a weakening of the basic coalition which has underpinned human rights reinforcement during the last decades.[32]

– Global markets raise the demand for international institutions, standardisation, and regulatory regimes. The negative impact of globalisation in terms of undermining human dignity and rights may occur precisely in war zones and conflict-prone areas where institutions are weak or non-existent, that is, in areas where global capitalism is unfettered due to the weakness of certain states, as well as ineffective international regulation. The latter point is developed further below.

It can be argued that globalisation trends affect human rights most negatively in regions and countries where there is little state control (no effective state) and a high degree of corruption. In such regions, a kind of predatory catastrophe capitalism has been developing. Reno describes how misrule and politicians' failures to meet even minimum popular expectations can lead to the collapse of order and the decline of external support. Such states then become a breeding ground for internal wars. However, even in these states rulers are able to wield power and control, despite the collapse of external support for the weak bureaucracy. Warlords or predatory rulers are served not by bureaucracies, but by business interests. Charles Taylor of Liberia was supported by Firestone Tire and Rubber's subsidiary even during a period of the early 1990s, when he did not control the capital. Laurent Kabila of Zaire was allegedly receiving "tax" support and logistical services from the Canadian-US-based mining company American Mineral Fields.[33]

The darker sides of globalisation in terms of exploitative alliances between dictators or warlords and economic investors seeking access to or control over natural resources are visible in collapsed and weak states in Africa such as Congo

31 In Denmark, otherwise a nation traditionally promoting international co-operation on human rights, a public debate evolved during 2005 between a law professor of the Faculty of Law at the University of Copenhagen, and researchers at the Danish Institute for Human Rights and at other universities, concerning the role of the European Court of Human Rights. While the law professor argued that the ECtHR had gone too far in its admission of cases and in broadening the scope of human rights, the researchers argued that the court was already restrictive in its approach. The professor also argued that the extension of areas under regional jurisdiction posed problems of democratic control.

32 *See* Forsythe, 2000, p. 7, who argues that the affluent liberal democracies of the Western world represented in the OECD (Organisation for Economic Co-operation and Development) have constituted a motor for the westernisation of international relations.

33 Reno, William, 2001. 'How Sovereignty Matters: International Markets and the Political Economy of Local Politics in Weak States', in Callaghy, Thomas, Ronald Kassimir, and Robert Latham (eds.): *Intervention and Transnationalism in Africa. Global-Local Networks of Power.* Cambridge University Press, pp. 197-205.

(DRC), Congo Brazzaville, Sierra Leone, Liberia, Somalia and to some extent Angola. However, it is less clear what the trends are in oppressive states where the bureaucracy is strong, sometimes respecting an oppressive rule of law, while also thriving on some form of corruption. In these cases, it would be more relevant to refer to oppressive and corrupt states rather than weak ones.

What is important in relation to reflections about how globalisation processes from above may impact on patterns of human rights protection is some understanding of the differentiated character of governance in respectively weak or collapsed states such as those just described, and in oppressive and corrupt ones. In fact, in terms of numbers, the latter are far more important than the former. Understanding how globalisation processes – economic and political – impact on societies and governance in respectively the OSCE region and in regions and states in Africa, South-, East- and South-East Asia, and Latin America seems to be the key to a deeper understanding of the prospects of human rights protection globally.

If a high level of corruption is generally an important indicator of bad governance, then the majority of states in the world where estimates of governance can be made are exerting quite bad or not very good governance.[34]

Table 1 records states with a relatively high level of corruption and examines the degree to which civil and political rights are respected in these states. Of the 56 states with a high degree of corruption, 46 , or 82%, exhibit a low level of civil and political rights compliance. No causal inferences are made between these two observations. What is significant, however, is that these indicators point to the existence of a large group of states that are corrupt as well as characterised by oppression. It would require a more detailed analysis than can be provided here to examine trends in some of these states. It should be clear, however, that both corruption and oppression pose serious threats to processes of reinforcing global governance and human rights protection in most continents. The indicators above remind us that the reinforcement of human rights in terms of institutional development and concerns with gross human rights violations takes place against a background which is not very promising. Cosmopolitanism, as Ignatieff observes, rests on a very fragile basis.

---

34 *See* Kaufmann, Daniel, Aart Kraay and Pablo Zoido-Lobatón. 2002. *Governance Matters II.* Policy Research Working Paper 2772, the World Bank, p. 19-21. Among the 159 states where estimates of corruption control could be undertaken covering the years 2000–2002, 42% were below the two lower quartiles in the scale measuring corruption control, 32% of the states were in the intermediate quartile, and 26% were in the upper range. Figures are based on perception surveys, and some of them are marked by high standard errors.

*Table 1. States with Poor Corruption Control and their Civil and Political Rights Compliance*

| | Control of corruption 2004 | Civil and Political Rights 2004 | | Control of corruption 2004 | Civil and Political Rights 2004 |
|---|---|---|---|---|---|
| Afghanistan | -1.33 | 7.0 | Libya | -0.91 | 7.0 |
| Albania | -0.72 | 5.0 | Macedonia | -0.52 | 4.5 |
| Algeria | -0.49 | 5.5 | Mali | -0.52 | 2.5 |
| Angola | -1.12 | 7.5 | Mexico | -0.27 | 6.0 |
| Argentina | -0.44 | 4.0 | Moldova | -0.86 | 4.5 |
| Armenia | -0.53 | 6.5 | Mozambique | -0.79 | 5.5 |
| Azerbaijan | -1.04 | 7.5 | Myanmar | -1.49 | 8.0 |
| Bangladesh | -1.09 | 6.0 | Nepal | -0.61 | 7.5 |
| Belarus | -0.91 | 6.5 | Nicaragua | -0.34 | 2.5 |
| Benin | -0.34 | 3.0 | Niger | -0.87 | 2.5 |
| Bolivia | -0.78 | 3.5 | Nigeria | -1.11 | 8.0 |
| Bosnia-Hrzg | -0.54 | 4.5 | Pakistan | -0.87 | 7.5 |
| Burkina Faso | -0.35 | 5.0 | Paraguay | -0.99 | 3.5 |
| Burundi | -1.16 | 7.0 | Peru | -0.35 | 3.5 |
| Cambodia | -0.97 | 8.0 | Romania | -0.25 | 5.5 |
| China | -0.51 | 7.5 | Russia | -0.72 | 7.5 |
| Cuba | -0.62 | 6.5 | Rwanda | -0.36 | 7.5 |
| Dom. Rep. | -0.50 | 4.0 | Sierra Leone | -0.88 | 6.5 |
| Ecuador | -0.95 | 5.0 | Sudan | -1.30 | 7.5 |
| Eritrea | -0.64 | 7.5 | Syria | -0.74 | 7.5 |
| Ethiopia | -0.85 | 7,5 | Tajikistan | -1.11 | 6.5 |
| Georgia | -0.91 | 6.0 | Tanzania | -0.57 | 5.0 |
| Guatemala | -0.74 | 5.5 | Thailand | -0.25 | 6.5 |
| Guinea | -0.81 | 6.0 | Togo | -0.92 | 5.5 |
| Haiti | -1.49 | 6.0 | Turkey | -0.23 | 7.0 |
| Honduras | -0.71 | 5.0 | Turkmenistan | -1.34 | 7.5 |
| India | -0.31 | 6.5 | Uganda | -0.71 | 7.5 |
| Indonesia | -0.90 | 7.0 | Ukraine | -0.89 | 7.0 |
| Iran | -0.59 | 8.0 | Uzbekistan | -1.21 | 7.5 |
| Jamica | -0.52 | 4.5 | Venezuela | -0.94 | 5.5 |
| Kazakhstan | -1.10 | 6.5 | Vietnam | -0.74 | 8.0 |
| Kenya | -0.89 | 5.5 | Yemen | -0.84 | 6.5 |
| Kyrgyz Rep. | -0.92 | 6.0 | Zambia | -0.74 | 6.0 |
| Lebanon | -0.51 | 6.5 | Zimbabwe | -1.01 | 7.5 |
| Liberia | -0.86 | 5.5 | | | |

Source: Kaufmann et al., 2005. Governance Matters IV. Danish Institute for Human Rights. Human Rights Indicators Database, civil and political rights. Note: The scale on governance measures performance from -2.5 to 2.5. Included in the table are those states which are found in the two lower quartiles of corruption control from a list of the performance of 204 states. The scale on civil and political rights measures country performance on a scale from 0–8, where 8 means that systematic violations take place in 8 out of 8 groups of civil and political rights measured in the index. A low number therefore indicates positive performance.

## 4 Human Rights Reinforcement From Below

A characteristic of the post-Cold War period has been the strengthening of transnational advocacy networks – activists beyond borders, as they have been called in the path-breaking study on international NGOs by Keck and Sikkink.[35] Two features may be said to be involved in these processes of reinforcing global agendas: first, growing co-operation between international and local NGOs, which is aptly described by Keck and Sikkink; and secondly, the appropriation by local NGOs of the human rights agenda as a platform for advocacy and social action. Such domestication of rights agendas often happens without a strong impetus from international NGOs.[36]

*Table 2. International NGO Growth and Issue Composition 1953–1993 (in percentages)*

| | 1953 (N=110) | 1963 (N=141) | 1973 (N=183) | 1983 (N=348) | 1993 (N=631) |
|---|---|---|---|---|---|
| **Human rights** | 30.0 | 27.0 | 22.4 | 22.7 | 26.6 |
| **Women's rights** | 9.1 | 9.9 | 8.7 | 7.2 | 9.7 |
| **Ethnic groups** | 9.1 | 8.5 | 9.8 | 10.6 | 4.6 |
| **International Law** | 12.7 | 13.4 | 13.7 | 7.4 | 4.1 |
| **Peace** | 10.0 | 14.2 | 7.7 | 6.3 | 9.4 |
| **Environment** | 1.8 | 3.5 | 5.5 | 7.5 | 14.3 |
| **Development** | 2.7 | 2.1 | 3.8 | 3.7 | 5.4 |
| **World order** | 7.3 | 2.8 | 6.6 | 8.9 | 7.6 |
| **Other** | 10.0 | 12.8 | 15.3 | 11.8 | 8.6 |

Source: Keck and Sikkink, 1998. Activists beyond Borders, p. 11. Based on Yearbook of International Organisations for the respective years. Note that in their own presentation of the table, Keck and Sikkink do not put the rows for human rights, ethnic group rights and women's rights in the above order.
Note: The figures in the table should be treated as indicative rather than as precise.

Table 2 shows the tremendous growth of international NGOs over the decades: the total number of organisations has more than quintupled between 1953 and 1993. The table also reveals that the *issue* composition did not change dramatically at the level of the NGOs operating internationally between these years. If the human rights agenda is composed of women's as well as ethnic group rights together with what are classified as human rights in the table, there is some decline in the importance

35 Keck, Margaret E. and Kathryn Sikkink, 1998. *Activists beyond Borders: Advocacy Networks in International Politics.* Cornell UP. See also the study by Boli, John and George M. Thomas, 1999. *Constructing World Culture: International Nongovernmental Organizations since 1875.* Stanford University Press, Stanford.

36 *See* the description by Richard Wilson, 1997, in *Human Rights, Culture and Context,* of how local NGOs and groups have taken the human rights agenda into their possession. Such processes are also known to the author of this article in respect of Georgia, Nigeria, and South India. There is no question that foreign finance and support are important in supporting human rights agendas in the South, but the fact that local NGOs define themselves within a rights-based agenda rather than within environmental or developmental agendas is hardly based on resource concerns, but rather on conceptions of justice and assessments of the most effective approach to take.

of organisational human rights agendas between 1953–63 averages and 1983–93 averages from 46.8% to 40.7% during the last two decades of the table. Updating this research for the present chapter is not entirely possible as the categories of the data sources are no longer the same. However, according to the data of the most recent *Yearbook of International Organizations*, the number of international organisations working with a human rights agenda tripled between 1992 and 2002.[37]

*Table 3. Local Organisations with a Human Rights Agenda 2002*

| | **Total Number of Organisations Recorded** | **Human Rights Organisations** | **Human Rights Organisations Founded Locally** |
|---|---|---|---|
| Uganda | 300 | 77 | 43 |
| Malawi | 42 | 29 | 28 |
| Niger | 29 | 28 | 28 |
| Morocco | 66 | 24 | 24 |
| Tamil Nadu | 109 | 15 | 15 |

Source: www.hri.ca; www.idealist.org; www.uia.org; www.onworld.net; www.peacewoment.org; www.soros.org; www.civilsoc.org
Note: Local Organisations are defined as those that are established in the country in question. The accuracy of some of the data has been checked in countries where the author and his colleagues had special insight into organisational development, for instance in Malawi and Afghanistan (the latter not included in the table). Not surprisingly, there is some degree of inaccuracy in the figures, particularly in a country like Afghanistan, from which data were excluded as they were deemed insufficiently reliable. In Malawi there were some problems of omission, but the order of magnitude as regards the high number of local organisations with a human rights agenda is correct.

It is more difficult to document the growth of *local* human rights organisations because accurate historical data are not available.[38]

Table 3 indicates the varying importance of the human rights agenda in the countries from respectively East and Southern Africa, West and North Africa and South Asia (using one state in India, Tamil Nadu, rather than the whole nation) during 2002. While in Niger in West Africa, the human rights agenda is present in every organisational mission statement, it is only modestly present as an organisational topic in most of the organisations in India (Tamil Nadu).[39] These differences are related to the historical development of human rights in different regions of the

37 UIA: Yearbook of International Organizations, 2003–2004. Research undertaken by Nina Svaneberg.

38 The data bases for this research were: www.hri.ca; www.idealist.org; www.uia.org; www.onworld.net; www.peacewoment.org; www.soros.org; www.civilsoc.org. The Internet sources record current organisations, some of which report their dates of establishment together with their mission.

39 Research was also undertaken on the development of human rights as a local agenda in Central Asia. However, some organisations cannot use 'human rights' concepts publicly and must refrain from making reference to human rights. The data sources also proved incorrect in a number of other respects in Central Asia.

world. From the data where human rights organisations report on their origins, it is possible to observe that the human rights agenda is connected to the process of democratic reform in regions where democratisation has taken place since the early or late 1990s. Thus, in East and Southern Africa, human rights organisations emerged during the 1990s following the process of constitutional reforms and multi-partyism. In West Africa, human rights organisations also developed with the emergence of democratisation. This happened in Niger as well as in Nigeria. In India – taking the state of Tamil Nadu as illustrative – where a democratic constitution has been in operation since independence, organisational agendas seem to have combined developmental and environmental concerns until very recently.[40]

The importance of the development of local human rights organisations is four-fold, it can be argued:

1. They institutionalise human rights values from below. Hence, they engage in local struggles over tradition, meaning and norms.
2. They contribute to human rights protection and awareness through litigation, campaigns and legal aid activities.[41]
3. They create linkages between the local and the global levels inasmuch as they engage in co-operation with and are protected and financed by international NGOs, bilateral or multilateral donors.
4. They fill in gaps where state authorities are ineffective or absent. In such processes of gap filling and social security action, they may contribute through acts of both representation and governance at the local level.[42]

---

40 Observations based on the net-data, but also on an evaluation of local organisation human rights work conducted by the author for Danida in Southern Africa (Malawi and Zimbabwe) and for the Norwegian Human Rights Fund in respectively Tamil Nadu and Nigeria. See Royal Norwegian Ministry of Foreign Affairs. *Evaluation of the Norwegian Human Rights Fund,* 1/2001.

41 In South India, local organisations were involved in actions for Dalits and for indigenous groups. They contributed to the reinforcement of rights through documentation, court action, public campaigns for land rights of indigenous groups, and advocacy at the national and international levels. See Royal Norwegian Ministry of Foreign Affairs. *Evaluation of the Norwegian Human Rights Fund,* 1/2001.

42 For a more elaborate description of both the problems and strengths of local civil society organisations' co-operation with international organisations, *see* Hans Peter Schmitz, 2001. 'When Networks Blind: Human Rights and Politics in Kenya.' See also William Reno, 2001. 'How Sovereignty Matters: International Markets and the Political Economy of Local Politics in Weak States.' For an analysis of local organisations and local governance, see Ronal Kassimir, 2001. 'Producing Local Politics: Governance, Representation and Non-State Organisations in Africa.' For an analysis of the way in which international NGOs may contribute to the creation of change in co-operation with international agencies and financial institutions, see Thomas Callaghy, 2001. 'Networks and Governance in Africa: Innovation in the Debt Regime.' All references in the volume: Callaghy, Thomas, Ronal Kassimir, and Robert Latham (eds.), 2001. *Intervention and Transnationalism in Africa: Global-Local Networks of Power.* Cambridge University Press.

Local NGOs and community organisations are therefore important in institutionalising change, not least when they co-operate and undertake advocacy vertically within states and within international organisations or cooperate horizontally among themselves in local networks and functional organisations of lobbying and advocacy. However, local organisations are not unproblematic. Their informal nature, flexibility and ease of mobilisation on issues is a strength. However, the more involved these organisations are in advocacy, the the greater the need for their accountability to be clarified in a political sense. This is a challenge not only for local organisations, but also for emerging structures and networks of global governance. Local organisations are definitely part of the new accountability agenda as described by Goetz and Jenkins (*see* section 2), not least as regards the strengthening of a more exacting agenda of social justice, but they also contribute to either global or local governance in ways that are often left unexamined.[43]

Another problem, apart from that of the representation and accountability of local NGOs, is the fact that, as indicated above, the latter are unevenly distributed. This means that structures of access to international institutions and other civil groups are skewed, often linked to either geo-political interests or to patterns of former colonial influence. Do local Indian or South American NGOs have some degree of access to international organisations like the World Bank? To some extent they may, but it can be asked whether Central Asian or Russian organisations have similar channels of access. Most likely, they do not. Emerging patterns of global governance therefore replicate existing lines of inequity that may serve to reinforce perceptions of inequities at the informal level.

There are therefore obvious problems of differential access to international institutions and well-known problems of representation and accountability on the part of local organisations that wield an influence beyond their borders. However, there are also very promising developments in the growing interactions from below with other civil society organisations across borders and vertically with international organisations. The most promising dimension is the development of the greater accountability of international institutions with respect to involving the participation of representatives of marginalised populations and their realisation of rights.

On a broader scale, the perspective of global governance offers a relevant alternative to what Thomas Pogge has described as "explanatory nationalism", that is, the convenient approach by citizens in wealthy countries of ignoring global interdependence and the way it hampers human rights realisation and of explaining the under-fulfilment of human rights from a perspective of local and national factors. Pogge's point of departure is the well-known fact that many people lack secure access to minimally adequate shares of public goods like physical integrity, adequate living standards, basic education and freedoms. He argues that the approach in resolving these issues must be national as well as international, and also non-legal as well as legal, because legal and even constitutional rights are insufficient to secure access to rights for the poor and uneducated. Pogge therefore argues that human

43 *See* Kassimir, Ronald, 2001, 104 passim.

rights must be embedded in social institutions not only by legal means, but also by moral and political ones.[44]

## 5 Conclusions: Improved Human Rights Enjoyment?

The globalisation debate currently revolves largely around security issues and terrorism. A second dimension of the globalisation debate is the relative importance and impact of the globalisation of economic and communication flows, that is, the de-linking of trade, investments and communication from territorial geography. However, there is a political and institutional dimension to globalisation which is often under-reported, namely the expansion of the role of international institutions and their influence in regulating flows of values and political and legal interaction, as well as trade and investments.

Since the end of the Cold War, important changes have occurred as a result of both economic and political globalisation. In this chapter, the concept of global governance has been used to describe the processes that are occurring. What is emerging is an institutionalisation of international politics through inter-state co-operation, through co-operation among international organisations and institutions, and through the interaction between local civil societies and the formalised institutions of national and international governance. A global civil society does not exist as a very structured network, but global civil society interactions have emerged, for instance, the global social summit. New dimensions of accountability are therefore emerging, some based on legitimate claims that are founded on the representation of local concerns, while others are less democratic in nature. The framework of global governance as used in this chapter has its strength in outlining new dimensions of accountability.

What is argued here is that the meaning of accountability is changing from a formal to a less formalised regime. Thus, international institutions can no longer be expected to respond to the concerns of governments alone, but must also take account of advocacy and lobbying by civil society groups. Some of these groups are value-based, for instance, based on human rights platforms rather than on strong backward linkages to rural areas and populations in their respective societies. However, what is also crucial in this regard is that international organisations and institutions depend on local actors in order not only to legitimise their agendas, but also to implement them. For business corporations and transnational investors, legitimation and certification through global standards and baseline codes are becoming increasingly important marketing strategies.

It has been the aim of this chapter to argue that these trends are important. It is fascinating that so much has happened on the global scene during the last two decades, while it seems that some of the developments are barely being noted by observers living in the middle of them.

44 See Pogge, Thomas. 2003. *World Poverty and Human Rights: Cosmopolitan Responsibilities and Reforms.* Polity, pp. 45-49, 56-58.

What does globalisation portend for human rights? While the trends described above are important, they should not be used to argue that a cosmopolitan world order, that is, an order based on the principles described by Held above, is around the corner. Examining human rights and corruption indicators tells a different story, namely that bad and oppressive governance is a salient feature of the majority of the world's states. Those who argue, like the US-based Freedom House, that freedom is on the march could take a sobering look at the figures for corruption and human rights violations.

Human rights reinforcement is therefore threatened not only in the darkest areas of the globe, where collapsed states, internal warlordism, and economic exploitation are undermining any notion of rights, but also more generally in those states where corruption and human rights violations are endemic.

There are therefore strong indications that the processes of globalisation can reinforce human rights threats in failed states. In addition, it can be hypothesised that the emerging structures of global governance based on human rights values have had little positive impact in a number of states such as those with initial conditions characterised by corruption and oppression. However, as this chapter has mostly been concerned with outlining and discussing processes, more elaborate analyses of impact would be necessary in order to substantiate these points.

These hypotheses aside, the chapter has made the argument that globalisation contributes to processes of global governance which in turn may engender human rights reinforcement through at least three important channels:

- In the interaction between local organisations acting in defence of rights and international institutions, that is, through processes where oppressive states are subject to what have been described as boomerang processes.
- In the interactions between local and international NGOs acting in defence of rights and on behalf of powerless groups, thus contributing to the emergence of a global civil society based on human rights values.
- In the interactions between state actors and international institutions seeking to reinforce respect for human rights and good governance from above.

The positive trends of human rights reinforcement are, however, feeble, because the international system of human rights monitoring is also weak. Human rights protection is potentially weakened by disagreements in the West between realists and liberalists, or conservatives and socialists, about the need for international and global governance and an international rule of law. The alliance between OECD states, international institutions and organisations, and local NGOs, which has been instrumental in promoting human rights, is not a firm and formalised one. From within the Western states, there are conservative forces working towards an agenda of nationalist and bilateral priorities.

In addition, it should also be emphasised that although global governance promotes the institutionalisation of human rights, there is no direct or simple link between the institutionalisation of human rights and their protection. The changing accountability that is emerging is still fragile as regards human rights protection. This is partly due to the fact that while human rights institutional development has expanded, the consolidation of institutional performance marked by a higher effectiveness of the human rights regime has not been achieved.

What is promising, however, is that the institutionalisation of human rights from below reinforces those who defend human rights, while also deepening human rights legitimacy locally. This is no longer a Western agenda; the activists beyond the borders have turned the agenda into a more universal one.

### References

Boli, John and George M. Thomas, 'Introduction', in Boli, John and George M. Thomas (eds.), *Constructing World Culture. International Non-Governmental Organizations since 1875*, Stanford University Press, 1999.

Clark, Ian, 'Globalization and the Post-cold-war Order', in Baylis, John and Steve Smith (eds.), *The Globalization of World Politics. An Introduction to International Relations*, pp. 634-647, 2001.

Donnelly, Jack, 'Human Rights, Globalization Flows, and State Power', in Brysk, Alison (ed.), *Globalization and Human Rights*, University of California Press, 2002.

Donnelly, Jack and Debra Liang-Fenton, 'Introduction', in Liang-Fenton, Debra (ed.): *Implementing US Human Rights Policy. Agendas, Policies, and Practices*, United States Institute of Peace Process, 2004.

Goetz, Anne Marie and Rob Jenkins, *Reinventing Accountability. Making Democracy Work for Human Development*, Palgrave, 2005.

Gready, Paul, 'Conceptualizing Globalisation and Human Rights: Boomerangs and Borders', *International Journal of Human Rights*, vol. 8, no. 3, 2004.

Habermas, Jürgen, 'Transition of International Law from a National to a Postnational Constellation', Translated into Danish from a presentation held in Istanbul 2003: 'Folkeretten i overgangen til den postnationale konstellation' in *Distinktion. Scandinavian Journal of Social Theory*, no. 8, 2004.

Halliday, Fred, 'Global Governance. Prospects and Problems' in Held, David and Anthony McGrew (eds.), *The Global Transformations Reader. Second edition*, Polity Press, 2003.

Held, David, Anthony McGrew, David Goldblatt and Jonathan Perraton, *Global Transformations. Politics, Economics and Culture*. Polity Press, 1999.

Held, David and Anthony McGrew, 'Political Globalization: trends and Choices', in Kaul, Inge, Pedro Conceicão, Katell le Gouven and Ronald U Mendoza (eds.), *Providing Global Public Goods. Managing Globalization*, UNDP, Oxford University Press, 2003.

Kaldor, Mary, 'Transnational Civil Society', in Dunne, Tim and Nicholas J. Wheeler (eds.), *Human Rights in Global Politics*, Cambridge University Press, 1999.

Kalder, Mary, 'The Idea of Global Civil Society', *International Affairs* 79, 2003.

Kaufmann, Daniel, Aart Kraay and Pablo Zoido-Lobatón, *Governance Matters II*, Policy Research Working Paper 2196, the World Bank, 1999.

Kaufmann, Daniel, Aart Kraay and Massimo Mastruzzi, *Governance Matters IV*, Policy Research Working Paper, the World Bank, 2005.

Kaul, Inge and Ronald U. Mendoza, 'Advancing the Concept of Public Goods', in Kaul, Inge, Pedro Conceicão, Katell le Gouven and Ronald U Mendoza (eds.), *Providing Global Public Goods. Managing Globalization*. UNDP, Oxford University Press, 2003.

Kaul, Inge, Pedro Conceicão, Katell le Gouven and Ronald U Mendoza, 'Why Do Public Goods Matter Today?' in Kaul, Inge, Pedro Conceicão, Katell le Gouven and Ronald U Mendoza (eds.) *Providing Global Public Goods. Managing Global.* UNDP, Oxford University Press, 2003.

Kaul, Inge, Pedro Conceicão, Katell le Gouven and Ronald U Mendoza, *Providing Global Public Goods. Managing Globalization.* UNDP, Oxford University Press, 2003.

Keck, Margaret E. and Kathryn Sikkink, *Activists beyond Borders: Advocacy Networks in International Politics*, Cornell UP, 1998.

Keohane, Robert O. and Joseph S. Nye, 'Introduction', in Nye, Joseph S. and John D. Donahue (eds.). *Governance in a Globalizing World*, Brookings Institutions Press, 2000.

Kjærum, Morten, 'National Human Rights Institutions Implementing human Rights', in Bergsmo, Morten (ed.), *Human Rights and Criminal Justice for the Down-Trodden: Essays in Honour of Asbjørn Eide*, Martinus Nijhoff, 2003.

Leftwich, Adrian, 'Governance, Democracy and Development in the Third World', in Corbridge, Stuart (ed.), *Development Studies. A Reader*, London/New York, E. Arnold, 1995.

Maher, Kristen Hill, 'Who has a Right to Rights? Citizenship's Exclusion in an Age of Migration', in Brysk, Alison (ed.).: *Globalization and Human Rights.* University of California Press, 2002.

Pogge, Thomas, *World Poverty and Human Rights. Cosmopolitan responsibilities and Reforms*, Polity, 2003.

Prakash, Aseem and Jeffrey A. Hart, 'Globalization and Governance: An Introduction', in Prakash, Aseem and Jeffrey A. Hart (eds.), *Globalization and Governance*, Routledge, 1999.

Rée, Stig, *Globale goder og udenrigspolitikkens praksis – en historisk, ledelsesteoretisk analyse*, 2003.

Reno, William, 'How Sovereignty Matters: International Markets and the Political Economy of Local Politics in Weak States', in Callaghy, Thomas, Ronald Kassimir, and Robert Latham (eds.), *Intervention and Transnationalism in Africa. Global-Local Networks of Power*, Cambridge University Press, pp. 197-215, 2001.

Rosenau, James N, 'Disaggregated Order and Disorder', in Hansen, Birthe and Bertel Heurlin (eds.), *The New World Order. Contrasting Theories*, McMillan Press, 2000.

Sano, Hans-Otto, 'Development and Human Rights: The Necessary, but Partial Integration of Human Rights and Development', *Human Rights Quarterly*, vol. 22, 3 August, pp. 734-52, 2000.

Sano, Hans-Otto, 'Er god regeringsførelse et globalt offentligt gode?', in Andersen, Erik André, Birgit Lindsnæs og Stig Rée (eds.), *På vej mod nye globale strategier. Offentlige goder og Menneskerettigheder*, Djøf-forlaget, 2005.

Schmitz, Hans Peter, 'Human Rights and Politics in Kenya', in Callaghy, Thomas, Ronald Kassimir, and Robert Latham (eds.), *Intervention and Trasnationalism in Africa. Global-Local Networks of Power*, Cambridge University Press, 2001.

Scholte, Jan Aart, 'The Globalization of World Politics', in Baylis, John and Steve Smith (eds.), *The Globalization of World Politics. An Introduction to International Relations*, Oxford University Press, 2001.

Udenrigsministeriet [Foreign Ministry], Danida, *Evaluering. Menneskerettigheder og demokrati. Et sammendrag*, København, Udenrigsministeriet, 2000.

UIA (Union of International Associations) *Yearbook of International Organizations. Guide to Global Civil Society Networks*, 2004-05.

UNDP, *Governance for Sustainable Human Development. A UNDP Policy Document.* UNDP, 1997.

Youngs, Richard, 'The European Union and Democracy Promotion in the Mediterranean: A New Disingenous Strategy', in Gillespie, Richard and Richard Youngs (eds.). *The European Union and Democracy Promotion. The Case of North Africa*, Frank Cass, pp. 40-62, 2002.

Waltz, Kenneth N., 'Intimations of Multipolarity', in Hansen, Birthe and Bertel Heurlin (eds.): *The New World Order. Contrasting Theories*, McMillan Press, 2000.

Weiss, Thomas G., 'Governance, Good Governance and Global Governance: Conceptual and Actual Changes', *Third World Quarterly*, vol. 21, no. 5, 2000.

World Bank, *Sub-Saharan Africa. From Crisis to Sustainable Growth. A Long Term Perspective Study*, The World Bank, 1989.

World Bank, *Governance. The World Bank's Experience*, The World Bank, 1994.

World Bank, *Reforming Public Institutions and Strengthening Governance: A World Bank Strategy*, The World Bank, 2000.

# 4. The Uneasy Balance between Individual Rights and the Necessity of Communities

*Sten Schaumburg-Müller*

The core of this chapter is an analysis of the relationship between the individual and the community in a human rights set up. It is my contention that this relationship has not been grasped adequately and that this inadequacy has wide practical implications, thus contributing to conceptual as well as factual turmoil. According to the analysis, human rights are attached to the individual, implying that the phrases group rights and natural rights are misnomers (section 1). However, rights are social and presuppose groups or communities (section 2). Consequently, there is a built-in tension between the individual, worthy of human rights protection, and the group, which is protector as well as violator of human rights (section 3). Often, human rights are seen in opposition to or together with the state, but as the Universal Declaration states, there are many human-rights-relevant communities, such as the family, society, association and international order (section 4). The relevance and even necessity of the many types of community for human rights are analysed further (section 5), and the points raised are used to analyse aspects of the present security agenda (section 6). The last part offers a conclusion and presents some overall perspectives (section 7).

## 1 Human Rights Are Individual

The first contention of this chapter is that human rights are individual and that any talk of human rights as collective rights or group right rights is conceptually mistaken, philosophically inconsistent and politically dangerous.

Human rights are simply rights attached to human beings, only to human beings and to all human beings. Zebras, gorillas, pigs and sheep may have rights in the sense that they are legally protected from extinction, maltreatment, etc., but such rights are not human rights. It may even be disputed whether it is appropriate at all to use the term 'rights' in relation to the legal protection of animals, as the animals themselves can never claim their rights, especially not towards other animals, but this is not at issue here. The point is that among animals and any other creatures, only humans can have human rights. But a corollary of this is that *all* human beings

*S. Lagoutte, H-O. Sano and P. Scharff Smith (eds.),* Human Rights in Turmoil, *pp. 71-96.*

have human rights as part of the very definition of those rights. Human rights are not dependent on any group affiliation, such as nationality, geographical location, religious belief, etc. (frequent denominators of various legal systems), nor on other distinctions such as income, colour, etc. This feature distinguishes human rights from other commonly occurring types of rights, such as rights attached to mainly territorially defined national legal systems, religious law and even international public law.

Human rights are only dependent on one affiliation, namely the affiliation to a natural species: *homo sapiens*.[1] It is in this way – and only in this way – that human rights can be said to be natural, in the sense that this type of right is attached to the natural species. By contrast, human rights are *not* natural in the sense that rights emerge directly from nature, in the way that natural-law philosophers claim. Human *rights* are not a natural fact; human *beings* are, and this natural fact defines the group which are the objects of those rights.

Thus, human rights represent liberation from any socially defined status, including nationality. This is spelled out in Article 2 (1) of the Universal Declaration: 'Everyone is entitled to all the rights and freedoms set forth in this Declaration, without distinction of any kind, such as race, colour, sex, language, religion, political or other opinion, national or social origin, property, birth or other status.' Human rights are only dependent on the natural status of being a human being.

In this way, human rights are truly universal, as is claimed in the title of the 1948 Declaration. Even though universality is also a feature of many other legal systems – indeed, the constitutional nation state could not function without rights being applied universally – universality within a nation state is somewhat limited and incomplete, as indicated in the 1789 French Declaration, which is not for humans as such but limited to French citizens,[2] thus representing a local universality and consequently not being truly universal. In this way, post-Second World War international human rights are more truly *human* rights, more real in the Hegelian sense.[3]

This approach also places the emphasis on gender as an important element of human-rights analysis, the two sexes being naturally grounded categories. Just as human individuals are natural facts, it is a fact that humans are divided into two natural subgroups: female and male.[4] This leaves human rights with an inherent

1 Whether rights are attached to the genus *homo* (thus including e.g. *homo neanderthalensis*), to the subgroup *homo sapiens* (thus including *homo sapiens idaltu*) or limited to *homo sapiens* is an interesting question, but presently without practical implications, as other species and subspecies are extinct. At any rate, 'rights' presupposes a species mastering complicated language and complex concepts.

2 'Déclaration des droits de l'homme et du citoyen', i.e. of the rights of man-and-citizen.

3 In Hegelian terms, one could say that human rights have left the natural-rights state-attached level and become abstract, universal human rights for all. However, this is only the antithesis, as their implementation, the *konkrete Freiheit*, is yet to be obtained at the global level.

4 The boundary is not impassable and some individuals are born with equivocal sexual characteristics. Still, the vast majority of humans are born with a clear sex which is a definite either/or, not a continuum.

problem of equality between the sexes. What, for instance, constitutes equality in relation to the foetus and newborn child? Joint decision as regards abortion? Custody rights to the newborn child also for the father, who has done nothing for approximately nine months? Man and woman have both contributed as necessary components in the procreation,[5] but in very different ways, which may call for differentiated rights rather than equal rights.

On the other hand, all cultures seem to have taken social differences much further than is supported by the natural differences (voting rights, to give just one example), and besides, differences attached to sex seem to be deeply embedded in culture and difficult to get rid of, probably due to the fact that they are regarded as natural.

Secondly, the approach brings the question of groups and collectives to the forefront. Collectives – as opposed to human beings – are not natural facts but social facts. Groups may, of course, be said to be natural in the sense that human beings live in groups. This simply means that *grouping* is natural and that it is natural for human beings to gather in groups; it does not render any particular kind of group natural. Neither people nor the state nor most other communities, except perhaps for family in the broad sense of the term, are natural phenomena. As regards states, this is obvious simply because the nation state is a rather recent historical phenomenon. Certainly in legal thinking states are often taken as natural, the assumption being that they are given or taken for granted just like human individuals. However, this is a conceptual mistake: humans are natural facts; collectives, including states, are social facts.

Thus, the shared Article 1 of the 1966 Covenants[6] involves a misconception or to be more precise, an inadequacy. The conception that 'all peoples have the right of self-determination' grasps, albeit inadequately, that rights presuppose a community and that the rights-rendering community must itself be autonomous in some sense. However, the rights-rendering community is not necessarily a 'people', as there are many other possible rights-rendering communities. Besides, a 'people' is neither a naturally given[7] nor an easily distinguishable entity, and therefore cannot represent the one and only community in which human rights can blossom. Politically, although the self-determination of peoples was a well-founded concept used against colonialism and for the right to decolonisation, it cannot serve as a broader

5 At least, this is still the case. A profound change in procreation techniques will inevitably entail changes in the law as well.

6 The International Covenant on Social, Economic and Cultural Rights and the International Covenant on Civil and Political Rights.

7 Søren Krarup, Danish nationalist essayist and Member of Parliament, refers to the 'historically given people', in *Dansen om menneskerettighederne* [Worship Human Rights], Gyldendal, 2000. This is correct in the sense that at a given historical moment one can with reasonable clarity – although not without blurred boundaries – identify a Danish people; but it is not correct in the sense that this 'given' is unchangeable or eternal. On the contrary, it is bound to change, intended or not. The perception of a people as given is a political tool in the sense that it can influence the way in which changes come about.

right for 'peoples',[8] nor is it an adequate concept for grasping the relationship between individual human rights and the necessary community.

This means that minority rights and indigenous peoples' rights are not human rights and that minority rights cannot be put in the same category as gender equality.[9] A 'minority' presupposes a state, which is not a natural entity like a human being, and unlike sex, a minority is not a natural phenomenon.

This does not mean, however, that minority and indigenous rights are irrelevant and that the only protection needed is human rights, nor that there are no connections between human rights and minority and indigenous rights. Of course, human rights can be interpreted in a more or less minority-sensitive way,[10] but this is not equivalent to their being of the same category. Lumping human rights and minority rights in the same basket probably stems from the notion that both are indispensable. This is correct, but categorising all indispensable rights as 'human rights' is neither an analytical advantage nor a necessity, as human rights can never be sufficient on their own as a means of ordering a society.

To sum up: human rights are individual. To speak of collective rights or group rights is a mistake, an abortive attempt to integrate the necessary social dimension into necessarily individualistic human rights. The social dimension is not a right, but a condition. Collective rights (state rights, minority rights, etc.) are important because they deal with the way we organise. But groups are not humans, nor are they natural. We can – to the extent that we can consciously organise our societal life – give different weight to different kinds of groups; and it seems quite clear that we have not found an appropriate balance between the various collectives involved, such as states, minorities and international society, let alone between the various collectives and individual rights. But conceiving the social dimension of rights as collective rights does not make it easier for us to solve these difficult legal-political problems.

## 2 Rights Are Social

The second contention of this chapter is that all rights are social in the sense that they presuppose a group, a collective, and that rights are a way of organising that group. The concept of 'rights' involves community in the same way as the concept of reality: "Thus, the very origin of the concept of reality shows that this conception essentially involves the notion of a community, without definite limits, and capa-

8 Jack Donnelly, *Universal Human Rights in Theory and Practice*, Cornell University Press, 2nd. ed., 2003, p. 222-223; Manfred Nowak, *CCPR Commentary*, N.P. Engel Publisher, 1993, p. 21-22.

9 Martin Scheinin's suggestion in 'Minority Rights: Additional Rights or Added Protection?' Morten Bergsmo (ed.), *Human Rights and Criminal Justice for the Downtrodden: Essays in Honour of Asbjørn Eide*, Martinus Nijhoff Publishers, 2003, p. 490.

10 Scheinin, *ibid.*, p. 490.

ble of a definite increase of knowledge."[11] Rights are not (necessarily) social in the sense of social rights under the ICESCR[12] or under the welfare state, but they are necessarily social in the sense that they are inter-subjective, working only between subjects who have formed some type of community or collective.

Habermas has analysed the refined understanding of *subjektive Rechte* within the modern state, from being a purely individually based concept to being one that advocates including the social element.[13] In the mid-nineteenth century, subjective rights were seen as being grounded in the individual. In the words of von Savigny, rights are 'the power pertaining to the individual person: an area in which his will rules', not unlike Locke's conception of natural individual rights.[14] Towards the end of the century, rights were seen as something conferred by the state. According to Rudolf Jhering, 'individual rights are powers of law conferred on the individual by the legal order', and similarly Bernhard Windscheid: "Right is a power or rule of will conferred by the legal order." Hans Kelsen pursued this state-based perception and conceived the subjective entitlement as authorised through orders by the sovereign, and as intimately attached to the existing legal order. In this way, the social aspect was understood solely in terms of a state.

After the war and the reign of the Nazis, there was an understandable return to the individualistic approach: "The idea of 'subjective right' carries on the view that private law and the legal protection grounded in it serve to maintain the individual's freedom in society" (Helmut Coing, 1959). This was followed by a renewed attempt to include the social: "More is required than a recognition of this private legal standing. Rather, it is just as important that one also integrates the individual by law into the ordered network of relationships.... In other words, one must develop and protect the legal institutions in which the individual assumes the status of member" (Ludwig Raiser, 1961). Thus, Raiser sought to attach the concept of subjective rights not only to the *Rechtsstaat* but also to the democratic welfare state (*Sozialstaat*) in which individuals are no longer subjects who merely have to obey orders, but equal members of society.

However, Habermas insists that these understandings are insufficient, first because they do not lift the focus from the individual and therefore do not see the necessary context, the fundamentally inter-subjective aspect of subjective rights. Secondly, the social, to the extent that it is included, is understood in form of an

11 Charles Sanders Peirce, *Collected Papers*, vol. 5, ed. by Charles Hartshorne and Paul Weiss, Harvard University Press, 1958-60, p. 311 (as referred to by Habermas, below, n. 13).

12 International Covenant on Economic, Social and Cultural Rights.

13 Jürgen Habermas, *Faktizität und Geltung: Beiträge zur Diskurstheorie des Rechts und des demokratischen Rechtsstaats*, Suhrkamp, 1993, pp. 112-116. Quotations from the English translation by William Rehg, *Between Facts and Norms*, Polity Press, 1996, pp. 85-88.

14 'All Men are naturally in ... a State of perfect Freedom to order their Actions, and dispose of their Possessions ... as they think fit.' John Locke, *Two Treatises of Government*, Second Treatise, Ch. II, § 4, 1st ed. 1690. Quotation from edition by Peter Laslett, Cambridge University Press, 1960, p. 309.

overarching state, which still neglects the fundamentally inter-subjective aspect of a right. Rather, "a right … is a relationship and a social practice …. Rights are social propositions … [and] … a form of social cooperation."[15] Rights are social in the sense that they presuppose cooperation between those involved, and in the wider sense in that they presuppose a group or community in which this cooperation can function.

Habermas's point of departure is the German *Zivilrechtsdogmatik*, but a similar analysis could be made of human rights. Individual human rights are not based in the individual or in nature, nor is the state the benevolent and omnipotent provider of rights. Rather, rights are – or have the potential to be – the social structuring of a more or less well-defined group or collective. Jack Donnelly expresses part of the point in this way: 'rights are a social practice' and 'individual rights are a social strategy',[16] although his point of departure is different.[17]

It is worth noting that Habermas thus offers a space between the Scylla of natural and the Charybdis of positive law. According to a strong tradition, subjective rights can only be based *either* in the given state order (positive law), as suggested by Jhering and many others, *or* – if positive law does not provide subjective rights – in 'nature', understood as the state of nature (Locke) or as the nature of the individual him- or herself.

It is obvious that human rights cannot simply be connected to positive law. Human rights are an operational concept even without a basis in any promulgated law, although, of course, positivation strengthens human rights and may even be seen as a necessary part of them.[18]

Historically, natural law served as the relevant (constructed) foundation, with John Locke and Hugo Grotius as its leading philosophers. However, with the hindsight of more than three hundred years of historical development and legal, philosophical and anthropological research, we can see that the reference to 'nature' in Locke's writings merely serves as a black-box reference to what is *not* positive law and what is *not* the state. But there are other alternatives to positive law than natural law, and other alternatives to the state than 'nature'. What is not state law is not necessarily 'natural' by any means. Law connected to other groups or collectives was only vaguely comprehensible in the seventeenth century, but is much clearer

15 *Ibid.*, p. 116 with a reference to F. Michelman, 'Justification and the Justifiability in a Contradictory World', *Nomos*, Vol. XVIII, 1986, p. 71 *et seq.* This article, however, contains no further analysis of the inter-subjectivity of law.

16 Donnelly, op. cit., p. 204 and p. 209, note 4, respectively.

17 'The source of human rights is man's moral nature, which is only loosely linked to the "human nature"', Donnelly, op.cit., p. 14.

18 In this way human rights can be seen as a Hegelian development – thesis: natural law; antithesis: positive law; synthesis: a Habermasian inclusion of both positions (thus constituting an *Aufhebung*). See G.W.F. Hegel, *Grundlinien der Philosophie des Rechts*, Verlag Ullstein GmbH, 1972 (1st edition 1821).

now: we know that there are other possible law-making groups than the state,[19] and we have experienced the reality of mankind as one social unit.

In the twentieth century – and probably even more in the twenty-first – it makes sense to conceive of humanity as a group and to see that it is exactly this group that makes universal human rights possible. This does not spell out human rights attached to other groups such as states (human rights protected in the constitution or other state law) or regions (human rights protected by regional arrangements such as the Council of Europe), but it does point to humanity as the prerequisite law-making group for universal human rights.

Thus, 'nature' has had the function of a black-box reference to something that is not a state and something that is not positive law. Now it is apparent, I maintain, that it is not nature either, but an emerging concept of mankind as a whole in legal terms (not only in moral or religious terms), a concept that had to develop from the horizon of the state in the eighteenth and nineteenth centuries, to the horizon of the inter-national in the twentieth century and – eventually – to the global level of the twenty-first century. Interestingly, the anthropologists of 1948 were unable to grasp mankind as a group either, but could only understand group and culture as being geographically limited. Fortunately, the drafters of the Declaration did not share the same scholarly bias.[20]

Twining has pointed out that the concept of the 'group' has been left out of legal philosophy, thus preventing an appropriate understanding of the law.[21] The same could be said of human rights philosophy. Not analysing the connection between group and human rights has led many astray in the wilderness of natural law.

My contention is that understanding that rights are social, that they are inter-subjective and that they are attached to a group enables us to cope better with certain problems, both theoretical and practical, in relation to individual (human) rights and the necessary community.

First, it is possible, although still difficult, to overcome the dichotomy between natural and positive law as insufficient positions. Much analytical effort can be directed towards activities other than defending inadequate positions.

Secondly, it enables us to analyse the various groups in legal terms, such as mankind (global level), regions, states, minorities (within states), sub-state groups (like tribes or peoples in Africa) and trans-border groups (like trans-national companies), and to analyse their mutual relations and their relations to individuals – rather than just leaving us with the simplistic terminology of 'state' and 'individual'.

Thirdly, it provides an improved point of departure for analysing the tension between the individual and the society in questions relating to security.

---

19 Ethnic groups are but one example. There is an abundance of literature on the topic of non-state law, and even a Commission on Folk Law and Legal Pluralism.

20 The American Association of Anthropologists, 'Statement on Human Rights', *American Anthropologist*, 1947, vol. 49 (4), pp. 539-43.

21 William Twining, *Globalisation and Legal Theory*, Butterworths, 2000, p. 166.

## 3 The Tension

The third contention of the chapter is that the collective, the very same entity that renders rights (including human rights) possible, is also the entity that threatens and violates those same rights. While it is true that rights are social and in that sense therefore presuppose a community (contention two, above), it is at the same time true that the same community is the principal violator of these rights.

If person A kills person B, this is in a sense a human rights violation (cf. the Universal Declaration Article 3, which provides for the right to life). But it is more obvious to talk about a human rights violation only when the collective (in contemporary law usually the state) becomes involved, either as the principal actor – A is a detainee beaten to death by B, a police officer – or as a non-actor by letting people get away with killing each other.[22]

In his analysis of the Universal Declaration Model of Human Rights, Donnelly points to the fact that the state is the principal protector and essential violator.[23] Earlier I emphasised the love/hate relationship between the state and human rights: on the one hand, human rights love the state because human rights require an entity to fulfil themselves. On the other hand, human rights hate the state because the state that is violating these rights.[24] The point is a valid one, but it is not restricted to the relationship between human rights and the state; it is also relevant for the relationship between human rights and any law-generating or even rights-rendering group. The state is neither the sole protector or violator of human rights, and sometimes it is not even the principal collective in relation to human rights protection or violation. Donnelly and my earlier analysis simply ignore the fact that there are many norm-producing entities,[25] as well as the possibility that these entities are or may be relevant and important in relation to human rights norms.

Besides the points that there are several communities relevant for human rights and that these communities all are potential protectors as well as potential violators, one can consider whether the tension also goes the other way round: are human rights only strengthening for the community because they are an efficient way of ordering a community, or do they also have a disintegrative function, thus threatening the cohesion of the community?[26] I shall not pursue this problem in the present chapter but only make a few preliminary remarks. First, rights are not de-

22 As an example, see *Özgür Gündem* v. *Turkey*, app. no. 23144/93, ECtHR 16 March 2000.

23 Donnelly, op. cit., p. 33.

24 *Internationale handelsrelationer i retsteoretisk belysning*. [International Trade Relations in the Light of Legal Theory], Jurist- og Økonomforbundets Forlag, 1997, p. 140.

25 Sally Falk Moore, in *Law as Process* (Routledge and Kegan Paul, 1978), talks about many 'semi-autonomous social fields' as norm-generating and norm-reproducing entities; cf. also the vast discussion on legal pluralism.

26 Peter Dews claims that a legalisation of social relations may singularise the individual and thus contribute to societal disintegration,: 'Law, Solidarity and the Task of Philosophy', in *The Politics of Human Rights*, ed. O. Savic for The Belgrade Circle Journal, Verso Books, London, 2002, pp. 84-100; see the discussion in Frederik T. Pedersen, 'Human

structive or disintegrative of communities but rather, they are often ways of mending disintegrated communities, answers to disintegration rather than its cause.[27] Secondly, there is always the possibility of abuse,[28] and the abuse of rights may, of course, be disintegrative and may even itself be an infringement of rights (cf. the warning in Art. 30 of the Universal Declaration that the human rights listed do not entail a right to destroy other rights). Thirdly, rights cannot fulfil the role of the only social relation. Thus, a family – and, I suggest, any other community – cannot function properly if it is only based on rights, though on the other hand rights may very well strengthen the cohesion that is already present. The right of a child not to be beaten even by its parents strengthens mutual respect between the child and its parents and with it their cohesion, in comparison to a family that is held together by dominance and power.

However, even if rights are an integrative factor, there is still a tension between the rights of the individual and the community. When dealing with this tension, it is important to be aware that there are several types of community. The Universal Declaration provides us with a wide range of collective entities that are relevant for human rights, and it is therefore worth examining these entities more closely.

## 4 A Human Rights Typology of Collectives

The 1948 Universal Declaration of Human Rights abandoned the limited horizon of seventeenth-century natural law, with its simplistic nature/state dichotomy, and opened up space for a variety of collectives in addition to the state, even though the state still plays a crucial role, to some extent behind the scenes.

The Universal Declaration is interesting as it is the first truly international human rights document (the documents abolishing slavery in the nineteenth century are also human rights documents, but the international aspect is limited to a few state parties), and it indicates the opening of a new era without the subsequent connection between human rights and international public law (*Völkerrecht*). This connection was, of course, necessary, since the Declaration was not binding and therefore incomplete in relation to the implementation of human rights. Yet, the close connection between human rights and international public law is not altogether a happy one, as states are not the only actors, whether in relation to threats to human rights or to their protection.

The Universal declaration lists the following collective entities:

---

Rights and Solidarity.: Two Creatures of the Modern World', paper presented to the IVR 2005 Conference in Granada.

27 See an earlier article, 'San Juan Chamula og verdenshistoriens bulldozer'. [San Juan Chamula and the Bulldozer of World History], on an indigenous people's right to culture versus the rights of the individual members of the group, from Chiapas, Mexico, *Retfærd*, No. 57, 1992, pp. 3-12.

28 For a general theory on the abuse of rights, see Jens Evald, *Retsmisbrug*, Jurist- og Økonomforbundets Forlag, 2001.

**(1)** Significantly, the first group to be mentioned is the *human family*, which appears in the first paragraph of the preamble. This is exactly an indication that humanity is the main relevant group in connection to human rights. Even the somewhat poetical framing, 'the human family', indicates a group that is more connected than merely being present at the same time at the same place. In this chapter, I shall not offer a more in-depth analysis of the internal coherence of various collectives – the *Gemeinschaft/Gesellschaft* discussion – but will just point to the fact that the term 'family' indicates a closer and more organic collective.

**(2)** Art. 16 (3) states that 'the *family* is the natural and fundamental group unit of society'. This rightly indicates that in a sense the 'family' is a natural fact: for humanity procreation is a necessity, and biologically human beings cannot do without approximately nine months' protection by the mother and several years of care, upbringing and protection, though not necessarily by the natural parents. In this way, the family is a natural necessity for human beings as opposed to other species such as sea turtles, which do not need any family. Of course, the family is also a social and cultural fact in the sense that it is culturally structured. Thus there may be single-unit adult families, nuclear families and their variants with same-sex social parents, or extended families including cousins, uncles, aunts, etc. with considerable influence. It is noteworthy that the Declaration is not specific as to the types of family that are included under human rights protection. The family is a necessity, but its type is bound to vary to a considerable degree.

**(3)** *Community* is mentioned three times: in Article 18 of the Universal Declaration, 'freedom of belief...in community with others'; in Article 27 (1), freedom to 'participate in the cultural life of the community'; and in Article 29 (1), 'Everyone has duties to the community in which alone the free and full development of his personality is possible.'

'Community' is not a precise entity and the term has slightly different meanings in the text of the Declaration. Still, it is a collective entity which is easily distinguishable from other collectives such as the family and the state, and moreover, it emphasises the importance for human beings to belong to a community or even to several communities. Freedom of belief – one of the four freedoms mentioned in Roosevelt's famous 1941 State of the Union address to the Congress – is thus inseparably connected to the notion of community. Religion and religious practice in broad terms simply involve a community, and the protection of solitary religious practice alone would obviously be inadequate. It is also obvious that the religious community is not equivalent to the state, although the wording of Article 27 does not exclude state churches. The 'community' mentioned in Article 27 concerning cultural life may be a more local community, but it is not conceptually linked to any geographical territory or size. Finally, the community to which individuals owe duties according to Article 29 is also undefined, and may mean a local community as well as the state or even the human community as a whole.

It is significant that Article 29 expressly states that the individual cannot function as a human being without belonging to a community. As I have argued, the same goes for the rights of the individual as well: the free and full development of human rights is only possible within some kind of community.

**(4)** *Association* connotes a voluntary and deliberately created collective, somewhat different from more naturally developed (*naturwüchsig*) communities like families and local communities. The Declaration provides for freedom of association, including the freedom not be compelled to belong to an association (Art. 20), and the freedom to own property in association with others (Art. 17).

**(5)** A *society* has organs (Preamble), and its fundamental unit is the family (Art. 16). The society and the state both have the duty to protect the family (this is not a duty exclusively of the state), and the right to social security is connected to being a member of society (Art. 22). Finally, the limitations of the various human rights are dependent on their being necessary in a democratic society (Art. 29). Thus, 'society' is a somewhat organic community with organs and units, definitely separable from the state (Art. 16), but in some respects it may be equivalent to the state.

**(6)** The *organs* of society (Preamble) as well as individuals have an obligation to strive for the promotion of human rights. These organs are more than just state institutions and they are some kind of collective unit, no doubt also including civic organisations and commercial associations.[29]

**(7)** It is no surprise that the *state* also appears in the Declaration. Member States are, of course, mentioned in the Preamble. After all, the Universal Declaration is a document of the General Assembly of the United Nations, an international community having states as its members. Article 13 (1) provides for free movement and residence within the borders of a state, and the right to leave and return to one's 'country' in Article 13 (2) is obviously related to exit from and entry into state entities. As mentioned above, the family is provided with protection by the state (Art. 16), and the social right to social security, connected with being a member of society, is dependent on 'the organisation and resources of each state' (Art. 22). Article 30 prescribes that 'nothing in this Declaration may be interpreted as implying for any State, group or person any right to engage in any activity or to perform any act aimed at the destruction of any of the rights and freedoms set forth herein.' This wording indicates that the state plays an important role in both the protection and the violation of human rights, but not exclusively so: other groups are also relevant.

To some extent, it can be argued that the state and the system of states is more than just expressly mentioned in the Declaration—–it is also presupposed as a manifest fact not worth mentioning. As an example, Article 11 speaks of national and international law, meaning domestic (state) law and law between states.

29 The 'UN Norms for Business' refer to the 'organs of society,' mentioned in the Universal Declaration.

**(8)** Beside the state, *people* and *nation* also appear in the Declaration, especially in the Preamble that refers to 'the peoples of the United Nations' and the 'peoples of member States and...the peoples of territories under their jurisdiction'. Human rights are described as a 'common standard of achievement for all peoples and all nations', and the Preamble also stresses the importance of 'friendly relations between nations'. In Article 21 (3), 'the will of the people' is set up as 'the basis of the authority of government'. The term *country* has also found its way to the Declaration, in Article 13 concerning the exit from and entry into a 'country', Article 21 (2) concerning the right to participate in the government of one's country, and Article 21 (2) concerning the right to 'equal access to public service' of the country.

Thus, 'state', 'people', 'nation' and 'country' are used sometimes in an interchangeable manner and sometimes with slight differences in meaning and connotation. They belong to the same level – as opposed to 'family', 'association', 'organ of society' and, at the other end of the scale, 'human family', etc. – their precise meaning and reference being neither absolutely clear, nor altogether ambiguous.

**(9)** Finally, Article 28 provides for 'a *social and international order* in which the rights and freedoms...can be fully realised'. Thus, human rights cannot be realised in a system strictly ordered by sovereign states; an international order is also a prerequisite. This is a logical consequence of the atrocities of the Second World War and especially those carried out by the sovereign state of Germany in relation to its own citizens. Human rights protection by the state is simply not enough.[30] Whereas some sort of international community is a prerequisite for the protection of human rights, it is by no means clear what kind of international order is required, or, to put it differently: the Universal Declaration's vision of a world order is not spelled out. In some way, this is a shortcoming. It is not enough to set up the rights and necessary communities, including the international one, but to leave out the question of how this community is to be structured in order to be able to provide human rights protection. But this can also be seen as an advantage: the international level *must* be developed, but how this is to be done is left to future generations.

## 5 Possible Conclusions from the Typology

From this typology of communities, from this variety of communities necessarily appearing in the first universal human rights instrument, a number of conclusions can be made. These are not to be understood as deductions, but rather as elaborations.

30 This acknowledgement can be viewed in Hegelian terms, criticising Hegel himself: the statement that "Der Staat ist die Wirklichkeit der konkreten Freiheit" (G.W.F. Hegel, *op. cit.*, § 260) is a limited truth – a 'truth', in the sense that freedom (or human rights) needs some kind of structure and community to realise it; 'limited', in the sense that the state is not sufficient for, and may be even detrimental to, its fulfilment. It is ironic that the conception of the state as the ultimate freedom was put forward by a German.

**(1)** First, there are many communities that are relevant for human rights. The Universal Declaration refers to a variety of them – family, association, society, state, people, international order, etc. – and it is therefore incorrect to grasp this fundamental human rights document as solely focused on the individual. As stated above, human rights are conceptually linked to the individual, and the Declaration certainly focuses on the individual as a holder of rights in contrast to collective entities. This does not entail an exclusive focus on the individual at the expense of the communities, but it does means that there is a certain relationship between the two. The Universal Declaration can be seen as a somewhat new way of understanding the relationship between individuals and communities: there are several relevant types of community, and all types in the Declaration are relevant to human rights, although of course not necessarily to the same extent. In this way, classical liberal contractarian philosophy is left far behind, as it is only able to understand one type of community, namely the state, and lumps all other non-state communities into a single basket labelled 'nature'.[31]

**(2)** Second, the relationship between individual and community is a universal phenomenon. It has been fashionable to proclaim that certain cultures are communitarian in deliberate opposition to the culturally linked, individualistic human rights.[32] But it is most inadequate to depict some societies or cultures as individualistic and others as communitarian. All societies or cultures have both individualistic and collectivistic features, albeit in different ways and on different levels, as the types of community and their relative importance will invariably differ. Therefore, the relevant task is not to group cultures on a scale of their respective individualism and collectivism (which is hardly possible), but to analyse the differences: where does one society stress individualism as opposed to another?

As an example, it is commonplace to depict European society as individualistic and African as more communitarian.[33] There is a grain of truth in this, but as an overall understanding is it nonsense. What is true is that different cultures may have different ways of dealing with the relationship between individual and community, and not least that the role and importance of the various communities differ. Thus, in Europe the extended family is not a central, social-structur-

31 John Locke, op cit., Second Treatise, Ch. II, 'The State of Nature'.

32 Former Singapore prime minister Lee Kuan Yew was an ardent proponent of Asian values. See Donnelly, op. cit., p. 107 ff.; Amartya Sen, 'Human Rights and Asian Values', *The New Republic*, July 14-July 21, 1997, at http://www.mtholyoke.edu/acad/intrel/sen.htm.

33 'The content of human rights ... has to bear ... African cultural fingerprints, which emphasises the group, duties, social cohesion and communal solidarity as opposed to rigid individualism'; Bonny Ibhawoh, 'Cultural Tradition and National Human Rights Standards in Conflict', in Kirsten Hastrup (ed.), *Legal Cultures and Human Rights*, Kluwers, 2001, p. 90. '[The] African conception of man is not that of an isolated individual, but an integral member of a group animated by a spirit of solidarity'; B. Obinna Okere, 'The Protection of Human Rights in Africa and the African Charter on Human and Peoples' Rights', *Human Rights Quarterly*, 1984, pp. 141 f.

ing community and is not the main provider of, for example, social security. In contemporary (northern) European societies instead, the welfare state is a very important entity, providing welfare, social security, law, human rights, etc. to individuals. African states generally do not have this capacity and cannot provide effective care, protection, law, human rights, etc. In African societies the relevant provider of social security, work, participation, etc. is rather the extended family.[34] Consequently, African communitarianism is not opposed to European, but may be different in character, not being more communitarian, but placing emphasis – for good or for bad – on other collective entities than the state. This misunderstanding – perceiving African societies as more communitarian – is probably linked to the further misunderstanding that states are natural entities on a par with individuals, not communities on a par with other collective entities.

In addition, one could mention many examples of African individualism and European collectivism. In Denmark, for instance, caring for the elderly is a task for the community, and it is carried out by the state and local authorities on the basis of tax payments. In Africa, the state does not have this capacity, and the burden of caring for the elderly is individualised. Legally, this has found its way into the African Charter, Article 27 (1), that imposes on the individual the duty to maintain his or her parents. Likewise, in Denmark the tasks of the administration (police, social security, etc.) and the courts are generally carried out with respect for the acts and laws in force, norms that are collectively agreed upon through democratic procedures. In Kenya, on the other hand, much is decided according to individual interests, implying that decisions are made not with respect to the general laws or the common interest, but in the interests of the individual. Thus, a law-enforcement officer may individualize the payment of fines by keeping the money rather than handing them over to the community.[35]

I am not claiming that European culture is more communitarian than African culture (let alone that it is possible to speak of any specific culture, be it European or African). My claim is that the concept of community is present in any culture, wherever human beings are involved, and that human rights cannot do without community, nor even without a variety of communities. Only when this is clear will it be possible to make profound analyses of the role and perception[36] of community and collective entities and their relationship to the individual in different cultures or locations. This is still a highly challenging task.

---

34 The HIV/AIDS pandemic has stretched the extended family far beyond its capacity. The implications for African communities have yet to be seen.

35 Kibutha Kibwana, Smokin Wanjala and Okechy-Owiti, 'The Anatomy of Corruption in Kenya'. *Legal, Political and Socio-Economic Perspectives*, Claripress Ltd., 1996.

36 The role and the perception may differ. See Fredrik Barth, 'Are Values Real? The Enigma of Naturalism in Anthropological Imputation of Values', in Michael Hechter, Lynn Nadel and Richard E. Michod (eds.), *The Origin of Values*, Aldine de Gruyter, 1993, pp. 31-46.

**(3)** Third, the various communities are not spelled out very clearly in the Declaration. This is logical in the sense that the Declaration is not a declaration of the necessity of communities, but of human rights. The appearance of the many communities, their relation to human rights and their importance for human rights protection are therefore presented more like assumptions than actual provisions. This is, of course, a weakness in the Declaration. It is rather easy to proclaim human rights as a common standard of achievement without indicating how goals concerning them are going to be reached. The Declaration proclaims human rights protection, but is rather silent concerning, or at best only vaguely indicates, how the protection can be implemented. This uncertainty, however, may also be seen as an advantage: the Declaration is not set on one way of organising human interaction in order to improve the human rights situation. The possible role of the various communities is still open and subject to analysis and even good ideas. As an example, the United Nations Human Rights Norms for Business, issued in 2003,[37] are turning attention to non-state actors such as companies as relevant and increasingly important participants in human rights protection. This is being advocated with reference to the Preamble of the Universal Declaration, in which the duty of 'every organ of society' to strive for the promotion of human rights is spelled out.

**(4)** Fourth, all types of community are likely to be relevant for human rights. The *family* is relevant for life, food and shelter (Art. 3 and 25), the *state* provides the 'competent national tribunals' (Art. 8), *society* provides the social order, the *human family* provides the international order without which human rights cannot be fully realised (Art. 28 and preamble), *associations* such as trade unions and *organs of society* such as companies are important participants in ensuring a 'just and favourable remuneration' (Art. 23 (3)), the *community* provides culture (Art. 27), etc.

It is important to be aware of the fact that the various types of community are not only relevant for human rights protection; they are all possible violators as well. Domestic violence and the sexual abuse of children within the family are unfortunately as universal as caring and protection (although not necessarily as widespread). Society is not always able to provide social order, as the cases of Somalia and Liberia show. Trade unions may prefer to look after the interests of the organisation rather than those of the individual, while business companies may violate human rights, for example, by disregarding claims for reasonable remuneration and by employing private security personnel, who proved to be as insensitive to human rights as the military and police during the dictatorships of the 1970s in Latin America and many other places. Even the human family in the shape of international society may be human rights violators, as was the case in Rwanda in 1994.

37 'Norms on the Responsibilities of Transnational Corporations and Other Business Enterprises with Regard to Human Rights', U.N. Doc. E/CN.4/Sub.2/2003/12/Rev.2 (2003).

All collective entities are relevant for human rights, although of course their roles are different. Still, whether private company, extended or nuclear family, or state, they share the strength of a community in relation to the weakness of the single individual. Donnelly's point that the state is the 'principal violator and essential protector'[38] is therefore only part of the whole picture: *all* collective entities are potentially both violators and protectors, though to varying degrees, depending on the strength of the particular community.

**(5)** Fifth, the state, even as a collective entity among other communities, plays a special role. The Universal Declaration contains or presupposes a system of states with national domestic law within the state and international public law (*Völkerrecht*) between states. 'Law' is simply either national or international law (Art. 11), and as a matter of course the tribunals are thought of as national tribunals (Art. 8). The Declaration also implies that this system was not fully developed at the time it was proclaimed because certain territories did not yet have their own domestic law, but were under foreign jurisdiction. The de-colonisation process was inherent in the Declaration as a perspective and an envisaged consequence.

It should be emphasised, however, that the Declaration does not attach human rights strictly to the system of a state-organised society. To some extent, this fact has been forgotten in the wake of later developments in which human rights were connected to the existing international legal system with international human rights conventions as the means of enhancing human rights. It was indeed logical, natural and even politically wise to tie human rights to the international level by drawing up human treaties in order to bind the states to human rights obligations. However, an international convention system is not sufficient, and there is nothing in the Declaration that restricts human rights protection to a state-oriented approach.

Thus, Donnelly's point that 'the contractarian notion of the state as an instrument for the protection, implementation, and effective realization of natural rights' in classical liberal theory is 'strikingly similar to the conception of the state in international human rights instruments'[39] does not apply fully to the Universal Declaration. The Declaration does not operate with natural rights and involves more types of community as instruments for the protection of human rights than just the state.

Habermas has characterised the state as an 'exceptionally successful format',[40] which is true also in relation to the protection and promotion of human rights. The state has been a vehicle for the rule of law, democracy, social security, freedom of speech, etc. However, this is not the whole picture; the state has also been exceptionally unsuccessful in some parts of the world, especially in some of the

38 Donnelly, op. cit., p. 35.

39 Donnelly, op. cit.

40 Jürgen Habermas, 'The Kantian project of the constitutionalisation of international law: does it still have a chance?', in *Law and justice in a global society*. IVR 2005. Anales de la Cátedra de Francisco Suárez,, p. 119.

former colonies, where it has not yet proved possible to establish a well-functioning state with the rule of law, democracy, social security, etc. Especially in Africa, the state has not developed the capacity to be the 'essential protector' of human rights, although it has unfortunately often been successful in performing the role of 'principal violator'.

An analysis and a rethinking of the various collective entities involved is a prerequisite in providing any improvement to the human rights situation in Africa and other places in which the state is not able to handle serious human rights problems.

In any case, the role of the state is changing, irrespective of the success of the format. It may be natural to understand the situation as post-Westphalian, that is, that the structuring of world society is no longer strictly attached to a system of sovereign states – even though it should be remembered that many states have never been fully included into the Westphalian system. Therefore, the Universal Declaration – with its more open and broader conception of a variety of necessary communities as regards human rights – may provide us with inspiration as to how to organise international society better, and more so than the human rights conventions closely connected to the Westphalian state structure.

**(6)** Sixth, the supra-state level of communities poses some problems. The Second World War and the atrocities committed by the states of Japan and Germany showed that national state-level protection of human rights is wholly insufficient. The creation of the United Nations and the adoption of the Universal Declaration indicated acknowledgment of the necessity of communities at the international level. Developments since the immediate post-war period have shown a tremendous growth in international or rather supra-state[41] collective entities, from regional political bodies, such as the Council of Europe and the European Union, to private commercial enterprises working across borders.

This development, important though it is for human rights, is itself not unproblematic, of course, in terms of politics (how is it possible to organise politics and democracy on a supra-state scale?), philosophy (how can we understand the supra-state level?),[42] law (how is law created at the supra-state level and how is it included in state law?), anthropology (what role does culture play in a period of globalisation?), etc. Let me point out a few problems relevant for an understanding of the relationship between communities and the individual.

One problem is that collective entities have to be invented. Most other types of community are fairly well-known – the family, the state, associations like NGOs and business companies – whereas the supra-state level is to a large extent being created at the present time. This is, of course, not impossible to do: human beings are creative and have throughout history been able to come up with new – and

41 The term 'international' implies relations between nations, a system of states. Developments have gone beyond this, the EU being the most obvious example.

42 The subject for the 2005 biannual conference of the *Internationale Vereinigung für Rechtsphilosohie* was exactly law and justice in a global society.

often better – ways of structuring their lives.[43] Still, problems of the legitimacy and efficiency of the new communities will always exist. The rejection of the EU Constitution Treaty in the French and Dutch referenda, the idea that the United Nations organisation is not only inefficient but downright superfluous, and the emergence of nationalistic political movements such as Pim Fortuyn in the Netherlands, the Danish People's Party in Denmark and the Bharatiya Janata Party in India all show a preference for well-known communities such as nations, states and religion, rather than the new and untested, more global, universalistic communities.

Another problem is the necessary inclusion of what are sometimes referred to as failed states, that is, states that are such in the formal sense, members of the United Nations, etc., but that nevertheless lack actual sovereignty, both externally (being highly dependent on foreign aid) as well as internally (having strong internal military factions or simply a malfunctioning state apparatus). In a way, they have never really been included in the Westphalian system of sovereign states. Strong, efficient states are probably capable of adapting to new circumstances with less emphasis on formal external sovereignty and more emphasis on creating an environment conducive to foreign investment etc. But it is highly questionable whether this change can take place in states that lack fundamental capacities, including human rights protection, and whose state apparatus is either non-existent (Somalia) or rather defunct (many Sub-Saharan African countries). To some extent, this could be ignored in a world society consisting of individual states, each doing things their way, but it becomes more of a problem in an inclusive world society. The problem has a bearing on human rights as well as on security, but apparently nobody knows what to do about it or sometimes even what to think about it. The German Habermas, one of the most influential philosophers of our time, ignores this problem, and the United Nations is in an awkward position, consisting of member states, some of which are defunct and thus part of the problem.

The vision of the ordering of a future world society is highly contested and raises questions not only of analysis and knowledge, but also of political will and power. At least three conceptions are influential in the global forum of ideas, all of them having some political structures and powers behind them.

One is an Islamic-fundamentalist ideology, whose aim is to create God's kingdom on earth. This vision probably does not have any chance of ordering the world, partly because it is exclusive in its ideology and therefore not attractive to the majority of humanity, and partly because it is not supported by any sufficiently strong power. However, it definitely has a chance of influencing the structuring of world society, as the ideology allows for violent means to be used in order to reach its goal.

Another vision is the neo-conservative or radical conservative idea of an empire with the USA in the lead. This ideology is in favour of human rights, democracy and the free market economy (although not necessarily in this order) and is therefore morally attractive. It is to some extent inclusive, inasmuch as human

43 The creation of the Westphalian system of sovereign states could be mentioned as an example of this adaptability.

rights, democracy and markets are for everybody. Besides, it has, if not sufficient, then at least enormous military power with which to fulfil its goals. Yet this vision has obvious shortcomings. As Habermas has pointed out,[44] pure military power is insufficient to combat terrorism, as conventional military power does not work fully in an asymmetrical war. Secondly, even a 'well-intended hegemon' will have structural problems in distinguishing its own national interest from the common human interest. Therefore, this vision will still be exclusive, unable to incorporate the views of 'the others', and in the end not very attractive for those who are excluded from influence over decision-making. After all, human rights do not function as grants, but require a degree of participation by those concerned.

The third vision is more conservative in the sense that it incorporates existing global structures without any wish for radical innovation, whether in the form of a caliphate or an empire. Instead it builds on existing international structures such as the United Nations and focuses on co-operation. There are, of course, different views as to the appropriate goal – world republic, republic of republics, etc.[45] – as well as the means. The vision is, or at least has the potential of being, inclusive, having cooperation as its base, rather than the exclusion based on religion or on security. It may, however, be weak in terms of military power – and therefore also in terms of political power.

Certainly, this 'visionology' could be much further elaborated, but hopefully it suffices to make at least one point clear: the vision of a cooperative world society is not likely to succeed if it only includes the community of states and ultimately supra-state entities. All relevant communities must be included, and the Universal Declaration can serve as an inspiration in this respect too, given its inclusion of a variety of communities necessary for human rights.[46]

It is tempting, but not advisable, to conceive of this development in Hegelian terms. Hegel was of the opinion that only the state could realise human freedom, making the point that freedom and human rights need a structure to fulfil them; natural law cannot do this on its own.[47] History, however, has shown that the state is not a sufficient human rights protector either, and that it could even be the principal violator, as shown by Hitler's extermination camps, so efficiently organised by the German state. Therefore, we need one more layer, namely the international level, which is able to bind states legally to their human rights obligations. The problem with this view is that there is no guarantee that the international community, which is needed as the protector of individual human rights, will not turn

---

44 Habermas, op. cit., p. 125-26.

45 For a cosmopolitan approach, see David Held, 'Principles of Cosmopolitan Order', in *Law and Justice in a Global Society*. IVR 2005. Anales de la Cátedra de Francisco Suárez, pp. 145-161 with references, whereas Habermas seeks to develop the Kantian approach: op cit., note 39.

46 On human rights in relation to sub-state communities, see *Human Rights in Development: Local Living Law*, Lone Lindholt and Sten Schaumburg-Müller, eds., Kluwer International, 2005.

47 Hegel, op. cit.

into a violator as well, if only by abstaining from interfering in certain situations where human rights are being violated. It is therefore requisite to reject a hierarchical framework and to include all relevant communities in the protection of human rights, including, of course, the international level (or rather, levels), but without excluding other and smaller communities.

## 6 Some Comments on Security

The analysis of the uneasy balance between individual human rights and the requirements of communities can, I believe, shed some light on the present security agenda. Terrorism and the fight against it both raise questions of human rights as well as the interests of communities, and especially the interest and capacity of the state. I make five points on this aspect of the problem.

**(1)** The relations between human rights and security are diverse: security of the person, that is, of the individual, is a human right as stated in the Universal Declaration (Art. 3). International order – which can be understood as involving international security – is also a human right (Art. 28). On a more general level, a certain degree of security is a precondition for human rights. Without security and order, human rights are threatened; war, civil unrest, civil war etc. entail gross violations of human rights, and the whole idea of human rights presupposes some kinds of reasonably stable institutions that are able to ensure individuals their rights.

The problem, of course, is that these stable institutions may be human rights violators themselves. If a state did nothing to protect its citizens from acts of terror, this would amount to an infringement of human rights,[48] but conversely the protective measures may be human rights violations themselves. This is a reflection of the double role of communities vis-à-vis human rights: the community, with its institutional capacity, is a necessity, a provider and a protector of human rights, as well as a potential violator.

However, the opposite is also true: human rights are a necessary means to obtain and sustain security. The UN Charter, Art. 55 puts it as follows: 'With a view to the creation of conditions of stability and well-being which are necessary for peaceful and friendly relations…the United Nations shall promote…universal respect for, and observance of, human rights and fundamental freedoms for all without distinction as to race, sex, language, or religion.' Art. 56 obliges member states to cooperate in achieving this aim. Thus, human rights are not (only) a goal in themselves but also a means to obtain stability and peaceful relations, in other words, security. This indicates that human rights violations are condemnable not only because of the violation of individual human dignity, but also because of their potential threat to security.

There is, of course, no one-to-one relationship between the two. Human rights-violating security measures do not necessarily create instability and insecurity, but they have the potential to do so – an important point represented in the

48 See the *Özgür Gündem* judgment, above, note 22.

UN Charter, but unfortunately much less represented in the contemporary security agenda.[49]

The Universal Declaration makes the same point in a warning in the Preamble: 'It is essential, if man is not to be compelled to have recourse, as a last resort, to rebellion against tyranny and oppression, that human rights should be protected by the rule of law.' Thus, human rights are not only a question of dignity and the rights of the individual, as stated in Art. 1, but also of avoiding rebellion and revolution, instability and insecurity and – seen from the perspective of the ruler – of being executed.[50]

Regarded in this way, neither human rights nor security are trumps in the sense that one overrules the other. Rather, there is an intriguing relationship between the two.

**(2)** According to my analysis, an understanding of human rights as natural is ill-founded, as 'nature' is not an inherent part of rights and cannot serve as a foundation. Secondly, 'nature' has served as a black-box reference to what could not be conceived previously: a collective as different from, and even extending beyond, the state.

The understanding of human rights as non-natural also has implications for the present security agenda. Importantly, human rights contain no natural definitions or limitations: they are man-made and can be altered by man. It may not be wise to make changes, less wise to make ad hoc changes and even more unwise to make ad hoc deviations according to the short-term needs of certain groups. But human rights are challengeable and debatable, first because we may not have found the very best answers to our problems, secondly because new problems may not be solved adequately by old methods, and thirdly because without being debated, human rights risk decaying into mere doctrine and taboo.[51]

It should be emphasised that questioning a particular human right, such as the right to privacy (Universal Declaration, Art. 12), is not equivalent to questioning the whole idea of human rights. Considering whether one right is an adequate solution to current problems in no way necessarily entails questioning human rights as such. Challenging the whole concept is certainly an option, but it should be remembered that questioning human rights as such is equivalent to questioning

---

49 For further discussion of this aspect, see 'Tre teser om retfærdig krig [Three theses on just war]', in Bo Kristian Holm (ed.), *Krig – dens legitimitet i religion og politik* [War – its legitimacy in religion and politics], Forlaget Anis, 2005.

50 Interestingly enough, this provides human rights with characteristics equalling the legal system in a modern state. As H.L.A. Hart has pointed out (*Concept of Law*, Clarendon, 1961), a citizen can abide by the law out of respect and a moral attitude, *as well as* out of sheer calculation. This is a strength, as it does not require a certain moral attitude by all members. The same goes for human rights: they can be followed out of respect for the dignity of the individual *and* out of calculation.

51 This argument is, of course, inspired by J.S. Mill's defence of freedom of speech in *On Liberty*.

humanity as a community, with far-reaching implications: it entails that there are no common interests, let alone room for the exchange of views and values.

In addition, the no-natural understanding leaves more room for democracy. If human rights are natural, it makes no sense to open them up to s democratic discussion – let alone a decision – on the more detailed content of such rights. The law of gravity is not a matter for democratic and political discussion either. The natural approach makes it more obvious for natural scientists or natural lawyers to make scholarly suggestions. As regards rights, the natural-law approach worked advantageously in the seventeenth century, but to use the same approach now is to ignore the experience of previous centuries, which has shown that democracy is a very efficient and effective way of generating law. The natural-law approach to human rights can only grasp democracy as being yet another right that is given naturally, thus without understanding the essential aspect of inclusion. Democracy is not only a right, but also an activity producing law and – ultimately – rights.[52]

It is remarkable that the natural-law approach seems to be more widespread in the USA. This is, no doubt, connected with its legal foundation, especially the Declaration of Independence, with its unmistakable traits of natural law, 'laws of nature', self-evident truths' and 'unalienable rights' being among the expressions it uses. The present US government is a part of this natural law tradition: democracy is a right, and where there is no democracy, America is ready to provide it by means of its superior military force, its commitment to democracy, and its willingness to make sacrifices, financially as well as in terms of soldiers killed and injured. The problem with this approach is that it conceives democracy merely as a (natural) right that can be granted benevolently: it is unable to conceive democracy as a necessarily inclusive process or a law- and rights-producing entity, and unable to understand community as an important aspect of 'rights'.[53] In this way, it is no coincidence that the military overthrow of Saddam Hussein was rather easy, whereas reconstruction has proven very difficult. it was simply anticipated that democratic reconstruction would follow naturally: it did not. Instead, various groups showed up: the Kurds, the Shiites, etc.

**(3)** The positive human rights law has some built-in experience and knowledge. As argued above, like any other law human rights are subject to debate, but this does not mean that actual prevailing human rights law is redundant. Blackstone put it as follows: 'We owe such deference to former times, as not to suppose that

52 At this juncture, I shall not venture into the complicated issue of democracy producing non-democracy, when, for example, the majority of voters prefer a non-democratic type of government. See, for example, the discussion in Roland Paris, 'Peace building and the Limits of Liberal Internationalism', *International Security*, vol. 22, 1997, pp. 54-89, especially pp. 75 ff.

53 See also the discussion above of the neo-conservative idea of an empire and Habermas's critique.

they acted wholly without consideration.'[54] Even though he ended up with a defence for a rather stiff, conservative legal system, the statement contains the point that a legal system or legal features to some extent contain considerations that should not be totally ignored.

As for menaces to security, the Covenant on Civil and Political Rights has provisions allowing for the suspension of certain rights 'in time of public emergency which threatens the life of the nation' (ICCPR, Art. 4). Evidently, the drafters were aware of the tension between human rights protection and security, and even though they were obviously focused on human rights issues, they arrived at the conclusion that in certain situations urgent security concerns could overrule certain individual rights. In order to invoke communal above individual human rights: (*a*) the situation must be serious (it 'threatens the life of the nation'); (*b*) the state of emergency must be publicly declared; and (*c*) not all rights can be derogated. By way of example, it would not be a violation of human rights to interfere with someone's privacy and detain them without trial, provided, of course, that the conditions for the state of emergency are (continuously) fulfilled. On the other hand, torture and retroactive criminal laws are ruled out, and even in a state of emergency there is an obligation to respect everyone as a person before the law and to respect freedom of thought, conscience and religion.

Neither the USA, nor Spain declared a state of emergency after the terrorist attacks on September 11$^{th}$ or March 11$^{th}$, respectively, even though the American situation in particular indicated emergency. Besides the successful attack on the Twin Towers of the World Trade Centre, there was an attack on the Department of Defence in the Pentagon and an attempted attack on the White House. A state of emergency is serious business, but its implementation need not be all-encompassing. On the contrary, deviations from current laws are allowed only 'to the extent strictly required by the exigencies of the situation.' Some detentions and interferences in telecommunications could be justified and acceptable within the prevailing human rights framework, even for a long period. Besides, the declaration of a state of emergency indicates in itself that the situation is exceptional and that the measures being taken are extraordinary and only meant for a limited period of time. Not declaring a state of emergency and embarking on detentions without trial and various forms of surveillance indicates a disregard for the human rights of the international community.

Furthermore, there seem to be problems not least with non-derogable rights: allegations of torture are so consistent that they are unlikely to be mere isolated incidents carried out by a few misguided individuals; recognition of the prisoners at Guantanamo Bay as persons before the law has been patchy; and some of the

54 Blackstone, William, *Commentaries on the Laws of England*, Vol. 1, Introduction, Sec. 3 (1795) (text can be found at. http://www.lonang.com/exlibris/blackstone/bla-003.htm).

publicised incidents from the Abu Ghraib prison indicate disrespect for conscience and religion.[55]

Thus, the USA and in principle also the other parties to the 'coalition of the willing', including the government of Denmark, have failed to defer to earlier times but instead suggested that the drafters of existing human rights law acted wholly without considerations relevant to present-day problems. As indicated above, this is not correct. In conclusion, the present security agenda not only entails violations of individual human rights, it may very well turn out to be counter-productive in the long run because it undermines legitimacy. Torture, the degrading treatment of prisoners and insults to religious symbols are signs of exclusion from the community and potential obstacles to international order.

**(4)** The Danish political scientist Ole Wæver has pointed out that categorising a situation as involving security is not a neutral act but an active invoking of particular interests.[56] Invoking 'security' is not (only) a way of understanding the situation, but also of moulding it into a special kind of situation that involves ultimate interests: survival is at stake. 'By saying "security", a state representative moves the particular case into a specific area, claiming a special right to use the necessary means to block this development.'[57] Wæver concedes that it is possible to use the word 'security' in other contexts, such as individual security or human security, but puts forward two objections: first, by making the concept all-encompassing – all problems are security problems (security of health, of food, etc.) – one deprives the concept any analytical content; and secondly, and more importantly, by deploying the concept of security, one risks playing the language game of security, thus invoking state security, ultimate means and the use of military force.[58]

In this way, the present global security agenda and the war against terrorism can be seen as attempts to strengthen the state vis-à-vis individual interests and other communities, and to revitalise the Westphalian state, which is under pressure in the present environment of globalisation and the relativisation of state power.[59] State security is thus a speech act which points to the relative weakness

---

55 *See* the recent report by Amnesty International, 'United States of America, Guantánamo and beyond: The continuing pursuit of unchecked executive power', 13 May 2005, http://web.amnesty.org/library/Index/ENGAMR510632005?open&of=ENG-IRQ

56 Ole Wæver, 'Securitization and Desecuritization', in *Concepts of Security*, Institute of Political Science, 1997, pp. 212 ff. Wæver is using John L. Austin's speech-act theory from his *How To Do Things With Words*, Harvard University Press, 1962. *Talking* about 'security' is, in this light, *doing* something about it.

57 Ibid., p. 221.

58 These are not only theoretical considerations. Security forces are no longer only used in traditional military actions, but also in providing or supporting both humanitarian and development aid, for example in Afghanistan.

59 Seen in this light, it is not surprising that the Danish People's Party did not support NATO's intervention in Kosovo, as it was based on universalistic ideas, but did support the US-led intervention in Iraq in 2003, which was based on state supremacy connected with moral rather than legal arguments.

of the emerging post-Westphalian world structure in guaranteeing the necessary order and security; it points to the state as the obvious agent as a provider of law, order and security; and – perhaps most importantly – it puts an end to disagreements and seeks to silence voices questioning the legitimacy of state action, or at least tries to do so.

(5) Terrorism is a menace to security as well as to human rights, to states as well as to individuals. One way of understanding terrorism is to see it as a reaction to the destruction of communities, precisely as Nazism and Fascism can be seen as reactions to globalisation and the destruction of communities in the late nineteenth and early twentieth centuries.[60] Thus, terrorism can be understood as a modern phenomenon exactly like Nazism and its perpetration of a holocaust: in both cases there is the skilful use modern technology, the exclusion of a group of other human beings from their own (conceived or constructed) community, the depiction of this group as a threat, and the reaction to supposedly lost communities.

It is hardly possible to avoid pressure on or even the loss of communities as the economy develops, but awareness of the necessity of communities should be possible, including of a variety of communities. Modernisation and industrialisation in Western Europe destroyed existing village communities, but new communities emerged, such as religious communities, trade unions, co-operative movements and the like. How future development can be directed towards the creation of these types of stabilising and fairly human rights-friendly communities, rather than the creation of communities such as the quasi-military youth gangs of Germany in the 1920s and 1930s and contemporary al Qaeda – groups that threaten individual human rights as well as collective security – is an obvious field for further consideration and research.

## 7 Concluding Remarks

My aim in the foregoing analyses has been to contribute to a clarification of the concept of human rights and provide at least some indication of the relationship between individual human rights and communities. The popular views of human rights as natural rights and of human rights as consisting of group rights as well are I believe, conceptually mistaken, and the resulting haziness and inadequacy has created problems for both scholarly traditions and legal-political processes in this field.

The individual human being needs the protection of the group, yet this very fact makes the group a potential threat to the individual. There may be several answers to this intriguing and perennial problem, but it is obvious to point out the existence of several types of communities, thus minimising the risk that one

60 Karl Polanyi, *The Great Transformation*, Beacon Press, 1970 (1st edition 1944), as referred to by Jürgen Habermas, 'Die postnationale Konstellation und die Zukunft der Demokratie', *Die postnationale Konstellation: Politische Essays*. Suhrkamp, 1998, p. 128.

community holds absolute and sovereign power over individuals. Hedley Bull has pointed out the balance of power as a means of stabilising the world order,[61] to which I add the necessity of other types of community as well, those indicated in the Universal Declaration. Communities other than the state are necessary, not as holders of human rights themselves – a view that ignores the potential of communities and sees them as vulnerable only in relation to the state – but as necessary fellow players in the games of power, security and human rights.

The role of the state, or at least its sovereignty, is diminishing. This may be seen as an advantage and as a step towards a more inclusive diversity of communities. But it obviously entails the risk of leaving us with less security rather than with more, because a new structure might not be able to develop into a new order.

As for the security agenda, which is part of the post-Westphalian development of diminished state sovereignty, asymmetric enemies, etc., it is vital that it does not end up only feeding on itself or being self-fulfilling, itself creating security problems that call for security solutions. In order to avoid this trap, it is important to take note of the suggestion made in this chapter, that human rights exist for the sake not only of individuals but also of communities. Ignoring human rights may be counter-productive even for security, and to a large extent the prevailing positivised international human rights have taken security issues into consideration. These considerations should therefore not just be ignored, but on the contrary, should be taken into account as human rights protection and security are developed further.

Secondly, communities play an important role in human rights as well as security matters. All communities, including the state, have potentially stabilising as well as destabilising features. It is important to include communities other that states in the human rights discourse, viewing communities (such as minorities and indigenous peoples) not only as potential problems in relation to the state, but also as important players capable of contributing to human rights protection and improvements in security. However, their potential as violators of human rights should not be ignored either.

Finally, a natural-law perception of human rights has so far been unable to include any understanding of communities, and it is therefore necessary, both philosophically and politically, to abandon what may have been conducive to human rights in the seventeenth and eighteenth centuries, but what is now rather an obstacle, and venture into the task of anchoring human rights in the diversity of human communities.

---

61 Hedley Bull, *The Anarchical Society: A Study of Order in World Politics*. Macmillan, 2nd ed., 1995, Ch. 5, 'The Balance of Power and the International Order'.

# 5. Human Rights on the Battlefield

*John Cerone*

## 1 Introduction

One of the most controversial and politically charged issues in current human rights discourse is whether and to what extent states are bound by their human rights obligations with respect to the conduct of their armed forces abroad in the context of armed conflict, occupation, and peace operations.

In the decades following the adoption and entry into force of the major human rights treaties, the capacity of states to project their power beyond their borders has dramatically increased. In the modern world, states are capable of mobilizing massive destructive power across the globe with increasing speed and efficiency. A crucial consequence of this enhanced military power is the increasing breadth of the state's impact on the enjoyment of human rights in territories far beyond its physical frontiers.

In addition to traditional situations of armed conflict, individuals today may find themselves in the power of states in fairly complex configurations. States are increasingly operating through multilateral frameworks, e.g. through coalitions or under the auspices of UN or regional peacekeeping operations with increasingly expansive mandates.

Further, states are now purporting to create zones beyond the reach of their human rights obligations. Detention facilities at Guantanamo Bay, on the high seas, and in secret locations raise controversial questions as to the nature and purpose of human rights norms. Indeed, efforts by powerful states to withdraw their military conduct from the purview of international law threaten to undermine the hard-won victories achieved by the international human rights movement during the past sixty years.

Whether such conduct is beyond the reach of the relevant states' obligations under international human rights law[1] is a question very much alive before interna-

1 This refers to international human rights law in the strict sense (i.e. not including humanitarian law and international criminal law). The present analysis will focus on the International Covenant on Civil and Political Rights (ICCPR), the International Cov-

*S. Lagoutte, H-O. Sano and P. Scharff Smith (eds.),* Human Rights in Turmoil, *pp. 97-131.*
 *ISBN 90 04 15432 9.*

tional courts and human rights mechanisms. Increasing numbers of cases involving alleged human rights violations committed in conflict situations outside the physical territory of the state are being adjudicated in various international fora. These institutions have already developed a varied jurisprudence, accepting extraterritorial application of human rights norms to the different scenarios to differing degrees.

Underlying the controversy are a number of complex legal questions, several of which have eluded definitive resolution. Chief among these questions is whether individuals affected by the conflict are among those whose rights states are obliged to secure. A common feature of human rights treaties is that the scope of beneficiaries[2] (i.e. those whose rights the state is obliged to respect and ensure) is typically limited to those within a state's territory or subject to its jurisdiction.[3] Based purely on an 'ordinary meaning' interpretation of the text, it is unclear how this would apply with respect to individuals outside of a state's territory. Even if a juridical basis for extraterritorial application is established, the question of positive obligations must still be resolved.

The complexity of answering these questions is further compounded in situations of collective action, giving rise to such questions as whether national contingents of multilateral operations retain their status as organs of their respective sending states.

The purpose of this chapter is to outline the issues underlying these questions, and to provide a framework for answering them. As a preliminary matter, section II examines the relationship between human rights law and international humanitarian law. Section III explores the nature of human rights obligations and the various modes of state responsibility in relation to human rights violative conduct. Section IV delineates a framework for understanding the application of human rights law in relation to individuals outside of a state's territory. Section V concludes the analysis by discussing implications of the present legal framework and suggesting principles to guide future jurisprudential development.

## 2 The Relationship between Human Rights Law and Humanitarian Law in Times of Armed Conflict and Occupation

Human rights law and humanitarian law (i.e. the law of armed conflict) are separate bodies of international law with distinct modes of application. While human rights law is primarily concerned with the way a state treats those within its domain,

---

enant on Economic, Social, and Cultural Rights (ICESCR), and their regional counterparts. Reference will also be made to relevant customary human rights law.

2 Use of the term beneficiaries is not intended to imply that individual human beings are not rights-holders under human rights law.

3 ICCPR, art. 2; European Convention of Human Rights, art. 1; American Convention on Human Rights, art. 1. While Article 2 of the ICCPR refers to all individuals within a State's territory *and* subject to its jurisdiction, the Human Rights Committee has interpreted these to be independent grounds for application of the Covenant. See, e.g., *Burgos/Delia Saldias de Lopez v. Uruguay*, Communication No. 52/1979 (29 July 1981), U.N. Doc. CCPR/C/OP/1 at 88 (1984).

"[h]umanitarian law aims at placing restraints on the conduct of warfare so as to diminish its effects on the victims of the hostilities."[4]

For much of the Twentieth Century it remained unclear whether human rights law would apply to a state's conduct during armed conflict or occupation, with some states having taken the position that these situations were governed by the *lex specialis* of humanitarian law, to the exclusion of human rights law. Others took the position that human rights law applied in full alongside humanitarian law. In support of their position, they noted that the International Covenant on Civil and Political Rights (ICCPR) and regional human rights treaties contain provisions permitting derogation from certain obligations in times "of public emergency which threatens the life of the nation," the inclusion of which implicitly recognizes that human rights law applies to all situations, subject to the possible derogation of certain obligations.[5]

Despite continuing objections on the part of a handful of states, a consensus is evolving in favor of this latter view. As stated by the International Court of Justice (ICJ) in its 1996 Advisory Opinion on the *Legality of the Threat or Use of Nuclear Weapons*:

> The Court observes that the protection of the International Covenant of Civil and Political Rights does not cease in times of war, except by operation of Article 4 of the Covenant whereby certain provisions may be derogated from in a time of national emergency."[6]

This position is shared by the Inter-American Commission on Human Rights (IACHR)[7] and the Human Rights Committee,[8] and has been echoed in political fora as well.[9]

---

4 *Prosecutor v. Kunarac, Kovac, and Vukovic*, Judgment (ICTY Trial Chamber, 2001). Other distinctions between human rights and humanitarian law include the subjects of obligations, the institutions competent to determine violations, the period of application, the scope of beneficiaries, the locus of application, the range of rights protected, and the sources of obligations.

5 ICCPR, art. 4. While states may derogate from certain human rights obligations when faced with a public emergency, strict limitations apply.

6 *Legality of the Threat or Use of Nuclear Weapons* ('Nuclear Weapons Opinion'), 1996 Advisory Opinion of the ICJ, para. 25.

7 *See Coard et al. v. the United States*, Inter-American Commission on Human Rights, Case 10.951, Report No. 109/99, September 29, 1999, ¶ 39. Given the pervasive phenomenon of cross-fertilization among international fora, particularly among human rights fora, it is not uncommon to cite jurisprudence from regional fora as precedent for universal regimes. Regional practice is also particularly useful since the regional institutions, the combined membership of which comprises a large proportion of UN member states, tend to be more active, and thus have broader bases of experience within their spheres of competence.

8 Human Rights Committee General Comment 31 ('HRC GC 31'). Concluding Observation of the Human Rights Committee, Israel, para. 11.

9 See Security Council Resolution 1265 (1999) ¶ 4.

As the ICJ clarified in a subsequent opinion:

> [T]here are thus three possible situations: some rights may be exclusively matters of international humanitarian law; others may be exclusively matters of human rights law; yet others may be matters of both these branches of international law."[10]

In situations where these branches of international law overlap, the ICJ,[11] the IACHR,[12] and the Human Rights Committee[13] have all concluded that the application of human rights law in times of armed conflict or occupation must be informed by the standards of humanitarian law. Thus, after noting that the "right not arbitrarily to be deprived of one's life" is non-derogable, the ICJ explained:

> The test of what is an arbitrary deprivation of life, however, then falls to be determined by the applicable lex specialis, namely, the law applicable in armed conflict which is designed to regulate the conduct of hostilities. Thus whether a particular loss of life, through the use of a certain weapon in warfare, is to be considered an arbitrary deprivation of life contrary to Article 6 of the Covenant, can only be decided by reference to the law applicable in armed conflict and not deduced from the terms of the Covenant itself.[14]

Once it is settled that human rights law does not cease to apply by reason of the inception of a state of armed conflict, it is easy to see how this body of law would apply to a state's regular forces in a situation of internal armed conflict. The situation becomes more complex, however, when states operate abroad, especially when acting through the context of collective action or with the assistance of private actors. The next two sections provide the necessary legal framework for understanding how human rights law applies in these circumstances.

## 3 The Nature of Human Rights Law: State Responsibility, Attribution, and the Obligation to Ensure

Human rights law, embedded in the inter-state structure of the international legal system, generally binds states, and states alone. Human rights treaties, such as the ICCPR, place responsibility for 'respecting and ensuring' human rights squarely

---

10 ICJ 2004 Advisory Opinion on the *Legal Consequences of the Construction of a Wall in the Occupied Palestinian Territory* ('Israeli Wall Opinion') at para. 106. The Court affirmed this approach in its December 2005 Judgment in *DR Congo v. Uganda*.

11 Israeli Wall Opinion at para. 106.

12 *See Coard*.

13 HRC GC 31, at para. 11.

14 Nuclear Weapons Opinion, at para. 25. Note, however, that the court does not invoke the *lex specialis* principle to abrogate the *lex generalis* of human rights law. Instead, it interprets human rights law so as to conform to the standards of humanitarian law.

upon states parties.[15] Thus, only conduct[16] attributable to the state can constitute an internationally wrongful act under these treaties, and only the state can be held responsible on the international plane for such violations.

At the same time, states are abstract entities, incapable of acting as such. The conduct of states is the conduct of individuals whose acts or omissions are attributable to the state. As such, the question of attribution not infrequently arises in disputes before human rights bodies.

As an initial matter, it is important to bear in mind that the question of whether an actor's conduct is attributable to a state is analytically distinct from the question of whether that conduct is internationally wrongful.[17] The rules of attribution form part of the law of state responsibility, which is codified in the International Law Commission's Draft Articles.[18] They are secondary rules of international law, as opposed to the primary rules of international law that place obligations upon states. As such, these rules are of a framework nature, generally applicable across the full spectrum of substantive international law and unconcerned with the separate question of whether the conduct at issue conforms to what is required by those substantive norms.

The first rule of attribution is that the conduct of an organ of a state, including that of any individual who is an official part of the machinery of the state,[19] or of an entity legally empowered by a state to exercise elements of governmental author-

15 ICCPR, art. 2. While the preambles of the ICCPR and ICESR both speak of duties of individuals, no normative content for this language has been determined. The idea of duties under human rights law is generally employed in the context of permissible restrictions on rights made through, e.g., claw-back clauses. See art. 19(3), ICCPR. Finally, although the African Charter on Human and Peoples Rights (ACHPR) sets forth duties in its operative text, these provisions have never been used by the African Commission to find individuals responsible for breaches of the Charter. Indeed, there are no procedures for alleging a breach of these duties.

16 Such conduct may consist of an action or omission. See ILC Draft Articles on Responsibility of States for Internationally Wrongful Acts 2001, art. 2. The rules of attribution set forth in the Draft Articles are declaratory of existing customary international law.

17 "As a normative operation, attribution must be clearly distinguished from the characterization of conduct as internationally wrongful. Its concern is to establish that there is an act of the State for the purposes of responsibility. To show that conduct is attributable to the State says nothing, as such, about the legality or otherwise of that conduct, and rules of attribution should not be formulated in terms which imply otherwise." (ILC Commentary to the Draft Articles at p.81) This distinction can be particularly difficult to discern in analyzing the extraterritorial application of human rights law. The European Court of Human Rights, as will be discussed below, has at times found the extraterritorial application of a primary rule to be triggered in part by a finding of attribution and has also linked the issue of attribution to the scope of this primary rule.

18 See ILC Draft Articles on Responsibility of States for Internationally Wrongful Acts 2001. The Draft Articles, adopted by the International Law Commission in 2001, represent the codification and progressive development of this area of international law.

19 See ILC Draft Articles, art. 4.

ity[20] is considered to be an act of that state. This would also include situations in which an organ is placed at the disposal of a state by another state and the organ is acting in the exercise of elements of the governmental authority of the former state.[21] The conduct of such actors is attributable to the state even where an actor's conduct is *ultra vires*, or beyond the scope of his or her authority, so long as he or she was acting in an official capacity.[22]

### *3.1 Attribution in the Context of Collective Action*

While the lines of responsibility are relatively clear when states act in an individual capacity in the course of a conflict, the issue of attribution becomes more complex in the context of collective action, particularly in light of the range of circumstances in which states may conduct collective operations.

States may simply deploy military forces jointly or through "coalitions of the willing", which may or may not have separate legal personality. They may also contribute troops to UN or NATO forces. Or they may deploy forces together with other states acting pursuant to a UN mandate, while retaining command and control. In these situations, chains of command may or may not be unified, states may or may not retain control over their contributed troops, and the lines of responsibility may be muddled as a result.

Given this complex array of possibilities, the issue of attribution must be assessed in light of the particular features of each operation. In general, the conduct of a state's military forces will be attributable to that state while those forces are acting in their national capacity. However, if troops are seconded to an intergovernmental organization, or another entity with separate international legal personality, such that they are acting on behalf of that organization or entity[23] and are no longer acting on behalf of their state of nationality, then their conduct may no longer be attributable to their state of nationality.[24]

---

20 Draft Articles, art. 5.

21 Draft Articles, art. 6. This rule is limited to situations in which "the organ, originally that of one State, acts *exclusively* for the purposes of and on behalf of another State and its conduct is attributed to *the latter State alone*." Draft Articles Commentary at 95 (emphasis added).

22 Draft Articles, art. 7. See also *Velasquez-Rodriguez* case, paras. 169-170.

23 While the law of State responsibility does not address the responsibility of intergovernmental organisations as such (see art. 57, Draft Articles), the rules discussed in this section may apply by analogy. At a minimum, intergovernmental organisations are responsible for the conduct of their own organs or officials. See Draft Articles Commentary at 361 ('[An intergovernmental] organization possesses separate legal personality under international law, and is responsible for its own acts, i.e., for acts which are carried out by the organization through its own organs or officials'). Regarding the responsibility of entities other than states in a peacekeeping context, see J. Cerone, 'Reasonable Measures in Unreasonable Circumstances.'

24 This is analogous to the situation referred to in article six of the Draft Articles where the organ of one state is placed "at the disposal of" another state. See ILC Commentary

In reality, the sending states of troops contributed to UN or regional peacekeeping operations retain a significant degree of control over their troops. In such situations, the precise scope of the troops' national capacity versus their intergovernmental peacekeeping capacity may be difficult to delineate. Indeed, it may be possible that the troops are operating in both capacities simultaneously, in which case their conduct may be attributable to their sending states as well as to the intergovernmental organization through which they have been deployed.

### 3.2 *Attribution of the Conduct of Non-state Actors*[25]

The conduct of non-state actors may also be attributed to a state under certain circumstances. The conduct of a non-state actor may be imputed to a state when the actor is in fact acting on the instructions of, or under the direction or control of, a state in carrying out the conduct;[26] when the actor is exercising elements of governmental authority in the absence or default of official authorities;[27] when the conduct is subsequently adopted by a state;[28] or when the conduct is that of an insurrectional movement that becomes the new government of a state.[29]

These standards establish a fairly high threshold of state involvement or, alternatively, *de facto* state action by non-state actors accompanied by state authorization or disengagement. Instances of simple complicity of state organs in the conduct of non-state actors are not sufficient to render such conduct attributable to the state under the traditional rules of attribution.[30]

---

to art. 57. However, this says nothing about the issue of member state responsibility for the conduct of intergovernmental organizations, which is a separate issue.

25 The phrase non-state actor is here used in a relative sense. It is meant to refer to any individual or entity that is not a *de jure* organ of the state whose obligations are under consideration. Thus, it may include *de jure* organs of other states or of intergovernmental organizations.

26 Draft Articles, art. 8. In the absence of specific instructions, a fairly high degree of control has been required to attribute the conduct to the state. According to the Commentary on the Draft Articles, 'Such conduct will be attributable to the State only if it directed or controlled the specific operation and the conduct complained of was an integral part of that operation. The principle does not extend to conduct which was only incidentally or peripherally associated with an operation and which escaped from the State's direction or control'. Commentary to Draft Articles, Report of the International Law Commission, 53rd Session, UN Doc. A/56/10 at 104.

27 Draft Articles, art. 9.

28 Draft Articles, art. 11. See also *U.S. v. Iran*, discussed infra.

29 Draft Articles, art. 10.

30 See, e.g., *Nicaragua v. U.S.*, ICJ Judgment (1986), (holding that provision of training, resources, and logistical support was insufficient for the conduct of the contras to be attributable to the United States).

### 3.3 The Use of Private Contractors

The use of private contractors in the recent conflicts in Iraq and Afghanistan has drawn increased attention to the relationship between the conduct of non-state actors and state responsibility. The rules of attribution contemplate two situations in which the conduct of private contractors may be attributable to the state.

The first is where the contractor is *de jure* acting on behalf of the state. This situation is covered by article 5 of the Draft Articles, which applies to entities that are empowered by the law of the state to exercise elements of governmental authority. Thus, the conduct of private contractors that are legally authorized to carry out public functions on behalf of the state will be attributable to the state. These entities essentially become assimilated to organs of the state when they are acting in their public capacity. Thus, their *ultra vires* conduct remains attributable to the state so long as they are acting in that capacity.

The second situation is where the contractor is in fact authorized to act on behalf of the state, without the official imprimatur of legal empowerment. In such situations, it does not matter whether the contractor is carrying out a public function. However, this situation would be governed by article 8 of the Draft Articles, which, as noted above, sets a fairly high threshold for attribution. In addition, as there is not necessarily any "official" capacity in such situations, the entity's conduct will not be attributable to the state if such conduct was contrary to the state's instructions.[31]

Thus, as noted above, the law of state responsibility sets a relatively high bar for attribution in these circumstances. However, the law of state responsibility admits the possibility of *lex specialis* where 'special rules of international law' may govern.[32]

### 3.4 Attribution in the Context of Human Rights Law

Special rules may be evolving through the practice of universal and regional human rights mechanisms. These institutions have increasingly found degrees of state involvement not rising to the level established for attribution under the Draft Articles to be sufficient to render the state responsible for the acts of non-state actors.

In the *Loizidou* case, for example, the European Court of Human Rights found that the Turkish army's "effective overall control" of northern Cyprus was sufficient

31 But see *Prosecutor v. Tadić*, 38 *ILM* (1999), 1518. In *Tadic*, the ICTY Appeals Chamber took the position that overall control of a hierarchically-organized non-state entity may be sufficient to assimilate that entity to a state organ, rendering all of its conduct attributable to the state. See infra.

32 Draft Articles, art. 55.

to impute[33] the conduct of the local administration to Turkey.[34] In adopting the "effective overall control" test and finding that it was therefore not necessary to determine whether Turkey actually exercised detailed control over the policies and actions of the authorities of the TRNC,[35] the European Court of Human Rights seemed to adopt a lower standard for attribution than that employed by the ICJ in the *Nicaragua* case and set forth in article 8 of the Draft Articles.[36]

However, an even lower standard for attribution in the context of human rights law may be evolving. A growing corpus of international human rights ju-

33 Note, however, that in *Loizidou v. Turkey (Preliminary Objections)*, app. no. 15318/89, ECtHR 23 March 1995, the Court essentially collapsed the issue of imputability with the question of the scope of Turkey's jurisdiction within the meaning of Article 1 of the European Convention. *Loizidou* at para. 57 ('It follows from the above considerations that the continuous denial of the applicant's access to her property in northern Cyprus and the ensuing loss of all control over the property is a matter which falls within Turkey's "jurisdiction" within the meaning of Article 1 (art. 1) and is thus imputable to Turkey'.) This of course becomes problematic in the context of peace operations involving collective action. The distinction between these questions was illustrated in *Bankovic and others v. Belgium and others*, app. no. 52207/99, ECtHR 12 December 2001, in which the Court found that it was unnecessary to consider the 'alleged several liability of the respondent States for an act carried out by an international organisation of which they are members' because the Court had already concluded that it was 'not satisfied that the applicants and their deceased relatives were capable of coming within the jurisdiction of the respondent States on account of the extra-territorial act in question' (paras. 82-83).

34 *Loizidou* at para. 56 ('It is not necessary to determine whether, as the applicant and the Government of Cyprus have suggested, Turkey actually exercises detailed control over the policies and actions of the authorities of the "TRNC". It is obvious from the large number of troops engaged in active duties in northern Cyprus ... that her army exercises effective overall control over that part of the island. Such control, according to the relevant test and in the circumstances of the case, entails her responsibility for the policies and actions of the "TRNC" ...').

35 Id.

36 This was expressly recognized by the ICTY Appeals Chamber in the *Tadic* judgment, in which it departed from the rule formulated by the ICJ for attribution of the conduct of organized, hierarchical groups. While the ICJ had held that the proper standard for attribution is 'effective control' over the group (*Nicaragua case*, ICJ Rep. 1986, 14), including direction and participation in the particular act to be attributed, the ICTY found 'overall control' to be sufficient and has not required direction or participation by the State in the specific conduct (Case IT-94-1, *Prosecutor v. Tadić*, 38 *ILM* (1999), 1518). In finding further that the State could be held responsible even for acts contrary to specific instructions, the ICTY Appeals Chamber noted that, generally speaking, 'the whole body of international law on State responsibility is based on a realistic concept of accountability, which disregards legal formalities and aims at ensuring that States entrusting some functions to individuals or groups of individuals must answer for their actions, even when they act contrary to their directives' (para. 121). The Appeals Chamber also made clear that it was applying its interpretation of the rules of attribution under the law of State responsibility, and was thus not relying on a *lex specialis* theory for its departure from the *Nicaragua* judgment.

risprudence and practice supports the proposition that the conduct of non-state actors may be attributable to the state where state actors are *complicit* in such conduct.[37]

An example of the application of this principle in human rights jurisprudence can be found in the *Massacre at Riofrío Case* of the Inter-American Commission on Human Rights. In analyzing whether the conduct at issue amounted to a violation of the right to life under the American Convention, the Commission found Colombia to be

> responsible for the acts of its agents as well as for those perpetrated by individuals who acted with their complicity to make it possible to carry out and cover up the execution of the victims in violation of their right not to be arbitrarily deprived of their lives, as established in Article 4 ...[38]

It should be noted, however, that cases in which human rights mechanisms have found complicity sufficient for attribution have generally involved state complicity in the conduct of non-state actors operating *within that state*. It is unclear

37 See, e.g., *Velasquez-Rodriguez* case; Decision Regarding Communication No. 155/96, African Comm. Hum. & Peoples' Rights, Done at the 30th Ordinary Session, held in Banjul, The Gambia from 13-27 October 2001, para. 61; Mass Exoduses And Displaced Persons, Report of the Representative of the Secretary-General, Mr. Francis Deng, Addendum, E/CN.4/1998/53/Add. See also *Cyprus v. Turkey* at para. 81 (noting that 'the acquiescence or connivance of the authorities of a Contracting State in the acts of private individuals which violate the Convention rights of other individuals within its jurisdiction may engage that State's responsibility under the Convention'). However, it should be noted that the European Court at times fails to distinguish clearly between human rights violative conduct that is attributable to the state and conduct of non-state actors that the state has failed to prevent or respond to. The lack of distinction may result in part from the formulation of article 1, containing the single obligation to secure rights, which would encompass both types of conduct, rather than being expressed as two distinct obligations (i.e., to respect and to ensure). There has been a parallel development in refugee law. *See Islam v. Secretary Of State For The Home Department; Regina v. Immigration Appeal Tribunal And Another; Ex Parte Shah (Conjoined Appeals)*, 25 March 1999, House of Lords, Lord Steyn.

38 *Riofrio Massacre*, Inter-American Commission on Human Rights, REPORT N° 62/ 01, CASE 11.654, COLOMBIA, April 6, 2001. In *Riofrío*, petitioners alleged that members of the Colombian army collaborated with a group of paramilitaries in the execution of a number of individuals in the municipality of Riofrío, Colombia. The Commission recalled that the Inter-American Court of Human Rights has noted that "[i]t is sufficient to show that the infringement of the rights recognized in the Convention has been supported or tolerated by the government." Having found evidence that "agents of the State helped to coordinate the massacre, to carry it out, and, as discovered by domestic courts, to cover it up," the Commission concluded that the "State is liable for the violations of the American Convention resulting from the acts of commission or omission by its own agents and by private individuals involved in the execution of the victims." It should be noted, however, that the actual conduct of State actors in this case would have met a higher standard than that adopted by the Commission.

whether the same standard would apply with respect to non-state actors operating abroad.[39]

### 3.5 *Caveat: Positive Obligations and the Attribution of Omission*

As noted above, the question of attribution is in principle separate from the content of international obligations. However, this distinction may become difficult to discern in the context of a failure of a state to fulfill positive obligations in relation to the acts of non-state actors. In such situations, it is essential to distinguish between whether the conduct of non-state actors is attributable to a state and the separate question of whether a state has failed to fulfill an affirmative obligation, should one be imposed by a primary rule of international law, in relation to the conduct of non-state actors.[40]

For example, in *US v. Iran*, the ICJ considered three grounds for finding Iran responsible in relation to the Embassy take-over and seizure of hostages carried out by a group of militants. First, it considered whether alleged incitement by Iranian officials accompanied by a failure to protect the embassy was sufficient to render the subsequent take-over of the embassy attributable to Iran. The Court found that this was not a sufficient basis for attribution.

The Court then considered whether the Iranian government's failure to protect the Embassy violated Iran's affirmative obligation to do so under the Vienna Conventions on Diplomatic and Consular Relations. The ICJ found that the failure of the Iranian authorities to take steps to protect the embassy violated this obligation. It is important to note that the court did not find that the failure to protect the embassy made the conduct of the militants attributable to Iran. The conduct at issue was the omission of the Iranian authorities – i.e. the failure of take steps to protect the Embassy. It was this conduct, this failure to act, that was not in conformity with what international law required, and Iran was therefore found to be in violation of its affirmative duty to protect the Embassy.

39 See discussion regarding the level of obligation under human rights law infra.

40 The difficulty in appreciating this distinction became apparent preceding the 2001 invasion of Afghanistan. In the aftermath of the September 11, 2001 attacks against targets in the United States, some scholars argued that *US v. Iran* stood for the proposition that acquiescence by a state in the conduct of non-state actors operating primarily within its territory was sufficient to find that conduct attributable to the state. That is clearly not the case under the rules of attribution as elaborated by the International Law Commission. While a state's responsibility may be engaged in relation to its own conduct – i.e. its own failure to take steps to prevent or respond to the acts of non-state actors, this is quite distinct from finding the conduct of the non-state actors to be attributable to the state. In the context of the 9/11 attacks, a finding that Afghanistan had breached its affirmative duty to take steps to prevent and respond to terrorist activity would give rise to an obligation on the part of Afghanistan to bring its conduct into conformity with its obligations and to make reparations. In contrast, to find that the 9/11 attacks were attributable to Afghanistan could give rise to the right of self-defense, justifying the use of armed force against Afghanistan.

Finally, the Court considered whether the subsequent praise of the militants by Iranian officials, together with a request by the Iranian government that the occupation of the Embassy be maintained, was sufficient to attribute the continuing occupation of the embassy and detention of the hostages to Iran. Here, the Court found that Iran adopted the conduct of the militants as its own, thereby translating the acts of the militants into acts of Iran. As explained by the Court, "The militants, authors of the invasions and jailors of the hostages, had now become agents of the Iranian State for whose acts the state itself was internationally responsible."[41]

Thus, the Court found attributable to Iran the conduct of two groups: the conduct of Iranian officials in failing to protect the embassy and also the conduct of the militants in taking over the embassy and detaining the hostages. The ICJ also emphasized the importance of the distinction between these two findings.[42]

The attribution of conduct consisting of omissions presents conceptual difficulties in part because conduct consisting of omissions is, in a sense, always attributable. As omission is a lack of action, an actor is not required. Hence, the state is essentially in a constant state of omission. However, in order for an omission to constitute a basis of responsibility, there must be a duty to act. The question of establishing a duty to act will turn on the content of the relevant primary rule. Thus, in these circumstances, the issue of attribution collapses into the content of the primary rule.

### 3.6 *The Obligation to Respect Versus the Obligation to Ensure*

The distinction between attribution of the conduct of non-state actors and a state's responsibility for its omissions in relation to the conduct of non-state actors has special significance in the context of human rights law. Where human rights violative conduct[43] is attributable to a state, the state will have breached an obligation of result and responsibility will arise immediately. Where such conduct is not attributable to a state, the question of whether human rights law has been violated will be determined by the quality of the state's response to this conduct, generally governed by a "best efforts" standard.

41 *US v. Iran* at para. 74.

42 "The Iranian authorities' decision to continue the subjection of the premises of the United States Embassy to occupation by militants and of the Embassy staff to detention as hostages, clearly gave rise to repeated and multiple breaches of the applicable provisions of the Vienna Conventions even more serious than those which arose from their failure to take any steps to prevent the attacks on the inviolability of these premises and staff." *US v. Iran* at para. 76.

43 By use of the terms "human rights violative conduct" or "human right violation", I do not refer to conduct that necessarily constitutes a violation of human rights law. I am using these terms to refer to conduct that would constitute an impermissible interference with one or more human rights if such conduct were attributed to the state. Thus, a human rights violation committed by a non-state actor whose conduct is not otherwise attributable to the state would not necessarily constitute a violation of human rights law.

As noted above, article 2(1) of the ICCPR states that "[e]ach State Party to the present Covenant undertakes *to respect and to ensure* to all individuals within its territory and subject to its jurisdiction the rights recognized in the present Covenant ..."[44] In its General Comments, the Human Rights Committee has construed this provision to oblige states to protect the rights contained in the Covenant against non-state interference.[45] In General Comment 31, the Committee stated:

> [T]he positive obligations on States Parties to ensure Covenant rights will only be fully discharged if individuals are protected by the State, not just against violations of Covenant rights by its agents, but also against acts committed by private persons or entities that would impair the enjoyment of Covenant rights in so far as they are amenable to application between private persons or entities. There may be circumstances in which a failure to ensure Covenant rights as required by article 2 would give rise to violations by States Parties of those rights, as a result of States Parties' permitting or failing to take appropriate measures or to exercise due diligence to prevent, punish, investigate or redress the harm caused by such acts by private persons or entities.

The regional human rights institutions have similarly interpreted comparable provisions[46] in their respective treaties.[47] In the *Velásquez-Rodriguez* case, the Inter-American Court of Human Rights found that agents who acted under cover of

---

44 Emphasis added. Customary law may entail a more limited level of obligation. It is unclear, for example, whether customary law requires states to "ensure" rights as that term has been interpreted by human rights mechanisms. For example, the US Restatement provides that a "state violates international law when, as a matter of policy, it practices, encourages, or condones any of the following: 1. Genocide, 2. Slavery or slave trade, 3. Murder or causing the disappearance of individuals, 4. Torture or other cruel, inhumane, or degrading treatment or punishment, 5. Prolonged arbitrary detention, 6. Systematic racial discrimination, or 7. A consistent pattern of gross violations of internationally recognized human rights". By limiting this obligation to situations when the State, "as a matter of policy, ... practices, encourages, or condones" the violations, this passage may be read to exclude an obligation to take affirmative steps to prevent or respond to violations by non-State actors, an obligation which clearly obtains under the major human rights treaties.

45 See, e.g., its General Comments 6, 10, 16, 17, 18, 20, 21, 27, 28, and 31.

46 See ACHR, art. 1(1); ECHR, art. 1. Article 1 of the European Convention requires the High Contracting Parties to "secure" the rights contained in the Convention. The European Court has interpreted article one to entail a scope of obligation similar to that encompassed by the phrase "to respect and to ensure" as interpreted by the Human Rights Committee. The African Commission on Human and Peoples Rights has gone farther, interpreting article 1 of the African Charter, which obliges states to "recognize" rights and to "adopt ... measures to give effect to them," to entail the obligations to respect, protect, promote, and fulfil the rights contained in the Charter. See Decision Regarding Communication No. 155/96, supra note X.

47 Id.; *Velásquez-Rodriguez*; Applic. 15599/94, *A v. U.K.*, report of 18 Sep. 1997; *Kiliç v. Turkey*, app. no. 22492/93, ECtHR 28 March 2000; *Jiménez v. Colombia*, Communication No. 859/1999, 25 March 2002, CCPR/C/74/D/859/1999 at para.s 7.2, 9.

public authority carried out the disappearance of Manfredo Velásquez. The Court stated, however, that "even had that fact not been proven, the failure of the State apparatus to act, which is clearly proven, is a failure on the part of Honduras to fulfill the duties it assumed under Article 1(1) of the Convention, which obligated it to ensure Manfredo Velásquez the free and full exercise of his human rights."[48]

In particular, the Court found that:

> An illegal act which violates human rights and which is initially not directly imputable to a State (for example, because it is the act of a private person or because the person responsible has not been identified) can lead to international responsibility of the State, not because of the act itself, but because of the lack of due diligence to prevent the violation or to respond to it as required by the Convention.[49]

The "due diligence" standard cited by the Court "has been generally accepted as a measure of evaluating a State's responsibility for violation of human rights by private actors."[50]

Thus, human rights violations committed by non-state actors may give rise to state responsibility even when there is no connection between the perpetrators and the state. The obligation to "ensure" rights under the major human rights treaties requires states to take reasonable, effective steps to prevent and to respond to human rights violations committed by non-state actors.[51]

---

48 *Velásquez-Rodriguez*, at para. 182.

49 *Velásquez-Rodriguez* case, at para. 172.

50 Preliminary report submitted by the Special Rapporteur on violence against women, its causes and consequences, Ms. Radhika Coomaraswamy, E/CN.4/1995/42, para. 103 (citing Moore, Int. Arb. 495 (1872)). Application of the 'due diligence' standard can be seen in the reports of UN special rapporteurs, UN special representatives, and the Secretary-General; comments, views, and concluding observations of human rights treaty bodies; reports on expert group meetings; resolutions of the Commission on Human Rights and the Economic and Social Council; Declarations by the General Assembly, and the writings of publicists. See J.Cerone, 'The Human Rights Framework Applicable to Trafficking in Persons and its Incorporation into UNMIK Regulation 2001/4', *International Peacekeeping. The Yearbook of International Peace Operations*, Volume 7, 2001, 43 – 98 (2002.

51 It should be noted, however, that the line between complicity sufficient for attribution and failure to exercise due diligence is highly fact-sensitive, and that these two modes of responsibility often blur into each other. In addition, state responsibility may also be engaged by the state's failure to provide an effective remedy in accordance with its treaty obligations. It is important to remember that although the same acts may implicate all three types of responsibility, these are separate modes of state responsibility and breaches of independent legal obligations. They offer separate bases of responsibility. The application of these various, related modes of state responsibility is illustrated in the *Riofrio* case described above. In that case, the Inter-American Commission found Colombia responsible for: violations of the rights to life and to humane treatment perpetrated by paramilitaries acting in complicity with state agents, violation of the right

As with the evolving jurisprudence finding complicity sufficient for attribution, much of the jurisprudence on responsibility for preventing and responding to violations committed by non-state actors has developed in the context of non-state actors operating within the relevant state's territory. It is unclear to what extent this interpretation of the obligation to ensure rights can be transposed to an extraterritorial context.

## 4 The Application of Human Rights Law in Relation to Individuals Outside the State's Territory

The great innovation of human rights law was that it regulated the way a state treated those within its jurisdiction. No longer could a state invoke the principle of non-intervention as an impermeable barrier to international scrutiny of its conduct vis-à-vis its own populace.

Conversely, the notion that international law took cognizance of and regulated a state's conduct on the territory of other states and toward foreign nationals was established long before the Universal Declaration of Human Rights was adopted. It is therefore somewhat ironic that a great controversy has erupted in recent years as to whether the norms of human rights law may be applied to a state's extraterritorial conduct.

Prior to the development of human rights law, international law was concerned almost exclusively with states' external conduct. Abuses committed within a state's territory were virtually invisible to international law unless the victim was a foreign national and the state of nationality was willing to espouse the claim on the inter-state level. Thus, human rights law filled a serious gap by regulating the way a state treated its own people. Human rights law has developed tremendously over the past few decades, and individuals are receiving increasing levels of protection against abuses committed by their own governments – levels of protection exceeding that afforded under the traditional law of state responsibility for injury to aliens. But is this protection to be afforded only vis-à-vis the state's own citizenry?

Relatively early on, it was made clear that human rights law applied to all those within the state's territory, even to those who were not nationals of that state, underscoring the universality of the concept of human rights. Thus, the heightened protection of human rights law applies irrespective of the nationality of the victim. A separate question is whether this protection applies irrespective of the physical location of the victim vis-à-vis the state.

Most of the jurisprudence of human rights bodies, which have greatly elaborated on the content of states' obligations under the various human rights treaties, has been developed in the context of alleged violations committed on the territory of the respective state party. Can these same standards be transposed onto the state's conduct abroad?

---

to judicial protection, and failure to ensure the rights protected under the Convention. *Riofrio.*

In order to answer this question, it is essential to closely examine the scope of human rights obligations.

### 4.1 *The Scope of Human Rights Obligations*

This section will provide a framework for delineating the scope of human rights obligations by examining three different parameters: the scope of beneficiaries, the range of rights applicable, and the level of obligation. The scope of beneficiaries refers to those individuals whose rights must be respected and ensured by the relevant state (or other subject of obligation under human rights law).[52] The range of rights applicable refers to the question of which rights apply in situations where the state may not be bound to recognize the full range of rights provided under treaty or customary law. The level of obligation refers to the degree of positive action a state must undertake in order to meet its obligations under human rights law.

It should be noted that the scope of obligation may vary depending upon whether the relevant source of law is treaty or custom as well as the context in which the state is operating.

#### 4.1.1 Scope of Beneficiaries

States parties to the ICCPR are not bound to respect and ensure the rights of all individuals everywhere. For example, it is clear that, absent special circumstances, states parties are not required to protect the rights of individuals living in other countries from violations perpetrated by the governments of those countries or by non-state actors operating there.

As noted above, a common feature of the major human rights treaties is that the scope of beneficiaries is typically limited to those within a state's territory or subject to its jurisdiction. While it was initially unclear whether this language could encompass a state's conduct abroad, the extraterritorial application of human rights treaties has now been clearly established in the jurisprudence of several international judicial and quasi-judicial bodies.

##### *4.1.1.1 The Approach of UN and UN-Related Institutions*

The Human Rights Committee has consistently held that the ICCPR can have extraterritorial application,[53] clearly demonstrating its understanding that a state's jurisdiction extends beyond its territorial boundaries. In particular, it has found that

52 In general, as states are the typical subjects of obligations under human rights law, states are referred to throughout the analysis. However, in most contexts, intergovernmental organisations may also be included to the extent that they may be deemed subjects of obligations under human rights law. Thus, throughout this analysis 'states' is used as short-hand for 'subjects of obligations under human rights law'.

53 See, e.g., Concluding observations of the Human Rights Committee : Israel. CCPR/CO/78/ISR. 21/08/2003. at para. 11; Human Rights Committee, Comments on United States of America, para. 19, U.N. Doc. CCPR/C/79/Add 50 (1995); Consideration of Reports Submitted by States Parties under Article 40 of the Covenant: Iran (Islamic Republic of Iran), para. 63, 30/07/93, CCPR/C/SR.1253.

the expressed scope of article 2(1) "does not imply that the State party concerned cannot be held accountable for violations of rights under the Covenant which its agents commit upon the territory of another State, whether with the acquiescence of the Government of that State or in opposition to it."[54]

In *Burgos / Lopez v. Uruguay*, the Committee held that Uruguay violated its obligations under the Covenant when its security forces abducted and tortured a Uruguayan citizen then living in Argentina. Following the command of Article 5(1) that "[n]othing in the present Covenant may be interpreted as implying ... any right to engage in any activity ... aimed at the destruction of any of the rights and freedoms recognized herein," the Committee reasoned that "it would be unconscionable to so interpret the responsibility under article 2 of the Covenant as to permit a State party to perpetrate violations of the Covenant on the territory of another State, which violations it could not perpetrate on its own territory."[55]

Initially, it was unclear whether the Committee's holding in *Burgos / Lopez* was strictly limited to extraterritorial violations committed against a state's own national, that factor providing a solid basis for finding that the victim was subject to the perpetrating state's jurisdiction. However, the Committee's recent practice makes clear that the Covenant applies to a state's conduct abroad even with respect to its treatment of foreign nationals.

In its General Comment 31, the Committee asserted that "a State party must respect and ensure the rights laid down in the Covenant to anyone within the power or effective control of that State Party, even if not situated within the territory of the State Party." Similarly, after affirming that the "enjoyment of Covenant rights is not limited to citizens of States Parties but must also be available to all individuals, regardless of nationality or statelessness, such as asylum seekers, refugees, migrant workers and other persons, who may find themselves in the territory or subject to the jurisdiction of the State Party," the Committee noted that "[t]his principle also applies to those within the power or effective control of the forces of a State Party acting outside its territory, regardless of the circumstances in which such power or effective control was obtained, such as forces constituting a national contingent of a State Party assigned to an international peace-keeping or peace-enforcement operation."

The Committee confirmed its position specifically in the context of armed conflict. In response to the Israeli government's assertion that the ICCPR did not apply outside of a state's territory, especially in the context of armed conflict or occupation, the Committee stated:

> Nor does the applicability of the regime of international humanitarian law preclude accountability of States parties under article 2, paragraph 1, of the Covenant for the actions of their authorities outside their own territories, including in occupied ter-

54 *Burgos / Delia Saldias de Lopez v. Uruguay*, para. 12.3. See also J. Cerone, 'Minding the Gap: Outlining KFOR Accountability in Post-Conflict Kosovo,' 12 *EJIL* 469 (June 2001).

55 *Id.*

> ritories. The Committee therefore reiterates that, in the current circumstances, the provisions of the Covenant apply to the benefit of the population of the Occupied Territories, for all conduct by the State party's authorities or agents in those territories that affect the enjoyment of rights enshrined in the Covenant and fall within the ambit of State responsibility of Israel under the principles of public international law.[56]

The Committee's position was endorsed in part by the International Court of Justice in its 2004 Advisory Opinion on *Legal Consequences on the Construction of a Wall in the Occupied Palestinian Territory.* In that case, the ICJ opined that the ICCPR, the International Covenant on Economic, Social, and Cultural Rights (ICESCR), and the Convention on the Rights of the Child applied to Israel's conduct in the Occupied Territories.

In particular, after citing the position of the Human Rights Committee, the Court found "that the [ICCPR] is applicable in respect of acts done by a State in the exercise of its jurisdiction outside its own territory." However, in contrast to the Human Rights Committee's broad reference to conduct by authorities "that affect [sic] the enjoyment of rights," the Court employs the more specific, and arguably circular, formulation "acts done ... in the exercise of its jurisdiction." It seems that the Court may have intended to establish a narrower standard in this respect. The Court did not cite General Comment 31 or its "power or effective control standard," even though that Comment was adopted by the Human Rights Committee several months before the ICJ rendered its Opinion.

The Court does not provide specific guidance as to what constitutes "acts done by a State in the exercise of its jurisdiction." While the Court clearly regarded this standard as having been met in the situation of occupation, the Court did not reject the Committee's broader interpretation. Indeed the Court cited *Burgos / Lopez,* referring to the arrests in those cases as exercises of jurisdiction. Thus, it would appear that an exercise of jurisdiction for the purpose of applying the ICCPR does not require as a pre-condition territorial control.

In contrast, the Court explicitly required territorial control to trigger application of the ICESCR. After noting that article 2 of the ICESCR does not contain a provision circumscribing the scope of states parties' obligations, the ICJ acknowledged that the rights enumerated therein are "essentially territorial." Nonetheless, the court found that "it is not to be excluded that it applies both to territories over which a State party has sovereignty and to those over which that State exercises territorial jurisdiction."[57] Here the Court appears to limit more narrowly the circumstances in which the ICESCR would apply extraterritorially. Rather than referring simply to the exercise of jurisdiction, the Court seems to require the exercise

56 Para. 11.

57 The Court cites with approval the finding of the CESCR that the "State party's obligations under the Covenant apply to all territories and populations under its effective control." While this may be interpreted to apply to effective control over either territories or populations, it is difficult to conceive of effective control of a population, as opposed to certain individuals, without territorial control.

of territorial jurisdiction, which implies control over territory and not just over individuals.[58]

### 4.1.1.2 *The Approach of Regional Human Rights Systems*

Regional human rights institutions have generated more extensive jurisprudence on this issue. Both the Inter-American and European Human Rights bodies have found that regional human rights treaties apply to extraterritorial conduct.

#### 4.1.1.2.1 The Inter-American Commission on Human Rights

The Inter-American Commission has applied a relatively low threshold for extraterritorial application of Inter-American human rights law, simply requiring control over the individuals whose rights have been violated. In *Coard et al. v. the United States*, the Commission examined allegations that the military action led by US armed forces in Grenada in October of 1983 violated a series of norms of international human rights and humanitarian law. In the course of its analysis, the Commission found that the phrase 'subject to its jurisdiction' "may, under given circumstances, refer to conduct with an extraterritorial locus where the person concerned is present in the territory of one state, but subject to the control of another state – usually through the acts of the latter's agents abroad."[59] The Commission further stated that "[i]n principle, the inquiry turns not on the presumed victim's nationality or presence within a particular geographic area, but on whether, under the specific circumstances, the State observed the rights of a person subject to its authority and control."

The Commission made clear that neither the victim's nationality nor geographic location were decisive, and set forth the criteria of authority and control over the victim. The petitioners in this case, having been taken into custody by US forces, were clearly under the authority and control of the United States.[60]

In *Alejandre v. Cuba*, petitioners alleged that a military aircraft belonging to the Cuban Air Force shot down two unarmed civilian light airplanes resulting in the deaths of the four occupants of those airplanes. The Commission examined the

---

58 As noted *infra*, the ICJ may be backing away from this position. See Section 4.1.2.

59 *Coard*, at para. 37. This standard was recently reaffirmed in a letter from the Inter-American Commission to the US government indicating precautionary measures in respect of detainees at Guantanamo Bay, Cuba. Detainees in Guantanamo Bay, Cuba; Request for Precautionary Measures, Inter-Am. C.H.R. (March 13, 2002). (citing string of cases).

60 Notwithstanding the broad language employed by the Commission, it could be argued that certain facts in this case limit the reach of its holding. Since the petitioners were placed in detention on military vessels of the United States, a finding of jurisdiction could be grounded on this fact alone. Similarly, petitioners had alleged that at the time they were arrested, the US had already consolidated its control over Grenada. It could thus be argued that it was this territorial control that enabled the Commission to find that the petitioners were under the authority and control of the US. However, the Commission made no mention of either of these facts in its analysis. *Alejandre*, a contemporaneous case, confirms that this was not an oversight.

evidence and found that the victims died as a consequence of direct actions taken "by agents of the Cuban State in international airspace."

In determining whether the victims were within the jurisdiction of Cuba, the Commission again cited the standard of "authority and control."[61] In this case, the victims were clearly not on Cuban territory or on any territory over which Cuba had any control. Nor were they in a Cuban vessel.[62] Nor were their bodies subsequently brought within Cuban territory. Further, while two of the victims were Cuban born, the other two were born in the United States. Thus, nationality could not serve as the jurisdictional link between the victims and Cuba. Authority and control in this case had to be found solely in the relationship between the agents of Cuba and the victims in the circumstances at the time of the incident.

The Commission found no evidence of any dialogue between the Cuban armed forces and the victims, stating, "At no time did [they] notify or warn the civilian airplanes, try to use other interception methods, or give them an opportunity to land." Nor were there any indicia of control other than the simple fact that the Cuban military aircraft had the victims in their cross-hairs. As noted by the Commission, their "first and only response was the intentional destruction of the civilian airplanes and their four occupants." Nonetheless, the Commission found this to constitute "conclusive evidence that agents of the Cuban State, although outside their territory, placed the civilian pilots . . . under their authority"[63] and held therefore that the victims were within the jurisdiction of Cuba for the purpose of applying its human rights obligations to the instant case.[64]

Thus, the Commission has established a relatively low threshold for the extraterritorial application of Inter-American human rights law. Indeed, it is hard to imagine a situation where human rights violations perpetrated by a state agent would fail to meet this test.

#### 4.1.1.2.2 The European Commission and Court of Human Rights

In contrast to the approach of the Inter-American system, the jurisprudence of the European Court of Human Rights has been more cautious, careful to avoid an

61 The Commission's language was almost identical to that used in *Coard*.

62 Their airplanes were US-registered.

63 It may be worth noting that the Commission used only the term "authority" in this context, and did not expressly find the victims to be under the "control" of Cuba. This may be interpreted to permit extraterritorial application in situations where individuals are subject to a state's authority, but are not necessarily within its control. Further, in the immediately preceding sentence, when restating the standard for extraterritorial application, the Commission stated, "The fact that the events took place outside Cuban jurisdiction does not limit the Commission's competence ratione loci, because, as previously stated, when agents of a state, whether military or civilian, exercise *power and authority* over persons outside national territory, the state's obligation to respect human rights continues..." (emphasis added). Note that the Commission makes no mention of control.

64 *Alejandre*.

interpretation that would render the European Convention applicable to all state conduct across the globe.

The European Court has set forth various standards for determining whether individuals are within the jurisdiction of Contracting States (i.e. states parties) for the purpose of applying the European Convention on Human Rights to their conduct abroad. It has found the Convention to apply where a Contracting State exercises effective overall control of territory beyond its borders,[65] as well as in certain other limited circumstances where agents of that state carry out a governmental function on the territory of another state.[66]

The early jurisprudence of the European Commission of Human Rights seemed to correspond more closely to the approach of the Human Rights Committee. In the case of *W.M. v. Denmark*,[67] in which a German citizen alleged human rights violative conduct on the part of the Danish ambassador in Berlin, the Commission found it clear that "that authorised agents of a State, including diplomatic or consular agents, bring other persons or property within the jurisdiction of that State to the extent that they exercise authority over such persons or property. In so far as they affect such persons or property by their acts or omissions, the responsibility of the State is engaged." While it ultimately did not find a violation in that case, the breadth of its language closely parallels that employed by the Human Rights Committee in *Burgos / Lopez*.

The European Court of Human Rights initially appeared to employ a similarly broad understanding of jurisdiction. In the case of *Drozd and Janousek v. France and Spain*[68] the applicant contended that French and Spanish judges who had been seconded to Andorran courts violated their rights under the Convention.

The Court began its analysis of whether the applicants came within the jurisdiction of France or Spain by re-stating the question as one of attribution:[69] "The

65 *Cyprus v. Turkey*, app. no. 25781/94, ECtHR 10 May 2001.

66 *Bankovic and others v. Belgium and others*, app. no. 52207/99, ECtHR 12 December 2001. As noted below, the jurisprudence of the European Court is presently in flux with regard to this issue. Recent cases seem to establish a lower standard.

67 *W.M. v. Denmark*, app. no. 17392/90, ECtHR 14 October 1992.

68 *Drozd and Janousek v. France and Spain*, app. no. 12747/87, ECtHR 26 June 1992.

69 As noted above, the European Court at times conflates the issue of attribution with the scope of beneficiaries; however, in principle these are distinct issues. Attribution is concerned with the link between the relevant subject of human rights law (generally, a state) and the individual (or entity) alleged to have perpetrated the violation of human rights law (by engaging in conduct that unjustifiably interferes with human rights). The scope of beneficiaries is concerned with the link between the relevant subject of international law and the victim of the human rights violation. However, ascertaining the existence and extent of the latter link may require the prior determination of an issue attribution. For example, to determine whether an individual is within a state's jurisdiction, it may be necessary to determine whether those who are exercising authority or control over those individuals are acting on behalf of that state. See J. Cerone, "Out of Bounds? Considering the Reach of International Human Rights Law", Working Paper of the Center for Human Rights and Global Justice at NYU School of Law (April 2006).

question to be decided here is whether the acts complained of by Mr Drozd and Mr Janousek can be attributed to France or Spain or both, even though they were not performed on the territory of those States." Although it ultimately found that the conduct of the judges was not attributable to France or Spain, the Court implied that had it been attributable, individuals over whom the judges exercised authority would have been within the jurisdiction of those countries.

However, in later cases, the Court seemed to take a somewhat different approach. In a series of cases relating to the Turkish occupation of northern Cyprus, the Court began to place greater emphasis on territorial control. In *Loizidou v. Turkey* (preliminary objections)[70], the Court began its analysis by identifying situations in which those outside of a state's territory could still be deemed within the jurisdiction of that state.

It first mentioned cases in which the extradition or expulsion of a person by a Contracting State could give rise to a human rights violation, "and hence engage the responsibility of that State under the Convention."[71] It then identified a second category, recalling that the "responsibility of Contracting Parties can be involved because of acts of their authorities, whether performed within or outside national boundaries, which produce effects outside their own territory," citing *Drozd v. Janousek.*

It then set forth a third situation in which the Convention could be found to apply extraterritorially:

> [T]he responsibility of a Contracting Party may also arise when as a consequence of military action – whether lawful or unlawful – it exercises effective control of an area outside its national territory. The obligation to secure, in such an area, the rights and freedoms set out in the Convention derives from the fact of such control whether it be exercised directly, through its armed forces, or through a subordinate local administration.

The Court then noted that "the applicant's loss of control of her property stems from the occupation of the northern part of Cyprus by Turkish troops" and that "it has not been disputed that the applicant was prevented by Turkish troops from gaining access to her property." The Court found therefore that "such acts are capable of falling within Turkish 'jurisdiction' within the meaning of Article 1 (art. 1) of the Convention."

In its judgment on the merits, the Court found that this extraterritorial jurisdiction had an extremely broad scope. The Court first found that the conduct of the TRNC was attributable to Turkey. This finding enabled the Court to view Turkish jurisdiction as encompassing all "[t]hose affected by [the] policies or actions" of the TRNC.

---

70 *Loizidou v. Turkey (Preliminary Objections)*, app. no. 15318/89, ECtHR 23 March 1995.

71 It should be noted, however, that this is not an example of extraterritorial application as the individual alleging a violation is actually within the territory of the state, as the Court expressly recognizes in *Bankovic*.

In the subsequent case of *Cyprus v. Turkey*,[72] the Court noted that the responsibility of Turkey, "[h]aving effective overall control over northern Cyprus, ... cannot be confined to the acts of its own soldiers or officials in northern Cyprus but must also be engaged by virtue of the acts of the local administration which survives by virtue of Turkish military and other support." This approach enabled the Court to find that "Turkey's 'jurisdiction' must be considered to extend to securing the entire range of substantive rights set out in the Convention and those additional Protocols which she has ratified, and that violations of those rights are imputable to Turkey." In adopting this approach, the Court essentially assimilated the TRNC to an organ of the Turkish state and the territory of northern Cyprus to Turkish territory for the purpose of applying the Convention.

Although the Court in the northern Cyprus cases focused its attention on the issue of territorial control, this did not seem to narrow in any way the other situations in which the European human rights institutions had found the Convention to apply extraterritorially, in particular the "exercise of authority" standard set forth in *W.M. v. Denmark*.

However, a subsequent, highly politically-charged case seemed to diminish the scope of the rule set forth by the Commission in *W.M. v. Denmark*. In the case of *Bankovic v. Certain NATO Member States*, the Court found that the applicants, relatives of individuals killed in the course of the NATO bombing of Serbia, were not within the jurisdiction of the respondent states. In rejecting the applicants' claims as being beyond the jurisdiction of Contracting States, the Court synthesized its prior holdings and set forth the various situations in which it found the European Convention to apply extraterritorially.

The Court noted that the European Convention would apply to a state's conduct abroad "when the ... State, through the effective control of the relevant territory and its inhabitants abroad as a consequence of military occupation or through the consent, invitation or acquiescence of the Government of that territory, exercises all or some of the public powers normally to be exercised by that Government."[73] To these two situations – the exercise of public powers either through effective control of territory or with consent – the Court added "other recognised

72 *Cyprus v. Turkey*, app. no. 25781/94, ECtHR 10 May 2001.

73 *Bankovic and others v. Belgium and others*, app. no. 52207/99, ECtHR 12 December 2001, at para. 71. The Court here seems to refer here to two standards. The first – effective control of territory – seems to be a reiteration of the rule expressed in the northern Cyprus cases. The second seems intended to encompass a standard implicit in *Drozd and Janousek*. Had the conduct of the judges in that case been attributable to France or Spain, it is likely that the Court would have found the Convention to apply. Note however, that the Court in that case simply stated that the "responsibility [of Contracting States] can be involved because of acts of their authorities producing effects outside their own territory." Similarly, in *Loizidou*, the Court reiterated that the "responsibility of Contracting Parties can be involved because of acts of their authorities, whether performed within or outside national boundaries, which produce effects outside their own territory," citing *Drozd v. Janousek*. In *Bankovic*, the Court recasts this principle in narrower terms.

instances of the extra-territorial exercise of jurisdiction by a State," including "cases involving the activities of its diplomatic or consular agents abroad and on board craft and vessels registered in, or flying the flag of, that State." The Court did not restate the broad "exercise of authority" standard of *W.M. v. Denmark*.[74]

Thus, the Court seemed to significantly narrow the scope of extraterritorial application of the Convention. The exercise of power and authority over persons would not be sufficient. The Court seemed to require territorial control (through military occupation), the performance of a public function with the permission[75] of the territorial state, or that the particular type of jurisdiction exercised be recognized in international law (i.e. cases involving diplomats or on vessels of the Contracting State). Ultimately, the Court found that none of the recognized standards for extraterritorial application were applicable in the instant case.

However, the Court's recent judgments show a trend toward convergence (or re-convergence) with the approach of the Human Rights Committee and Inter-American Commission. In *Issa v. Turkey*,[76] a case concerning the conduct of Turkish forces in northern Iraq, the Court again listed situations in which the European Convention would apply extraterritorially. In addition to the "effective overall control" standard of the northern Cyprus cases, the Court seemed to resurrect the "power and authority" standard. Citing the Commission's decision in *W.M. v. Denmark*, it stated, "a State may also be held accountable for violation of the Convention rights and freedoms of persons who are in the territory of another State but who are found to be under the former State's authority and control through its agents operating – whether lawfully or unlawfully – in the latter State." The Court implies that this rule has been a consistent part of it jurisprudence, but that would seem not to be the case.[77]

---

74 Presumably, the Court intended *W.M.* to be encompassed as a case "involving the activities of its diplomatic or consular agents abroad." However, this would seem to be a narrower interpretation of the standard applied in that case. In *W.M.*, the Commission found it clear that "that authorised agents of a State, *including diplomatic or consular agents*, bring other persons or property within the jurisdiction of that State to the extent that they exercise authority over such persons or property." (Emphasis added.) This seems to imply that it was not limited to acts of diplomatic or consular agents.

75 The Court thus appeared to exclude conduct committed against the wishes of the territorial state, unless imposed through military occupation of the territory. This stands in stark contrast to the finding of the Human Rights Committee that the expressed scope of article 2(1) "does not imply that the State party concerned cannot be held accountable for violations of rights under the Covenant which its agents commit upon the territory of another State, whether with the acquiescence of the Government of that State *or in opposition to it*." *Burgos/Lopez*, para. 12.3.

76 *Issa and others v. Turkey*, app. no. 31821/96, ECtHR 16 November 2004, Final 30 March 2005

77 Of the various cases cited for this standard, none are the Court's own cases. Indeed, the *Issa* Court cited cases of the Inter-American Commission and Human Rights Committee from which the Court had distanced itself in *Bankovic*, and even adopted the reasoning of the Human Rights Committee in *Burgos / Lopez*, stating, "Accountability in such situations stems from the fact that Article 1 of the Convention cannot be

While this is a welcome development, it begs the question of the continued necessity of territorial control. If the exercise of power and authority over individuals is sufficient to find those individuals within the jurisdiction of the Contracting State, then it would seem nonsensical to retain the higher standard of effective control over territory. Presumably, anyone within territory under the effective control of a state would also be under that state's power and authority. Thus, after *Issa*, it would appear that the distinctions among the various standards cited by the European Court over the past decade have lost much of their significance in the context of determining whether individuals may fall within the jurisdiction of a Contracting State. However, these distinctions may still be relevant in determining other dimensions of the scope of that Contracting State's obligation as explained below in Sections B and C.

#### 4.1.1.2.3 Regionality

One element in particular of the European Court's jurisprudence warrants closer inspection. In the *Bankovic* case, the Court noted that "the Convention was not designed to be applied throughout the world, even in respect of the conduct of Contracting States." It found that "the Convention is a multi-lateral treaty operating . . . in an essentially regional context and notably in the legal space (*espace juridique*) of the Contracting States." As the Federal Republic of Yugoslavia was not a party to the Convention, it did not comprise part of this legal space.

However, a number of considerations support a finding that regional human rights obligations do apply to a state's conduct beyond regional frontiers. Chief among these is the notion of universality. The very idea of human rights supports a finding that they would apply vis-à-vis all human beings. Although regional human rights norms are generated and formulated within a regional framework, they purport to be universally applicable.[78] As such, the focus of human rights law generally is on how states ought to behave with respect to any human being under their control. Thus, it is clearly established in the jurisprudence of all regional human rights bodies that human rights obligations apply irrespective of the nationality of the victim.[79]

The regional nature of the treaty speaks not to the scope of beneficiaries, but to the willingness of states within the region to agree to a particular treaty regime

---

interpreted so as to allow a State party to perpetrate violations of the Convention on the territory of another State, which it could not perpetrate on its own territory." This formulation is almost identical to that used by the Human Rights Committee in *Burgos / Lopez*, which the Court had criticized in *Bankovic*.

78 The preamble to the European Convention makes clear that the standards enunciated in that treaty are derived from the Universal Declaration and reaffirms the "profound belief [of the Contracting States] in those fundamental freedoms which are the foundation of justice and peace *in the world*," not just the region (emphasis added). The preamble of the American Declaration of the Rights and Duties of Man similarly employs the language of universality, asserting that "[a]ll men are born free and equal, in dignity and in rights."

79 *Coard*; see also *Alejandre* at para 23

and system of collective enforcement. As expressed in the preamble of the European Convention, "the governments of European countries which are like-minded and have a common heritage of political traditions, ideals, freedom and the rule of law, [were resolved] to take the first steps for the collective enforcement of certain of the rights stated in the Universal Declaration."

Finally, the European Court's jurisprudence is itself in flux with respect to this issue. The Court has diminished the force of its "legal space" argument. In *Issa*, the Court found that Turkish troops had been carrying out cross-border military operations "aimed at pursuing and eliminating terrorists who were seeking shelter in northern Iraq." The Court noted that if Turkey "could be considered to have exercised, temporarily, effective overall control of a particular portion of the territory of northern Iraq" and if it could be shown that "at the relevant time, the victims were within that specific area," then "it would follow logically that they were within the jurisdiction of Turkey (and not that of Iraq, which is not a Contracting State and clearly does not fall within the legal space (*espace juridique*) of the Contracting States..." The Court essentially equates being within the jurisdiction of Turkey with being within the legal space of the Contracting States for the purpose of applying the Convention. This could be interpreted as relegating the legal space argument to circularity, at least in situations where Contracting States exercise a degree of territorial control.

#### *4.1.1.3 Customary Human Rights Law*

Finally, this limitation of scope may not apply with respect to those human rights norms that have evolved into customary international law. Thus, all states may be bound by these norms in their dealings with anyone anywhere. The US JAG Operational Law Handbook ("JAG OLH"), for example, provides that the customary law of human rights applies to US armed forces wherever they may act.[80]

### 4.1.2 Range of Rights Applicable

Under human rights treaties, the range of rights applicable within a state's territory will normally be the full range of rights set forth in each treaty. However, this may not be the case when the state is operating abroad. In such situations, the range of applicable rights may be limited by the scope of the state's authority or control in the circumstances. In general, it may be reasoned that as human rights law is generally predicated on a state's authority and presumed capacity to control individuals and territories,[81] a state's human rights obligations while acting abroad would

80 Maj. Derek I. Grimes, ed., 'Operational Law Handbook, The Judge Advocate General's Legal Center and School' (2005) ("JAG OLH"), chapter 3 ('Human rights law established by treaty generally only binds the state in relation to its own residents; human rights law based on customary international law binds all states, in all circumstances'). It should be noted, however, that the US rejects extraterritorial application of the ICCPR.

81 *Bankovic*.

not be as extensive as when it acts on its own territory. Similarly, it may be the case that the application of certain rights requires a higher threshold of control.

As noted above, the ICJ appeared to establish different thresholds of application for the International Covenants. While the exercise of jurisdiction was sufficient for application of the ICCPR, the ICJ explicitly required *territorial* control to trigger application of the ICESCR. After noting that article 2 of the ICESCR does not contain a provision circumscribing the scope of states parties' obligations, the ICJ acknowledged that the rights enumerated therein are "essentially territorial." Nonetheless, the court found that "it is not to be excluded that it applies both to territories over which a State party has sovereignty and to those over which that State exercises territorial jurisdiction." Here the Court appears to limit more narrowly the circumstances in which the ICESCR would apply extraterritorially. Rather than referring simply to the exercise of jurisdiction, the Court seems to require the exercise of territorial jurisdiction, which implies control over territory and not just over individuals.

It may be that this approach is linked to the nature of economic and social rights. In general, these rights are thought to require an expansive and more highly defined conception of the state. In situations of extraterritorial conduct, this conception is not necessarily applicable – the full apparatus of the state is not readily available; nor is the level of control as great as that exercised by a state within its own territory.

It should be noted, however, that the ICJ's recent jurisprudence may indicate a movement away from this approach. In *DR Congo v. Uganda* the Court seemed to adopt a single standard for the application of all human rights treaties. Although the regional institutions provide little express guidance on this issue, the European institutions have indicated that the exercise of certain rights may be linked to territorial control, and have implied that such rights may not apply in situations falling short of territorial control.

Thus, in *W.M. v. Denmark*, in response to the applicant's allegations that he was deprived of his right to move freely on Danish territory and that he was expelled without a decision being taken in accordance with law, the European Commission observed that "although, as stated above, a State party to the Convention may be held responsible either directly or indirectly for acts committed by its diplomatic agents, the provisions invoked by the applicant must be interpreted in the light of the special circumstances which prevail in situations as the one which is at issue in the present case." Noting that "as the applicant, while the incident took place, was not on Danish territory," the Commission held that "the provisions invoked by him are not applicable to his case."

In *Cyprus v. Turkey*, where the European Court found that Turkey had territorial control over northern Cyprus, the Court found the full range of Convention rights to be applicable. After finding that Turkey, by virtue of its effective overall control of northern Cyprus, was responsible for the conduct of the local authorities there (i.e. the TRNC), the Court held, "It follows that, in terms of Article 1 of the Convention, Turkey's 'jurisdiction' must be considered to extend to securing the entire range of substantive rights set out in the Convention and those additional

Protocols which she has ratified ...." This seems to imply that in situations falling short of effective overall control, Contracting States may be bound to observe a narrower range of rights.

More generally, the jurisprudence of regional institutions seems to indicate that the scope of a state's obligations vary with the scope of the authority and control exercised. In *W.M v. Denmark*, the European Commission found it clear from the "constant jurisprudence of the Commission that authorised agents of a State, including diplomatic or consular agents, bring other persons or property within the jurisdiction of that State *to the extent that* they exercise authority over such persons or property. *In so far as* they affect such persons or property by their acts or omissions, the responsibility of the State is engaged."[82] This seems to imply that a state's exercise of extraterritorial jurisdiction has a variable scope. Similarly, the European Court, in formulating the question of whether extraterritorial conduct of the state has fallen within the scope of article 1, has variously referred to individuals, acts, matters, or property being within the jurisdiction of the particular state. It seems then that individuals may come within the jurisdiction of a state's jurisdiction to various degrees. For example, where a state brings an individual into its jurisdiction through a particular act, without having control generally over that individual or over the territory within which that individual may be found, it would seem then that the individual is within the jurisdiction of that state only for the purpose of that act.

As these institutions have linked their findings of "jurisdiction" to the scope of a state's authority and control over people or territory, it may thus be argued that the range of rights states are bound to respect is dependent upon the level of that State's control.[83]

---

82 Emphasis added.

83 This also seems to be the case with respect to customary human rights law. In general, customary law recognizes a narrower range of rights than that provided under treaty law. Further, the extraterritorial application of customary human rights law may be subject to limitations analogous to those applicable to human rights treaties. For example, the US JAG OLH notes that when the US carried out detention operations in Haiti as part of Operation Uphold Democracy, US forces complied with the customary human rights norms implicated by that operation, including freedom from arbitrary detention. JAG OLH ('Along this line, the Joint Task Force (JTF) lawyers first noted that the Universal Declaration of Human Rights does not prohibit detention or arrest, but simply protects civilians from the arbitrary application of these forms of liberty denial. The JTF could detain civilians who posed a legitimate threat to the force, its mission, or other Haitian civilians'). The Handbook notes that detainees were also 'entitled to a baseline of humanitarian and due process protections', including 'the provision of a clean and safe holding area; rules and conduct that would prevent any form of physical maltreatment, degrading treatment, or intimidation; and rapid judicial review of their individual detention'. The US did not, however, 'step into the shoes of the Haitian government, and did not become a guarantor of all the rights that international law requires a government to provide its own nationals'. As the US rejects extraterritorial application of human rights treaties, the Handbook refers here solely to customary law.

Nonetheless, the European Court appeared to dismiss this possibility in *Bankovic*, flatly rejecting the applicants' "claim that the positive obligation under Article 1 extends to securing the Convention rights in a manner proportionate to the level of control exercised in any given extra-territorial situation." The Court stated its view that "the wording of Article 1 does not provide any support for the applicants' suggestion that the positive obligation in Article 1 to secure 'the rights and freedoms defined in Section I of this Convention' can be divided and tailored in accordance with the particular circumstances of the extra-territorial act in question."

This position seems difficult to reconcile with the notion that a state's exercise of jurisdiction may be limited to a narrow scope. Indeed, in the Court's later jurisprudence, it seems to back away from the rigidity of this statement.[84]

However, another approach is to focus the inquiry not on the question of which rights the state is obliged to secure, but instead on the level of obligation upon states with respect to those rights, as discussed below.

### 4.1.3 Level of Obligation

As noted above, the obligation to "respect and ensure" rights, or, in the words of the European Convention, to "secure" rights, entails a substantial degree of positive obligation.[85]

As with the range of rights, the level of obligation may also be limited where the state operates abroad. The level of obligation may similarly be tied to the scope of a state's extraterritorial activities or authority to act. In particular, it is arguable that human rights obligations requiring the adoption of affirmative measures may be more limited in an extraterritorial context.

This position finds support in the international jurisprudence cited above. In the *Israeli Wall Opinion*, as noted above, the ICJ found that the ICCPR "is applicable in respect of acts done by a State in the exercise of its jurisdiction outside its own territory." While the Human Rights Committee had referred to "conduct by the State party's authorities," the Court used the phrase "acts done by a State." This difference in terminology may have some significance. While the term "conduct" is broad enough to encompass both actions and omissions,[86] the term "acts" may be read to preclude the latter. Under this interpretation, only negative obligations would be applicable to Israel's conduct.

As to the scope of obligation imposed on Israel by the ICESCR in the Occupied Territories, the Court stated, "In the exercise of the powers available to it [as the occupying Power], Israel is bound by the provisions of the International Covenant on Economic, Social and Cultural Rights." Thus, the scope of its obligation under the ICESCR may be co-extensive with the scope of its authority as an occupying Power. The Court noted further that Israel "is under an obligation not

84 See, e.g., *Ilascu and others v. Moldova and Russia*, app. no. 48787/99, ECtHR 8 July 2004.

85 As indicated above in Part 3, customary international law may entail a lower level of obligation.

86 See supra Part 3.

to raise any obstacle to the exercise of such rights in those fields where competence has been transferred to Palestinian authorities." Thus, with respect to matters within the scope of Palestinian authority, the Court implies that Israel is bound only by negative obligations. This would seem to imply, *a contrario*, that the scope of Israel's obligation in matters within its authority, and beyond the authority of the Palestinians, encompasses positive obligations. This would seem to indicate that as Israel cedes control, the scope of its obligation is decreased from one encompassing positive and negative obligations to one entailing only negative obligations. Ultimately, however, the Court analyzed Israel's conduct exclusively in the context of negative obligations, finding that "the construction of the wall and its associated régime impede [sic]" the exercise of a number of rights under both Covenants. Nonetheless, its language setting forth the applicable law was broad enough to accommodate positive obligations in principle.

Similar language has been employed by the regional institutions. In *Alejandre*, the Inter-American Commission recalled that "when agents of a state, whether military or civilian, exercise power and authority over persons outside national territory, the state's obligation to respect human rights continues." Again, it is worth noting that the Commission referred only to the obligation to respect rights. It did not mention the obligation to ensure rights. It may be that this was not intended to imply that Cuba would be limited to negative obligations. However, to date the Commission's finding of extraterritorial application of human rights obligations has been limited to finding violations of negative obligations.

The European Court seems to admit the possibility that a state's obligations may encompass positive obligations in an exterritorial context, at least in situations of territorial control. In *Cyprus v. Turkey*, the European Court noted that since Turkey had effective control over the territory of Northern Cyprus, "its responsibility could not be confined to the acts of its own agents therein but was engaged by the acts of the local administration which survived by virtue of Turkish support. Turkey's 'jurisdiction' under Article 1 was therefore considered to extend to securing the entire range of substantive Convention rights in northern Cyprus."[87] In using the term "securing" instead of "respecting" the Court may have implied that positive obligations were entailed. While the European Convention does not use term "respect" in its article 1, it could have employed this term as it is used by other human rights bodies if it wished to limit the scope of obligation to negative duties. The Court then addressed the question of whether Turkey was required to protect rights from private interference in northern Cyprus. It determined that it would address this issue on a case by case basis in light of the violation alleged.[88] In analyzing alleged violations by third parties, the Court found that Turkey's responsibility would be engaged if the applicant could establish a "policy of acquiescence" on the part of the TRNC. It would thus appear that a mere failure to respond to perpetration of violations by non-state actors would be insufficient to trigger responsibility. The omission would be culpable only if it were pursuant to a policy of

87 *Bankovic* at para. 70 interpreting its findings in *Cyprus v. Turkey*

88 *Cyprus v Turkey* at para. 81

acquiescence. This approach blurs the distinction between negative and positive obligations.

In *W.M. v. Denmark*, as noted above, the European Commission seemed to admit the possibility of a variable scope of obligation, and this could be interpreted to apply to the degree of positive obligation entailed. In that case, the applicant contended that Denmark bore responsibility for human rights violations perpetrated by DDR police because the Danish Ambassador had summoned the police who arrested the applicant. In analyzing the responsibility of Denmark in relation to human rights violations perpetrated by the DDR authorities, the Court recalled "that an act or omission of a Party to the Convention may exceptionally engage the responsibility of that State for acts of a State not party to the Convention where the person in question had suffered or risks suffering a flagrant denial of the guarantees and rights secured to him under the Convention," citing the *Soering*[89] case. The Commission found, however, "that what happened to the applicant at the hands of the DDR authorities cannot in the circumstances be considered to be so exceptional as to engage the responsibility of Denmark." Clearly, the Commission was of the view that the Danish Ambassador was under no positive obligation in these circumstances to protect the applicant from the DDR authorities. Indeed, it seems Denmark was similarly free of any negative obligation to refrain from handing him over to the police.

However, in *Bankovic*, the European Court seemed to reject the possibility of a varying level of obligation. The Court rejected the applicants' claim that the scope of a Contracting State's obligation was proportionate to its degree of control, asserting that "the applicants' submission is tantamount to arguing that anyone adversely affected by an act imputable to a Contracting State, wherever in the world that act may have been committed or its consequences felt, is thereby brought within the jurisdiction of that State for the purpose of Article 1 of the Convention." The Court dismissed this possibility.

As phrased by the Court, this proposition does indeed seem unreasonable. To hold states responsible for extraterritorial consequences of their conduct that were neither intended nor foreseeable seems both unworkable and unrealistic. But it certainly would not be unreasonable to admit the possibility of world-wide application of the Convention where a state was the direct perpetrator of a violation, fully aware of the consequences of its conduct.

As noted above, subsequent jurisprudence seems to indicate that *Bankovic* was anomalous. In the *Issa* case, in support of its inclusion of the "power and authority" standard, the Court stated, "Accountability in such situations stems from the fact that Article 1 of the Convention cannot be interpreted so as to allow a State party to perpetrate violations of the Convention on the territory of another State, which it could not perpetrate on its own territory." As with the *Israeli Wall* case and the *Alejandre* case, the word employed by the Court implies a context of violation of a negative obligation. Here, the Court refers to "perpetration," which could be read as encompassing only affirmative interference with rights, as oppose to a

89 *Soering v. The United Kingdom*, app. no. 14038/88, ECtHR 7 July 1989.

failure to adopt positive measures of protection. While this use of language may not have been intentional, it fits a pattern among human rights bodies of employing the language of negative obligations when finding extraterritorial application based on a standard of power or authority or control over individuals (and not over territory).

Thus, it would seem that there may be an identifiable trend toward recognizing varying levels of obligation. In particular, it may be that negative obligations apply whenever a state acts extraterritorially, but that the degree of positive obligations will be dependent upon the type and degree of control (or power or authority) exercised by the state. This is not inconsistent with these institutions' general jurisprudence on positive obligations. Such obligations are limited by a scope of reasonableness even when applied to a state's conduct within its territory; there is no reason why application to a state's extraterritorial conduct would not similarly be bounded by a scope of reasonableness,[90] such that the adoption of affirmative measures is only required when and to the extent that the relevant party *de jure* or *de facto* enjoys a position of control that would make the adoption of such measures feasible. Ultimately, any such inquiry would be highly fact-sensitive.

This approach would preserve the integrity of the respective treaties[91] and would vindicate the universal nature of human rights, which is proclaimed in the preambles of all of the human rights treaties considered in this analysis. At the same time, it would not place unreasonable burdens on states parties. Due to the very nature of negative obligations, states would be bound by those obligations only to the extent they affirmatively acted in the relevant sphere. Similarly, positive obligations would apply only in circumstances in which it would be reasonable for the state to take affirmative steps in light of its level of authority, control, and available resources. Thus, where there is only a limited connection between a state and an individual, the state would not be required to undertake the same degree of positive action, if any, to protect that individual's rights as it would if the individual were subject to a broader degree of control by the state, such as in situations of territorial occupation.

---

90 Similar reasoning is implicit in the jurisprudence of human rights mechanisms finding that the obligation to ensure rights against violations by private actors is bounded by a scope of reasonableness. For example, in the *Velazquez-Rodriguez* case, the Inter-American Court of Human Rights noted that this obligation was not absolute; the standard is one of 'due diligence'. The Court also recognized that '[i]t is not possible to make a detailed list of all such measures, since they vary with the law and the conditions of each State Party' (para. 175). In essence, the inquiry under the American Convention is whether the State party acting in good faith undertook steps that were reasonable in the circumstances. See also *Ilascu*.

91 By not "dividing them up," in the words of the *Bankovic* Court. Nor is this approach inconsistent with the textr of these treaties. See J. Cerone, "Out of Bounds? Considering the Reach of International Human Rights Law", Working Paper of the Center for Human Rights and Global Justice, NYU School of Law (April 2006).

### 4.1.4 Application in the Context of Armed Conflict, Occupation, and Peace Operations

It thus appears that states remain bound by human rights law even when engaged in hostilities far from their home territories. Even during the invasion phase of an armed conflict, it would seem that a state would exercise sufficient control over any individuals with whom its forces come in contact for those individuals to fall within the scope of beneficiaries of that state's human rights obligations. This, however, does not mean that the content of those obligations would be the same as if the individuals in question were within the home territory of that state. The scope of the obligation, at least in terms of the level of obligation as explained above, will vary with the degree of control exercised in the circumstances. Once an individual is taken into detention by the state, the degree of control over the individual will clearly have increased. Similarly, if a state's armed forces effectively occupy a territory, it is likely that the state's obligations will entail a substantial positive dimension.

#### *4.1.4.1 Collective Action*

This question becomes further complicated in the context of collective action. In such cases, while the collective entity may exercise control over the individual alleging a human rights violation, it is unclear whether such an individual may be deemed within the 'jurisdiction' of any of the individual states contributing personnel or otherwise participating in the collective entity. In applying a control-based standard to determine the scope of beneficiaries of states' obligations under human rights treaties, it is arguable that the analysis should start from the position of the individual to determine whether his or her relationship to the relevant authority meets the control-based standard, and then to address separately the question of attribution of the entity's conduct to a subject of obligations under human rights law.[92]

The Human Rights Committee has determined that obligations under the ICCPR continue to apply in full in the context of collective action. In General Comment 31 it stated:

> This principle also applies to those within the power or effective control of the forces of a State Party acting outside its territory, regardless of the circumstances in which such power or effective control was obtained, such as forces constituting a national contingent of a State Party assigned to an international peace-keeping or peace-enforcement operation.[93]

---

92 In this context, it is particularly important to distinguish the question of the scope of beneficiaries from the issue of attribution. It would seem most appropriate to determine whether the collective entity exercises the necessary degree of control, and then to focus only on the issue of attribution.

93 Para. 10.

Note, however, that this statement may go too far. As noted above in Section III, the issue of attribution must be considered whenever organs of a state are assigned to peace operations. If armed forces are placed entirely and exclusively at the disposal of an intergovernmental organization, their conduct may no longer be attributable to the sending state.[94] However, it is arguable that in such circumstances, the troops would no longer be "forces of a State Party."

Nonetheless, if it is determined that the contingent is placed at the disposal of an intergovernmental organization such that the sending state is not deemed responsible for the contingent's conduct, this does not mean that there is no subject of international law that may be held responsible for violations that may be committed. The United Nations, for example, has a large measure of international legal personality,[95] and can bear responsibility on the international level for the conduct of its agents.[96] In addition, where serious violations of human rights law overlap with international criminal law, the individual perpetrators themselves may be held directly responsible under international law.

## 5 Conclusions

International judicial and quasi-judicial bodies have provided answers to many of the important legal questions described in the introduction to this chapter. Nonetheless, there remain significant gaps that provide ample opportunity for these institutions to further elaborate on what is required of states in situations of armed conflict and occupation.

It is now clearly established that both human rights law and humanitarian law are simultaneously applicable in situations of armed conflict and occupation, and that their relationship is that of a *lex generalis* to a *lex specialis*. However, there is

---

94 The distinction between these questions was recognized in *Bankovic*, in which the European Court found that it was unnecessary to consider the 'alleged several liability of the respondent States for an act carried out by an international organisation of which they are members' because the Court had already concluded that it was 'not satisfied that the applicants and their deceased relatives were capable of coming within the jurisdiction of the respondent States on account of the extra-territorial act in question' (paras. 82-83).

95 *Reparation for Injuries Suffered in the Service of the United Nations* (Advisory Opinion) (ICJ 1948).

96 In general, as intergovernmental organizations have no territory, it may be useful to analogize to situations of extraterritorial application of human rights law. However, where an intergovernmental organizations acts as the government of a territory (as in, e.g., the UN Interim Administrations in Kosovo and East Timor), it may be more appropriate to analogize to infraterritorial application with respect to treatment of individuals within that territory. For further analysis of this topic see, J. Cerone, 'Reasonable measures in unreasonable circumstances: a legal responsibility framework for human rights violations in post-conflict territories under UN administration' in Nigel White and Dirk Klaasen (eds), *The UN, Human Rights and Post-Conflict Situations* (2005).

little detailed guidance on what this means in context. Does it essentially mean that where the norms overlap the norms of humanitarian law prevail? If so, does the assertion that human rights law continues to apply lose much of its legal significance?

The extraterritorial application of human rights law has also been clearly established such that, in principle, a state's human rights obligations will continue to apply even when it is engaged in hostilities far from its home territory. However, international jurisprudence has yet to produce clear criteria for when extraterritorial application is triggered or clear parameters for determining the scope of a state's human rights obligations when it acts abroad.

Nonetheless, the following principles may underlie a general trend in human rights jurisprudence. The first is that the negative dimension of human rights obligations, at least with respect to those rights that are not "essentially" territorial in the words of the ICJ, will apply to a state's conduct in relation to all those who are directly affected by that conduct anywhere in the world. The second principle is that the positive dimension of these obligations will be based upon the degree of control exercised by the state, subject to a standard of reasonableness.

# 6. Terrorism and Human Rights

*Peter Vedel Kessing*

## 1 Introduction

In recent years much has been said and written on the problematic relationship between terrorism and human rights. Several commentators have maintained that human rights are being trampled under foot in the fight against terrorism.[1] In a similar vein, a considerable number of international NGOs like Amnesty International and Human Rights Watch report that the fight against terrorism is being used to legitimise extra-judicial killings, encroachments on opponents of torture, and other kinds of state terrorism.[2]

Likewise, several human rights monitoring bodies have expressed their profound concern at the situation. In a joint statement of June 2003, a number of UN special rapporteurs and experts expressed "alarm at the growing threats against human rights, threats that necessitate a renewed resolve to defend and promote these rights ... and ... profound concern at the multiplication of policies, legislation and practices increasingly being adopted by many countries in the name of the

1 See e.g. Colin Warbrick, 'The European Response to Terrorism in an Age of Human Rights', *European Journal of International Law (EJIL)*, Vol. 15, No. 5, 2004, p. 989–1018, and Anthea Roberts, 'Righting Wrongs or Wronging Rights? The United States and Human Rights Post-September 11', *EJIL*, Vol. 15, No. 5, 2004, p. 722–749 and Philip B. Heymann, 'Civil Liberties and Human Rights in the Aftermath of September 11', *Harvard Journal of Law and Public Policy*, Spring 2002, p. 25, and 2 Academic Research Library p. 441

2 See, e.g., Amnesty International, *Human Rights Under Sustained Attack in the 'War on Terror'*, 2 November 2005, http://web.amnesty.org/library/Index/ENGEUR450502005 (visited on 8 November 2005), and Human Rights Watch, *Anti-terror Campaign Cloaking Human Rights Abuse*, 16 January 2002, http://hrw.org/english/docs/2002/01/16/global3690.htm (visited on 8 November 2005).

*S. Lagoutte, H-O. Sano and P. Scharff Smith (eds.),* Human Rights in Turmoil, *pp. 133-162.*
 *ISBN 90 04 15432 9.*

fight against terrorism, which affect negatively the enjoyment of virtually all human rights – civil, cultural, economic, political and social."[3]

During the annual session of the UN Human Rights Commission in 2004, the Commission decided to appoint a special independent rapporteur on the protection of human rights and fundamental freedoms in the fight against terrorism. The rapporteur was appointed for a one-year period, during which he identified "a broad range of human rights that have either come under increasing pressure or are being violated by states in the context of national and international counter-terrorism initiatives", including *inter alia*:[4]

- the principle of nullum crimen sine lege (broad and imprecise definitions of terrorism and terrorist-related offences);
- the right to liberty and security of persons, including the right to humane treatment (the definition of torture, possible excuses for torture, non-refoulement where there is a risk of torture, etc.);
- the rights to due process and to a fair trial (military commissions and the like);
- the right to property (compilation of lists and freezing the assets of terrorists);
- the right to privacy (information collection and sharing);
- the principle of non-discrimination (techniques to screen terrorist suspects).

The special rapporteur further recommended that "the Commission of Human Rights should consider the creation of a special procedure with a multidimensional mandate to monitor states' counter-terrorism measures and their compatibility with international human rights."[5]

Upon this basis, at its sixty-first session in April 2005, the UN Human Rights Commission decided to appoint a "rapporteur on the promotion and protection of human rights and fundamental freedoms while countering terrorism" for a period of three years.[6] The new special rapporteur has been given a very comprehensive and broad mandate, including among others the following duties:

- gathering information from governments, victims, organisations and others, including through country visits, on alleged violations of human rights while countering terrorism;
- identifying and promoting best practices on measures to counter terrorism that respect human rights; and

3 Joint statement of UN Special Rapporteurs/Representatives, Experts and Chairpersons of the working groups on the special procedures of the United Nations Commission on Human Rights, 30 June 2003, A/58/120, Annex 2.

4 See *Protection of Human Rights and Fundamental Freedoms While Countering Terrorism*, 7 February 2005, E/CN.4/2005/103, p. 27.

5 Ibid.

6 See Resolution, UN Commission on Human Rights, *Protection of human rights and fundamental freedoms while countering terrorism*, 15 April 2005, E/CN.4/2005/L.88.

- making concrete recommendations on the promotion and protection of human rights and fundamental freedoms while countering terrorism, including, at the request of states, the provision of advisory services or technical assistance on such matters.

As can be seen, there is considerable documentation that the fight against terrorism has entailed quite extensive encroachments and violations of the human rights obligations of states. Indeed, there is no doubt that the increased focus on the fight against terrorism has brought the practical implementation of human rights into turmoil, which also seems to have happened at a more theoretical and conceptual level.

The purpose of this chapter is therefore to assess how this increased focus on terrorism has influenced human rights as a concept and their scope of application. The chapter does not pretend to offer an exhaustive analysis of all the relevant problems, but it does aim to present a broader picture of certain current trends and to illustrate them with examples.

Section 2 analyses how considerations pertaining to human rights protection have been incorporated into the existing international and regional instruments against terrorism. At this formal level there is no doubt that states are obliged to respect human rights and international humanitarian law in their efforts against terrorism. Section 3 emphasises the political will to respect human rights in national and international efforts against terrorism. It has become clear that the considerable focus on security issues since 11 September 2001 has led to an extensive marginalisation of human rights, restricting them to retrospective judicial control. In consequence, doubt has arisen as to the protection of human rights in a number of contexts (section 4). First, there is doubt as to whether the fight against terrorism in general supersedes human rights (section 4.1). Secondly, there is uncertainty as to the application of human rights (section 4.2). Thirdly, there is doubt as to the interpretation and scope of human rights protection (section 4.3). Finally, section 5 offers a summary of the chapter.

## 2 The Formal Protection of Human Rights and International Humanitarian Law in Anti-Terrorism Instruments

The international community has tried for years – long before 11 September 2001 – to develop a Comprehensive Convention on Terrorism containing a generic definition of terrorism and an obligation to criminalize terrorism as well as to prosecute terrorists or extradite them for prosecution in other states. So far attempts to reach agreement on such a convention have failed, mainly due to the lack of agreement on a generic definition of terrorism.[7]

---

7 Negotiations on the Convention are now continuing in a special Ad Hoc Committee established by the UN General Assembly in 1996. The present draft for a Comprehensive Convention can be found in *Report of the Ad Hoc Committee Established by*

### 2.1 Definition of Terrorism

The first attempts to codify a generic definition of terrorism date back to 1937, to the League of Nations' Convention for the Prevention and Punishment of Terrorism. In this Convention terrorism is defined as:

> All criminal acts directed against a State and intended or calculated to create a state of terror in the minds of particular persons or a group of persons or the general public.[8]

However, the Convention was never ratified by a sufficient number of states and consequently never entered into force. Since then a number of attempts to reach agreement on a generic, abstract definition of terrorism have been undertaken within the UN, all of which have failed.[9]

In the present draft Comprehensive Convention on Terrorism, terrorism is defined as follows:

> Article 2
> 1. Any person commits an offence within the meaning of this Convention if that person, by any means, unlawfully and intentionally, causes:
>    (a) Death or serious bodily injury to any person; or
>    (b) Serious damage to public or private property, including a place of public use, a state or government facility, a public transportation system, an infrastructure facility or the environment; or
>    (c) Damage to property, places, facilities, or systems referred to in paragraph 1 (b) of this chapter, resulting or likely to result in major economic loss,
>
> when the purpose of the conduct, by its nature or context, is to intimidate a population, or to compel a Government or an international organisation to do or abstain from doing any act.[10]

However, as pointed out by Cassesse (2005), it is not so much the definition itself which causes disagreement,[11] but the question of which exceptions ought to apply to it.

---

*General Assembly Resolution 51/210 of 17 December 1996, Sixth Session (28 January-1 February 2002)*, Fifty-seventh Session. Supplement No. 37 (A/57/37).

8 19 *LNOJ* 23 (1938). See also http://www.unodc.org/unodc/terrorism_definitions.html

9 See *inter alia* A. R. Perera, "Reviewing the UN Conventions on Terrorism: Towards a Comprehensive Terrorism Convention", and Cyrille Fijnaut, Jan Wouters and Frederik Naert, "Legal Instruments in the Fight Against International Terrorism, A Transatlantic Dialogue", in Brill (2004), pp. 567–587.

10 The current draft Comprehensive Convention can be found in *Report of the Ad Hoc Committee Established by General Assembly Resolution 51/210 of 17 December 1996, Sixth Session* (28 January-1 February 2002), Fifty-seventh Session. Supplement No. 37 (A/57/37).

11 See Antonio Cassese, *The International Response to Terrorism*, International Law, Oxford University Press, 2005, p. 465. Cassese thus states that today there is general

### 2.2 The Exceptions Which Ought to Apply to the Definition

There are two issues in particular upon which states are not able to agree.

First, some states have argued that the definition of terrorism should exclude freedom fighters and groups fighting an occupying force. While older UN resolutions on terrorism often contained a clause reaffirming the right to self-determination, as an implicit acceptance that terrorism could be applied in the fight for self-determination,[12] no recent resolutions from either the UN General Assembly or the UN Security Council include such a clause. On the contrary, terrorism is condemned in no uncertain terms: it is explicitly pointed out that terrorism is a crime irrespective of where it is committed, by whom or for what purpose.[13] Likewise the present draft Comprehensive Convention states that

> criminal acts within the scope of this Convention are under no circumstances justifiable by considerations of a political, philosophical, ideological, racial, ethnic, religious, or other similar nature.[14]

In spite of this growing consensus that no political aim – nor the right to self-determination – can justify terrorism, the issue still remains controversial. This can be illustrated by the adoption of the EU Framework Decision on Combating Terrorism of 2002.[15] Article 1 of the Framework Decision contains a definition of terrorism which does not include any disclaimer for freedom fighters and the like. However, the European Council wished to clarify that acts carried out with the

---

agreement on the very definition of terrorism and that it is to be considered part of customary international law. The fact that there is still (some) uncertainty concerning exceptions to the definition does not change this.

12 See *inter alia* General Assembly Resolution 27/3034 (1972), General Assembly Resolution 32/147 (1977), General Assembly Resolution 34/145, (1979), General Assembly Resolution 36/109, (1981) and General Assembly Resolution 38/130, (1983). These resolutions condemn terrorism and add, "the continuation of repressive and terrorist acts of colonial, racist and alien regimes in denying people their legitimate right to self-determination and independence and other human rights and fundamental freedoms". See also Malvina Halberstam, *The Evolution of the United Nations' Position on Terrorism: From Exempting National Liberation Movements to Criminalizing Terrorism Wherever and by Whomever Committed*, Columbia Journal of Transnational Law 2003.

13 See a number of UN resolutions adopted by the UN General Assembly from 1985 and thereafter, *inter alia* General Assembly Resolution 40/61, (1985), General Assembly Resolution 50/53, (1995), General Assembly Resolution 51/210, (1996), General Assembly Resolution 52/165, (1997), General Assembly Resolution 53/108, (1999), General Assembly Resolution 55/158, (2001); see also resolutions from the UN Security Council, *inter alia* Security Council Resolution 1269, (1999) and Security Council Resolution 1373, (2001). See also Malvina Halberstam, ibid.

14 See article 5 of the draft Comprehensive Convention on terrorism, above, note 10.

15 Council Framework Decision of 13 June 2002 on combating terrorism (2002/475).

purpose of bringing a country democracy and human rights shall not be considered terrorist acts pursuant to Article 1.[16]

Secondly, the other major issue which has caused disagreement over a generic definition of terrorism is the issue of state terrorism. The majority of international terrorism instruments do not address state terrorism as such. Indeed, many implicitly seem to exclude it.[17] Certain commentators have argued that terrorism committed by states should also be covered by a generic definition of terrorism and by a comprehensive convention on terrorism.[18]

Interestingly, the current draft Comprehensive Convention includes references to state terrorism, and it could arguably be claimed that the current draft seems to include it. Thus, it follows from the current wording of the preamble

> that the suppression of acts of international terrorism, including those which are *committed or supported by States*, directly or indirectly, is an essential element in the maintenance of international peace and security and the sovereignty and territorial integrity of States [emphasis added].[19]

State terrorism is also discussed in the report of the UN High-level Panel on Threats, Challenges and Change of 2004.[20] It stresses that since 1945, an ever stronger set of norms and laws – including the Charter of the United Nations, the Geneva Conventions and the Rome Statute for the International Criminal Court – has regulated and constrained states' decisions to use force and their conduct in war. In contrast, the norms governing the use of force by non-state actors have not kept pace with those pertaining to states. Against this background, the Panel argues that it is not necessary to include state terrorism in a generic definition of terrorism.

---

16 Gade, Lauland, Schjønning and Sørensen, *Det politimæssige og strafferetlige samarbejde i den Europæiske Union*, DJØF 2005, pp. 314-315.

17 See, e.g., Helen Duffy, *The 'War on Terror' and the Framework of International Law*, Cambridge University Press 2005, p. 35.

18 See Christian Tomuschat, *The Individual Threatened by the Fight Against Terrorism?* http://www.rewi.hu-berlin.de/jura/ex/tms/sp/warschau.pdf: "Obviously, such a convention [the Comprehensive Convention on Terrorism] would be useless if it did not, at the same time, take into account terrorist acts undertaken by state authorities. A convention focusing exclusively on terrorist offences committed by private individuals would be blind in one eye." Likewise M. Cherif Bassiouni, 'Legal Control of International Terrorism: A Policy-oriented Assessment', 43 *Harvard Int'l Law J.*, Winter 2002, p. 102: "The exclusion of state actors' unlawful terror-violence acts from inclusion in the overall scheme of terrorism control highlights the double standard that non-state actors lament and use as a justification for their own transgression. This disparity of treatment between state and non-state actors is plainly evident, and constitutes one of the reasons for the attraction of adherents to non-state terrorist groups."

19 See above, note 10.

20 United Nations High-level Panel on Threats, Challenges and Change (2004). *A More Secure World: Our Shared Responsibility*, pp. 158-163.

State terrorism in times of armed conflict and the correlation between anti-terror conventions and international humanitarian law have been other related matters of dispute. Terrorism is criminalized in the Geneva Conventions;[21] the question is therefore whether state terrorism (a state's excessive use of force) during armed conflict should also be covered by anti-terrorism conventions.

In the UN Convention Against Terror Bombings, mentioned below, this dispute is resolved by making the two sets of rules mutually exclusive: the anti-terror provisions are not applicable during armed conflict, when international humanitarian law is applied instead.[22] A similar procedure is suggested in the draft Comprehensive Convention on Terrorism.[23] However, this procedure has been criticised, for example, due to the considerable difficulty in determining precisely when the situation amounts to an "armed conflict" pursuant to international humanitarian law – an uncertainty which can lead to doubts as to which of the two sets of rules is applicable.[24]

Conversely, other organisations – for example the International Committee of the Red Cross (ICRC) – stress that the simultaneous application of the two sets of rules during armed conflict can be problematic, as there might be a risk that conduct which is criminalized pursuant to the anti-terror conventions is not criminalised – or is actually legal – according to international humanitarian law.

### 2.3 *A New Consensus on the Definition of Terrorism*

In spite of all these disagreements, a higher degree of international consensus on the definition of terrorism and its exceptions seems to have developed in recent years. In 1999, the following general definition of terrorism was included in the International Convention for the Suppression of the Financing of Terrorism:

> (b) Any other act intended to cause death or serious bodily injury to a civilian, or to any other person not taking an active part in the hostilities in a situation of armed conflict, when the purpose of such act, by its nature or context, is to intimidate a

---

21 See *infra* section 2.4.

22 Article 19(2) of the Convention states: "The activities of armed forces during an armed conflict, as those terms are understood under international humanitarian law, which are governed by that law, are not governed by this Convention, and the activities undertaken by military forces of a State in the exercise of their official duties, inasmuch as they are governed by other rules of international law, are not governed by this Convention."

23 See draft article 18, above, note 5. However, international humanitarian law contains its own specific prohibition of terrorism, which I elaborate on below.

24 See Christian Walter, above, note 9, p. 20, who instead proposes that anti-terror conventions should also be applied during armed conflict, together with international humanitarian law (IHL), but with IHL as *lex specialis* in case of problems.

> population, or to compel a Government or an international organisation to do or to abstain from doing any act.[25]

The UN High-level Panel report from 2004[26] and the UN General Secretary report *In Larger Freedom* from 2005[27] also seem to have contributed to creating a stronger consensus on a generic definition of terrorism and – perhaps not least – on the possible exceptions to this definition. Both reports suggest that the definition should exclude state terrorism and not contain any "freedom fighter clause".[28] This raises some well-founded hope that in the near future it will be possible to reach agreement on a definition and, following this, on the Convention itself.

### 2.4 International Instruments on Counter-Terrorism

In the absence of a comprehensive convention on terrorism, States have still agreed on a number of conventions which define certain specific acts as terrorism and oblige the States to criminalize and prosecute such acts.

25 See Article 2 of the Convention. While this definition only includes "death or serious bodily injury to a civilian" as possible acts of terror, Article 2 in the present draft Comprehensive Convention also includes "damage to public or private property". The definition in the draft Comprehensive Convention is thus more extensive.

26 United Nations High-level Panel on Threats, Challenges and Change (2004), *A More Secure World: Our Shared Responsibility*, section 164, suggests the following definition of terrorism: "any action, in addition to actions already specified by existing conventions on aspects of terrorism, the Geneva Conventions and Security Council Resolution 1566 (2004), that is intended to cause death or serious bodily harm to civilians or non-combatants, when the purpose of such act, by its nature or context, is to intimidate a population, or to compel a Government or an international organisation to do or to abstain from doing any act."

27 The UN Secretary General agrees to the definition as recommended in the report from the High-level Panel; see UN Secretary-General, *In Larger Freedom: Towards Development, Security and Human Rights For All*, 21 March 2005, A59/2005, par. 91.

28 Ibid., par. 91, which reads: "It is time to set aside debates on so-called 'State terrorism'. The use of force by States is already thoroughly regulated under international law. And the right to resist occupation must be understood in its true meaning. It cannot include the right to deliberately kill or maim civilians."

There are twelve international legal instruments pertaining to terrorist acts. Five of these relate to aviation security,[29] two to terrorism on the sea,[30] two to nuclear terrorism,[31] and four to other specific terrorist acts.[32] In April 2005, the UN General Assembly adopted a new convention, the Convention for the Suppression of Acts of Nuclear Terrorism, which has not yet entered into force.[33]

As another example of this thematic, subject-specific approach to terrorism, the prohibition against terrorism in international humanitarian law (IHL) is significant. In parallel to the instruments that deal with terrorism in peacetime, terrorism has also been criminalized during armed conflict in international humanitarian law. Terrorism is criminalized in article 33 of the Fourth Geneva Convention, article 51 of the First Additional Protocol and article 13 of the Second Additional Protocol. From these instruments it appears that:

> The civilian population as such, as well as individual civilians, shall not be the object of attack. Acts or threats of violence the primary purpose of which is to spread terror among the civilian population are prohibited (article 13 of the Second Additional Protocol).

In the *Galic* case from 2003, concerning the siege of Sarajevo and random attacks on the civilian population, the International Criminal Tribunal for the Former Yu-

---

29 The *Tokyo Convention on Offences and Certain Other Acts Committed on Board Aircraft*; 1963 (177 States parties); *The Hague Convention for the Suppression of Unlawful Seizure of Aircraft*, 1970 (177 States parties); *The Montreal Convention for the Suppression of Unlawful Acts against the Safety of Civil Aviation*, 1971 (179 States parties); *The Montreal Protocol for the Suppression of Unlawful Acts of Violence at Airports Serving International Civil Aviation, supplementary to the Convention for the Suppression of Unlawful Acts against the Safety of Civil Aviation*, 1988 (142 States parties); *The Montreal Convention on the Marking of Plastic Explosives for the Purpose of Detection*, 1991 (101 States parties).

30 *The Rome Convention for the Suppression of Unlawful Acts against the Safety of Maritime Navigation*, 1988 (102 States parties); *The Rome Protocol for the Suppression of Unlawful Acts against the Safety of Fixed Platforms Located on the Continental Shelf*, 1988 (95 States parties).

31 *The Vienna Convention on the Physical Protection of Nuclear Material*, 1979 (96 States parties). The convention is currently being revised and updated: see Deliberations on the UN-backed conference in July 2005: www.un.org/apps/news/story.asp?NewsID=14873&Cr=terrorism&Cr1, A new convention.

32 *The New York Convention on the Prevention and Punishment of Crimes against Internationally Protected Persons, Including Diplomatic Agents*, 1973 (144 states parties); *The New York International Convention Against the Taking of Hostages*, 1979 (136 states parties); *The New York International Convention for the Suppression of Terrorist Bombings*, 1997 (116 states parties); *The New York International Convention for the Suppression of the Financing of Terrorism*, 1999 (109 states parties).

33 See *International Convention for the Suppression of Acts of Nuclear Terrorism*, 4 April 2005, A/59/766. The Convention will enter into force when it has been ratified by twenty-two states.

goslavia was the first international court to deal with a case concerning terrorism committed during armed conflict. The Tribunal defines terrorism as a war crime as:

1. Acts of violence directed against the civilian population or individual civilians not taking direct part in hostilities causing death or serious injury to body or health within the civilian population.
2. The offender wilfully made the civilian population or individual civilians not taking direct part in hostilities the object of those acts of violence.
3. The above offence was committed with the primary purpose of spreading terror among the civilian population.[34]

According to this definition, terrorism contains an objective element consisting in murder or serious injury to body or health inflicted upon civilians, and a subjective element consisting in the specific intent to spread terror among the civilian population.

Similar objective and subjective elements form part of the new definitions of terrorism in peacetime in the EU Framework Decision of 2002, the UN Convention for the Suppression of the Financing of Terrorism, the present draft Comprehensive Convention on Terrorism, and the recommendations of the UN High-level Panel and the UN Secretary General.[35] Accordingly, there seems to be a high degree of similarity between the definition of terrorism during armed conflict and the definition of terrorism in peacetime.

In addition to the international instruments on counter-terrorism, a number of regional counter-terrorism instruments have been adopted.[36] The most recent

---

34 See ICTY, Trial Chamber Judgment, *Prosecutor* v. *Stanislav Galic*, 5. December 2003, IT-98-29-T, p. 748.

35 In these definitions the intent, however, can refer *either* to "intimidate a population *or* to "compel a Government or an international organization to do or to abstain from doing any act". In the draft Comprehensive Convention, the harm can also relate to "public or private property". The peacetime definitions thus seem somewhat broader than the definition under IHL.

36 *Arab Convention on the Suppression of Terrorism*, 22 April 1998; *Convention of the Organisation of the Islamic Conference on Combating International Terrorism*, 1 July 1999; *European Convention on the Suppression of Terrorism*, 27 January 1977; *OAS Convention to Prevent and Punish Acts of Terrorism Taking the Form of Crimes against Persons and Related Extortion that are of International Significance*, 2 February 1971; *OAU Convention on the Prevention and Combating of Terrorism*, 14 July 1999; *SAARC (South Asian Association for Regional Cooperation) Regional Convention on Suppression of Terrorism*, Katmandu 4 November 1987; *Treaty on Cooperation among States Members of the Commonwealth of Independent States in Combating Terrorism*, Minsk 4 June 1999.

regional convention on terrorism is the Council of Europe (CoE) Convention on Prevention of Terrorism, adopted in May 2005.[37]

Anti-terror conventions, whether regional or international, contain a number of common features:[38]

- description of criminal offences;
- obligation to incorporate these offences into domestic penal legislation;
- obligation to submit for prosecution;
- establishment of the principle "extradite or prosecute";
- conventions as the basis for extradition (i.e. the offences are deemed to be included in existing bilateral extradition treaties);
- rejection of the political motivation clause.

The new CoE Convention on Prevention of Terrorism differs from other international and regional anti-terrorism conventions by specifically trying to *prevent* terrorism. While the other conventions define and criminalize specific acts of terror such as attacks against aviation safety, the new CoE Convention defines and criminalizes acts which can *lead to* terrorism, but which do not in themselves constitute acts of terror, including public provocation to commit a terrorist offence (article 5), recruitment for terrorism (article 6) and training for terrorism (article 7).

Even though earlier anti-terror conventions often also oblige states to criminalize acts of incitement and complicity – such as "provocation, recruitment and training for terrorism" – there seems to be no doubt that the new CoE Convention contains the most far reaching criminalization.

### *2.5. Respect for Human Rights*

A number of the conventions mentioned above include specific clauses to the effect that persons suspected of having committed an act of terror criminalized in the convention should be ensured fair treatment and respect for their human rights.

The *international* conventions thus include the following clauses:

- fair treatment clauses in seven conventions;
- human rights references in three conventions (1997, 1999 and 2005);
- humanitarian law references in two conventions (1979 and 1997);
- anti-discrimination clauses in three conventions (1963, 1997 and 1999);
- diplomatic protection clauses in all conventions (except in 1979 "Nuclear convention").

37 See Council of Europe, *Convention on the Prevention of Terrorism*, 16 May 2005, CETS No. 196. The convention will enter into force when it has been ratified by six states; see article 23 of the Convention. For the Convention, see: http://conventions.coe.int/Treaty/EN/Treaties/Html/196.htm

38 See also United Nations Office on Drugs and Crime, *Legislative Guide to the Universal Anti-terrorism Conventions and Protocols*, UN, New York 2003.

The protection clause in the most recent international anti-terror convention from 2005 – the "International Convention for the Suppression of Acts of Nuclear Terrorism" – reads as follows:

> Article 12. Any person who is taken into custody or regarding whom any other measures are taken or proceedings are carried out pursuant to this Convention shall be guaranteed fair treatment, including enjoyment of all rights and guarantees in conformity with the law of the State in the territory of which that person is present and applicable provisions of international law, including the international law of human rights.

An identical provision is contained in the draft Comprehensive Convention,[39] but with an additional phrase following "including the international law of human rights": "and in particular, the Standard Minimum Rules for the Treatment of Prisoners." The Standard Minimum Rules for the Treatment of Prisoners contain several rules for the treatment of persons deprived of their liberty[40] but constitute a non-binding instrument ("soft law"). With the new reference to these rules in the draft Comprehensive Convention, they become part of the Convention and thus become binding ("hard law").

If this addition actually becomes part of the provision in the new Comprehensive Convention against Terrorism, it will be considered quite a far-reaching protection of the rights of the terror suspect. Indeed, legally speaking, persons deprived of their liberty under suspicion of terrorism will be better protected than persons who are deprived of their liberty under suspicion of other kinds of crime (in which case the Standard Minimum Rules will only be considered soft law).

In addition to these international and regional conventions, the UN Security Council has adopted a number of resolutions on fighting terrorism. The most important of these continues to be Resolution 1373 of 28 September 2001.[41] The resolution was adopted pursuant to Chapter 7 of the UN Charter concerning "action with respect to threats to the peace, breaches of the peace and acts of aggression". Such decisions are directly binding on all UN member states. It follows from the UN Charter that steps required to implement the decisions of the Security Council to maintain international peace and security should be taken by all the members of the United Nations.

---

39 See above, note 2, article 12.

40 UN Standard Minimum Rules for the Treatment of Prisoners can be found at http://www.ohchr.org/english/law/treatmentprisoners.htm.

41 UN Security Council Resolution 1373 (2001), UN SCOR, 4385th meeting, UN Doc, S/RES/1373(2001), 28 September 2001. The UN Security Council adopted the first resolution on terrorism in 1999 – SC Res. 1269 (1999) – before work against terrorism under the aegis of the UN became restricted to the UN General Assembly. See Clémentine Olivier, 'Human Rights Law and the International Fight against Terrorism: How do Security Council Resolutions Impact on States' Obligations under International Human Rights Law? (Revisiting Security Council Resolution 1373)' in *Nordic Journal of International Law*, 73, 2004, pp. 399-419.

Resolution 1373 obliges all UN member States to:

- prevent terrorism;
- criminalize acts of terror and the financing thereof in national legislation;
- ensure that persons who plan, finance or carry out acts of terror are actually prosecuted and punished;
- ensure that there are no places or countries where persons responsible for the execution of terrorism can avoid prosecution ("no safe havens");
- strengthen international cooperation, including the exchange of information with a view to fighting and punishing acts of terror.

The resolution also establishes a Counter-Terrorism Committee (CTC), to monitor state parties' implementation of the obligations in the resolution.

The resolution does not contain references to human rights standards or to international humanitarian law. However, in the subsequent Resolution 1456 of the Security Council it is explicitly stated that anti-terror measures "should be in accordance with international law, in particular human rights, refugee, and humanitarian law".[42]

In sum, there is no doubt that states are obliged to respect human rights and standards of humanitarian law in their efforts against terrorism. This is explicitly stated in most – and in all the most recent – international and regional anti-terror instruments. In this respect, it does not make sense to make the issue of human rights and the fight against terrorism an issue of finding the right balance between the two, as is sometimes stated. As demonstrated, there is simply no basis for balancing between the two considerations. Human rights must always be observed in the fight against terrorism. It is quite another issue that *within* the human rights system – and under the monitoring of the established human rights bodies – there is a possibility to balance between considerations (concerning a large number of rights, rights which can be limited or derogated from). Indeed, there is no doubt that human rights must be observed and respected in the fight against terrorism. However, the question remains whether there is the political will to impose and implement these human rights considerations.

## 3 The Political Will to Implement Human Rights Obligations

Since 11 September, there has been a decrease in the political will to implement human rights obligations. Two tendencies can be identified: first, to give less political attention to human rights concerns (section 3.1); and secondly, to restrict human rights review to judicial bodies (section 3.2).

### 3.1 *Less Political Attention to the Protection of Human Rights*

While the 1990s, after the end of the Cold War and its bloc policy, were characterised by considerable political will to strengthen and give priority to human rights,

42 SCR 1456 (20 January 2003).

the same political support for human rights does not seem to have been forthcoming since 11 September 2001.

Jack Donnelly claims that the policy of a given state generally seems to be dictated by three categories of consideration.[43] First, considerations concerning the economic interest of the state, then considerations concerning state security and finally other considerations, including respect for and protection of human rights. While the 1990s showed a relatively high degree of "equilibrium" between the three categories of considerations, Donnelly finds that since 11 September security considerations have become *the* decisive and dominant consideration, forcing the other two categories, including consideration for human rights, into the background.

A comparison between the degree of state reporting to and cooperation with, respectively, the UN Counter-Terrorism Committee (CTC) and the UN Committee Against Torture (CAT) illustrates how states have increasingly given priority to the fight against terrorism.

The content of the obligations in Security Council Resolution 1373 (SC 1373) concerning the fight against terrorism and the UN Convention Against Torture are extraordinarily similar. Both instruments oblige states to prevent, criminalize, prosecute and punish acts of torture, to exclude "safe havens", and to strengthen international cooperation against torture and terrorism. Like SC 1373, the Torture Convention establishes a committee––the UN Committee against Torture––to monitor and ensure that state parties comply with the obligations of the Convention. The UN Convention Against Torture is binding for 134 countries at the moment. Like UN member states, which are obliged to follow SC 1373, states that have ratified the UN Convention Against Torture are obliged to follow and live up to the obligations stated in this Convention. However, in practice huge differences can be observed in the efficiency of implementation and observance of the two instruments by the state parties to these.

According to Resolution 1373, within three months of the adoption of the Resolution – that is, before 27 December 2001 – states should report "precisely and clearly" to the CTC on which concrete legislative and administrative measures they have implemented or intend to implement in order to live up to the obligations of the Resolution.

It is remarkable that 117 states – considerably more than half of the 191 member states of the UN – actually observed the three-month deadline and reported to the CTC before the first deadline on 27 December 2001. As of 30 June 2003, only about two years after the adoption of the resolution, all 191 member states had reported once to the Committee, 154 states had reported twice to the Committee

43 Jack Donnelly, 'International human rights: unintended consequences of the war on terrorism' in Thomas G. Weiss, Margaret E. Crahan and John Goering (eds). *Wars on Terrorism and Iraq*, Routledge 2004, p. 99.

(eighty-one per cent), and thirty-five states had reported three times (eighteen per cent).[44] This can only be categorised as a very high degree of compliance.[45]

Quite the contrary, states have been much more relaxed as to their obligation to report to the UN Committee Against Torture. According to the Torture Convention, states should report to the CAT no later than one year after ratification of the convention, and then every fourth year. As of today, thirty-seven countries have still to deliver their first report to CAT, thirty-four countries have not fulfilled their reporting obligations for more than five years and fifty-one state reports are more than five years delayed.[46] As of May 2005 the CAT has received a total number of 180 state reports, with a further 190 reports overdue.

In other words, over a period of three months the number of state reports submitted to the CTC was almost as high as the number of reports submitted to the CAT during ten years. The reporting system has thus proved a very efficient and well-functioning instrument for monitoring states' efforts in relation to the fight against terrorism. The same can certainly not be said for the protection of human rights.[47]

### 3.2 *The Marginalization and Restriction of Human Rights Concerns*

Simultaneously with the strong political focus on security issues and the fight against terrorism, a general animosity towards the inclusion of human rights concerns in the political and administrative process for preparing anti-terror measures can be detected, both internationally and nationally. Some suggest that the human rights review of politically agreed anti-terror measures must be conducted only after the fact, and only by judicial bodies. This implies a restriction of human rights concerns.

At the *international* level, this trend can be illustrated by the fact that the CTC has consistently maintained – despite persistent and urgent requests from the UN

---

44 'Letter dated 15 July 2003 from the Chairman of the Security Council Committee established pursuant to resolution 1373 (2001) concerning counter-terrorism addressed to the President of the Security Council,' UN Doc, S/2003/710, section 4.

45 By 30 June 2005, the Committee had received 601 reports from member states and others. They included 191 first reports from member states, 166 second reports from member states, 127 third reports from member states, 94 fourth reports from member states and 14 fifth reports from member states. See *Work Programme of the Counter-Terrorism Committee (1 July-30 September 2005)*, S/2005/421, 29 June 2005, par. 5.

46 'Report of the Committee against Torture,' Annual Report, 1 November 2002, UN GAOR, 27–28th Sessions, UN Doc, A/57/44.

47 Looking at the entire degree of reporting to the six UN human rights committees (CESCR, CCPR, CERD, CEDAW, CAT, CRC), it appears that 325 states have not fulfilled their obligations to report to one or more of the six human rights committees for more than five years and 593 state reports were due more than five years ago. See 'Methods of Work Relating to the State Reporting Process,' Second Inter-committee Meeting of the Human Rights Treaty Bodies, Geneva, 18–20 June 2003, HRI/ICM/2003/3, 11 April 2003.

High Commissioner for Human Rights[48] – that it will not include human rights concerns in its assessment of the anti-terror initiatives that states implement to live up to SC 1373. The reason for this is that the UN system already has an extensive monitoring system (both treaty-based and charter-based) in place, which should be able to assess whether there is cause for concern from a human rights point of view. However, there does seem to be an increasing willingness to include human rights aspects in the CTC's work.[49]

It is mainly in connection with the practical implementation of obligations stemming from SC Resolution 1373 that states may come into conflict with human rights obligations. It would therefore be relevant for the CTC to include human rights issues in their assessment when carrying out country visits. However, judging from the documents that are publicly available, this does not seem to happen.[50]

At the *national* level, there also seems to be a general trend for legislators and administration to be inclined, to a large degree, to leave a more thorough human rights assessment of anti-terror initiatives to subsequent review and control by the judiciary. In consequence, legislators and state administrators have developed, adopted and implemented questionable anti-terror legislation and initiatives, while indicating that it is the responsibility of the judiciary to decide subsequently whether the legislation or initiatives contain a possible conflict with human rights or other international obligations.

Whereas the trend until and through the 1990s was to include human rights considerations in political and administrative processes – the so-called mainstreaming of human rights considerations – the trend since 11 September of the human rights monitoring bodies seems to be rather to restrict human rights concerns to subsequent review.[51]

---

48 See *inter alia* UNHCHR's *Note to the Chair of the Counter-Terrorism Committee: A Human Rights Perspective On Counter-terrorist Measures; and Proposals for "Further Guidance" for the Submission of Reports Pursuant to Paragraph 6 of Security Council Resolution 1373 (2001) (intended to supplement the Guidance of 26 October 2001).*

49 In SC Resolution 1535 (26 March 2004) the CTC was charged to liaise with "the office of the UNHCHR and other organizations competent in matters related to human rights and counter-terrorism". There is also information to the effect that "an expert on human rights, humanitarian law and refugee law" will be included in the staff of the Directorate for CTC. Finally the Danish Government, which is chairing the CTC for a two-year period, has stated that one of the Danish priorities for the work of the CTC is to "promote the human rights aspect of the CTC's work"; see Danish Government Report to the Folketing, *Redegørelse af 9/6 05 om indsatsen mod terrorisme.*

50 The first country visit was carried out in March 2005, to Morocco. In addition to representatives from the Counter-terrorism Directorate under the CTC, experts from the International Criminal Police Organization (INTERPOL), the World Customs Organization, the Financial Action Task Force and the European Union also participated in the visit. See above, note 30. While several "security experts" participated, no dedicated human rights expert took part in the visit.

51 Colin Warbrick, 'The European Response to Terrorism in an Age of Human Rights', *European Journal of International Law*, Vol. 15, No. 5., pp. 989–1018, at p. 1016: "The

In sum, it can be said that 11 September has provoked, on the one hand, a trend towards less political focus on human rights concerns and more on security considerations, and on the other hand, a trend towards relegating human rights concerns to subsequent review by judicial and human rights bodies. This strong political focus on security considerations, together with the toning down and restriction of human rights considerations, can cause concern and entail a considerable risk of over-reaction. As Ignatieff stresses, politicians are bad at "balancing threat and response" because "the political costs of under-reaction are always going to be higher than the costs of over-reaction."[52]

## 4 Doubt About Human Rights Protection in Three Areas

In general, the decrease in the political willingness to implement and enforce human rights obligations has led to doubts about human rights protection in three areas.

First, there is doubt as to whether the fight against terrorism in general might supersede human rights concerns. According to some, a state's human rights obligations must yield to the obligation of the state to prevent terrorism. The human rights system is out-dated and inapplicable, and has to be reformulated and toned down in this new security situation. There is a need for a "securitisation" of human rights.

Secondly, there is uncertainty in some quarters as to how human rights ought to be applied. Here, no general rejection of human rights is intended. However, it is disputed whether human rights are applicable in special situations, including for example during armed conflict or when a state is acting outside its own territory.

Thirdly, there is doubt over what the interpretation and "level" of human rights protection ought to be. There are those who maintain that, although human rights obligations must be respected in the fight against terrorism, a restrictive interpretation of these rights is still necessary, often in contradiction to the interpretations of human rights monitoring bodies.

These areas of concerns are analysed in the next three parts.

### *4.1 The Fight against Terrorism May Supersede Human Rights*

Only a very few states have *officially* adopted the view that counter-terrorism supersedes human rights. As a matter of fact, there has been no increase in the number of states that derogate from their human rights obligations with reference

human rights implications of some of the [counter-terrorism] initiatives scarcely seem to have been considered (or, worse, if considered, disregarded). Human rights law at best then becomes reactive, trying to provide *ex post facto* remedies for persons who have suffered serious violations of their rights."

52 See Michael Ignatieff, *The Lesser Evil: Political Ethics in an Age of Terror*, Edinburgh University Press 2004, p. 58.

to the terror threat.[53] On 18 December 2002, however, Great Britain decided to derogate from its obligations under article 5 of the EHRC and article 9 of the ICCPR in order to be able to deprive foreigners of their liberty. This measure concerned foreigners who could not be deported from Great Britain (for fear of violation of their human rights in the country of destination) and who, according to the British Government, presented a terror security threat, though there were not sufficient grounds to initiate criminal prosecutions against them. This derogation was, however, overruled by the British House of Lords in December 2004, and Great Britain therefore withdrew the derogation on 15 March 2005.[54]

At a more general level, some states have argued that it follows from Article 103 of the UN Charter[55] that the obligations to fight terrorism contained in SC 1373 – which contains no reference to human rights – supersede other international obligations, including human rights obligations.

In December 2001 the UN Human Rights Committee examined the fifth periodic report of Great Britain to the Committee, expressed its concern at the far-reaching consequences of British anti-terror legislation and questioned its compatibility with British obligations in the human rights area. However, the British side "invoked Article 103 of the UN Charter to argue that its obligations to the Counter-Terrorism Committee under Security Council Resolution 1373 took precedence over its obligations to the Human Rights Committee."[56] The same perception seems to form the basis of a response in January 2003 from the Danish Prime Minister in answer to a question from the Danish Red Cross.[57] The issue is no longer so urgent, however, as the Security Council, by subsequent Resolution SC

53 See UN Sub-Commission on Human Rights, *Questions of Human Rights and States of Emergency; List of States Which Have Proclaimed or Continued a State of Emergency*, 7 July 2005, E/CN.4/Sub.2/2005/6.

54 UN Sub-Commission on Human Rights, above note 54, at p. 7.

55 Article 103 of the UN Charter reads: "In the event of a conflict between the obligations of the Members of the United Nations under the present Charter and their obligations under any other international agreement, their obligations under the present Charter shall prevail."

56 Human Rights Committee, "Summary Record of the First Part of the 1963 Meeting: United Kingdom of Great Britain and Northern Ireland," 23 October 2001, UN ESCOR, 73rd Session, UN Doc, CCPR/C/SR 1963.

57 See letter of 7 January 2003 from Prime Minister Anders Fogh Rasmussen to President Freddy Karup Pedersen and Secretary General Jørgen Poulsen, Danish Red Cross, available at www.ft.dk, annex to the Legal Affairs Committee: "Finally, I can inform you that some of these international law issues are being discussed in the UN International Law Commission. The Commission has started to analyse the collision of norms which may arise between, on the one hand, the states' obligations under current international conventions, and on the other hand, the obligation which rests with the UN member states in cases where the UN Security Council has adopted binding measures on the basis of the UN Charter. Article 103 of the UN Charter states that the UN Charter and the measures implemented based upon it shall prevail in such a situation."

1456 (2003), has stated unequivocally that the obligation to fight terrorism should be conducted with full respect for human rights.[58]

Nevertheless it is still doubtful whether states should be able to extricate themselves from their human rights obligations by referring to the fact that the action in question was implemented in accordance to a binding decision of the Security Council and to the precedence of these decisions pursuant to Article 103.

First, this seems to depend on whether it was really the clear intention of the Security Council to overrule other international obligations, including human rights:

If it appears that the Council was intending to lay down a rule irrespective of the prior obligations of States, in general or in particular, then that intention would prevail; if, conversely, it appears that the Council was intending to base itself on existing legal rules or an existing legal situation, then its decision ought certainly to be interpreted taking those rules into account.[59]

Secondly, it has been argued that Security Council resolutions – as a secondary legal instrument adopted in the context of the UN Charter – are subordinated to the provisions of the UN Charter[60] and thus could not be used to restrict human rights obligations. This view seems to have been confirmed indirectly by the European Court of Human Rights in the recent *Bosporus Airways* case from June 2005.[61] The Court did not refrain from reviewing whether the Irish authorities' detention of a Yugoslav plane constituted a violation of the EHRC, in spite of the fact that Ireland, pursuant to the sanctions against Yugoslavia adopted by the UN Security Council, was obliged to detain the plane. The decision seems to make it clear that states cannot excuse themselves from their human rights obligations by referring to the fact that they are merely implementing a binding decision of the UN Security Council.

Finally, it has been submitted that, at the very least, Article 103 cannot be understood to imply that Security Council resolutions can take precedence over norms which hold the status of peremptory norms – *jus cogens*.[62] This view was

---

58 See also identical human rights references in *SC Resolution 1566 (2004) and SC Resolution 1624 (2005)*. However, Security Council Resolution 1540 (2004), which also imposes certain obligations on states in relation to fighting terrorism, omits any reference to either human rights or international humanitarian law.

59 M. Wood, *The Interpretation of Security Council Resolutions*, (1998) 2 Max-Plank Yearbook of UN Law 92.

60 Pursuant to Article 24 (2) "the Security Council shall act in accordance with the purpose and principles of the United Nations", and pursuant to Article 1 of the Charter, it is one of the purposes of the United Nations to "promot[e] and encourag[e] respect for human rights and for fundamental freedoms for all without distinction as to race, sex, language, or religion."

61 See *Bosporus* v. *Ireland*, app. no. 45036/98, ECtHR 30 June 2005.

62 See Alexander Orakhelashvili, 'The Post-War Settlement in Iraq: The UN Security Council Resolution 1483 (2003) and General International Law', *Journal of Conflict and Security Law*, December 2003, Oxford University Press; and Clémentine Olivier, 'Human Rights Law and the International Fight against Terrorism: How do Security

confirmed in a recent decision by the Court of First Instance of the Court of Justice of the European Communities in the case *Ahmed Ali Yusuf et al* v. *the Council of the European Union*.[63] The case concerned a Swede of Arab origin, whose funds had been frozen in November 2001 by the European authorities after a Sanctions Committee of the UN Security Council – pursuant to an Article 103 Security Council resolution – had put him on a list of alleged terrorists. Yusuf claimed that the sanctions were in breach of the Treaty of Rome, which states that EU law cannot lead to disciplinary actions against single individuals. He also asked to be allowed to prove his innocence in a court of law. The Court found that:

> International law ... permits the inference that there exists one limit to the principle that resolutions of the Security Council have binding effect: namely, that they must observe the fundamental peremptory provisions of *jus cogens*. If they fail to do so, however improbable that may be, they would bind neither the Member States of the United Nations nor, in consequence, the Community.
>
> The indirect judicial review carried out by the Court in connection with an action for annulment of a Community act adopted, where no discretion whatsoever may be exercised, with a view to putting into effect a resolution of the Security Council may therefore, in some circumstances, extend to determining whether the superior rules of international law falling within the ambit of *jus cogens* have been observed, in particular, the mandatory provisions concerning the universal protection of human rights, from which neither the Member States nor the bodies of the United Nations may derogate because they constitute 'intransgressible principles of international customary law.'[64]

The case has now been appealed to the Court of Justice of the European Union.

The question of whether the fight against terrorism should supersede human rights protection is also hotly debated among scholars. Some of them argue that, since 11 September, we are in a new situation which demands us to reconsider and tone down the protection of human rights. Ignatieff presents the following dilemma:

> Whether a country facing a terrorist emergency should base its public policy exclusively on its own constitution and its own laws, or whether it has any *duty* to pay atten-

Council Resolutions Impact on States' Obligations under International Human Rights Law? (Revisiting Security Council Resolution 1373)', *Nordic Journal of International Law*, 73, 2004, pp. 399-419.

63 See judgments of the Court of First Instance, *Ahmed Ali Yusuf, et al.* v. *Council of the European Union and Commission of the European Communities*, Case T-306/01 and Case T-315/01, 21 September 2005.

64 Ibid., pp. 281-2.

> tion to what other states have to say and what international agreements and conventions require [emphasis added].[65]

Ignatieff concludes that, in such a situation, states cannot be bound by international human rights standards.

Similarly, other scholars have asserted that it is no longer possible to maintain the absolute prohibition against torture.[66] Dershowitz has thus argued for the necessity of being able to torture in order to fight terrorism (the "ticking bomb" situation). He proposes to legalise the use of torture by court order, so the police – as is the case with telephone wiretapping, search and seizure, and the like – can request the court's permission to use torture in concrete cases.

In addition, there exist several weighty examples of circumstantial evidence showing that certain states in practice have *unofficially and covertly* allowed their efforts against terrorism to supersede human rights obligations. There have been several persistent allegations concerning the USA's "extraordinary rendition" of terrorists in order to obtain information, that is, the transfer of individuals – without recourse to the *regular legal procedures* of extradition, removal, exclusion, etc. – to a foreign state where it is reasonable to expect that the individual will be subjected to torture and other forms of ill-treatment.[67] Likewise, the USA is under persistent allegations of operating secret detention centres in a number of countries.[68]

### 4.2 *When Are Human Rights Applicable?*

In this second developing line of argument, it is a given that efforts to counter terrorism must consider and respect states' human rights obligations. However, the situations in which human rights apply and the precise scope of human rights protection are intensely debated.

#### 4.2.1 Previous Experience of Fighting Terrorism while Respecting Human Rights

Terrorism is not a new phenomenon. The world knew terrorism before 11 September 2001. Europe has decades of experience of fighting terrorism and handling

---

65 See Michael Ignatieff, *The Lesser Evil: Political Ethics in an Age of Terror*, Toronto: Penguin, 2004, p. 7.

66 Alan M. Dershowitz, *Why Terrorism Works*, New Haven, Conn.: Yale University Press 2002, pp. 131–163. See also Mirko Bagaric and Julie Clarke, 'Not Enough (Official) Torture in the World? The Circumstances in Which Torture is Morally Justifiable', *University of San Francisco Law Review*, July 2005.

67 See, e.g., The Association of the Bar of the City of New York and Center for Human Rights and Global Justice, *Torture by Proxy: International and Domestic Law Applicable to "Extraordinary Renditions"*, November 2004.

68 See, e.g., Council of Europe, Committee on Legal Affairs and Human Rights, *Alleged secret detentions in Council of Europe member states*, Information Memorandum II, 22 January 2006. Can be found on: http://assembly.coe.int/Main.asp?link=/CommitteeDocs/2006/20060124_Jdoc032006_E.htm

the issues that can arise when states must prevent and fight terrorism, while at the same time respecting human rights obligations.[69] It has thus been stated "that no part of the world has more experience with terrorism than Europe."[70] Consequently, as early as 1960, the European Court of Human Rights in the case *Lawless v. Ireland* ruled on whether counter-terrorism measures violate the rights set forth in the human rights conventions. The Court has since ruled on similar issues several times.[71]

Furthermore, in 2002 the Council of Europe developed guidelines on Human Rights and the Fight against Terrorism.[72] These guidelines are mainly based on case law from the European Court of Human Rights. It has been argued that they could also be applied outside Europe, including by the UN.[73]

### 4.2.2 A New Type of Terrorism Leading to a New Situation

It is often argued, however, that terrorism has changed fundamentally since 11 September 2001, and that consequently, the experience and guidelines which for instance the European Court of Human Rights has elaborated no longer carry the same relevance. Whereas terrorism was earlier predominantly nationally or regionally based, it has now assumed a much more transnational character. In addition, it is also argued that the methods and means used by terrorists are quite similar, in strength and intensity, to actual armed attacks.

In tune with this development, efforts to counter terrorism have also changed fundamentally. First, before 11 September, the fight against terrorism took place in a peacetime context and therefore made use of normal tools, such as the intelligence services, law enforcement and criminal procedural initiatives. Secondly, these efforts against terrorism predominantly took place on the territory of the state concerned.[74] Normal police and criminal procedural cooperation with other

69 During the last fifty years, a number of European states have been the victims of acts of terror, including Germany, Ireland, Italy, the Netherlands, Spain, France and the United Kingdom.

70 See John Hedigan, "The European Convention on Human Rights and Counter-Terrorism", *Fordham International Law Review*, January 2005.

71 Ibid. For a detailed presentation of these cases, see also Colin Warbrick, "The Principles of the European Convention on Human Rights and the Response of States to Terrorism", *European Human Rights Law Review*, 2002, Vol. 3, pp. 287–314.

72 In 2005 the Council of Europe (CoE) initiated a process to revise and possibly update the guidelines of 2002. In May 2005 an expert meeting was arranged in the CoE to assess the implementation of the guidelines and suggest possible areas to update.

73 The UN Sub-commission on Human Rights decided at its session in July 2005 to establish a working group to develop guidelines similar to the European ones. See UN Sub-Commission on Human Rights, *Working group to elaborate detailed principles and guidelines, with relevant commentary, concerning the promotion and protection of human rights when combating terrorism*, E/CN.4/Sub.2/2005/L.44, 8 August 2005.

74 See also Silvia Borelli, "Casting Light on the Legal Black Hole: International Law and Detentions Abroad in the 'War on Terror'", *IRRC*, Volume 87, No. 857, March 2005.

states in order to prevent and fight terrorism existed, of course, but actual extraterritorial use of power in order to fight terrorism was infrequent.[75]

A number of the anti-terror initiatives taken since 11 September 2001 have been introduced under circumstances in which states are acting outside their own territories in situations similar to armed conflict, the wars in Afghanistan and Iraq being the most obvious examples. In addition, terrorism has also caused increased debate about who can commit human rights violations. Consequently, the fight against terrorism has entailed renewed or stronger doubts as to the scope of application of human rights.

The human rights obligations of a state are generally defined by the following parameters: *ratione personae* (based on person), *ratione loci* (based on place) and *ratione materiae* (based on content). It seems that all these parameters have been somewhat influenced by and exposed to increased debate after 11 September. Consequently there is increased doubt as to (1) whether private persons can commit human rights violations (*ratione personae*), (2) whether human rights apply during armed conflict (*ratione materiae*), and finally (3) whether states are bound by human rights when acting outside their own territory (*ratione loci).*

These questions are not really new; they were discussed in human rights circles even before 11 September. It does, however, seem irrefutable that 11 September and the ensuing fight against terrorism have raised renewed and increased doubts about these questions. I refer to this in further detail below.

### 4.2.3 *Ratione Personae*: Can Private Persons Violate Human Rights?

It is a well-established fact in human rights theory and practice that states are under a human rights obligation to protect people within their jurisdiction from terrorist acts. Indeed, there is a positive human rights obligation upon states to prevent and prosecute such acts.[76] Nevertheless, it is strongly disputed whether terrorist acts in themselves can be classified as human rights violations.

This disagreement – which appears to have a clear regional basis – emerged (among other places) at the 59th session of the UN General Assembly in December

---

75 This has happened, though, for example with Israel's operations in the occupied territories, as well as Turkish military operations in Northern Iraq.

76 See, e.g., the Council of Europe 'Guidelines on Human Rights and the Fight against Terrorism', 11 July 2002. See also the European Court of Human Rights decision in *Kiliç* v. *Turkey*, app. no. 22492/93, ECtHR 28 March 2000, par. 62, which states: "The Court recalls that the first sentence of Article 2 § 1 of the European Convention for the Protection of Human Rights and Fundamental Freedoms enjoins the State not only to refrain from the intentional and unlawful taking of life, but also to take appropriate steps to safeguard the lives of those within its jurisdiction.... This involves a primary duty on the State to secure the right to life by putting in place effective criminal-law provisions to deter the commission of offences against the person, backed up by law-enforcement machinery for the prevention, suppression and punishment of breaches of such provisions. It also extends in appropriate circumstances to a positive obligation on the authorities to take preventive operational measures to protect an individual or individuals whose life is at risk from the criminal acts of another individual...."

2004. The Assembly adopted a resolution on human rights and terrorism by a recorded vote of 127 in favour and fifty against. The fifty opposing states were all from the group of West and East European states. These states could not accept the view expressed in the resolution: that terrorist acts perpetrated by non-state actors as such can be defined as human rights violations.[77]

Several states consider acts of terror committed by non-state terror groups as violations of human rights. According to this view, human rights basically constitute a protection of human dignity; as acts of terror constitute one of the most serious attacks on human dignity, the concept of human rights must be understood or interpreted as a protection against such acts of terror.

On the contrary, the group of Western and Eastern European states maintains that under international law, only states are legally responsible for protecting human rights and only states can be responsible for violating human rights obligations. Terrorist acts may constitute crimes under international criminal law, but they are not violations of human rights *per se*.

### 4.2.4 *Ratione Materiae*: Do Human Rights Apply during Armed Conflict?

Traditionally, human rights and international humanitarian law have been considered as two distinct sets of rules applicable in two different situations: human rights in peacetime, international humanitarian law during armed conflict. As soon as an international armed conflict arises, human rights protection automatically ceases and international humanitarian law (IHL) takes over.

There is no doubt that IHL only applies during armed conflict, as stated explicitly in the common article 2 of the four Geneva Conventions. On the contrary, human rights applicability during armed conflicts is not explicitly regulated in human rights conventions. However, ICCPR article 4, par. 1 allows state parties to derogate from some of the rights stipulated in the Covenant "In time of public emergency which threatens the life of the nation". A similar possibility exists in ECHR Article 15 in time of "war or other public emergency threatening the life of the nation". Conversely, it is possible to conclude that human rights conventions are – unless states have derogated from their obligations – also applicable during armed conflicts.

This basic assumption has been confirmed by the practice of the UN General Assembly and the UN Human Rights Commission,[78] and of some human rights

77 See General Assembly Resolution, *Human Rights and Terrorism*, 22 March 2005, A/RES/59/195. See also Commission on Human Rights Resolution, *Human Rights and Terrorism*, E/CN.4/2004/44, par. 5.

78 For example, in connection with the Iraqi occupation of Kuwait in 1990, where both bodies criticized Iraq for human rights violations, including violations of the ICCPR in occupied Kuwait. See UN General Assembly Resolution of December 18 1990, concerning *The Situation of Human Rights in Occupied Kuwait*, A/Res/45/170, par. 1, which: "condemns the Iraqi authorities and occupying forces for their serious violations of human rights against the Kuwaiti people and third-State nationals and, in particular, the continued and increasing acts of torture, arrests, summary executions, disappearances and abduction in violation of the Charter of the United Nations, the

bodies and the International Court of Justice (ICJ).[79] Most recently a resolution of the UN Human Rights Commission stressed that "human rights law and international humanitarian law are complementary and mutually reinforcing".[80]

However, some states still invoke the traditional distinction between the respective scopes of IHL and HRL. For instance, the State of Israel is of the opinion that

> the two systems, which were codified in separate instruments, remained distinct. The law of armed conflict applied in situations where generally recognised human rights norms could not be applied owing to the fact that the normal government-citizen relationship did not prevail. Any attempt simultaneously to apply the two regimes could only be detrimental to both.[81]

A similar view was defended by the USA during the debate on the Resolution on Protection of the Human Rights of Civilians during Armed Conflict in the UN Human Rights Commission in April 2005. According to the USA representative, IHL and HRL "were separate and conceptually distinct areas of law".[82] The USA maintained that the two systems of rules were therefore mutually exclusive.

One example of how IHL, according to the United States, can supersede normal human rights obligations is the imprisonment of Al-Marri, a citizen of Qatar. Al-Marri was not captured in or near the battlefield. He resided legally in the USA as a university student with his wife and children when he was arrested shortly after 11 September 2001 as a "material witness in the investigation of the September 11 attacks". In 2003 President Bush declared him an "enemy combatant", and he has since then been imprisoned without charge and *incommunicado* for more than two years on an American navy vessel in South Carolina.[83]

In sum, although the prevailing assumption seems to be that IHL and HRL are not mutually exclusive but can be applied simultaneously during armed conflict, there is no doubt that 11 September and the subsequent fight against terrorism

---

International Covenants on Human Rights, other relevant human rights instruments and the relevant instruments of humanitarian law".

79 See ICJ, *Legal Consequences of the Construction of a Wall in the Occupied Palestinian Territory*, Advisory Opinion, 9 July 2004, par. 106.

80 Commission on Human Rights, *Protection of the Human Rights of Civilians in Armed Conflict*, April 15 2005, E/CN.4/2005/L.82. Fifty-one states voted in favour of the resolution, one against (USA), and one abstained (Japan).

81 See HRC, Summary Record of the 18th Meeting, 15 May 2003; see also Second Periodic Report of Israel, E/C.12/2003/SR.18, 4 June 2003, par. 23.

82 See UN Press Statement of 20 April 2005: "Michael Peay (USA), speaking in an explanation of the vote before the vote, said the United States…had been constrained to call

> for a vote because the text conflated and confused the two separate bodies of international humanitarian law and international human rights law. They were separate and conceptually distinct areas of law."

83 See Human Rights Watch, Cruel Confinement of 'Enemy Combatant' in United States available at: http://hrw.org/english/docs/2005/08/08/usdom11612.htm

have created more doubt and debate about the application of human rights during armed conflict.[84]

#### 4.2.5 *Ratione Loci*: Extraterritorial Application of Human Rights?

The original logic behind the concept of human rights was to protect individuals against arbitrary intervention from the authorities in the *territorial state* in question. But since 11 September and the increased focus on fighting international terrorism – including the use of so-called "preemptive strikes" undertaken outside of the territory of the striking state – there has been a certain tendency towards the acts of states increasingly having consequences for individuals who are *outside* the territorial borders of the state in question. In the longer term, this development could contribute to undermining the importance of human rights and the protection which they can give to individuals.

Defining the scope of human rights in such a situation has given rise to an intense debate and a number of decisions and statements from both national judicial bodies and international human rights bodies, regarding whether and to what extent states are bound by human rights conventions when acting outside their own territory.[85] Not surprisingly, a certain reluctance can be detected among states and government representatives to concede or acknowledge the extraterritorial application of the human rights conventions.

The USA has thus consistently maintained that human rights conventions, including the ICCPR, which the USA has ratified, do not apply to it extraterritorially.

Similarly it has been the view of the UK that the UN's Torture Convention can not apply extraterritorially.[86] The British government has also put forward the opinion that the ECHR does not apply when the UK acts outside of its own territory: "the UK Government does not believe that the European Convention on Hu-

---

84 It is, however, more questionable – though I shall not discuss the issue here – how the two sets of rules can play together in concrete terms during armed conflict and how the obvious conflicts between the two sets of rules can be resolved.

85 Here I include, as extraterritorial acts, only those acts which states actually undertake outside their own territory. Acts undertaken by states within their own territory that may have consequences in the territory of other state are thus not included here as cases concerning extraterritorial application of the Convention. Likewise, I exclude cases concerning deportation to torture or inhuman or degrading treatment; see the decision of the European Court of Human Rights in *Soering v. The United Kingdom*, app. no. 14038/88, ECtHR 7 July 1989.

86 See the UK's response to members of the UN Committee Against Torture in connection with the Committee's consideration and assessment of the Fourth Periodic Report of the UK to the Committee, November 17-18 2004, p. 22: "In essence the United Kingdom believes that those parts of the Convention which are applicable only in respect of territory under the jurisdiction of the state party cannot be applicable in relation to actions of the UK in Afghanistan and Iraq."

man Rights is applicable to our operations in Iraq. We are awaiting a High Court judgment on this issue and...the *Bankovic* judgment is key to our argument." [87]

Some states seem to believe that a human rights void – and actually a void of judicial review – exists when states act outside their own territory. In this view, states are not bound by the human rights obligations which they have otherwise assumed. However, recent decisions and statements from human rights bodies seem to invalidate this view. Consequently there seems to be a trend towards the increased recognition of extraterritorial application of the human rights conventions, as illustrated by recent decisions of the European Court of Human Rights[88] and statements of the UN Committee Against Torture.[89] The International Court of Justice (ICJ) has also recognised, in very general terms, the extraterritorial application of the ICCPR.[90] A British High Court decision also found that the ECHR is binding for British troops when managing detention centres in Iraq.[91]

In sum, terrorism itself and states' initiatives in fighting terrorism have caused considerable renewed and intensified debate on the application of human rights, with some states – headed by the USA – arguing in favour of limiting the scope of human rights.

### 4.3 Doubt Concerning the Interpretation and Level of Human Rights Protection

In the last ideological trend to be mentioned here, it is conceded that human rights are not superseded by the fight against terrorism, and that the rights should not be dispensed with because special conditions prevail. Accordingly, efforts against terrorism should take place within the human rights system and through the application of and respect for human rights standards. In this view, human rights protection depends on the interpretation and level of protection provided by the human rights standards. Here a tendency has been observed for states to try to limit the level of protection. Human rights apply – but at a lower level.

In general terms it is said that the fight against terrorism has entailed a limitation on the level of human rights protection at national level in three ways: through legislative changes which encroach upon human rights protection, through the more restrictive interpretation of existing rules, and through actual discretion-

87 Ibid., p. 23.

88 See, e.g., *Öcalan* v. *Turkey*, app. no. 46221/99, ECtHR 12 March 2003; *Ilascu and Others* v. *Moldova and Russia*, app. no. 48787/99, ECtHR 8 July 2004; *Issa and Others* v. *Turkey*, app. no. 31821/96, ECtHR 16 November 2004.

89 See *Conclusions and Recommendations of the Committee Against Torture, United Kingdom of Great Britain and Northern Ireland, Crown Dependencies and Overseas Territories*, CAT/C/CR/33/3, 10 December 2004, par. 4(b).

90 See International Court of Justice, *Legal Consequences of the Construction of a Wall in the Occupied Palestinian Territory*, 9 July 2004, General list No. 131, par. 109.

91 See *Al Skeini and Others* v. *Secretary of State for Defence*, Case No. CO/2242/2004, High Court of Justice, Queen's Bench Division, Royal Courts of Justice, 14 December 2004.

ary power.[92] Indeed, a number of human rights allow states legitimately to limit the scope of their human rights obligations (limitation) or temporarily to derogate from them in compelling situations of emergency or security threats (derogation).

This restrictive interpretation of human rights is most conspicuous and causes most concern in relation to absolute rights – such as the prohibition against torture and other ill-treatment – which can under no circumstances be balanced against security considerations. Even in relation to these absolute rights, there are several examples of states' restrictive interpretations under the influence of the new security situation.

An excellent example of this is the torture memos written in 2002 and 2003 by the US Department of Defence and Department of Justice.[93] The memos attempt to reinterpret the international prohibition against torture on several points, including assigning the term "torture" to absolutely extraordinary circumstances and correspondingly characterising less extreme methods of interrogation as legal methods of interrogation. "Torture" is thus confined to extreme acts which involve pain which is "difficult to endure", a pain that must be "equal in intensity to the pain accompanying serious physical injury, such as organ failure, impairment of bodily function, or even death" as formulated by a legal "task force" under the Department of Defence.[94] This definition is without doubt contrary to the practice of both international and regional human rights bodies.

Another example of a restrictive re-interpretation of human rights is the absolute prohibition on returning persons to countries where they risk exposure to torture or other inhuman treatment. This prohibition has come under considerable pressure since 11 September. Several states have returned individuals to countries

---

92 This view is expressed by several authors, including Vojin Dimitrijevic: "The dangers to the enjoyment of human rights resulting therefrom [from terrorism] belong to three categories. First, there is the tendency to restrict existing rights by formal legislative action. Laws are amended and new legislation introduced reducing rights and freedoms 'abused' by terrorists in order to limit the terrorists' freedom of action and to facilitate their apprehension and punishment. Second, existing legislation is reinterpreted in a generally restrictive fashion, sometimes in a discriminatory manner, affecting both persons prone to terrorist violence and members of the general public. Third, the general climate of panic, fear and suspicion infects law enforcement agencies and influences their judgment and behaviour when exercising their discretionary power." Vojin Dimitrijevic´, Terrorism and Human Rights after 2001, in Morten Bergsmo (ed.), Human Rights and Criminal Justice for the Downtrodden: Essays in Honour of Asbjørn Eide", Martinus Nijhoff Publishers 2003, p. 603-620 (p. 614).

93 The memoranda mentioned are available at http://texscience.org/reform/torture/. The restrictive interpretation of the prohibition against torture which is argued in several of these memoranda was largely rescinded by a memorandum from the US Department of Justice of 30 December 2004.

94 See Donald Rumsfeld, Secretary of Defense, *Working Group Report on Detainee Interrogations in the Global War on Terrorism*, 6 March 2003. This interpretation and other limitations to the international prohibition against torture were, however, rescinded by the Department of Justice in December 2004; see US Department of Justice, *Legal Memorandum*, 30 December 2004.

where they risk being exposed to torture, justifying the legitimacy of this procedure with reference to their receipt of diplomatic guarantees from these countries that the individuals in question will not be exposed to torture. This also includes countries which are known for their widespread and systematic use of torture. The UN Special Rapporteur on Torture expressed his concern at this development in a press release in August 2005, occasioned by the advanced plans of the UK to return a number of such individuals: "The Special Rapporteur fears that the plan of the United Kingdom to request diplomatic assurances for the purpose of expelling persons in spite of a risk of torture reflects a tendency in Europe to circumvent the international obligation not to deport anybody if there is a serious risk that he or she might be subjected to torture."[95]

## 5 Summary

In spite of the fact that it appears clearly and explicitly from both international and regional anti-terror instruments that the fight against terrorism can only take place if human rights are fully respected, there is extensive documentation that a number of human rights have been violated in states' fight against terrorism. A decisive explanation is that human rights concerns are not being given the same international and national political priority they once were. Human rights have been given a lower priority and have been marginalized and to some degree restricted to judicial and human rights arenas for subsequent control. This has resulted in human rights generally coming under pressure on three fronts: the argument that human rights are being superseded by terrorism, a trend that sees the scope of human rights as limited due to special conditions or situations, and finally a trend towards a restrictive interpretation and limitation of the level of human rights protection.

These developments all give cause for concern. First, these stratagems against human rights not only affect the terrorists, but also our societies in a much broader sense, and threaten to undermine our most fundamental principles of openness, freedom, the rule of law, and respect for and protection of the rights of individuals.

Secondly, one can with good reason question whether "sacrificing" human rights is the right way to prevent and fight terrorism. As a number of sources have pointed out, it seems reasonable to assume that the fact that suspected terrorists have been treated with complete disregard for international law, and especially for human rights principles, has increased rather than limited the supply of potential terrorists.

In March 2005, the UN Secretary General published a first draft of a comprehensive strategy on the prevention of terrorism, which contemplates fighting and preventing terrorism through a combination of short-term security initiatives like increased control, surveillance and the seizure of financial assets, as well as

95 UN Special Rapporteur on Torture, Diplomatic Assurances Not an Adequate Safeguard for Deportees, 23 August 2005. http://www.unhchr.ch/huricane/huricane.nsf/view01/9A54333D23E8CB81C1257065007323C7?opendocument

long-term initiatives such as strengthening human rights and development.[96] This appears to be the most sustainable and effective way of combating terrorism.

96 The strategy contains five elements – the "five Ds": i) dissuade disaffected groups from choosing terrorism as a tactic to achieve their goals; ii) deny terrorists the means to carry out their attacks; iii) deter states from supporting terrorists; iv) develop states' capacity to prevent terrorism; and v) defend human rights in the struggle against terrorism.

# 7. Humanitarian Intervention and State Sovereignty: A Social Constructivist Analysis*

*Helle Malmvig*

The many humanitarian interventions during the 1990s caused renewed debate about the extent to which the state-based order is changing and what the concept of state sovereignty means today. In general terms there are two principal schools of thought within this debate: the (neo)realist school and the idealist/neo-liberalist school. According to the realist view, sovereign states remain the primary building blocks of the international system. Sovereign states are viewed as the most important international actors, and the nation state is taken to constitute the basic reference point for our identities and loyalties. According to the idealist view, by contrast, humanitarian intervention, globalisation and the spread of human rights are seen as phenomena that are gradually changing the state-based order, replacing it with a new one based on common values and individual rights (DUPI 1999, p. 16).

However, this chapter will propose a third perspective on the relationship between state sovereignty and humanitarian intervention. It will argue that humanitarian intervention should not be seen as a practice which is eroding or infringing the principle of state sovereignty, but rather one that is shaping the very content and meaning of state sovereignty.

The discipline of International Relations provides the starting point for this chapter. Its theoretical basis is social constructivism, and more specifically Foucaldian discourse analysis (Foucault 1972). This means, in the context of this chapter, that state sovereignty will be examined as a discourse, and humanitarian intervention analysed as one of those discursive practices which creates and gives meaning to state sovereignty. *Discourse* can in general terms be defined as a particular way of talking about and understanding the world. A discourse is a particular pattern (of speech) that makes our existence and actions meaningful (Winther, Jørgensen and Phillips, p. 9; Malmvig 2002, p. 15). Discourse analysis is thus a way of analys-

* This chapter is based on a previous article in *Cooperation and Conflict* vol. 36, no. 3, 2001: 'The Reproduction of Sovereignties: Between Man and State During Practices of Intervention', pp. 251-272.

*S. Lagoutte, H-O. Sano and P. Scharff Smith (eds.),* Human Rights in Turmoil, *pp. 163-180.*

*ISBN 90 04 15432 9.*

ing how the world is constructed sociologically and how it is given meaning. It is, as Åkerstrøm Andersen has explained, a second-order enquiry rather than a first-order enquiry (Åkerstrøm 1999, p. 12). Therefore, it is not the aim of this chapter to say anything about what state sovereignty really is (first-order enquiry), or to define which activities ought to be categorised as humanitarian interventions. Instead, it will analyse how researchers in International Relations, representatives of international organisations and political leaders speak and give meaning to state sovereignty and intervention (second-order enquiry).

This chapter is divided into three sections and has three principal arguments. The first section examines how state sovereignty and intervention are conceptually linked. The second section analyses how humanitarian interventions have been legitimised in recent years. Analytically, the chapter distinguishes between three different strategies which have been used to legitimise humanitarian intervention: genocide, crimes against humanity and gross violations of human rights. Each of these strategies has different discursive effects, but they all have in common the fact that they refer to an inviolable sovereign subject. The analysis is primarily based on how NATO's intervention in Kosovo in 1999 was justified, but it also draws on examples from interventions in Bosnia and northern Iraq in 1998. These three ways of legitimising interventions is often discussed in the form of a dilemma or conflict between the principles of human rights and state sovereignty. The third section of the chapter, however, argues that humanitarian interventions should not just be viewed as a deviation from the principle of state sovereignty, but that legitimisations of interventions also give (new) meaning to what it means to be a sovereign state and underline the continued importance of the principle of state sovereignty. In this way, the chapter also points to the growing importance of human rights in the international sphere, not in the sense of being a substitute for – or a competing principle to – state sovereignty, but as one of the defining elements of what it means to be a legitimate sovereign state today.

## 1. State Sovereignty and Intervention

This section will first describe how state sovereignty and intervention are mutually dependent concepts. Secondly, it will demonstrate how state sovereignty and intervention function as a binary pair, and how this relationship necessitates that interventions are legitimised. Legitimations of interventions presuppose that interventions are problematic and abnormal events in international politics which demand justifications and explanations, whereas state sovereignty is perceived as a part of the good and normal affairs of international politics which does not require any further explanation. The analysis is based on a reading of the International Relations literature as a particular discourse. This discourse is not, however, limited to scholars of International Relations; it is also (re)produced by state officials, diplomats and international organisations.

How are intervention and state sovereignty linked conceptually? According to conventional thinking in International Relations, state sovereignty and intervention function as opposing concepts, in that intervention is defined as a *violation of state sovereignty* (see, e.g., Vincent 1974; Little 1975; Bull 1984; Akehurst 1984; Jackson 1990; Krasner 1993; Hoffmann 1996). According to this definition, intervention is derived from state sovereignty. This means that studies of intervention often come to assume – although often implicitly – the meaning and existence of state sovereignty. In order to define or identify something as an intervention, state sovereignty must already be assumed. Without state sovereignty, it seems impossible to speak of an intervention, since who would then be the object of the intervention, and what would be violated or transgressed (Weber 1995; Malmvig 2002; Malmvig 2006). The concept of state sovereignty thus becomes the starting point for any understanding of the concept of intervention. As Ramsbotham and Woodhouse paradigmatically put it: 'To approach the classical debate about forcible humanitarian intervention, the natural place to begin is with the core concept of state sovereignty (Ramsbotham and Woodhouse 1996, p. 33).'

The relationship, however, goes both ways. Just as the conceptual meaning of intervention depends upon state sovereignty and can only be understood against the backdrop of the latter, so the meaning of state sovereignty depends on the concept of intervention. Interventions are one of the international acts or practices that give meaning and content to state sovereignty (Weber 1995). Interventions demarcate the line between what is considered an internal affair which falls within the realm of state sovereignty and what is considered to be an international affair that falls outside a state's sovereignty. In other words, when the international community, the UN or a certain government is justifying a specific intervention as a humanitarian one, these international actors are at the same time constructing what it means to be a legitimate sovereign state. They are establishing – although only temporarily – a specific understanding of the authorities, rights and competencies that should belong to a sovereign state (Weber 1995; Malmvig 2006).

State sovereignty and intervention are not just mutually dependent; the two concepts also function as a binary pair (Derrida 1978). That is to say, the relationship between them is characterised by a series of dichotomies, such as 'up/down', 'normal/abnormal', 'peaceful/dangerous' and 'order/disorder'. State sovereignty supposedly resides on the side of the 'normal and good' of this binary pair, while intervention is viewed as an abnormal, problematic and potentially dangerous action, which threatens international order and demands explanation and legitimation.

Why is state sovereignty predominantly perceived as a good thing and as part of the normal international political order? Primarily, this is because the principle of state sovereignty is presumed to guarantee – even to be synonymous with – national and international order. Within the two main schools of thought in International Relations – (neo)realism and idealism/liberalism – the main emphasis is on the importance of *internal order* and hierarchy, that is, the authority and monopoly of the means of violence which the state possesses internally with respect to its citizens. In the absence of internal sovereignty, it is presumed that civil war, instability and violence will erupt, a state of anarchy, of a war of all against all, as Hobbes described it in his *Leviathan*. In other words, state sovereignty is seen as a fundamental good because it is assumed to ensure peace and order inside the state's territorial borders (see also Banks and Shaw 1991; Bartelson 1995).

But state sovereignty is also presumed to be a guarantee of *international order*. According to the English school, state sovereignty – and especially its counterpart, the principle of non-intervention – is viewed as a necessary condition for peace and order (see, e.g., Vincent 1974, pp. 40 ff.; Bull 1977; Wight 1977; Brems Knudsen 1999).[1] The norm of non-intervention guarantees states' right to self-determination and formal equality, and protects each individual state against interference from outside powers. Without the norm of non-intervention, it is presumed that cooperation between states would be much more difficult and that war and instability would occur much more frequently.

Given this understanding of the many benefits of state sovereignty and the principle of non-intervention, intervention is in general viewed as a risky, dangerous and exceptional action in International Relations. It is seen as a practice which in the long run may undermine both national and international order, thereby leading to more violence and suffering than the intervening states or the international community sought to combat in the first place (DUPI 1999, p. 114). To simplify somewhat, one might say that interventions are seen as undermining because they have the potential to diminish a state's and its nation's independence, while also violating that state's sovereign right to protect its own people and to define the moral and political values that apply internally.[2]

This widespread conception of the relationship between state sovereignty and intervention means that interventions are perceived as exceptional international actions that require their own special form of justification. It also means that when international actors legitimise a particular intervention, they come to reproduce this understanding of sovereignty as belonging to the good and normal state of affairs, and of interventions as being exceptional and dangerous. In other words, the process of legitimising intervention presupposes that state sovereignty is part of normal political life among states, and that interventions are problematic actions that require justification. If this conception were not presumed – at least implicitly – then there would be no need at all to justify interventions. As Parekh has argued:

> The very concept of intervention would not make any sense, and the need to justify it would not arise, unless states were assumed to be sovereign and entitled to immunity from external interference. Justifying intervention on strictly humanitarian grounds alone also makes sense only on such an assumption. (Parekh 1997, p. 56)

This implies, moreover, that the legitimisation of interventions always contains a paradox. On the one hand, any legitimisation of intervention will inherently rec-

1 In this sense there is a certain circularity to this argument, since international order, like the principles of non-intervention and state sovereignty, is thought to guarantee order in sovereign states.

2 As Stanley Hoffmann describes it, "In a world of sovereign states, sovereignty protects one against outsiders trying to topple the government, or to set up a puppet regime or to impose their views of what is good and right" (Hoffmann 1996, p. 19).

ognise the principle of state sovereignty as a necessary and essential part of international relations, otherwise there would be no need to legitimise the action in the first place. On the other hand, intervention is also defined as a violation and transgression of state sovereignty. Intervention is, at one and the same time, a violation and a recognition of the principle of state sovereignty.

## 2 Defying the Normal Political Logic: Three Legitimisation Strategies

> Since genocide is almost always committed with the connivance, if not the direct participation of state authorities, it is hard to see how it could be prevented without intervening in a state's internal affairs. (UN General Secretary Kofi Annan, Ditchley Park, UK, 26.06.1998)

As explained above, the legitimisation of interventions contributes to the construction of state sovereignty as part of good and normal political life, and the conception of interventions as problematic actions that violate that normality and therefore necessitate justification.

But which events or acts can legitimise a transgression or disregard of state sovereignty? Interventions can, in principle, be legitimised in innumerable ways, and they have historically been justified by a wide variety of strategies. Cynthia Weber, for example, has investigated how interventions during the last two hundred years have been based upon widely divergent conceptions of what it means to be a sovereign state. At the beginning of the 1800s, interventions were legitimised by reference to such considerations as ensuring the European monarchies' safety against popular uprisings and revolutions, while at the beginning of the 1900s it was a people's right and will to be democratically represented that often were used to legitimise them (Weber 1995). Martha Finnemore has similarly shown how the meaning of humanitarian intervention has changed over time, because the definition and understanding of what it means to be 'human' and part of humanity have changed historically. Thus, at the beginning of the 1800s it was only white Christians who were considered to be part of humanity: the protection of blacks and slaves, for example, was not perceived to be a sufficient ground for humanitarian intervention. It was only with the wave of de-colonisation in the middle of the twentieth century that 'the West/White Christians' began to understand the concept of 'humanity' in more universal terms (Finnemore 1996, p. 155). The issue of what constitutes a humanitarian intervention and what counts as a sufficient ground for intervention are thus not independent of time and place. Every time and place will have its own understanding of the type of arguments that are considered valid and authoritative (Malmvig 2006).

If we look at how recent interventions in Kosovo, Bosnia or northern Iraq have been legitimised, it is striking how the intervening states did *not* refer to national security interests, insist on territorial demands, or appeal to military strength and status in order to legitimise the use of force. These interventions were instead justified with reference to their humanitarian purpose and necessity.

Analytically one can distinguish between three discursive strategies with which humanitarian interventions were legitimised in the 1990s. 'Strategy' should in this context be understood not as an intentional act or a cynical plan which state representatives apply in order to convince their populations of the validity of an intervention, but rather as a particular manner of combining and assigning meaning to certain subjects, concepts and objects (Foucault 1972). Each of these strategies presumes the existence of a sovereign and inviolable subject: 1) the 'crimes against humanity' strategy is based on an understanding of *humanity* as a sovereign subject; 2) 'genocide' is based on an understanding of the *nation* or a *people* as sovereign subjects; and 3) 'gross and massive violations of human rights' is based on the *individual* as a sovereign subject.

These three strategies are all powerful ways of legitimising an intervention,[3] as they all demand and necessitate some kind of action and response. They all serve to make action imperative. It appears obvious that 'something must be done' when crimes against humanity, genocide or gross violations of human rights take place.[4] In other words, it is very difficult not to 'do something' when these three strategies are invoked. One might say that each of these strategies *in and of itself* acts as a justification. They do not require further argumentation, but constitute their own reasoning.[5] This was clear, for example, with respect to the intervention in Kosovo. In that case, Western governments argued that 'we' must act (intervene), that the situation in Kosovo left the international community with no other choice when a people's basic rights and identity were being violated.

> Can the outside world simply stand by when a rogue state brutally abuses the basic rights of those it governs? Allow ethnic cleansing or stop it. That remains the choice. (Tony Blair, 17.05.1999, Atlanta)[6]
>
> After witnessing Milosovic's thugs who were massing to unleash an ethnic slaughter once again on the people of Kosovo, we knew we would not sit on the sidelines of history and remain indifferent to cruelty and misery being inflicted. We had no choice but to act. (U.S. Secretary Cohen, 25.05.1999)

---

3 Ethnic cleansing is, in this context, similar to genocide, but it is not codified in international law and is not nearly so closely associated with the Holocaust (see also Malmvig 2002).

4 Lene Hansen has likewise argued in connection with genocide that "constructing a situation as constituting genocide situates it in a special realm. It constructs it as something 'we' should not allow to let happen ... genocide overrides, in short, all other considerations" (Hansen 1998, p. 167).

5 This explains correspondingly why, when reasons are given for why the international community ought to become involved or utilise intervention, an effort is often made to avoid references to genocide or crimes against humanity. By way of example, Campbell (1998a, p. 99-109), Hansen (1998) and Kuusisto (1999) have shown how the USA in particular avoided speaking of the war in Bosnia in terms of genocide.

6 Unless otherwise specified, all quotations come from the United States Information Agency.

Although crimes against humanity, genocide and human rights violations in and of themselves legitimise and necessitate an international reaction, it is certainly not given which type of international action should be set in motion. As it often has been pointed out in the literature on humanitarian interventions, gross violations of human rights and brutal oppression have occurred in many places across the world without leading the international community to intervene. In that sense, 'crimes against humanity', 'genocide' and 'human rights violations' are not magic words and phrases. There is no simple causal or lineal relationship between the three strategies and the type of response that international actors set in motion. For example, it was far from certain how the international community would react with respect to the conflicts in Kosovo and Bosnia at the beginning of the 1990s. The fact that the international community in the end carried out humanitarian interventions in both conflicts should also be attributed to those defining discursive battles – preceding the interventions in 1995 and 1999 – over what was 'actually occurring' in Bosnia and Kosovo and how the international community should and could react (see, e.g., Campbell 1998; Hansen 1998).[7] In both cases, one of the decisive factors was the ability to determine that all peaceful means and solutions had been exhausted (Malmvig 2002). Therefore, it is only to the extent that intervention is perceived as the only remaining course of action – and thus becomes identical with action – that the three strategies make it obvious that military intervention must be undertaken.

What makes these three legitimisation strategies so powerful? How can they justify an action that is usually seen as illegitimate in international relations? In general terms, this is due to the fact that they construct and build upon an absolute conceptualisation of the three subjects' nature and status. As explained above, humanity, peoples and individuals are all perceived as having inviolable and sovereign identities, which makes crimes against humanity, genocide and human rights violations absolute wrongs. In other words, it is the three subjects' existence and integrity that is violated in cases of genocide, crimes against humanity, and human rights violations. Because of the presumption that these three subjects possess a predetermined and inviolable identity, therefore, violations of their identities must be prevented. Thus, it can be argued that the logic of these three strategies functions in the same manner as the logic connecting state sovereignty and intervention. Intervention is perceived as a violation of a state's sovereignty – i.e. the state's identity – while human rights violations, genocide and crimes against humanity are perceived as violations of an individual's, a people's or humanity's sovereign identity.

The three strategies are not, however, equally powerful, since they produce different types of responsibility, scope and identity with respect to the different subjects. The sections below will briefly sketch out how the three strategies are distinguishable from each other. The aim is to describe the discursive rules that apply to each of the three strategies and to show their different political effects. It must

7 Prior to 1994, Bosnia was seen primarily as a civil/ethnic war rather than a case of ethnic cleansing or genocide.

be emphasised, however, that it is neither the legal definition nor the underlying humanitarian law that I wish to shed light upon here, but rather the way in which the three strategies have been used and granted meaning in relation to the political legitimisation of interventions in the 1990s. It should also be added that although the three strategies are analytically distinct and operate differently, they are often used simultaneously. During the Kosovo intervention, for example, they were all used to justify NATO's intervention. At an analytical level, therefore, it is appropriate to differentiate between the three strategies, though in practice they will often overlap and be closely linked to each other.

## 3 The Three Strategies

### *3.1 Construction of Responsible Subjects*

The first distinction that can be drawn between the three strategies concerns who is being referred to as the responsible actor and perpetrator of a violation. All three strategies are in this regard dependent on the identification of a responsible subject behind the act. This actor can, in principle, take many different forms and may be constructed in multiple ways. Thus, one can speak of both individual actors and collective actors. *Who* is assigned responsibility naturally has important implications, since a line can accordingly be drawn between guilty and innocent, good and evil, victim and perpetrator.[8] The establishment of responsibility also enables the intervening states to align themselves on the side of the 'innocent ' and the 'victims' while directing the intervention against the 'perpetrators' or 'evil'. These dichotomies, for instance, played an important role with respect to the intervention in Kosovo.

> It is important to remember that we have no quarrels with the Serbian people ... in a sense they are victims of this tragedy too. (President Clinton, 15.04.1999)

> Nato's objective is not to harm innocent Serbs, but to stop the attacks in Kosovo. (US Secretary of State Albright, 25.03.1999)

> We have no fight with the Serbian people and it has now been made very clear that their leadership is, as the indictment says, responsible for these heinous crimes. (US Secretary of State Albright, 27.05.1999)

8 In the case of civil war or humanitarian catastrophe, however, it is much more difficult to use these binary codes. As Campbell, for one, has argued, the conflicts in Bosnia, Rwanda, Chechnya, Somalia and Sudan were all characterised by difficulties in drawing clear lines between "good" and "evil", "victim" and "perpetrator" (Campbell 1998b). The same was equally true in connection with the massacres in Algeria in the 1990s (see Malmvig 2002).

This attribution of responsibility made it possible to discuss NATO's intervention in terms of an action directed against the Serbian leaders – primarily Milosovic – rather than the Serbian people, who instead were referred to as innocent. As the Defence Minister of Germany at the time put it, 'We are not fighting against the Serbian people, we are fighting against the last dictator in Europe' (Rudolph Scharping, 24.05.1999).

This form of individualisation of responsibility was also applied in relation to the US's and the UK's legitimation of the intervention in northern Iraq in 1998. Here, Saddam Hussein – just like Milosovic – was referred to as the actor truly responsible for the oppression in Iraq, in contrast to the Iraqi people, who were viewed as innocent and repressed. During the civil war and ethnic cleansing in Bosnia, however, the responsibility was primarily placed with a collective actor. Here, blame and responsibility were often ascribed to entire ethnic groups, in particular to the Bosnian Serbs.

While political and/or moral responsibility can be placed with collective actors – such as a nation, an ethnic group or a religious group – responsibility in the legal sense requires individualisation (Foucault 1995, p. 245). Only individuals are subject to prosecution and can be brought before a court of law (Dillon 1998, p. 550). This means that when international law is used as a reference point, the range of possible actors to whom responsibility can be assigned becomes narrower. There is often a certain tension, therefore, between political and legal responsibility, as is reflected in the following quotes regarding the Kosovo intervention.

> As for Yugoslav President Milosevic he is *politically* responsible for the atrocities in Kosovo. (James Rubin, 07.04.1999)

> A data base of individual names is being created, but overall responsibility for what is going on in Kosovo reaches back to the political and military leadership in Belgrade – specifically, Yugoslav President Slobodan Milosovic. (US Amb. Scheffer, 25.05.1999)

During the intervention in Kosovo, Western leaders argued that legal responsibility should be assigned to specific individuals, while overarching political responsibility should be assigned to the government in Belgrade.

In relation to human rights violations, however, another type of logic applies. Human rights violations can rarely be traced back to a specific individual, but more often are considered to be the responsibility of states and their governments (Campbell 1998b). It is presumed, as a rule – both politically and legally – to be the state which has the responsibility for supervising and controlling what goes on within its own territory, as well as the responsibility to protect its own citizens. When a people are subjected to gross violations of human rights, it is therefore states and governments who are accused and judged, rather than single individuals.

### 3.2 *Intentionality and Extent*

The other distinction that can be drawn between the three strategies concerns how widespread the violation is, the intention behind it, and the degree to which it is planned and systematic. As described above, all three strategies presume that the violation can be traced back to a responsible actor. There must be, in other words, someone who has intended the result: it should not be the unintentional consequence of other events such as natural disasters or war. The intent behind the act is also given a prominent position in the Convention on Genocide: 'genocide means any of the following acts committed with intent to destroy, in whole or in part, a national, ethnical, racial or religious group' (DUPI 1999, p. 111). When reference is made to crimes against humanity or genocide, therefore, it is a prerequisite that the systematic and intentional nature of the acts can be established. The importance given to intention and planning was also very visible with respect to NATO's legitimation of the intervention in Kosovo:

> We are witnessing the largest forced deportation in Europe since the time of Hitler and Stalin. This exodus is not the result of spontaneous acts of brutality. It was planned in Belgrade and is co-ordinated from Belgrade. (Robin Cook, 19.04.1999, House of Commons)

> Nine of every ten Kosovar Albanians have now been driven from their homes, thousands murdered, at least 100,000 missing ... over 5,000 cities torched. All this has been carried out, you must understand, according to a plan carefully designed months earlier in Belgrade. (President Clinton, 14.05.1999)

In political discourse, however, it is also seems as if a certain scale or systematisation is demanded in order to refer to violations in terms of genocide. As David Campbell has pointed out, this proviso of scale and systematisation is not part of international law; but genocide is for many closely tied to the history of the Holocaust and the systematic mass murders of Nazi Germany. That is to say, "Holocaust's uniqueness determines for many what counts and does not count as genocide" (Campbell 1998a, p. 101).

Reference to violations of human rights, however, does not require that the violation is premeditated or carried out on a large scale. Human rights violations can be arbitrary and few in number, and are not associated with the experiences of the Holocaust in the same way as ethnic cleansing and genocide. Human rights violations are, as it were, easier to neglect or to turn into less significant kinds of violations, which do not necessitate an international reaction or response.

But by referring to *gross and massive* violations of human rights, such violations can become more serious infringements which border on crimes against humanity and therefore also require international measures and action. For example, UN Secretary General Kofi Annan stressed, in relation to the intervention in Kosovo, that gross and systematic breaches of human rights demanded that the international community become involved: 'We have learnt that the world cannot stand aside when gross and systematic violations of human rights are taking place' (Annan, 19.09.99). When a French government diplomat justified the British, French and American bombings of northern Iraq in 1998, he similarly argued that violations of human rights may be so extensive that they constitute crimes against humanity: 'Violations of human rights become a matter of international interest when they take on such proportions that they assume the dimension of crimes against humanity' (quoted in Brems Knudsen 1999, p. 180).

### 3.3 *Difference and Identity*

The third element that differentiates the three strategies from one another concerns who is constructed as a victim – and thus as an object – of the three types of violation. As mentioned in the introduction, genocide constructs people as objects of violations, crimes against humanity constructs humanity as an object, and human rights violations constructs individuals as objects of violations. Thus, with respect to all three strategies, people, humanity and the individual are taken to constitute sovereign subjects whose particular identities are to be protected and kept intact.

Which specific identity these three subjects is ascribed is, however, decisive for how forcefully a humanitarian intervention can be legitimised. Generally speaking, the three types of subject may be seen as either different from or similar to the intervening states. If the subject of violations is articulated as being 'like us' or as a part of 'us' – that is, the states leading the intervention – the violations can be seen not just as attacks on a particular group's identity, but also as attacks on 'our' existence and values. During the Kosovo intervention, for example, it was often emphasised that the Kosovar Albanians were just like 'us', and that if 'we' failed to react against the atrocities committed against the Kosovar Albanians, 'we' would lose a part of our (human) selves.

> Behind these images is a reality of people no different in their fundamental rights or humanity than you and me. (US Secretary of State Albright, 20.04.99.)

> We ourselves become less human when we do not respond to human misery or do not raise our voices in protest to atrocities and crimes against humanity. (Clinton, 14.05.99)

Since the idea of crimes against humanity presupposes that humanity as a whole is (symbolically) violated, such acts can be articulated as attacks against everyone, in contrast to genocide or human rights violations that are perceived as infringements against particular peoples or individuals . As the former American President Clinton explained in the quotation above, we become less human if we do not act against crimes against humanity. In this sense, it can be argued that crimes against humanity will support the use of armed force by the international community – or a particular group of countries – in order to stop such crimes to a greater extent than will references to genocide or violations of human rights.

However, a given group of individuals or people can also be represented as having the same characteristics and values as the intervening states. In that case, references to genocide or to violations of human rights can appear to be ways of legitimising an intervention that are equally powerful as crimes against humanity. Lene Hansen has shown, for instance, in her analysis of the intervention in Bosnia, how Bosnia was articulated – in one of the dominant Western discourses – as part of Europe and the European 'Self'. Intervening against the ethnic cleansing thus also became a question of protecting 'our' own identity and future (Hansen 1998). Cynthia Weber has similarly shown, in her historical analysis of interventions and state sovereignty, how the intervening actors often ascribe the same desires, aspirations and characteristics to the people of the target state as those of the intervening actors. This may enable those intervening, among other things, to claim that they represent and speak on behalf of the oppressed people in that state (Weber 1995).

In relation to the legitimisation of the Kosovo intervention, both strategies were employed. On the one hand, the oppression and persecution of the Kosovar Albanians was constructed as an affront to the integrity of the whole of humanity, and therefore to all of 'us'. On the other hand, the conflict was also articulated as the violation of a particular ethnic group's rights, identity and existence. The Kosovar Albanians were not, however, viewed as being radically different from the Western NATO states. On the contrary, Western government leaders and commentators often emphasised that the Kosovar Albanians had the same values of freedom, tolerance and democracy as the Western states (Malmvig 2002). This representation of the identity of the Kosovar Albanians thus stood in stark contrast to the way in which the various ethnic groups in the Balkans had been described and characterised by the West only a few years earlier. At the beginning of the 1990s, it was not unusual for politicians, academics and commentators to refer to the ethnic groups in the Balkans as inherently barbaric, violent or driven by a special kind of intolerant nationalism (Campbell 1998; Hansen 1998). Preceding the NATO-led intervention in Kosovo, however, much was done to change these earlier images and representations of the Balkan peoples. The US president, for instance, stressed that earlier demonisations of the Balkan countries had been used as excuses for not intervening much earlier in the conflict, and that the West should now acknowledge that the Balkan peoples were also capable of living in a civilised and peaceful manner:

> And we do no favours to ourselves … when we justify looking away from this kind of slaughter by oversimplifying and conveniently, in our own way, demonising the whole of the Balkans by saying that these people are simply incapable of civilised behaviour with one another. (President Clinton, 14.05.99)

In sum, recent legitimisations of humanitarian interventions have been based on and have furthered the idea of the individual, the people or humanity as sovereign and inviolable subjects, whose existence and integrity the international community must protect and uphold. Genocide, crimes against humanity and gross violations of human rights constitute three different strategies, each of which provides powerful legitimisation for why the intervening states need to use exceptional means to stop violations and infringements. As demonstrated above, the three strategies can be seen as distinct strategies in that they refer to different types of identity, different responsible actors and different degrees of planning and extent. Yet all three strategies presume that the subjects in question have a fixed and inviolable sovereign identity. They all share the idea of human sovereignty.

This means, as I shall spell out below, that when interventions are legitimised with reference to the principle of human sovereignty, they appear to conflict with the principle of state sovereignty. Humanitarian interventions are therefore often debated in terms of an irresolvable dilemma.

## 4 An Irresolvable Dilemma?

> States are now widely understood to be the servants of their peoples, and not vice versa. At the same time, individual *sovereignty* – and by this I mean the human rights and fundamental freedoms enshrined in our charter – has been enhanced by a renewed consciousness of the right of every individual to control his or her destiny. (Kofi Annan in Financial Times, 10.01.2000, italics added)

In general the conflict between the principle of state sovereignty and the principle of human sovereignty is discussed in terms of a zero-sum game or an irresolvable dilemma. Either the international community must accept that humanitarian interventions violate the principle of state sovereignty, or the international community must accept that human sovereignty is violated through acts of genocide, crimes against humanity or gross violations of human rights.

Ideally, however, these two primary foundations of modern enlightenment thought – the sovereign human being and the sovereign state – are not taken to be in conflict. Rather, the sovereign state is thought to be a precondition for the sovereign individual (Ashley 1995, p. 110; Bartelson 1995). As Kofi Annan also points out in the quotation cited above, the sovereign state should ideally be the guarantor and protector of peoples and individuals. However, when a state commits gross violations and crimes against its own citizens, a conflict arises between these two sovereign foundations. This means that the intervening actors must choose to protect either the principle of state sovereignty or the principle of human sovereignty. But both choices entail equally unfortunate consequences, hence giving rise to the dilemma.

This well-known dilemma has been a focal point of much of the literature on humanitarian interventions (Bull 1984; Lyons and Mastunduno 1995b; Hoffmann 1996; Ramsbotham and Woodhouse 1996; Parekh 1997; DUPI 1999; ICISS 2001). It was also at the centre of the academic debates on the Kosovo intervention's legitimacy and legality. NATO's intervention in Kosovo illustrated in a nutshell the dilemmas and divisions the international community faces with respect to humanitarian interventions (Simma 1999; Guichard 1999; Cassese 1999; Pharo 2000).

On the one hand, very few questioned whether the international community should hinder ethnic cleansing in Kosovo and thus prevent a repetition of those atrocities which the international community had witnessed in Bosnia just a few years earlier. On the other hand, there was no UN mandate for the intervention or the use of force, and many feared that NATO's intervention would set a dangerous precedent for the future, thus undermining the principle of non-intervention and the international order in the long run.

Opponents and those sceptical of NATO's intervention therefore pointed out that humanitarian justifications can easily be misused by powerful states that are primarily concerned with their own national interest. By setting aside the principle of non-intervention for the sake of humanitarian concerns, we risk producing more war and disorder in the long term and undermining less powerful states' rights to decide their own national and political affairs. In short, opponents of the Kosovo intervention pointed to the benefits and advantages of the principles of state sovereignty and non-intervention.

Supporters of NATO's intervention, conversely, argued that the principle of non-intervention should not justify the international community sitting passively by while thousands of people were being violently repressed and killed. As one scholar, for instance, asked: 'Should one sit idly by and watch thousands of human beings being slaughtered or brutally persecuted ... only because the existing body of international law proves incapable of remedying such a situation?' (Cassese 1999). The Danish Minister of Foreign Affairs at the time likewise emphasised that the principle of state sovereignty should not be seen as a carte blanche or shield behind which dictatorial regimes could carry out gross violations of human rights, without the international community intervening (Helveg Pedersen, Chatham House, 17.02.2000).

In other words, both supporters and opponents of the intervention in Kosovo seemed to be caught in a zero-sum game, where they were proposing to disregard the rights and integrity of either sovereign states or sovereign individuals.

This dilemma between the individual and the state, order and justice, law and morality, has in many ways paralysed the debate about state sovereignty and humanitarian interventions. When humanitarian interventions are discussed in terms of a dilemma, it is assumed from the outset that we are in an either/or situation. Humanitarian interventions are represented as a definite choice in favour of human sovereignty at the expense of state sovereignty.

Yet, as described in the first part of this chapter, intervention is also one of the international practices which help to define the limits and meaning of what it means to be a sovereign state, as well as a sovereign individual, people or humanity. Thus, although humanitarian interventions are legitimised with reference to the integrity and sovereignty of humans – in the form of individuals, peoples or humanity – this type of humanitarian justification should not only be seen as an erosion or undermining of the principle of state sovereignty.

Intervention is also a practice – albeit a paradoxical one – that grants meaning to state sovereignty. Intervention is at the same time a violation of the state sovereignty principle, one of those international actions that contributes to constructing and re-constructing the definition of state sovereignty. By legitimising intervention, the intervening actors simultaneously reproduce the principle of state sovereignty as an essential part of the international order and violate that very same principle. In so far as much of the literature and recent debates on humanitarian interventions interpret interventions as a sign that the principle of state sovereignty is becoming increasingly obsolete, they manage to overlook the paradox and meaning-producing significance of humanitarian interventions.

## 5 Conclusion

This chapter began by questioning respectively the (neo)realist and idealist/liberalist understandings of the relationship between state sovereignty and intervention. In the idealist/liberalist version, interventions are predominantly seen as a sign that the state-based world order is about to change, and that humanitarian values can potentially replace the notion of national interests. In the (neo)realist version, however, humanitarian interventions are not seen as practices that have altered the international order noticeably. States are still the main actors in the international system, and it is they who first and foremost take care of their own people's security and interest.

However, this chapter has offered a third perspective, arguing that interventions both reproduce the importance of state sovereignty and at the same time are one of those international practices that are contributing to a (re)definition of what it means to be a sovereign state. This implies that intervention can be seen as a particular type of international practice which draws a line between what can legitimately be considered an internal affair and what should be considered an international affair, which rights and competencies a state has and which it does not have, under what circumstances a state can legitimately be said to represent its people's will and values, and when it does not. In other words, humanitarian interventions do not necessarily undermine state sovereignty in favour of human sovereignty, but rather help to create a particular conceptualisation of what it means to be a sovereign state today. This conception has – as Cynthia Weber and Martha Finnemore, among others, have pointed out – changed historically; and one of the ways in which the conception of state sovereignty has changed is precisely through interventions and the public debates which follow in their wake (Weber 1995; Finnemore 1996 and 2003).

In this sense, it can be said that neither the (neo)realist nor the idealist/liberalist perspective fully encompasses the contradictions and changes that are at play with respect to humanitarian interventions. Even though the idea of the sovereign and inviolable state is not about to disappear (the realist view), it is nevertheless clear that humanitarian interventions are contributing to changing the state-based international order (the idealist/liberalist view). This change does not mean that state sovereignty is about to wither away and disappear, but that the meaning of state sovereignty has changed. Today, state sovereignty is also understood to be a question of the state having to respect basic human rights and humanitarian values if it wants to avoid sanctions and reprisals or, in the final instance, immediate intervention. In this way, human rights have emerged as one of the defining characteristics of legitimate statehood today.

### References

Akehurst, Michael, 'Humanitarian Intervention', in Bull, Hedley (ed.), *Intervention in World Politics*, Oxford, Clarendon Press, pp. 95-118, 1984.

Ashley, Richard, 'The Powers of Anarchy: Theory, Sovereignty, and the Domestication of Global Life', in Der Derian, James (ed.), *International Theory: Critical Investigations*, London, Macmillan, pp. 94-129, 1995.

Bartelson, Jens, *A Genealogy of Sovereignty*, Cambridge, Cambridge University Press, 1995.

Brown, C., *International Relations Theory. New Normative issues.* Hertfordshire, Harvester Wheatsheaf, 1992.

Brown, C., 'Human Rights', in Baylis, J & Steve Smith (eds.), *The Globalization of World Politics*, Oxford, Oxford University Press, pp. 469-482, 1998.

Bull, Hedley, *The Anarchical Society: A Study of Order in World Politics*, London, MacMillan Press, 1977.

Bull, Hedley, *Intervention in World Politics*, Oxford, Oxford University Press, 1984a.

Bull, Hedley and Adam Watson, *The Expansion of International Society*, Oxford, Oxford University Press, 1984b.

Campbell, David, *National Deconstruction. Violence, Identity and Justice in Bosnia*, Minneapolis, University of Minnesota Press, 1998a.

Campbell, David, 'Why Fight: Humanitarianism, Principles, and Post-structuralism', *Millennium*, 27, 3, pp. 497-521, 1998b.

Charvet, John, 'The Idea of State Sovereignty and the Right of Humanitarian Intervention', *International Political Science Review*, 18, 1, pp. 39-48, 1997.

Constantinou, Costas, 'Before the Summit: Representations of Sovereignty on the Himalayas', *Millennium*, 27, 1, pp. 23-53, 1998.

Danish Institute of International Affairs (DUPI), *Humanitarian Intervention: Legal and Political Aspects*, Gullanders Bogtrykkeri Skjern for DUPI, Copenhagen, 1999.

Derrida, Jacques, *Writing and Difference*, London, Routledge, 1978.

Derrida, Jacques, *Politics of Friendship*, London & New York, Verso, 1997.

Dillon, Michael, 'Criminalising Violence Internationally', *Millennium*, 27, 3, pp. 543-567, 1998.

Finnemore, Martha, 'Constructing Norms of Humanitarian Intervention', in Katzenstein, Peter (ed.), *The Culture of National Security: Norms and Identity in World Politics*, New York, Colombia University Press, pp. 153-185, 1996.

Foucault, Michel, *The Archaeology of Knowledge and the Discourse on Language*, New York, Panthenon Books, 1972.

Foucault, Michel, *Discipline and Punish. The Birth of the Prison*, New York, Vintage Books, 1995.

Foucault, Michel, 'Governmentality', *Ideology and Consciousness*, 6, 1979.

Foucault, Michel, *The Order of Things: An Archaeology of the Human Sciences*, London, Routledge, 1991.

Giddens, Anthony, *Nation State and Violence. Volume Two of a Contemporary Critique of Historical Materialism*, Cambridge, Polity Press, 1985.

Hansen, Lene, *Western Villains Or Balkan Barbarism? Representations and Responsibility in the Debate over Bosnia*, Copenhagen, Institute of Political Science, 1998.

Hinsley, F. H., *Sovereignty*, Cambridge, Cambridge University Press, 1986.

Hoffmann, Stanley, 'The Problem of Intervention', in Bull, Hedley (ed.), *Intervention in World Politics*, Oxford: Clarendon Press, pp. 7-28, 1984.

Hoffmann, Stanley, *Janus and Minerva, Essays in the Theory and Practice of International Politics*, Westview, Boulder, 1993.

Hoffmann, Stanley, *The Ethics and Politics of Humanitarian Intervention*, Notre Dame, Indiana, University of Notre Dame Press, 1996.

ICISS, *The Responsibility to Protect: Report of the International Commission on Intervention and State Sovereignty*, 2001.

Jackson, Robert, *Quasi-States: Sovereignty, International Relations, and The Third World*, Cambridge, Cambridge University Press, 1990.

James, Allan, *Sovereign Statehood: The Basis of International Society*, London, Allen and Unwin, 1986.

Keohane, Robert, 'Hobbes's Dilemma and Institutional Change in World Politics: Sovereignty in International Society', in Holm, Hans-Henrik & Georg Sørensen (eds.), *Whose World Order? Uneven Globalization and the End of the Cold War*, Boulder, Westview Press, pp.165-186, 1995.

Krasner, Stephen D., 'Westphalia and All That', in Goldstein, Judith & Robert Keohane (eds.), *Ideas and Foreign Policy: Beliefs, Institutions, and Political Change*, Ithaca and London, Cornell University Press, pp. 235-264, 1993.

Linklater, A., 'The Evolving Spheres of International Justice', *International Affairs*, 75, 3, pp. 473-483, 1999.

Little, Richard, *Intervention: External Involvement in Civil Wars*, Totowa, NJ, Rowman & Little field, 1975.

Little, Richard, 'Liberal hegemony and the realist assault', in Banks, Michael & Martin Shaw (eds.), *State and Society in International Relations*, Hertfordshire, Harvester Wheatsheaf, pp. 19-38, 1991.

Lyons, Gene M. and Michael Mastanduno (eds.), *Beyond Westphalia? State Sovereignty and International Intervention*, Baltimore & London, The John Hopkins University Press, 1995a.

Lyons, Gene M. and Michael Mastanduno, 'State Sovereignty and International Intervention: reflections on the Present and Prospects for the Future', in Lyons, Gene M. and Michael Mastanduno (eds.), *Beyond Westphalia? State Sovereignty and International Intervention*, Baltimore and London, The John Hopkins University Press, pp. 250-266, 1995b.

Malmvig, Helle, *Sovereignty Intervened: Constitutions of state sovereignty during interventionary and non-interventionary practices in Kosovo and Algeria*, Copenhagen, Institute of Political Science, 2002.

Malmvig, Helle, *State Sovereignty and Intervention: A Discourse Analysis of Interventionary and Non-interventionary Practices in Kosovo and Algeria*, London, Routledge, 2006.

Morgenthau, Hans J., *Politics among Nations: The Struggle for Power and Peace*, New York, Alfred A Knopf, 1973.

Ohmae, K., *The End of the Nation State: The Rise of Regional Economics*, New York: Free Press, 1995.

Parekh, Bhikhu, 'The Dilemmas of Humanitarian Intervention: Introduction', *International Political Science Review*, 18, 1, pp. 5-7, 1997.

Piertse, Jan N., 'Sociology of Humanitarian Intervention: Bosnia, Rwanda and Somalia Compared', *International Political Science Review*, 18, 1, pp. 71-93, 1997.

Ramsbotham, Oliver, 'Humanitarian Intervention 1990-5: a Need to Reconceptualize?' *Review of International Studies*, 23, pp. 445-468, 1997.

Ramsbotham, Oliver and Tom Woodhouse, *Humanitarian Intervention in Contemporary Conflict*, Cambridge, MA, Polity Press, 1996.

Ratner, Steven and Jasner Abrams, *Accountability for Human Rights Atrocities in International Law: Beyond the Nurenberg Legacy*, Oxford, Clarendon Press, 1997.

Roht-Arriaza, Naomi, 'Institutions of International Justice', *International Affairs*, Spring, 1999.

Rosenau, James N., 'Sovereignty in a Turbulent World', in Lyons, Gene M. and Michael Mastanduno (eds.), *Beyond Westphalia? State Sovereignty and International Intervention*, Baltimore and London, The John Hopkins University Press, pp. 191-227, 1995.

Rosenau, James N., *States and Sovereignty in a Globalizing World*. 1998/1. Copenhagen, DUPI, 1998.

Ruggie, John Gerard, 'Territoriality and Beyond: Problematizing Modernity in International Relations', *International Organization*, 47, 1, pp. 139-174, 1993.

Sieff, Michelle and Leslie Wright, 'Reconciling Order and Justice? New Institutional Solutions in Post-Conflict States', *International Affairs*, Spring, 1999.

Vincent, Raymond John, *Nonintervention and International Order*, Princeton, Princeton University Press, 1974.

Walker, R. B. J., *Inside/outside: International Relations as Political Theory*, Cambridge, Cambridge University Press, 1993.

Walzer, M., *Thick and Thin: Moral Argument at Home and Abroad*, Notre Dame, University of Notre Dame Press, 1994.

Weber, Cynthia, *Simulating Sovereignty: Intervention, the State and Symbolic Exchange*, Cambridge, Cambridge University Press, 1995.

Wheeler, Marc, 'On the Hazards of Foreign Travel for Dictators and other International Criminals', *International Affairs*, 75, 3, pp. 599-619, 1999.

Wheeler, Nicholas and Justin Morris, 'Humanitarian Intervention and State Practice', in Fawn, Rick and Jeremy Larkins (eds.), *International Society after the Cold War: Anarchy and Order Reconsidered*, London, MacMillan Press, pp. 135-171, 1996.

Wight, Martin, *Systems of States*, London, Leicester University Press in association with LSE, 1977.

# 8. Manoeuvring in the Turbulent Sea of Human Rights and Religion: Religious Communities Approaching Human Rights

*Eva Maria Lassen*

## 1 A Meeting in the Summer of 1946

In May 1945, the German occupation of Denmark came to an end and the Danish Jews returned from their refuge in Sweden. A little more than a year later, the Danish Chief Rabbi, Max Friediger, went to Oxford to attend a conference organised by the Council of Christians and Jews, an organisation established during the war in reaction to the Nazi atrocities.

Upon his return from Oxford, the Chief Rabbi gave an enthusiastic account of the events he had witnessed. The main purpose of the conference, he wrote in the Jewish magazine *Jødisk Samfund* ("Jewish Society"),[1] was to discuss the burning issue: "How may the chaotic condition in which humanity lives at the moment be brought to a standstill and be replaced by love of one's neighbour?" (1946, p. 1).

The Council of Christians and Jews, he noted, agreed on the following principles as the foundation for fruitful cooperation between Christians and Jews: international laws must exist and apply to everyone; human rights must be respected and minorities protected; international cooperation between all nations must be developed and the creation of international institutions supported in order to sustain a just world peace; and within its own borders, every nation must support a just social order (1946, p. 2).

According to the Danish Chief Rabbi, the gist of the conference was that religion is the great unifier of humanity, as well as the basis for the universal acknowledgement of human rights:

> It should be religion which binds people together as well as the belief that we are all God's children ...; while acknowledging the existence of dogmatic differences between religions, humanity should be able to unite in the belief that human dignity as well as

1 Chief Rabbi Friediger, 'Verdenskonferencen af 'The Council of Christians and Jews'', *Jødisk Samfund* 15 September 1946. The quotations are my translations from the Danish.

*S. Lagoutte, H-O. Sano and P. Scharff Smith (eds.),* Human Rights in Turmoil, *pp. 181-200.*
 ISBN *90 04 15432 9.*

> human rights and duties have their origin in God as humanity's Creator…; freedom is a good which is created by God and that no human being must be deprived of." (pp. 2-4)

Also characteristic of the tone of the conference was a complete Christian denunciation of and detachment from the Holocaust: Nazism's fight against Judaism was a monstrous attack on Christianity (p. 2).

The Danish Chief Rabbi's experience of religiously based attempts to promote human rights in the immediate aftermath of the Second World War was not unique: there are many examples of religious voices being raised in the debate taking place at the time about the creation of universal human rights and about religion being seen as a positive instrument in the promotion of human rights.[2]

Today, this still applies and on a larger scale: numerous religious leaders, communities and denominations try to conceptualize human rights in the context of their religions in order to accommodate human rights or at least to formulate their understanding of them. Indeed, as will be argued in this chapter, an undercurrent of religiously anchored attempts to understand, accommodate or promote human rights, as well as a willingness to address those conflicts which exist between the religious and the human rights spheres, is having a settling influence on the otherwise turbulent sea of human rights and religion in the modern world. It will also be argued that this general undercurrent must be qualified and seen in the context of concrete situations unfolding at specific times in particular countries and regions. In this way, local variations and the political and cultural climate facing the members of particular religions in particular contexts can be taken into account.

Thus, this chapter takes a different approach than a predominant trend in public discourse – as may, for instance, be observed in the media as well as on the political stage in a number of European countries – which often emphasises the problematic nature of religious values and practices in relation to the human rights field, and which frequently presents these values and practices as being at odds with human rights. In this way, the chapter aims to supply more nuances to the complex picture of the relationship between human rights and religion. The chapter will take a modern as well as a historical perspective.

## 2 Outline

The chapter falls into two parts. Part One focuses on general tendencies in the development of the relationship between human rights and religion. Starting with a brief sketch of the pessimistic view of the role played by religion in the human rights field and the possible undermining of human rights by religious discourses and practices, the chapter moves on to present a different view – offered among others by the UN Secretary General, Kofi Annan – suggesting a much more posi-

2 See, e.g., the impact of Jewish (in the sense of "intersecting religious, cultural, ethnic, and national identities" (Cotler 1996, p. 237)) organisations in the creation of the Universal Declaration of Human Rights. Cotler 1996, p. 245 ff.

tive approach to the role of religion in the human rights sphere. The view of Kofi Annan is placed in the context of one particular construction of a historical link between religious traditions and human rights, as well as a number of significant views formulated by selected religious communities. There then follows a discussion of religious activism in support of human rights and of such dialogues between religions which have human rights as a core issue. The focus will subsequently be on some of the areas in which religious communities wish to take human rights in certain directions, which may differ from those envisioned by the mainstream human rights community. This brings us to areas of discrepancies or outright conflicts between religious traditions and human rights, and attempts by the followers and leaders of different religious traditions to deal with these conflicts. Throughout the first part of the chapter, the argument will be illustrated and supported by means of discussions of a number of important Jewish, Christian and Muslim approaches to human rights.

Part Two will focus on the particular by returning to the starting point of this chapter, namely the position of Danish Jews in the aftermath of the Second World War. We shall see how the Danish Jewish community, then the best known Danish minority, approached human rights in the post-war period, and how Danish Jews positioned human rights in the context of their particular situation.

## 3 Part One. A Modern Perspective on the General: Religious Communities Approaching Human Rights

Over the last decades, debates involving politicians, the media, scholars, religious communities and individuals have focused on the various problems that religious traditions generate for the promotion and implementation of human rights. There are many religious practices which are arguably deeply problematic to human rights, such as gender inequality, undemocratic ecclesiastical structures, difficulties linked to the right to change religion, honour killings, female circumcision and blood money – to name but a few on a very long list. These debates are, for instance, flourishing currently in a number of member states of the European Union (see Lagoutte and Lassen 2006, p. 33ff). To this should be added the claimed or actual role of religion in global problems, notably the role of Islam in international terrorism.

While these debates may sometimes paint too grim a picture, they nevertheless reflect the fact that, in a number of areas, fundamental differences exist between religious practices and human rights, and that some of these differences have the nature of conflict. What is not always evident from these debates, however, is the fact that the religious communities are very often proclaimed supporters of human rights and that they are frequently actively involved in mapping out and attempting to solve some of the problems linked to discrepancies between human rights and religious practices.

### 3.1 *Religions in Favour of Human Rights*

Human rights are a modern invention; religions go back thousands of years. Even so, there is a connection between the two phenomena, indeed a very strong one, if we are to believe the UN Secretary General, Kofi Annan:

> Human rights, properly understood and justly interpreted, are foreign to no culture and native to all nations. The principles enshrined in the Universal Declaration of Human Rights are deeply rooted in the history of humankind. They can be found in the teachings of all the world's great cultural and religious traditions [...] Tolerance and mercy have always and in all cultures been ideals of government rule and human behaviour. Today, we call these values human rights." (Statement by Secretary-General Kofi Annan on the fiftieth anniversary year of the Universal Declaration of Human Rights, 10 December 1997, the University of Tehran, Iran. Source: UN home page).

Kofi Annan's view, which is not infrequently repeated by himself and often echoed by other UN officials,[3] represents a particular reconstruction of the history of human rights. Whether it is valid as an understanding of religious traditions and the history of human rights is in itself a highly interesting question, but for the purposes of this chapter what is more significant is that representatives of world religions have to a large extent contributed themselves to the establishment of the view that human rights and religious traditions are intertwined.

Often, however, the historical link is constructed differently from the global reconstruction of Kofi Annan. Thus, we may find religious leaders who claim that their particular religion is the mother of human rights. An illustrative example of a Christian claim to the genesis of human rights is Pope John Paul II's speech to the European Court and Commission of Human Rights in 1988, in which he stated that:

> The human rights of which we are speaking draw their vigour and their effectiveness from a framework of values, the roots of which lie deep within the Christian heritage which has contributed so much to European culture. These founding values precede the positive law which gives them expression and of which they are the basis. They also precede the philosophical rationale that the various schools of thought are able to give to them.[4]

---

3 See, e.g., the opening address of the then UN Commissioner of Human Rights, Mary Robinson, at the Symposium on Human Rights in the Asia-Pacific Region, January 1998. Quoted from Robinson 1998, p. 254 f.

4 John Paul II: Address to the European Court and Commission of Human Rights, October 1988. Quoted from Filibeck 1994: 41. As the Pope's statement illustrates, the understanding of the relationship between Christianity and human rights is often linked to a perception of the human rights history, according to which the genesis of human rights can be traced back to biblical antiquity. Sometimes this understanding includes biblical as well as Greek-Roman antiquity, as in the following quotation of the Nobel Peace prize-winner, the Catholic bishop Carlos Belo of East Timor: "the Stoics … emphasised

Equally, Muslim claims to the genesis of human rights are found in the foreword to the Universal Islamic Declaration of Human Rights, adopted by the Islamic Council of Europe in 1981:

> Islam gave to mankind an ideal code of human rights fourteen centuries ago. These rights aim at conferring honour and dignity on mankind and eliminating exploitation, oppression and injustice.[5]

This declaration, as well as the Cairo Declaration on Human Rights in Islam of 1990, express a particular, conservative Islamic understanding of human rights, which in a number of areas (for instance, with regard to the family, women's rights, religious freedom, and property and inheritance rights) clash with those human rights that come across in international conventions.[6]

Finally, Jewish voices which trace human rights back to Judaism are also raised, for instance in the words of an orthodox Jew:

> Historians agree that our current standard of ethics stems from the Jewish ethic. ... Today, we are witnessing the most dramatic results of Abraham's strategy in action. ... It was only once the people of Europe began actually reading the Bible and discussing what it had to say to them, that the concepts of human rights, social responsibility, the value of life and eventually the ideal of world peace, took a front seat in civilization's progress. (Tzvi Freeman)[7]

What is important is to be aware of the following: first, a growing number of leaders of the world religions see human rights as a concept which in different ways plays an integrated role in the continuous development of their respective religions (e.g. Tergel 1998 Chapters 3-8).

Secondly, praise of human rights is frequent, echoing Pope John Paul II, who called The Universal Declaration of Human Rights "one of the most valuable and significant documents in the history of law",[8] and there have been numerous official expressions of support of human rights declared by leaders of religious denominations.

---

the dignity of all men. However, it was not until later, through the influence of Christianity, that the idea of the human dignity took root in our culture .... The concept of the human dignity of every man was thus of divine (Trinitarian and Christological) origin in Judaeo-Christian thought, or of purely moral origin in lay philosophical thought" (1998, p. 59).

5 Source: website alhewar.com/ISLAMDECL. See also Tergel 1998, p. 102.

6 For a legal overview of Islamic approaches to human rights, see Brems 2001, p. 183-94.

7 'What's so Terrible about Idolatry?' *Chabad-Lubavitch's website*, 7 December 2001.

8 John Paul II, Message to H.E. Mr Didier Opertti Badàn, President of the 53rd Session of the United Nations General Assembly. Quoted from Pontifical Council for the Family, 'The Family and Human Rights'. Source: www.vatican.va

It is, of course, very difficult to assess the extent to which statements such as that above may hide a situation where the representatives of religions pay lip service to the notion of human rights, whether for political or other purposes. Any assessment must depend on an evaluation of the concrete case. But our third point suggests that in many instances a serious consideration of human rights lies behind such praise of them:

Thirdly, it is common to see religious communities *take responsibility for the promotion of human rights*. Religious activism related to human rights takes place and has taken place at very different levels and with very different starting points. To give an example, Jewish approaches to human rights have been strongly influenced by discrimination against Jews and their persecution. Jewish groups and individuals were directly involved in or influential lobbyists during the drafting process of the Universal Declaration of Human Rights, as well as a number of other important human rights documents.[9] Historically, one of the worst human rights violations committed against Jews was the denial of their religious rights (notably by means of forced conversions), and it is often in the area of religious freedom and minority rights that Jewish organisations and individuals were active in the early days of international human rights law.[10] Jewish involvement in the promotion of human rights is to a very large extent disconnected from Judaism proper, including the Jewish religion, but in the Jewish self-perception, support for human rights has often been seen as a reflection of Jewish values, both cultural and religious (e.g. Cotler 1996, p. 236).

Clusters of denominations within the same religion work together to promote human rights. An example is the Conference of European Churches, an organisation working within Europe to promote human rights in collaboration with European and international institutions. It carries out work monitoring the United Nations, the Organisation for Security and Cooperation in Europe, the Council of Europe, and the institutions of the European Union, particularly in the area of human rights and religious freedom.[11] Similarly, Lutheran churches express joint support for human rights, notably through the Lutheran World Federation.[12] The

9 Jewish NGOs played a crucial role in the development of the Convention on the Protection and Punishment of the Crime of Genocide (1948), the International Covenant on Political and Civil Rights (1966), the International Covenant on Social, Economic and Cultural Rights (1966), and the International Convention of the Elimination of All Forms of Racial Discrimination (1965). For post-war Jewish contributions to the development of international human rights documents, see also Cotler 1996, p. 245-9.

10 Cf. Cotler (1996, p. 294): "it is arguable that it was the early internationalization of Jewish NGO advocacy around religious human rights that may have inspired the Jewish contribution to the development of international human rights law as a whole."

11 The Conference has 126 members of Orthodox, Protestant and Old Catholic denominations in Europe, a large number of which are established churches, for instance the Church of England and the Church of Sweden. For the activities of the organisation, see www.cec-kek.org.

12 For concrete initiatives of the Federation, for instance with regard to the fight against apartheid and the struggle for women's rights, see Tergel 1998, p. 259-95.

World Council of Churches is another umbrella organisation supporting human rights in concrete cases, for instance women's rights and poverty reduction.[13]

Finally, it should be mentioned that religious support for human rights works in both directions. First, the implementation of human rights can be enhanced by the support of religious communities. Secondly, the preservation of religious communities may be supported by human rights, notably freedom of religion.

### 3.2 Religions in Dialogue about Human Rights

Against the background of a world history marred by frequent religious conflicts, the fact that dialogues, whether institutionalised or not, are today taking place among religions is in itself ground-breaking. And interestingly in the context of this chapter, the starting point for these dialogues is often human rights. Thus, representatives of the three monotheistic religions of Judaism, Christianity and Islam frequently find that they share the same appreciation of fundamental notions of human rights, the example *par excellence* being the notion of dignity. This view has, for instance, repeatedly been taken by the Roman Catholic Church.[14] An example of inter-religious dialogues dedicated to finding shared ways to promote universal human rights is the already mentioned International Council for Christians and Jews, the ICCJ. Today, this is an umbrella organisation of 38 national Jewish-Christian dialogue organisations world wide that specifically addresses issues "of human rights and human dignity deeply enshrined in the traditions of Judaism and Christianity" (as expressed in the organisation's mission statement). In recent years, the ICCJ and its member organisations have become increasingly engaged in the "Abrahamic dialogue", i.e. a dialogue between Jews, Christians and Muslims. A main focus is human rights.[15]

Another example of the inter-religious dialogue aimed at finding shared ways to promote universal human rights is "The International Conference on Human Rights and Our Responsibilities toward Future Generations", held on Malta in

13 For this organization, including its practical human rights initiatives, see Tergel 1998, p. 203-95.

14 "We must remain convinced that any assault on human dignity, even the most remote one, has repercussions, imperceptible but real ones, on the life of everyone; for an indelible bond unites all human beings. This bond exists for all believers – Christians, Moslems and Jews – and is derived from their faith in the one true God who, as Father of all men, is the source and foundation of human dignity. For those who have been called to share Christian faith, this bond is summed up in the words: 'we are all brothers in Jesus Christ.'" John Paul II: Address to the European Court and Commission of Human Rights, 8 October 1979. Quoted from Filibeck 1994, p. 49.

15 In the summer of 2003, for instance, the ICCJ held two international conferences, one of them addressing the issue of "Imagining the Other: Jews, Christians and Muslims in modernity: between self-determination and the imagined other", the other the issue of "Human rights, women and religion: current perspectives" (the ICCJ Women's conference). Source: www.ICCJ.org.

the spring of 1999.[16] The conference's terms of reference were identical with the UNESCO Declaration on the Responsibilities of the Present Generations Towards Future Generations of 1997, viewed in an inter-religious perspective, and focusing on three world religions, namely Judaism, Christianity and Islam. The participants – scholars as well as representatives of governments, national human rights institutions, and United Nation institutions – agreed on a Final Statement, which emphasised the importance of honouring the differences between the religions at the same time as working towards "the discovery of shared respect for the Universal Declaration of Human Rights and a commitment to further dialogue on these themes from the perspective of three faiths." The statement encouraged religious communities "to lend their influences" to eliminating human rights disasters, and, in their endeavour to create a united stand of the world religions against violations of human rights, to approach their own religious traditions critically.[17] Since it was a Euro-Mediterranean conference, the participants focused on the three monotheistic religions, but it also underlined the importance of the involvement of all religions in the promotion of human rights.

Finally the "Global Ethics" projects should be mentioned, where representatives of the world religions typically work together on issues of global interest, including human rights (see Lassen 2001, p. 182).

16 The conference was organized by the Future Generations Program in collaboration with the Mediterranean Academy of Diplomatic Studies and the United Nations Educational, Scientific and Cultural Organization (UNESCO).

17 "2. On the basis of extensive discussions among participants drawn from the monotheistic religions of the Book that prevails in the Euro-Med region, it is agreed that interfaith dialogue on the basis of their spiritual traditions is an essential step on the path toward healing inter-civilizational wounds and conflicts. As our own experience confirms, interfaith dialogue clarifies our identity, including shared values and a shared commitment to uphold human rights, which in turn is one key to the protection of the needs and interests of future generations.... 4. It is also agreed that it is essential to consider the differences as well as the similarities among religions in the course of such a dialogue. It must be made clear that it is not the purpose of such a dialogue to merge spiritual identities or to promote a syncretist approach to religion. On the contrary, this statement celebrates the diversity among distinct religious perspectives, and it commends at the same time familiarity and appreciation of spiritual otherness, and the discovery of shared respect for the Universal Declaration of Human Rights, and a commitment to further dialogue on these themes from the perspectives of three faiths.... 11. In concluding, we believe that the well-being and happiness of future generations depend crucially on what we do now and in the years and decades ahead in keeping with our religious commitments. We affirm this approach in relation to the Euro-Med region, but we also seek to reach out beyond, and engage other world religions in carrying forth this commitment to uphold the life prospects and hopes of future generations for all people in the world.

### 3.3 *Theological Wrestling with Human Rights*

The religious support of human rights exists amid the already mentioned discrepancies between human rights norms and religious norms. This religious ambiguity vis-à-vis human rights has been accurately depicted by Charles Villa-Vicencio – professor of religious studies, one of the most important Christian ethicists in South Africa, and a leading anti-apartheid activist during apartheid – who describes the potentially liberating force of religion in connection with his studies of the role of religion in South Africa's transition from apartheid to democracy:

> The amazing thing about religion is that it has the capacity to renew itself. Just when a particular religion seems to be an established part of a particular oppressive ideology, resources are discovered in that same religion that enable it to be renewed.[18]

Religions therefore have a capacity to renew themselves. Acknowledging this fact, another aspect has to be taken into account when dealing with human rights: denominations, especially conservative denominations within the different religions, may face seemingly insurmountable obstacles in accommodating concrete human rights, even in those cases where the denominations have a genuine wish to do so. One example is Orthodox Judaism, which is facing some substantial challenges with regard to human rights, particularly in relation to the status of women. Particularly problematic is the phenomenon of *aguna*, the wife to whom her husband is refusing to grant a divorce or whose husband has disappeared.[19] It may be argued that this phenomenon is, properly speaking, only a human rights issue in countries where Jewish law is the law of the state, namely the state of Israel (Lagoutte and Lassen 2006). The point here, however, is that while many attempts to solve the problem at the same time as preserving the principles of Orthodox Judaism have been made, none of them has proved fully satisfactory, neither from a human rights perspective nor from a religious point of view.[20]

At a different level, religious communities often try to influence the future development of human rights, not infrequently attempting to take them in directions that differ from those envisioned by the mainstream human rights community. An example is the Roman Catholic Church, which has been very active in trying to influence the future shape of human rights in the area of the family. This, for instance, is the case with the right to divorce, which a number of human rights lawyers have

18 Villa Vicencio 1996: 531. The author discusses how the religious exclusiveness of diverse religions has been challenged by the universalism, inclusiveness and openness of the same religions (notably Christianity, Judaism, Buddhism, Islam and Hinduism).

19 The literature on the problem of equal access to divorce in Jewish law is extensive. For an overview of the problem and a discussion of some of the concrete attempts at solving it, see Berger and Lipstadt 1996: 313 ff.

20 For attempts to solve the problem of *agunot*, see e.g. Lagoutte and Lassen (2006, p. 38ff.).

suggested should be included in the human rights catalogue.[21] The Catholic Church uses many resources to fight such arguments, claiming that a just society resting on human rights cannot include the right to divorce (Lassen 2005, p. 90f).

In this process of renewing or reaffirming religious teaching in wrestling with human rights, scholarly contributions have added depth to the debate. In increasing numbers, theologians are explicitly engaging in studies of the relationship between human rights and religious traditions. This may, for example, be illustrated by Christian Protestant theology. The relationship between human rights and different branches of Protestantism, for instance Lutheran theology, has been the subject of many studies.[22] Generally speaking, interpretations of the Bible have played an important part in the approaches of Protestant churches to human rights. In the middle of the twentieth century, New Testament scholarship and the phenomenon of human rights were to be profoundly influenced by the same historical experiences. The establishment of international human rights law took place against a background of the European Holocaust, and by the same token the Holocaust came to change New Testament scholarship. In the aftermath of the Second World War, an exegesis formerly tainted by anti-Jewish sentiments was replaced by an exegesis that was often genuinely sensitive to Judaism. Similarly, modern theology on mission activities usually has respect for religious freedom as well as a readiness to dialogue with other religions as its point of departure.[23] Another example is women's studies, which have a central position in modern biblical exegesis. "Feminist theology", for instance, has become an important part of biblical exegesis, challenging a previously male-oriented scholarship. This development goes hand in hand with the development of women's rights (Lassen 2004, p. 53ff)

To sum up, religion and human rights are often presented – for instance, in the European media and political discourse – as being inherently and regularly in conflict. By looking at the relationship from a different angle, a more complex picture emerges. Thus a willingness by the representatives of religions to engage in debates on human rights has been demonstrated together with the existence of numerous measures taken by religious communities, leaders and lay people actively to promote human rights, as well as to develop strategies to deal with discrepancies between religious traditions and modern human rights.

Such general tendencies must be seen in the context of concrete attempts by religious communities and individuals to manoeuvre in the often turbulent sea of religion and human rights. This is the subject of the second part of this chapter, where the focus is on Denmark in the immediate post-war years.

---

21 See Lassen 2005, p. 90, note 11.

22 See, e.g., the Danish theologian Svend Andersen, who explores the relationship between human rights thinking and Lutheran theology in 'Human Rights and Christianity: A Lutheran Perspective' (Andersen 2005, p. 98-104). See also Tergel 1998, p. 274f. For a historical approach to the relationship between human rights and Protestantism, see Collinson 1995, p. 21-54.

23 See, e.g., the "interfaith dialogue programs" of the Lutheran World Federation (source: www.lutheranworld.org).

## 4 Part Two. A Historical Perspective: Human Rights and the Danish Jews in the Post-War Years

In 1948, Denmark made an international commitment to human rights by adopting the Universal Declaration of Human Rights. In what follows, the emerging universal human rights will be discussed first from the perspective of Danish society at large, including Danish legal culture. This will provide us with the necessary insight into the ambience within which the Jewish community in Denmark dealt with issues linked to human rights.[24]

### 4.1 *Human Rights in Denmark in the Post-War Period from the Perspective of Danish Lawyers and the Media*

In the post-war years, certain Danish *lawyers* believed that human rights came from "the outside" and they demonstrated a certain scepticism of the notion itself.[25] A more common opinion, however, was that human rights were "obvious" in Denmark (Nørregard 2004, p. 79f). In other words, the Universal Declaration of Human Rights, together with the European Convention for Human Rights ratified by Denmark in 1953, provided a guarantee that for the most part already existed. In the mind of the *politicians* at the time, human rights did not stand out as something very significant, as was reflected in the absence of an extension of the human rights catalogue in the amended Danish constitution of 1953.

In the following decades, the view mentioned above that human rights fitted well into Danish legal tradition continued to dominate the legal field. Illustrative of this is one of the first legal writings in Danish about human rights, written in 1968 by two international lawyers, Ole Espersen and Isi Foighel. They explained the Danish ratification of the European Convention of Human Rights in the following way:

> It is remarkable that the European Convention was adopted as early as 1950 and ratified in 1953. It is particularly noteworthy because precisely this convention...places greater burdens on the states than the United Nations. The explanation is probably first and foremost that, as mentioned in the preamble, the European states have a common heritage of political traditions, ideals, freedoms and fundamental legal principles. From the condition that the fundamental legal principles are common and build upon the same traditions and freedoms, it follows that the necessary changes in the domestic law of the individual states after ratification of the convention will be fewer in number. (1968, p. 9; my translation)

---

24 The analysis of the Danish-Jewish approach to human rights is largely based on analyses of *Jødisk Samfund* ("The Jewish Community"), Mosaisk Troessamfund's monthly community magazine. In what follows, the translations of quotations from *Jødisk Samfund* and from Danish newspapers are mine.

25 For an analysis of these views, see Nørregaard 2004, p. 79.

Again, in this view, human rights are embedded in what already exists and expressed in the country's common share in Europe's "political traditions, ideals, freedoms and fundamental legal principles".

Taking this view into consideration, it is not surprising that Denmark's adoption of the Universal Declaration of Human Rights in 1948 took place without much prior or subsequent debate in Denmark. It is interesting, however, to listen to the voices, some positive, some sceptical, in the limited debate that *did* take place. Substantial parts of this debate were carried out in the national newspapers. To give an example, the correspondent of the national newspaper the *Berlingske Tidende* did not take kindly to the Universal Declaration of Human Rights. Asking how such a declaration could be *common* to the entire world, he went on:

> Should a piece of paper really have the power to obtain for the individual who lives in the East the freedoms enjoyed by individuals in the West? Or is it conceivable that we in the West would be content with the freedoms and rights enjoyed by the individuals in the East? With the broad text and the nice list of the many rights so much desired by human beings, there will be ample opportunity for numerous transgressions and disappointments. One should have been satisfied by the short biblical commandment about loving your neighbour as a guideline for interaction between human beings and between nations. (*Berlingske Tidende*, 2 December 1948)

Other newspapers had a more positive attitude to the Universal Declaration, for instance *Politiken*, of which the leading article read: "Let us be happy with these human rights and let us hope that they will be interpreted in the right way" (13 December 1948). *Information*, a newspaper that dedicated a series of articles to the background and progress of the UN General Assembly in Paris, saw the Universal Declaration as "an important tool to promote human rights" (*Information* "Kronik" 13 December 1948).

What is common to these newspaper contributions is that the values, the legal order and the guarantees of the individuals underpinning human rights are perceived as something which *other* nations in particular need (not least nations under the domination of the Soviet Union).[26] In this connection, it should be mentioned that, as early as 1948, the debate about human rights was coloured by the emerging Cold War. This is reflected in the Danish newspapers, which emphasise the different approaches to human rights of the Western democracies and the Soviet Union, respectively, and take sides over the issue.[27]

---

26 See, e.g., *Berlingske Tidende*, 2 December, 'Tegn paa voksende Respekt i Kreml for Vestens Styrke' by Erhardt Larsen, correspondent in Paris.

27 See, e.g., the article quoted above: *Berlingske Tidende*, 'Et lident inspirerende dokument', 2 December 1948.

### 4.2 *The Jewish Minority in Post-War Denmark*

The Danish-Jewish population has always been very small in number, approximately 7,000 individuals in 1948. Most Jews who were religiously affiliated belonged to Mosaisk Troessamfund, an Orthodox community. Historically, anti-Semitism existed in Denmark but on a smaller scale than in a majority of other European countries, and the rescue of Denmark's Jews from the Holocaust resulted in an outpouring of warm feelings between the Jews on the one hand and the majority population and representatives of state institutions on the other. In this connection, it should be kept in mind that the grimmer aspects of the Danish government's dealings with *non-Danish* Jewish refugees, which have particularly come to light in recent years,[28] were little known at the time, let alone discussed. Equally, it is only in recent decades that the rescue of the Danish Jews has been subject to more nuanced and complex interpretations. Some of these have been much more critical than the original construction of the historic events which emphasised the heroic efforts of Resistance fighters and other Danes, a historical construction which, in its romanticised form, is very influential to this day in the international perception of the rescue of the Danish Jews.[29]

Many Danes were active in the rescue of the Jewish population, and the famous Pastoral letter read out in all churches belonging to the Danish Evangelical Lutheran Church (*Folkekirken*) in German-occupied Denmark in October 1943, protesting against the persecution of the Jews, cemented the attitude of the Danish Church to the "Jewish question":

> The attitude of the Evangelical Lutheran Church in Denmark towards the Jewish question.
>
> Wherever Jews are persecuted for racial or religious reasons, it is the duty of the Christian Church to protest against such persecution...because it conflicts with the understanding of justice rooted in the Danish people and settled through centuries in our Danish Christian culture. Accordingly, it is stated in our constitution that all Danish citizens have an equal right and responsibility towards the law, and they have freedom of religion, and a right to worship God in accordance with their vocation and conscience and so that race or religion can never in itself become the cause of the deprivation of anybody's rights [to] freedom or property.
>
> Irrespective of diverging religious opinions, we shall fight for the right of our Jewish brothers and sisters to keep the freedom that we ourselves value more highly than life.[30]

28 See here in particular Rünitz 2005.

29 See here in particular the important work of Sofie Lene Bak 2001.

30 Signed on behalf of the bishops by Bishop Fuglsang Damgaard on 29 September 1943; quoted from Mogensen 2003, p. 44-45.

This feeling of solidarity between the Christian majority and the Jewish minority in Denmark continued after the war.[31]

### 4.3 *"Human Rights Are of Invaluable Importance to Jews": Danish-Jewish Views on Human Rights*

The Danish-Jewish community was enthusiastic in its support of human rights. This is reflected in a number of articles in *Jødisk Samfund* in the second half of the 1940s, for instance in an article in the June issue of 1949 praising the Universal Declaration as the first attempt in history to introduce a "moral constitution" of the world. The article stresses that "human rights are of invaluable importance to Jews now and in the future", at the same time proudly emphasising Jewish efforts to create legally binding human rights ("Mrs Roosevelt og 'Menneskerettighederne'" by *TM. Jødisk Samfund*, June 1950, pp. 4-5).

Partly reflecting the shared experience of racism, exile and persecution, and partly reflecting a sense of belonging to the Jewish people, Mosaisk Troessamfund's declared support of human rights resembles what we find world wide in Jewish communities and among Jewish individuals in the 1930s and the following decades (see above).

In 1949, Mosaisk Troessamfund debated whether it should join the World Jewish Congress (WJC) as a member. The WJC, an organisation founded in 1936 to fight Nazism, acted in the immediate aftermath of the war on behalf of Jews and Jewish communities world wide to promote the establishment of legally binding international human rights. The organisation therefore lobbied in connection with the drafting of the Universal Declaration of Human Rights and argued unsuccessfully for the right of petition as an instrument to protect human rights (Cotler 1996, p. 245 ff).[32]

Interestingly, the Danish Mosaisk Troessamfund, although supporting the aims of the WJC, refrained from joining the organisation as a member. The caution of the Danish community was grounded in the concern that the Danish majority might consider such an affiliation a breach of loyalty vis-à-vis the Danish people. Thus, at a meeting of the Assembly of Delegates of Mosaisk Troessamfund in October 1950, the chairman expressed the view that the Jewish community ought not take part in an organisation, the activities of which involved an independent foreign policy:

31 As, for instance, expressed in a letter addressed to the Jewish community in 1946 by Bishop Fuglsang, the author of the Pastoral Letter. Reproduced in *Jødisk Samfund*, December 1946.

32 The WJC's focus on human rights can also be observed in several articles in *Jødisk Samfund*. See e.g. 'Mrs Roosevelt og 'Menneskerettighederne' ' by TM, *Jødisk Samfund*, June 1950, p. 5. 'Hvad er W.J.C.' ('What is W.J.C.?') by E. Hilb, *Jødisk Samfund*, December 1948, p. 8-9.

> We are Danes and must follow Danish politics and can therefore not be active members in an organisation, thereby risking finding ourselves in opposition to the Danish government .... We have a rarely obtained a happy position in this country. No one thinks about whether we are Jews or not, and if we wish to maintain this situation, we must make sure not to bring ourselves into a position which under certain circumstances may appear dubious .... The Board of Delegates therefore considers it unfortunate to make a closer connection to Congress than is presently the case. However, if we can contribute without endangering Danish interests, we are willing to do so." ("Meeting in the Assembly of Delegates", *Jødisk Samfund*, November 1950, p. 8-9)

Although this argument prevailed at the time, it gave rise to conflict. It was argued, for instance, that the activities of the World Jewish Community were exclusively linked with human rights and that the Danish public could have nothing against Mosaisk Troessamfund defending the interests of Jews world wide in the area of "humanitarian work".[33]

### 4.4 *The Question of Assimilation*

The question of assimilation is integral to human rights in relation to minorities because it touches on the right of minorities to exercise their own norms and practices. Whereas the demand for complete assimilation into the majority population opposes minority rights as well as some specific rights (notably religious freedom), the borderline between reasonable and necessary integration and acceptable non-assimilation is today constantly under debate in European countries, in the media, the courts and among politicians.[34] It was debated in the post-war period as well.

The question of assimilation – here understood in the sense of the complete adaptation of the Jewish minority to the majority's norms and practices[35] – came up from time to time in the Danish media in the second half of the 1940s. Thus in October 1946, an article was published in the major national newspaper, *Berlingske Aftenavis*, by the Hungarian-born author Arthur Koestler. In this article, Koestler foresees that a legally recognized Jewish state will be established in Palestine, and he suggests two alternatives for the Jews of the world: they must either become *completely assimilated* into their respective countries (thus preventing future atrocities against them), or *emigrate* to Palestine to become "Hebrew citizens".[36] In another

---

33 See, for instance, the intervention of Welner, 'Meeting in the Assembly of Delegates', *Jødisk Samfund* November 1950, p. 9.

34 Often it is debated in connection with discussions about concrete religious practices which are visibly different from practices carried out by the majority population. The headscarf is a notable example. See here Lagoutte and Lassen (2006).

35 For a discussion of assimilation and integration in the context of the Danish-Jewish minority, see, e.g., Kragh 2005, p. 17.

36 'Løfternes Land' ('The land of promises') by Arthur Koestler. "Kronik" in *Berlingske Aftenavis* 4 October 1946.

newspaper, *Information*, a similar request was made earlier in the same year: the Danish Jews should assimilate themselves to the Christian majority.[37]

Not surprisingly, these suggestions met with opposition from the Jewish community, including Markus Melchior, who was to be appointed chief rabbi of the Danish-Jewish community the following year. Two aspects of his response in *Jødisk Samfund* are worth mentioning. First, he asserts the rights of Jews in the countries where they presently live, emphasising the statement in the Balfour Declaration of 1917, according to which "nothing shall be done which may prejudice the civil and religious rights of existing non-Jewish communities in Palestine, or the rights and political status enjoyed by Jews in any other country."[38]

Secondly, it is interesting that one of Melchior's arguments against assimilation is not based on its disadvantages for the Jews, but rather on its disadvantages for *Danish society as a whole*: complete assimilation would be detrimental to Danish society and the Danes. Thus he emphasised the value for society of *diversity*:

> If the nations in which midst the Jews live as citizens knew what is best for themselves, they would not desire or require such assimilation. A nation is rich and strong because of the diversity in its composition. The more spiritual the regimentation, the greater the boredom, and the less flexibility and potential for development. It is the many colours which create the beauty of a painting, the many sounds which make beautiful music. There have been times in the modern Jewish history of emancipation when certain countries granted the Jews citizenship with the expectation that they would soon be absorbed into the majorities of these countries. But this is, as indicated, an unreasonable expectation, and the Jews are guilty of a misunderstanding if they think that they will prove their love of the fatherland by giving up their Jewish character. This character is indeed the true gift they can offer their fatherland. Through this they bring that nuance to their fatherland's culture, literature and work for society of every kind, which is what the fatherland expects and needs. Even though it may sound paradoxical, the truth is this: the more faithful the Jews remain to themselves, the better citizens and the more genuine patriots they are able to become. ("Assimilation" by M. Melchior, *Jødisk Samfund*, October 1946, p. 4)

Melchior was by no means totally opposed to what he called "assimilation", but he used this term in a way that nowadays would most often be referred to as *integration*, as is clear from the following quotation:

> It is not the purpose to eliminate healthy and natural assimilation, without which we could not exist at all. Human beings have so much in common, and they are to a degree in need of learning the good from one another, that Jews and Christians, wherever they live, have to assimilate themselves to one another. The art of being a human being con-

37 For a comment on and reference to the contributions in *Information*, see M. Melchior, 'Assimilation', *Jødisk Samfund*, October 1946, p. 3.

38 Quoted from the Avalon Project of Yale Law School: 20th Century Documents. www.yale.edu./lawweb/avalon.

> sists, however, in understanding where the reasonableness of melting together ends, and where the duty to be oneself begins. (*Jødisk Samfund*, October 1946, p. 4)

In sum, in asserting the right of the Jews not to assimilate more than what can reasonably be required, Melchior is basing his argument partly on the rights of the minority, and partly on the presumed benefits of non-assimilation for Danish society as a whole.

Melchior's views did not go undisputed among members of the Jewish community, and the issues he raised in this and other articles were discussed in other connections. For instance, the discussion of a double loyalty developed further in the above-mentioned debate about the possible affiliation of Danish Jews with the World Jewish Congress.[39]

To conclude: in Denmark in the post-war years, the emergence of international human rights (as reflected in the media and among lawyers) was largely seen as being more relevant to other countries than to Denmark, whether this view was based on the perception that Denmark already possessed the basic characteristics of human rights, or because human rights were seen as part of the emerging Cold War. On the whole, the notion of human rights did not loom large in the public sphere in the immediate post-war years. Among members of the Danish-Jewish minority, however, whole-hearted enthusiasm for the emerging human rights was certainly expressed, since human rights were seen as central to the protection of the Jews in the future.

Despite the positive atmosphere between the majority population and the Jewish minority in post-war Denmark, the Danish Jews were not always immune from finding themselves in situations which demanded caution and careful consideration or from being confronted with issues that were problematic regarding the preservation of a distinct Jewish identity. One example of this is Mosaisk Troessamfund's support of human rights, which had to be balanced with the need to manoeuvre in the particular context of Danish society. This led to a pronounced caution in supporting the World Jewish Congress. Another example is the right to preserve religious traditions and practices, which was challenged from time to time, as we have seen through examples from the Danish newspapers.

### 4.5 *Contemporary Perspectives*

In recent years, Mosaisk Troessamfund has continued to express its support of human rights, as, for instance, in the community's statutes:

> The community supports the principles of the protection of human rights and fundamental freedoms, as written down in the European Convention of Human Rights, which works to promote tolerance and understanding between human beings, and which fights xenophobia, racism and anti-Semitism." (my translation).

39 See, e.g., 'Meeting in the Assembly of Delegates', *Jødisk Samfund*, November 1950, p. 8-9.

The community also makes use of human rights to assert the right of Jews to practice Jewish customs. A recent example is the statement of Mosaisk Troessamfund submitted to the Danish Ministry of Justice concerning the proposal of Dyreetisk Nævn (the Board of Animal Ethics) to ban ritual slaughter in Denmark. A substantial part of the statement's argument against this prohibition is based on a discussion of human rights and the practice of the European Court of Human Rights.[40] Generally speaking, Jewish objections to legal and non-legal attempts to curb religious practices are taken seriously by the majority population, including the media and lawmakers. However, the Jewish community is no longer in the spotlight as the most visible minority group in Denmark. In recent decades, demographic and religious changes have taken place due to Muslim immigration. This, in its turn, has shifted the focus away from the Jews and to the Muslims, who from time to time are confronted with critical voices concerning their religious practices. In effect, if indirectly, when Danish Jews defend the right to perform those Jewish practices that are similar to those of Muslims, for instance male circumcision or ritual slaughter, the rights of Muslims are defended as well.

## 5 Conclusion

When the relationship between religion and human rights is discussed, it is the many obvious and often very visible problem areas that are frequently to the fore. By demonstrating the involvement of the representatives of religions, religious leaders and lay people in debates on human rights, as well as the commitment of numerous religious institutions and individuals to promote human rights and to develop strategies to deal with discrepancies between them and religious traditions, this chapter has aimed to add nuances to the bleak picture regularly painted of the relationship between human rights and religion. Such general tendencies were linked to a study of the human rights approach of Mosaisk Troessamfund, the main congregation of Jews in Denmark in the post-war years, offering an early example of how religious communities and individuals may manoeuvre in the often turbulent sea of religion and human rights.

The more positive picture of the relationship between religion and human rights that emerges from analyses of the involvement of religious institutions in the latter is relevant to the future development of human rights for several reasons, among them the following. First, the active involvement of religious institutions in attempts to solve problems growing out of discrepancies between religious traditions and human rights is a critical step in the direction of finding sustainable solutions (cf. Lagoutte and Lassen 2006). Secondly, since religious institutions form part of civil society, their position on human rights issues plays an important role in the implementation of human rights.

40 Mosaisk Troessamfund, 'Vedr. J.nr. 2005-5432-0007: høring over Det Dyreetiske Råds udtalelse om rituelle slagtninger', Copenhagen, 15 April 2005.

### References

Andersen, S., 'Human Rights and Christianity: A Lutheran Perspective', in Binderup, L. and T. Jensen (eds.), *Human Rights, Democracy and Religion*, Odense, University of Southern Denmark, pp. 98-104, 2005.

Bak, S. L., *Jødeaktionen oktober 1943: Forestillinger i offentlighed og forskning*, Copenhagen, Museum Tusculanum, 2001.

Belo, C. F. X., 'The Dignity of the Individual', in B. van de Heijden and B. Tahzib-lie (eds.), *Reflections on the Universal Declaration of Human Rights: A Fiftieth Anniversary Anthology*, The Hague/Boston/London, Martinus Nijhoft Publishers, pp. 59-63, 1998.

Berger, M.S. and D.E. Lipstadt, 'Women in Judaism from the Perspective of Human Rights', in J. Witte and J.D. van der Vyer (eds.), *Religious Human Rights in Global Perspective, Vol. 1*, The Hague/Boston/London, Martinus Nijhoff Publishers, pp. 295-321, 1996.

Brems, E., *Human Rights: Universality and Diversity*, The Hague, Boston, London, Martin Nijhoff Publishers, 2001.

Collinson, P., 'Religion and Human Rights: The Case of and for Protestantism', in O. Hufton (ed.), *Historical Change and Human Rights*, The Oxford Amnesty Lectures 1994, New York, Basic Books, pp. 21-54, 1995.

Cotler, I., 'Jewish NGOs and Religious Human rights: A Case Study', in J. Witte and J.D. van der Vyer (eds.), *Religious Human Rights in Global Perspective: Religious Perspectives, Vol. 1*, The Hague/Boston/London, Martinus Nijhoff Publishers, pp. 235-94, 1996.

Espersen, O., and I. Foighel, *Menneskerettighederne*, Copenhagen: Den danske UNESCO-nationalkommission, 1968.

Filibeck, G., (ed.), *Human Rights in the Teaching of the Church: From John XXIII to John Paul II*, Vatican City, Libreria Deitrice Vaticana, 1994.

Glendon, M. A., *A World Made New: Eleanor Roosevelt and the Universal Declaration of Human Rights*, New York, Random House, 2001.

Johnson Everett, W., 'Human Rights in the Church', in J. Witte and J. van der Vyer (eds.), *Religious Human Rights in Global Perspective*, The Hague, Boston, London, Martin Nijhoff Publishers, Vol. 1, pp. 121-42, 1996.

Krag, H., in H. Goldstein (ed.), *Til et folk de alle høre... Den jødiske minoritet i Danmark*, Copenhagen, Gyldendal, pp. 11-28, 2005.

Küng, H. and K.J. Küschel (eds.), *A Global Ethic: The Declaration of the Parliament of the World Religions*, London, New York, Continuum, 1993.

Lagoutte, S. and Lassen, E. M., 'Meeting the Challenge: Redefining Europe's Classical Model for State Intervention in Religious Practices', *Netherlands Human Rights Quarterly*, vol. 24, no 1, March, pp. 33-59, 2006.

Lassen, E. M., 'International Human Rights Law and the Bible: Two Norm-setting Standards of the Modern World', in L. Binderup and T. Jensen (eds.), *Human Rights, Democracy and Religion*, Odense, University of Southern Denmark, pp. 84-97, 2005.

Lassen, E. M., 'Women, Religions, and Human Rights', in I. B. Mæhle and I. M. Okkenhaug (eds.), *Women and Religion in the Middle East and the Mediterranean*, Oslo, UNIPUB, pp. 49-68, 2004.

Lassen, E. M., 'World Religions, World Values: In Dialogue with the Bible', in K. Hastrup (ed.), *Human Rights on Common Grounds: The Quest for Universality*, The Hague/London/New York, Kluwer Law International, pp. 177-94, 2001.

Lauren, P. G., *The Evolution of International Human Rights: Visions Seen*, Philadelphia, Penn, University of Pennsylvania Press, 1998.

Mogensen, M., 'October 1943: The Rescue of the Danish Jews', in M. Bastholm Jensen and S.L.B. Jensen (eds.), *Denmark and the Holocaust,* Copenhagen, Institute for International Studies, Dept. for Holocaust and Genocide Studies, pp. 33-61, 2003.

Mayer, A. E., *Islam and Human Rights*, London, Pinter Publishers, 1991.

Novak, D., 'Religious Human Rights in Judaic Texts', in J. Witte and J. van der Vyer (eds.), *Religious Human Rights in Global Perspective,* The Hague, Boston, London: Martin Nijhoff Publishers, Vol. 1, pp. 175-202, 1996.

Nørregaard, M., *Menneskerettighedskonventionens anvendelse mellem private*, Copenhagen, Forlaget Thomson, 2004.

Robinson, M., 'The Universal Declaration of Human Rights: The International Keystone of Human Dignity', in B. van de Heijden and B. Tahzib-lie (eds.), *Reflections on the Universal Declaration of Human Rights: A Fiftieth Anniversary Anthology*, The Hague/Boston/London, Martinus Nijhoft Publishers, pp. 253-60, 1998.

Rünitz, L., *Af hensyn til konsekvenserne: Danmark og flygtningespørgsmålet 1933-1940*, Odense, Syddansk Universitetsforlag, 2005.

Sugirtharajah, R. S. (ed.), 'Postcolonial Perspectives on the New Testament and Its Interpretation', *Journal for the Study of the New Testament*, 73, 1999.

Tergel, A., *Human Rights in Cultural and Religious Traditions*, Uppsala, Acta Universitatis Upsaliensis, 1998.

Villa-Vicencio, C., *A Theology of Reconstruction: Nation-Building and Human Rights,* Cambridge, Cambridge University Press, 1992.

Villa-Vicencio, C., 'Identity, Difference and Belonging: Religious and Cultural Rights', in J. Witte and J. van der Vyer (eds.), *Religious Human Rights in Global Perspective*, The Hague, Boston, London, Martin Nijhoff Publishers, Vol. 2, pp. 517-38, 1996.

Witte, J., 'Introduction', in J. Witte and J. van der Vyver (eds.) *Religious Human Rights in Global Perspective*, Vol. 1, 1996.

# 9. Freedom from Want: Globalisation and Social Security

*Hatla Thelle*

In January 1941 the American President, Franklin D. Roosevelt, formulated the four freedoms that were to become an important source of inspiration for the human rights system as we know it today.[1] The third of them – the freedom from want – was included seven years later as articles 22-27 of the Universal Declaration of Human Rights (UDHR) of December 1948, which were eventually elaborated and codified in their own instrument, the International Covenant of Economic, Social and Cultural Rights (ICESCR), which entered into force in 1976. Social and economic rights were, from the very beginning, of the same value and formulated at the same level as other human rights, though they got caught up in the ideological struggles of the Cold War period (Craven 1995, pp. 16-22). After the collapse of communism in Eastern Europe and the Soviet Union, the interdependence of all human rights was reconfirmed in the Vienna Declaration of 1993.

Social rights are protected by social policies adopted by states around the world. In the course of globalisation, however, the protection of people's basic livelihoods has increasingly been challenged by the free movements of labour and capital. The improvement of rights protection and expansion of market forces are two movements that converge in the state, each of them at times pulling in opposite directions, at other times supporting each other. Rights protection presupposes a strong state, while a truly free market works to weaken the state. The state serves as the regulator with the duty of ensuring some degree of balance between the living conditions of different groups in society. This regulatory function can be carried out in different ways, and the different systems more or less comply with international human rights standards.

The term 'globalisation' will be used here for the rapidly increasing economic integration between different regions which has taken place during the last three decades. In its present form, it has both positive and negative implications for people around the world. During the course of globalisation, immense wealth has been created as a result of transactions across borders and many people have acquired new

1 Freedom of speech, freedom of religion, freedom from want, and freedom from fear.

*S. Lagoutte, H-O. Sano and P. Scharff Smith (eds.),* Human Rights in Turmoil, *pp. 201-220.*
 *ISBN 90 04 15432 9.*

jobs and better living conditions, but wealth is still unevenly distributed, and other groups of people have found themselves less and less able to subsist through their former channels. Some scholars analyse globalisation in the long run as a progressive force that is conducive to social development (Bhagwati 2004), while others fear that market forces might lead to the commoditisation of social services (Lamarche 2004, p. 114) and thus increase the inequality and exclusion of marginalized groups (Bauman 1998, p. 71). These two radically opposing views and frozen opinions of an ideological nature are softened by voices seeking to tap the immense potential of globalisation and to use it in the interests of everyone (WCSDG 2004), instead of just the 'mobile elite', to use Zygmunt Bauman's term (Bauman 1998, p. 19).

Vulnerable groups of people with few resources are faced with the most serious social risks, and the right to basic social security is an important safeguard for them. Following this line of thought, the present chapter will discuss the current challenges created by globalisation for the effective protection of the right to social security and will ask what role a rights-based approach can play in strengthening such protection. First, social rights as a specific category of rights will be defined and their role in the human rights regime discussed. It will be shown how the idea of economic and social rights has been contested throughout the sixty-year history of the modern human rights regime. Then, the concepts of social policy and welfare theory will be explained, and the relationship between human rights and social policy discussed. The subsequent two sections will assess the negative and positive impacts of globalisation in relation to the protection of social security around the globe. Examples will then be used to illustrate the dilemmas and problems in expanding social safety nets. Lastly, a balance will be sought between the movements and counter-movements related to social protection in the era of globalisation from around 1980 until today.

## 1 Background

### *1.1 Social Rights as Human Rights*

As soon as UDHR had to be translated into legally binding instruments soon after its adoption, political and ideological disagreements began and have continued ever since, affecting the issue of the tension between freedom and security. The socialist states, led by the Soviet Union, stressed social rights as part of their commitment to egalitarian redistributive goals, while the Western world tended to favour civil rights in accordance with its ideals of freedom and democracy. In the beginning, in 1950, the UN Economic and Social Council (ECOSOC) proposed that human rights were interdependent and that all categories of rights should be contained within one document.[2] However, on the basis of Western claims, the arguments were ignored by the General Assembly (UNGA), which asked the Commission of

2 General Assembly Resolution 421 E (V) of 4 December 1950: 'When deprived of economic, social and cultural rights, man does not represent the human person whom the Universal Declaration regards as the ideal of the free man'.

Human Rights to draft two covenants dealing respectively with civil/political and economic/social rights.[3] These were adopted in 1966, but only came into force in 1976.[4] But the idea of the indivisibility and interdependence of all human rights continued to figure in official documents and public rhetoric, as confirmed in the declarations of the two international conferences on human rights held in Teheran in 1968 and in Vienna in 1993.[5]

Decisive for the division into the two categories of civil/political and economic/social rights were arguments for the different nature of the two types of right, creating different demands on states and the need for different instruments:

> It was expected that states who did not want to undertake the obligations arising from economic, social, and cultural rights would be willing to ratify an instrument which contained only civil and political rights. (Eide et al. 2001, p. 10)

Civil rights were understood to be 'negative', 'immediate', 'justiciable', 'precise' and – not least important – 'cheap'; social rights were 'positive', 'programmatic', 'non-justiciable', 'vague' and – again, not least important – 'expensive'. In other words, civil rights only demanded states not to interfere with individual freedoms, and violations could easily be brought to court. Social rights, on the contrary, oblige governments to provide social services that are costly, and violations cannot easily be brought to court.

The difference has been widely discussed,[6] and the idea of a rigid categorisation of rights has lost ground since the end of the Cold War. New developments, furthermore, point to an increase in the judicial enforcement of economic and social rights. Some 'new' nations like South Africa and countries in the former Soviet Bloc, like Hungary and Lithuania, have included economic, social and cultural (ESC) rights directly as justiciable rights in their constitutions, while many more countries have constitutional articles which relate to ESC rights. In South Africa

---

3 In the so called 'separation resolution' no. 384 (XIII) of 29 August 1951.

4 A certain number of ratifications have to be deposited before a convention enters into force; e.g. for ICESCR the number was thirty-five ratifications, and the Convention accordingly came into force on 3 January 1976.

5 The Proclamation of Teheran, 13 May 1968, para 13: 'Since human rights and fundamental freedoms are indivisible, the full realisation of civil and political rights without the enjoyment of economic, social and cultural rights is impossible. The achievement of lasting progress in the implementation of human rights is dependent upon sound and effective national and international policies of economic and social development.' And the Vienna Declaration, 25 June 1993, para 5: 'All human rights are universal, indivisible, interdependent and interrelated. The international community must treat human rights globally in a fair and equal manner, on the same footing, and with the same emphasis.'

6 See, e.g., Martin Scheinin, 'Economic and Social Rights as Legal Rights', in Eide et al. 2001: 41 ff. The justiciability of socio-economic rights is affirmed in the Maastricht Guidelines on Violations of ESCR (*Human Rights Quarterly* 20, 1998: 726). See also Hunt 1996 and Koch 2003.

several famous cases have been tried in the Constitutional Court on the right to housing and medical treatment, but in most jurisdictions ESC rights are recognised as directives to state policies in relation to which individuals cannot claim violations in court (Circle of Rights 2000, p. 211). In these cases ESC rights can be covered by other laws or protected indirectly through the application of certain civil rights, as has been the case in Canada and Germany (Liebenberg 2001).

However, critics of this duality do not claim that there are no differences between the two categories; the concern is that social rights receive too little attention from legal circles (Koch 2003, pp. 38-39). Opposition to the civil/social dichotomy rests on the practical observation that different rights interact in everyday life, alternately being instruments for or consequences of each other. The right to vote and to be elected is linked to the right to education; the right to life is guaranteed through fulfilment of the right to health; the right to assembly is a precondition for enjoyment of the right to join a trade union, etc. This acknowledgment has led human rights bodies to adopt an integrated approach, where especially the European Court of Human Rights has found that on the one hand social rights can be tried in court, and on the other hand social policy measures can be essential for the protection of certain civil rights.

But all in all, the judicial enforcement of economic and social rights is still a new phenomenon in national legal systems. The above exposition shows that the existence and validity of social rights have in reality been questioned since their very birth; they are now under added pressure from more recent challenges posed by the rapid economic integration of the countries around the globe. Before dealing with these pressures, a brief discussion of measures and policies for protecting social rights will be in place.

### 1.2 Social Policy Theory

The blooming of the welfare-state concept as an ideology and as political practice in the Western world since the mid-1950s created a new social science discipline addressing state involvement in the provision of social welfare, usually known as 'social policy' or 'social policy theory'. The field of social policy theory is concerned with *the role and capacity of the state* as well as *the needs and properties of individuals* and thus involves a range of disciplines within the social sciences and the humanities, such as sociology, anthropology, economics, law, psychology and history. The area is also characterised by strong links to politics and ethics, as it touches upon redistributive justice and such fundamental moral questions as the obligation of the rich to help the poor, individual responsibility, compassion and social order.

Two key problem areas are central to the discussion of the ideal balance between the state and the individual in relation to the responsibility for subsistence:

- the balance between state and non-state actors, the latter most typically involving the market, civil organisations and the family;
- the relationship between contribution to society and protection from society.

Protection for those who cannot protect themselves has in all societies in all eras been taken care of by a mixture of the wider community and the close family. The distribution of responsibility between these entities can be very different, constituting degrees on a scale going from the (almost) total state engagement seen in many socialist countries before 1989, to liberal, everyone-for-himself regimes like the US – or the UK from 1979 to 1997 – with limited state engagement. Most societies lie somewhere in between these two extremes. Societies with relatively little public protection are exposed to the danger of creating a huge, impoverished class of citizens that in turn can threaten political legitimacy and social stability. On the other hand, strong state involvement can impede economic development by creating dependency and pacifying, even destroying, individual initiative, as happens as a result of the highly redistributive mechanisms of socialist systems (Havel 1985). Redistribution is basically a problem of available resources, technical competence and political will, but it can be restricted by and criticised on account of the fear of the negative consequences of rising dependency. This criticism has mostly been levelled at socialist systems, but it has also been put forward in the Western debate on new trends in social protection, as in Denmark, where even the Social Democrats in the 1990s argued for cuts in social spending on exactly these grounds.

The mix of concerns can be depicted as a triangle of state/market/family or as a continuum from more to less state engagement; in either case it is a question of a flow rather than of opposites. The dichotomies public/private and state/non-state have often been conceived as absolute questions of either/or, but this view has been challenged in the last decades through the development of social policy studies, especially in relation to Third World countries (Cook and Cabeer 2000, p. 3) and the new Asian economies, where the distinction between public and private sectors has been considered unhelpful or at least irrelevant.

Another crucial distinction, especially pertaining to a human rights approach, is whether social support is contingent on individual contributions in the form of work or money, or is unconditional. Most societies provide little or no social support without demanding a previous contribution, but here a continuum is also involved, some countries giving more, some less unconditional support.

In 1990 three different welfare regimes were identified by Gøsta Esping-Andersen using a triple distinction pertaining to Western political cleavages between *liberal*, *conservative* and *social democratic* welfare regimes (Esping-Andersen 1990). The liberal regime is found in the Anglo-Saxon countries (US, and the UK under Thatcher) and is characterised by a low degree of state intervention, the promotion of market solutions, and individual (as opposed to family) responsibility. Typical conservative regimes are found in Continental European countries like Germany, France and Austria, which base welfare on compulsory social insurance schemes differentiated among occupational status groups, and where responsibility is placed with the family. Social democratic regimes are found in the North European countries that build their welfare on universal coverage based on citizenship and funded by corporate and income taxes. These models can, with some flexibility (Thelle 2004, pp. 80-81), be used for all the dominating social and cultural systems ('civilisations') in today's world. In the developed world, all three regimes exist today; in post-communist countries, social security has hitherto been linked to the guarantee of full employment; while in the developing world, social rights are still protected basically via non-state actors like the community, the family and the informal sector. In countries that are moving from planned to market economies, we now see a tendency to adopt a model close to the conservative regime in Esping-Andersen's classification. In poor countries, the establishment of any viable and effective state provision of social security is hampered by weak state capacity, poverty and aid conditionalities, as will be discussed below.

### 1.3 A Rights-Based Social Policy

The basic paragraphs on social security in the international human rights system are article 25 of the UDHR, which promises everyone the right to 'security in the event of unemployment, sickness, disability, widowhood, old age or other lack of livelihood in circumstances beyond his control'; and article 9 of the ICESCR, which, as the shortest article in the whole Covenant, states that 'The States Parties to the present Covenant recognise the right of everyone to social security, including social insurance'. As can be seen, both documents use a very short and general wording, which could be connected to the extensive regularisation of the area by another UN organisation, the International Labour Organisation (ILO).

The principal document within the ILO system is Convention No. C102 *Social Security (Minimum Standards) Convention* of 1952, describing social security as consisting of several services or risks which are by now considered the basic elements of all social policies: medical care and benefits in case of sickness; family benefits; and benefits in case of unemployment, old age, employment injury, childbirth, invalidity and death of provider. The ILO list is repeated in the reporting guidelines for ICESCR article 9, confirming the strong links between the two instruments. ILO Convention No. C102 provides a general framework, which has been elaborated by a whole range of subsequent conventions aimed at specific situations (Lamarche 2002, p. 91). Likewise in the ICESCR, social security is not only dealt with by article 9, but also relates to most of the other substantive articles in the Covenant (paras. 6-12), except the right to education and the right to take part in cultural life (paras. 13-14). Some of these are more specific in their demands for state policies, like 'safe and healthy working conditions' (para. 7), 'reduction of infant mortality' and 'prevention and control of epidemic diseases' (para. 12). But all contain a certain degree of vagueness, as international documents must in order to allow for 'national and regional particularities', in the words of the Vienna Declaration.[7]

More clarity can be found in the General Comments of the Economic, Social and Cultural Rights (ESCR) Committee. One General Comment (no. 3) defines

7 *Vienna Declaration*, 25 June 1993, para 5: 'While the significance of national and regional particularities and various historical, cultural and religious backgrounds must be borne in mind, it is the duty of States, regardless of their political, economic and cultural systems, to promote and protect all human rights and fundamental freedoms....'

state obligations, others refer to rights for special groups of people, like the disabled (no. 5) or the elderly (no. 6), or to the understanding of a specific right like housing (nos. 4 and 7) or health (no. 14). These comments, as well as the declarations mentioned above and other core documents, lay down a set of common principles defining requirements for a social policy based on the concept of human rights:

- Legislation is to be supplemented with administrative, financial and educational measures.
- Basic services shall be attainable and affordable for everyone without discrimination.
- Judicial remedies shall be available in cases of violations.
- Public participation shall be guaranteed and institutionalised.
- Core obligations can be defined for each right and shall be complied with immediately.
- Reliable and adequate institutions for collecting and analysing data shall be established.

Nevertheless, a certain lack of equality is a cross-cutting weakness in most documents and in the institutionalised systems for social security around the globe, despite the general human-rights principle of universality and the overarching prohibition against discrimination. The basic ILO texts favour people attached to the labour market and excludes non-formal workers and the self-employed, while all social systems in the world have some kinds of conditions attached to the enjoyment of social benefits – some more some less. Apart from employment, residence and citizenship are factors which are often used to categorise people into those who can and who cannot receive state support. No system is truly universal or protects the rights of everyone without distinction. As mentioned above, increased inequality is one of the observed consequences of the globalisation process, but on this point the human rights standards offer only limited help. Other features, however, like access to remedies and the right to participation in policy-making, are important contributions to fulfilling the goal of basic social guarantees, as, for example, we saw in the expanded use of legal remedies at the domestic level (Liebenberg 2001). But what role do these contributions play in the era of globalisation? I shall now turn to the question of the forces working for and against a continued or strengthened protection of the right to social security in today's world.

## 2 Movements and Counter-Movements

### *2.1 Movement: Globalisation and Social Security since 1980*

The state-regulated welfare systems of the West, dominated by two competing models of development – welfare-state capitalism and socialism – began to change more or less dramatically from around 1989, with the fall of the Iron Curtain. Both models were committed to full employment and socio-economic security. But in the last decades, new developments have affected the prospects for the protection of social rights in different ways. In the capitalist countries, new trends have emerged in the form of neo-liberal policies in the fields of economics, characterised by cuts in public spending and by privatisation, and social policies, characterised by selectivity and commoditisation. In the socialist countries, the centrally planned economy, with its imbedded welfare provisions, was replaced by the market economy, and social services were increasingly commercialised. In the developing world, public spending on welfare was restricted by the new aid policies of the developed countries. In all these movements we see a tendency towards restricting the role of the state and securing the autonomy of the market (Ghai 1999, p. 246). Furthermore, the link between participation in the labour market and entitlement to social security has been strengthened in most areas at the expense of the idea of social rights as a universal entitlement, irrespective of social status (Clasen 2001, p. 2). According to the UNDP progress has been made in reducing poverty, (HDR 2000, p. 34), but there is a widespread consensus that global income inequality has reached 'grotesque levels' (HDR 2003, p. 39), while income inequality between citizens in the world probably increased during the 1990s. The measurement of inequality across the globe is extremely difficult and the trends are ambiguous, but UNDP nevertheless dares to draw the above conclusions. The challenges for existing systems of social welfare and for the prospects for an expansion of distributive justice in developing and transitional economies manifest themselves in a number of ways in the different regions of the world.

In the *European Union* a Social Charter was adopted in 1989 by eleven of the twelve member states. Great Britain did not join in the declaration of the charter, which was a legally non-binding document signalling the willingness of the eleven countries to work together to secure the social dimension of the expansion of the free market. The UK signed only after New Labour came to power in 1997. Nevertheless, the basic thinking and practical policies on social security have been debated intensely during the last two decades. The ageing of populations as well as the introduction of a whole group of new, poorer members into the European community[8] have awakened both governments and people to new realities. Lifestyles and family structures have also changed, so the former systems, based on the idea that a single male in life-long employment supports his family,[9] has become outdated. There is widespread recognition that the existing systems will not be able to accommodate the heavier burden of larger unproductive segments in society. Therefore new, economically sustainable policies are having to be designed, which must also be accompanied by changes in values and morality; and a convergence between the different social systems in Europe is taking place (Moreno 2001, p. 93). As a consequence the balance between rights and duties has changed: unemployment policy is increasingly referred to as 'activation' policy; responsibility for caring for the sick and the elderly is being transferred back to the family or the private

8 The EU Enlargement Declaration, adopted in Copenhagen in December 2002, allowed Cyprus, the Czech Republic, Estonia, Hungary, Latvia, Lithuania, Malta, Poland, Slovakia and Slovenia to become members of the EU.

9 The so-called 'bread-winner bias' denied entitlement to social benefits to women and to people in part-time or informal jobs (UNRISD 2000: 3-4).

sector; and philanthropy is re-emerging in the form of non-profit and voluntary organisations being incorporated into the provision of services, etc.

Within Europe systems still differ, though. At one end of the continuum from less to more state involvement, neo-liberalism dominated British policy after the Conservative Margaret Thatcher became prime minister in the UK in 1979. Under her governments, social reforms shifted responsibility from the public to the private sector, nationalised industries were privatised, and individual entrepreneurship was encouraged and rewarded. England's political and economic system moved closer to the US's (especially in relation to the direction that American politics took from the Reagan administration in 1981 onwards) and thus away from its continental European neighbours' (Stokke 2004, p. 41). After Thatcher the direction did not change radically. Tony Blair's New Labour focused on activation measures and placed an equal stress on rights and duties, gradually converging with the rest of Europe in a move away from universal policies towards more selective systems.

Even in the *Nordic countries*, with their hitherto universal social security schemes, a new ideology and understanding of social problems have taken shape. One dominant trend has been that the duty aspect has become more prominent than before, and stronger conditions have been attached to the granting of social benefits. In Denmark new social legislation was passed from the late 1980s on, according to which unemployed workers are now required to enrol in activation measures as a precondition for receiving unemployment benefits, and recipients of early retirement or invalidity benefits have to undergo periodic tests of their ability to work. The demands for contributions in return for social benefits and for further means testing are new in their current form, and their introduction is linked to both increased immigration and internal pressures like the ageing of the population (Jæger and Kvist 2004, p. 63). Similar developments have taken place in the other Nordic countries (Dalberg-Larsen 1995, p. 29). Notwithstanding this, the commitment to universal tax-based welfare systems is still strong, despite the adaptations, and despite the fact that social equality was ranked as having the lowest significance for the Danish population as compared to other European countries according to the European Social Survey.[10]

In the *former communist countries* of Eastern Europe, Central Asia and China, the transition to a market economy caused severe cuts in public spending on social services and the establishment of selective social-security systems paid by the social partners in the labour market (employers and employees). Vulnerable groups, like people without a job and the elderly, lost out in the process. Before the demise of communism, the welfare policies of Eastern Europe and Central and East Asia were characterised by a unity of social and economic policy (Brooks and Thant 1998, p. 418; Deacon and Szalai 1990). Welfare was then also linked to employment,

10 The European Social Survey (ESS) is a biennial multi-country survey covering over twenty nations. The project collects and analyses huge amounts of data on social development in the EU countries and is funded jointly by the European Commission, the European Science Foundation and academic funding bodies in each participating country. Web-page: http://ess.nsd.uib.no

but as the systems were dedicated to full employment, in reality almost everybody received social benefits through their work-places. The state guaranteed its citizens a job, and with the job followed the right to free medical services, primary schooling, housing, pensions, etc. But by the mid-1990s all these countries had adopted new legislation on social protection, which was characterised by a diversification of service provision through the devolution of responsibilities to local governments, marketisation and the support of voluntary charitable activities. For the urban population social security funds were established for employees, covering the most important welfare items like health care and pensions. Employers and employees paid in contributions to the funds and received benefits according to their contributions (Thelle 2004, p. 85). But for great numbers of people, notably the unemployed and farmers, no effective social-security systems have been set up.

In *the developing world*, since 1980 the Bretton Woods institutions (the World Bank and the International Monetary Fund) have promoted the so-called structural adjustment policies (SAP) as a condition for member states to receive loans. These policies are characterised by the 'liberalisation' of the economy, meaning the encouragement of privatisation and reduced protection for domestic industries. The role of the state is minimised, and public spending severely discouraged. With public spending restricted, governments are unable to support health care schemes, free schooling or social security programmes for their citizens. The SAPs have been heavily criticised over the years by international NGOs and governments in developing countries for increasing poverty levels and the dependence of developed countries.[11] The policies are now under serious debate within international financial institutions, and SAPs are gradually being replaced by policies promoting good governance and poverty alleviation. The worst effects of these policies are addressed in the institution of a special procedure, discussed below as a 'counter-movement'.

The most expensive and therefore economically and politically sensitive aspect of social security are *pension systems*, and the ageing of populations worldwide has put the design and reform of pension systems high on the international agenda. Protection in old age is also one of the recurring items in all documents on the protection of social rights produced by the UN and the ILO, and has been so since the beginning of the history of social security systems, in Germany in the 1880s (Scheinin 2001, p. 211). The increasing proportion of old people has been haunting Europe and the international community like a spectre, and concern for the detonation of a so-called 'demographic time bomb' has led to grim predictions of the breakdown of the modern welfare state in the developed nations (Castles 2001, pp. 141-142). In the developing world, support for old people is still largely the responsibility of the family or closer community. However, the issue has been the subject of intense scholarly research in the last decades, and international organisations are beginning to provide recommendations to states about it.

---

11 www.globalissues.org/TradeRelated/SAP; www.whirledbank.org/development/sap; www.saprin.org

In 1994 the World Bank launched a plan for pension reforms, encouraging the replacement of universal public pensions with contribution-based schemes (World Bank 1994). The plan has been quite influential, especially in Latin America and the former East European countries. Notably the experience of Chile, which had already replaced universal pension schemes with a system based on savings and corporate insurance in 1981, have been studied widely, also in Asia. In 2004 a 'Pension Reform Primer' was published, providing a practical tool for policy-makers who want to introduce the suggested 'Defined Contribution Pension' scheme (Modigliani 2004). This system is characterised by the principle that the number of pension payments depends on contributions over the years, that is, throughout their working lives pensioners themselves save the money they will receive as pensions.

The pension system advocated by the World Bank fits very well with the demands of a free market economy, and is in opposition to the universal pension schemes based on redistribution, in which present generations pay for earlier ones. A very powerful international organ thus supports the establishment of a certain kind of social structure, which reduces the responsibility of governments and transfers the protection of social rights to the market and civil society. And new pension systems, introduced across the globe, are following this pattern (Overbye 2001, p. 180), as is reflected in the examples from Asia discussed below.

The converging trends mentioned above are all contributing to the pressure placed on state-regulated welfare systems; they thus pose a danger to the existing protection of social rights and minimise the possibility of establishing new effective systems in countries which previously did not have any. The trends were all set in motion from around 1980, and they are based on the same ideology of neo-liberalism, public-choice theory or the 'new right' breaking with the idea that a moral state should assume responsibility for the implementation of economic and social rights (Stokke 2004, p. 41ff.). It can – and has been – argued that not all that happens in the world is necessarily caused by globalisation (Bhagwati 2004, p. 29), and in some of the examples mentioned above the challenges to systems of social security come from other sources than economic integration – for example, demographic growth and ageing populations – factors that certainly also constitute threats to systems of social protection. It can be said that it is the expanded market economy, liberal ideology and demographic transition taken together that are undermining egalitarian social systems. As a counter-current, efforts to establish global minimum social standards and a new emphasis on the ideas of rights and public participation work in the opposite direction.

### 2.2 *Counter-movements: Global Social Responsibility*

The pressure on social livelihoods in the era of increased market integration has caused a growing recognition of poverty as a violation of human rights, and the international community has in many ways expressed concern over the fact that 'the benefits of globalisation are unevenly shared while its costs are unevenly distributed.'[12] Many documents and reports on the issue commence with and refer to the Millennium Declaration (MD), adopted by the UN General Assembly on 8 September 2000, which lays down a number of concrete goals within the areas of security, development, environment and good governance, and a number of special goals meeting the needs of Africa, all to be realised by 2015.[13] Several of the seven objectives pertain to social rights, such as the goals to halve the proportion of the world's population living on less than one dollar a day, to halve the proportion of people with no access to clean drinking water, to ensure that all children will be able to complete primary schooling, to reduce child mortality, and to stop the spread of AIDS. Numerous programmes and initiatives have been designed since the turn of the millenium to achieve these goals.

Concerning the fate of people in poor countries, the UN Commission on Human Rights (UNHRC) has initiated one of its so-called *special procedures* to assess the impact of SAPs on the governments' ability to adopt policies and programmes for the enjoyment of economic, social and cultural rights. Since 1998 an independent expert on SAPs has been appointed,[14] and the Economic and Social Council has established a working group on SAPs to work on policy guidelines to serve as basis for dialogue between human rights bodies and financial institutions. The mandate of the independent expert was renewed for the period 2003-2006 after he submitted a report to the 60th session of the UNHRC in February 2004.[15] The report reviews the initiatives taken by the WB and the IMF to grant debt relief for the poorest countries if they commit themselves to poverty-reduction strategies. The conclusion is that these initiatives are far from sufficient to ensure sustainable development, and donors are being encouraged to work especially towards strengthening the capacity of public expenditure management and the integration of human rights considerations into national budgeting and monitoring processes.

In May 2001, the treaty body that deals especially with the rights in question, the ESCR Committee, contributed to the discussion by adopting a statement on 'Poverty and the ICESCR', expressing the view that poverty in itself constitutes a denial of human rights and that the Covenant should be used to enhance poverty-reduction strategies.[16] Another UN measure has especially targeted the corporate sector. The Global Compact (GC) was launched by the UN Secretary General in July 2000 as 'a voluntary international corporate citizenship network initiated to support the participation of both the private sector and other social actors to advance responsible corporate citizenship and universal social and environmental principles to meet the challenges of globalisation.' The GC is based on ten principles from the fields of human rights, labour and the environment, the first one encompassing social rights by demanding that 'businesses should support and re-

12 Commission on Human Rights, Resolution 2001/27.
13 Many of the Millenium goals appeared earlier in the Plan of Action from the Social Summit in Copenhagen in 1995.
14 Since 2000 called 'the independent expert on SAPs and foreign debt.'
15 E/CN.4/2004/47.
16 E/C.12/2001/10.

spect the protection of internationally proclaimed human rights.'[17] The GC is underpinning a complex network with many ramifications based on the concept of Corporate Social Responsibility (CSR). Within this framework, companies are held responsible for human rights violations occurring during their operations – and these will often belong to the category of economic and/or social rights. Standard setting and consumer pressure are parts of the varied strategies pursued by human rights NGOs and activist lawyer firms in the endeavour to make companies act in a more socially responsible way.

Catering to the interests of employees, the ILO established a so-called World Commission on the Social Dimension of Globalisation in February 2002, which published a report two years later (WCSDG 2004). The establishment of the Commission was inspired by a wish to extend the benefits of globalisation to more people and to foster a consensus instead of the existing public debate of 'frozen opinions' (WCSDG 2004, p. ix). The mandate of the commission was 'to respond to the needs of people as they cope with the unprecedented changes that globalisation has brought to their lives, their families, and the societies in which they live.' The report received support from the UN through the adoption of a resolution[18] linking the report and the Commission to the Millennium Declaration. Subsequently the EU Commission joined in by publishing a communication to the EU Parliament, describing a range of actions undertaken in regard to the social aspects of globalisation. The communication is very positive both in relation to the economic gains of globalisation and the Union's ability to live up to the goals of the Millennium Declaration. It is said that 'the EU has already developed initiatives and policies to address the social dimension of globalisation both in Europe and elsewhere',[19] the question now being merely to strengthen this dimension in light of the WCSDG report. In spite of its somewhat propagandistic tone, the publication of the communication proves that the EU Government considers it important to address social issues, *inter alia* expressed through support for the ESS project (see n. 10, p. 209).

In the academic field, efforts followed the Copenhagen Social Summit back in 1995. A Globalism and Social Policy Programme (GASPP) was established in 1997 in collaboration between the University of Sheffield (UK) and the National Research and Development Centre for Welfare and Health, Helsinki. The programme aims to investigate the implications of globalisation on social policy, and it works on the assumption of the possibility and even desirability of formulating a global social policy based on universalist and redistributional values and principles. The criterion for entitlement to social benefits is no longer to be citizenship, as globalisation has outdated the territorial bases for citizenship, but the issue of an

17 www.un.org/Dpts/ptd/global.htm.

18 A/RES/59/57.

19 Communication from the Commission of the EU to the European Parliament, the Council of Ministers, the European Economic and Social Committee and the Committee of the Regions. *The Social Dimension of Globalisation – the EU's policy contribution on extending the benefits to all.* COM(2004)383 final.

international citizenship with associated rights and duties is raised. The scholars in the program are actually quite optimistic about the future for this policy, stating this year that, "Now even within the World Bank there is some evidence that the case for a universal approach to social welfare provision is again being recognised" (Deacon 2005). The GASPP has been very active in discussing and lobbying for a socially responsible form of globalisation. For the past five years it has edited the journal *Global Social Policy*, which is not only an academic exercise, but also serves a global policy-making audience. The programme publishes recommendations to governments and participates in networks and alliances with partners in the South.

The quest for a more human and equitable kind of globalisation is thus taking place in many different forums, shaping agenda setting and putting policy recommendations forward. Some of these have been mentioned here, but there are others, like the boards of the WB and IMF; the annual meetings of the UN specialised agencies, notably the ILO, WHO and UNESCO; various UN summits relating to social issues; project support generated from large foundations like Ford, Rockefeller and the Soros Open Society Institute; and numerous academic gatherings and professional settings putting forward recommendations and interacting with national governments. Many of these initiatives are coming directly from the human rights system itself, and though some of them have a stronger human rights focus than others, they all refer to human rights thinking being their basic value in one or another way. The question is to what degree they are able to secure a basis of social security for vulnerable groups and societies in the era of globalisation. Two cases will be discussed to illustrate how complex the answers are.

## 3 Case Studies

The patterns and movements circulating around people and creating social safety nets for them are complex and diversified. On the one hand, relatively unconditional (universal) social protection is still restricted to just a few countries, and the possibilities for expanding these kinds of social security systems are not great, trends which do not further protection of the poor and marginalised groups. Many post-communist and some developing countries are adopting new policies, where survival still basically depends on relations with the formal labour market, or on family support. *East Asia*, with China as its largest country, provides one example. On the other hand, the threat of the breakdown of existing systems may not be as serious as feared by some observers. Foreseen threats to social security caused by global or regional economic integration and exposure to the international market have in some cases proved to be exaggerated. The *European Union* provides one such case.

### 3.1 A Welfare Model with East Asian Characteristics

In Asia, the sustainability of Western welfare models is questioned, and other models have been suggested. Asia has been the region with the world's fastest economic growth during recent decades and it is often suggested that it will be the new economic centre of the 21st century (Frank 2001). The rapidly growing economies in East and South-East Asia have followed a different path than Western Europe, and many of them have been able to combine growth and political stability without introducing democratic systems based on public participation.

The rise of Asian economic power began with Japan after World War II, followed by rapid growth in the 'four little tigers'[20] from the mid-1960s, and then by Malaysia, the Philippines, Indonesia and Thailand from the early 1990s. In these countries spectacular economic growth has been followed by a more equitable income distribution during the last three decades (Xin Meng 2000, p. 133). The growth has in large part been export-led, with the state playing an important role as the regulator of a market economy, and spending on social welfare has been tightly controlled. In spite of its limited investments in social welfare schemes, the region has seen a high level of political stability and no substantial decline in income equality in South-East Asia, though in China inequality is rising rapidly (Tang 2000). This is an ideal combination seen from the politician's point of view: peace and prosperity on a small state budget, a fact which invoked the interest of scholars and social policy-makers in Western societies, where existing institutions for the provision of social welfare were being questioned. In the mid 1990s the 'low-spending "welfare states" of East and South-East Asia not only attracted increasing attention among Western scholars and politicians, but were actually pointed out as potential welfare models for the West' (Hort and Kuhnle 2000, p. 164).

Even though the picture changed somewhat during the Asian crisis of 1997, there is general agreement that some kinds of social welfare institutions are being shaped in part of the region. The common elements of the Asian systems are based on the strategic priority of rapid industrialisation on the one hand and an authoritarian political regime on the other. Welfare policy is linked more often than not to support for the political legitimacy of the regime in question, and what exists of social welfare mechanisms in these countries is said to be characterised by:

- An authoritarian or paternalistic political rule
- Low government spending on social welfare
- Attachment to non-statutory welfare, i.e. dependence on family and community
- Weak development of the notion of social rights or entitlements
- Social insurance favoured over tax-based pay-as-you-go models
- Exclusive support to elite groups and lack of popular participation

China, as the biggest country in Asia, is, together with Vietnam, special in being both a (post-) communist society and in having a basically Confucian cultural orientation. Regarding social policy, the Chinese Government has adopted new policies, which are a mixture of social insurance and savings. The system demands that employers and employees pay into funds at the level of local government. The funds cover pensions, health care, and in some cases maternity leave and unem-

20 Hong Kong, South Korea, Taiwan and Singapore.

ployment. But the system only covers urban people with employment in the formal sector.[21] People without formal employment in the cities have to make do with a small 'minimum living standard subsidy', which is difficult to obtain, and as a rule peasants do not have the protection of social security benefits at all (Thelle 2004). Other post-communist societies have adopted similar systems, governed by the principles of selectivity, contributions in return for social benefits, and meagre or inaccessible minimum living benefits.

Development in Asia is not governed by basic human rights principles, but rather pursues a path well fitted to the needs of international capital. Foreign investment in turn provides a certain rise in living standards, which may affect some weak groups too, but it does not guarantee a livelihood for everyone.

### *3.2 EU Enlargement*

In another example, Europe, there were fears that the increased integration of the European Union would drag the whole region down with respect to the protection of marginalised groups. Conservative political forces warned against further social and economic integration and pointed to the threat of losing welfare protection in the earlier members of the European community. But researchers have, to some extent, found the fear exaggerated and concluded that 'institutional resilience and the vested interests that welfare-state institutions cater to' are seen as meeting the challenges of increased economic interaction (Kvist 2004, p. 316). In 2002 the EU was enlarged by ten new member states. This triggered similar debates and policy concerns as did the global integration of economic and social systems discussed above. The European Union is basically a free-market zone securing unrestricted movement of capital and labour. The ten new states were considerably poorer than the EU's existing fifteen members, and their accession raised questions within and among the old member states concerning how to manage a potentially massive inflow of new workers within the existing – and different – systems of social security. Would the accession lead to widespread welfare migration, putting pressure on social security provision and levels of benefits in the better-off European societies? Would the enlargement lead to the famous 'race to the bottom' within the rich part of Europe?

Earlier enlargements of the EU in the mid-1980s involving the then poorer southern neighbours of Portugal, Spain and Greece were not followed by considerable migration, though the same concerns were expressed at that time. Research carried out at this early stage also indicates that welfare migration has not taken place at the level feared after the latest round of enlargement. On the contrary, there is a growing feeling that immigration should be welcomed as a way of fighting the ageing of the population in the EU's former fifteen states (Krieger 2004). But European countries have reacted to their fears by introducing temporary measures restricting the free movement of labourers and their access to social benefits in

21 This means either employed in state/collective enterprises or having a labour contract with a private employer.

the host countries. According to the Accession Treaty, the old member states are allowed to restrict the movement of workers for a period of up to seven years, and most countries have done so through the introduction of quotas, demands for registration, documentation of job offers, etc. Only labour migration is restricted, however: migration for residence, study or other purposes is not included, as these forms of migration do not create social security entitlements. The different EU countries have integrated their policies, so when one country adopts restrictions, other countries will discuss similar policies in order not to become more attractive to 'social tourists' than their neighbours (Kvist 2004, p. 311-312). But until now the fear of mass migration has proved unfounded, and researchers assess that even without restrictive measures, migration would not pose a serious problem within Europe, even though increased integration might lead to 'some redistribution of population' (Salt 2003, p. 4).

The fear of social dumping and a 'race to the bottom' (Hort and Kuhnle 2000) has also been mentioned in relation to the globalisation process as such. But in the case of Europe, at least, it seems that ingrained institutions are slow to change. The problem is that the developing world does not have the institutions with which to resist accumulated international capital.

## 4 Balancing

Thus, on a global scale, pressure on social security from the internationalised market economy is being met with opposition from international movements lobbying for a 'global social policy', just as rapid industrialisation within the European and Anglo-Saxon countries during the late 1800s produced a labour movement and with it development of the social policies we know today. The present chapter has aimed to investigate the role that the idea of social security as a *right* is playing in meeting challenges for the protection of social rights in the future. The rights approach was defined as state policies securing free and equal access to basic means of livelihood based in law, formulated with the participation of the population at large, and guaranteeing remedies in cases of violation. Most documents and initiatives mentioned above support the human rights concept in general terms, but when it comes to the policies proposed and adopted at both the international and the national levels, the emphasis on the constitutive elements of a rights-based social policy is less dominant.

Many discussions centre on poverty alleviation as a national and international responsibility from above, but are less concerned with guarantees for public participation or the creation of effective remedies securing a movement from below (see also Hans-Otto Sano in this volume). The social policies in the melting pot in a large part of the world like China and the former Soviet Bloc are based on contributions and only sporadically guarantee public participation and systems for effective remedies. The trend of social policies in the old world is moving towards means-testing and away from universal principles. International recommendations to developing countries are based on reductions in public social spending by governments. The causal connection between globalisation and the observed threats to social security is not direct and clear cut. Many different factors interact in shaping the world as it looks today, but it is difficult not to link the facts that, on the one hand, more economic power is being vested in private capital that operates relatively freely across borders than in state budgets with only national reach, and on the other hand, that social inequality persists and may even be on the rise, in spite of spectacular economic growth in many regions.

The validity of social rights as such has in fact been questioned throughout the history of the human rights regime. The rights are vaguely defined, and the most detailed codification allows for the different treatment of different groups of people. The challenges of globalisation have come on top of general doubts that social rights are not 'real' human rights, but subject to political decisions regarding priorities of resource allocation. Social rights are thus exposed to a double jeopardy, from claims that they belong to the political realm and are not a matter for the legal system, to the actual weakness of states in providing sufficient social security for their citizens; and the incapacity of states is underpinned by globalisation.

On the other hand, rights thinking as such can challenge the degradation of social justice caused by economic globalisation. Some scholars think the human rights regime provides the 'nearest thing to a coherent challenge' (Ghai 1999, p. 250; Felice 2003, p. 232-234). Bob Deacon likewise stated in 1998 that the mere existence of human social rights empowers people to demand them of their governments, even though developed countries often do not live up to their own rhetoric (Deacon 1998). As pointed out elsewhere in this volume too, many initiatives indicate the emergence of vibrant and dynamic counter-movements which are struggling to introduce a more socially responsible attitude into the world community.

### References

Bauman, Z., *Globalization. The Human Consequences*, London, Polity Press, 1999.

Bhagwati, J., *In Defence of Globalization*, Oxford, UK, Oxford University Press, 2004.

Blanpain, R. (ed.), *The Council of Europe and the Social Challenges of the XXIst Century*, Bulletin of Comparative Labour Relations, The Hague, Kluwer Law International, 2001.

Brooks, D. H. and Thant, M., *Social Sector Issues in Transitional Economies of Asia*, Oxford, UK, Oxford University Press, 1998.

Castles, F. D., 'Public Expenditure and Population Ageing: why families of nations are different' in Clasen, J. (ed.), *What Future for Social Security? Debates and Reforms in National and Cross-national Perspective*, The Hague, Kluwer Law International, pp. 141-155, 2001.

*Circle of Rights. Economic, Social and Cultural Rights Activism: A Training Resource*, Washington D.C., International Human Rights Internship Program and Asian Forum for Human Rights and Development, 2000.

Clasen, J. (ed.), *What Future for Social Security? Debates and Reforms in National and Cross-national Perspective*, The Hague, Kluwer Law International, 2001.

Craven, M., *The International Covenant on Economic, Social and Cultural Rights. A Perspective on its Development*, Oxford, Clarendon Press, 1995.

Cook, S. and Kabeer, N. (eds.), 'Social Policy in the South: Revisioning the Agenda', *IDS Bulletin*, vol. 31, no. 4, 2000.

Dalberg-Larsen, J., 'The Nordic Welfare Model – What Separates the Nordic Countries from the Rest of Europe?' in *Re-Conceptualizing the Welfare State*, proceedings from symposium in connection with Maastricht II, 28-30 September 1995, Copenhagen, The Danish Centre for Human Rights, pp. 22-32, 1995.

Deacon, B., 'Social Rights and Globalization' in *Copenhagen Papers*, no. 3, A European Regional Forum on Social Development, 5-6 November 1998, Paris, 1998.

Deacon, B., *Globalization and Social Policy: the Threat to Equitable Welfare*, United Nation's Research Institute for Social Development (UNRISD), Geneva, Occasional Paper 5, 2000.

Deacon, B. 'From "Safety Nets" Back to "Universal Social Provision": Is the Global Tide Turning?' in *Global Social Policy*, vol. 5, no. 1, April, 2005.

Deacon, B. and Julie Szalai (eds.), *Social Policy in the New Eastern Europe. What Future for Socialist Welfare?*, Aldershot, Avebury, 1990.

Eide, A., Krause, C. and Rosas, A. (eds.), *Economic, Social and Cultural Rights. A Textbook. Second revised edition*, Dordrecht, Martinus Nijhoff Publishers, 2001.

Esping-Andersen, G., *The Three Worlds of Welfare Capitalism*, Cambridge, Polity Press, 1990.

Felice, W. F., *The Global New Deal. Economic and Social Human Rights in World Politics*, Lanham, Boulder, etc., Rowman & Littelfield Publishers, Inc., 2003.

Frank, A.G., *Re-ORIENT : global economy in the Asian age*, Berkeley, California, University of California Press, 2001.

GASPP (Globalism and Social Policy Programme).

Ghai, Y., 'Rights, Social Justice and Globalization in East Asia' in Bell and Bauer (eds.), *The East Asian Challenge for Human Rights*, Cambridge, Cambridge University Press, pp. 241-263, 1999.

Havel, V. et al., *The Power of the Powerless. Citizens Against the State in Central-Eastern Europe*, Edited by John Keane, London, Hutchinson, 1985.

HDR 2000, *Human Development Report*, New York, UNDP, 2000.

HDR 2003, *Human Development Report*, New York, UNDP, 2003.

Held, D. et al., *Global Transformations – Politics, Economics and Culture*, Cambridge/Oxford, Polity Press, 1999.

Hort, S.E.O. and Kuhnle, S., 'The Coming of East and South East Asian Welfare States?' in *Journal of European Social Policy*, vol. 10, no. 2, pp. 162-184, 2000.

Hunt, P., *Reclaiming Social Rights. International and Comparative Perspectives*, Aldershot, Dartmouth, 1996.

Jæger, M. and Kvist, J., 'Det sociale medborgerskab' (Social Citizenship) in Koch and Thelle (eds.), *Sociale Menneskerettigheder* (Social Human Rights), Copenhagen, Akademisk Forlag, 2004.

Koch, I. E., 'The Justiciability of Indivisible Rights' in *Nordic Journal of International Law*, Vol. 72, pp. 3-39, 2003.

Krieger, H., *Migration Trends in an Enlarged Europe*. Report from European Foundation for the Improvement of Living and Working Conditions, Dublin, 2004.

Kvist, J., 'Does EU enlargement start a race to the bottom? Strategic interaction among EU member states in social policy' in *Journal of European Social Policy*, vol. 14(3), pp. 301-318, 2004.

Lamarche, L., 'The Right to Social Security in the International Covenant on Economic, Social and Cultural Rights' in Chapman and Russell (eds.), *Core Obligations: Building a Framework for Economic, Social and Cultural Rights*, Oxford, UK, Hart Publishing, pp. 87-114, 2002.

Liebenberg, S., 'The Protection of Economic and Social Rights in Domestic Legal Systems' in Eide, A., Krause, C. and Rosas, A. (eds.), *Economic, Social and Cultural Rights. A Textbook. Second revised edition*, Dordrecht, Martinus Nijhoff Publishers, pp. 55-84, 2001.

Modigliani, F. and Muralidhar A., *Rethinking Pension Reform*, Cambridge, Cambridge University Press, 2004.

Moreno, L., 'Europeanisation and Decentralisation of Welfare "Safety Nets"' in Clasen, J. (ed.), *What Future for Social Security? Debates and Reforms in National and Cross-national Perspective*, The Hague, Kluwer Law International, pp. 87-100, 2001.

Nowak, M., 'The Right to Education' in Eide, A., Krause, C. and Rosas, A. (eds.), *Economic, Social and Cultural Rights. A Textbook. Second revised edition*, Dordrecht, Martinus Nijhoff Publishers, pp. 245-271, 2001.

Overbye, E., 'The Redistributional Impact of a World Bank "Pension Regime"' in Clasen, J. (ed.), *What Future for Social Security? Debates and Reforms in National and Cross-national Perspective*, The Hague, Kluwer Law International, pp. 179-194, 2001.

Salt, J., *Current Trends in International Migration in Europe*, Strasbourg, Council of Europe, 2003.

Scheinin, M., 'Economic and Social Rights as Legal Rights' in Eide, A., Krause, C. and Rosas, A. (eds.), *Economic, Social and Cultural Rights. A Textbook. Second revised edition*, Dordrecht, Martinus Nijhoff Publishers, pp. 29-54, 2001.

Stokke, H., 'What is Left of State Responsibility? Turning State Obligations into State Responsibility in the Field of Economic, Social and Cultural Rights' in *Human Rights in Development. Yearbook 2002*, Leiden/Boston, Martinus Nijhoff Publishers, pp. 37-70, 2004.

Tang, K., *Social Welfare Development in East Asia*, Hampshire, Palgrave, 2000.

Thelle, H., *Better to Rely on Ourselves. Changing Social Rights in Urban China since 1979*, Copenhagen, NIAS Press, 2004.

UNRISD, *Social Policy in a Development Context*. Report of the United Nations Research Institute for Social Development (UNRISD) International Conference, 23-24 September 2000, Tammsvik, Sweden, 2000.

World Commission on the Social Dimension of Globalization (WCSDG), *A Fair Globalization. Creating Opportunities for All*, Geneva, ILO, 2004.

World Bank, *Averting the Old Age Crisis: Policies to Protect the Old and Promote Growth*, New York, Oxford University Press, 1994.

Xin, M., *Labour Market Reform in China*, Cambridge, Cambridge University Press, 2000.

# 10. Prisons and Human Rights: The Case of Solitary Confinement in Denmark and the US from the 1820s until Today

*Peter Scharff Smith*

## 1. Prisons, Human Rights, and the Use of Solitary Confinement

It is still today questioned in various parts of the world whether prisoners have rights, or whether the ordinary rights of a citizen or a human being cease to exist once an individual is detained inside prison walls. In fact, one does not have to venture far back into history in order to find this situation in democratic states. In 1871 a now famous judgment was passed in Virginia in the United States, which declared that a convicted felon "is *civiliter mortuus*; and his estate, if he has any, is administered like that of a dead man". A prisoner was accordingly "civilly dead" and inmates were simply "slaves of the State".[1] This and other cases created the foundation of what was later termed the "hands-off" doctrine, according to which US courts only intervened in extreme cases. Otherwise penal institutions were "virtually abandoned...to the unchecked power of their administrators".[2] As late as 1958 the Supreme Court accordingly refrained from entering "the domain of penology".[3] The hands-off doctrine was in other words practised by US courts for around a century, but during the early 1960s a number of prisoners' rights became established through court cases.[4] This was also the case in several other countries, and the 1960s and 1970s became a period of intensive reforms and changes of attitude

1 *Ruffin v. Commonwealth* 1871. Quoted from Hans Jørgen Engbo 'Menneskerettigheder under afsoning af fængselsstraf' in Jepsen og Lyhne (ed.), *Retspolitiske udfordringer*, 2003, p. 286. See also Michael Jackson, *Prisoners of Isolation*, University of Toronto Press, 1983, p. 82.

2 Edgardo Rotman 'The Failure of Reform' in Morris and Rothman (ed.), *The Oxford History of the Prison*, Oxford University Press 1998, p. 171.

3 *Gore v. US* 1958. Quoted from Engbo 2003, p. 286.

4 According to Norval Morris "federal and state courts" in the US applied the hands-off doctrine until "the early 1970s"; Norval Morris 'The Contemporary Prison' in Morris and Rothman (ed.), *The Oxford History of the Prison*, Oxford University Press 1998, p. 219.

*S. Lagoutte, H-O. Sano and P. Scharff Smith (eds.),* Human Rights in Turmoil, *pp. 221-248.*
 *ISBN 90 04 15432 9.*

in the area of prisoner rights.[5] In 1974 the US Supreme Court, for example, stated that there "is no iron curtain drawn between the Constitution and the prisons of this country". The significance of prisoner rights was spelled out even more clearly in a Canadian judgment of 1969, according to which "an inmate of an institution continues to enjoy all the civil rights of a person save those that are taken away or interfered with by having been lawfully sentenced to imprisonment".[6]

Following the Second World War, a human rights framework for securing prisoner rights has also evolved, which includes, for example, the UN Standard Minimum Rules for the Treatment of Prisoners of 1955, the International Covenant on Civil and Political Rights of 1966, the Convention against Torture and Other Cruel, Inhuman or Degrading Treatment or Punishment of 1984, the UN Basic Principles for the Treatment of Prisoners of 1990, which were revised in 2006, and the European Prison Rules (a regional document).

But the issue of prisoner rights is still contested. Even in states which accept the basic premise of prisoners having rights, extending these rights beyond official law into the reality of the prison might be difficult. In England, for example, judges "are disinclined to intervene in many areas of prison life, notwithstanding the introduction of the Human Rights Act [in] 1998".[7] The same well-known problem of human rights implementation (versus official adherence to conventions etc.) has also been noticed in the Danish context. As a Danish prison governor pointed out, it is "remarkable that the convention [ECHR] is so invisible in the daily application of law among the authorities responsible for executing punishment".[8] In the US the concept of prisoner rights is itself being contested at the moment. The government has been "playing fast and loose with the international law of war" in its treatment of detainees, and, according to an English Professor of Criminal Justice, the practice of detention without trial is both "deeply troubling and in deep trouble".[9] An institution like the detention facility at Guantanamo Bay could, from a historical point of view, be interpreted as a revival of the "slaves of the State" philosophy expressed in Virginia in 1871.

The tendency either to question and oppose human rights or not to prioritise implementation in this area is unfortunate since prisons – as a specific type of institution – tend to provide ample opportunity for violations of human rights. This is well known from social-psychological experiments as well as from the turbulent history of the prison. In the words of the international expert on prison reform,

5 "The heyday of the prisoners' rights movement roughly spanned the period from 1960 to 1980", according to James B. Jacobs, 'Prison Reform amid the Ruins of Prisoners' Rights' in Michael Tonry (ed.), *The Future of Imprisonment*, Oxford University Press 2004, p. 183. Concerning the US, *see* also Rotman 1998, and concerning Germany, *see* Liora Lazarus *Contrasting Prisoners' Rights: A Comparative Examination of Germany and England*, Oxford University Press 2004, pp. 34 et seq.

6 Both quotes are taken from Engbo 2003, pp. 286 f.

7 Lazarus 2004, p. 3.

8 Engbo 2003, p. 309 (translated by the author).

9 Clive Walker, 'Prisoners of "War All the Time"', in *European Human Rights Law* Review, no. 1, 2005, pp. 51 et seq.

Vivien Stern, "prison is a prime place for dehumanization".[10] As the current English Chief Inspector of Prisons described the situation, "in our prisons, things that would be unacceptable in any other context can become accepted and even built in to the system".[11]

The use of solitary confinement in prison systems is a good example of such a phenomenon, a practice which is unthinkable in almost any other context than the prison.[12] But the isolation of individual prisoners is nevertheless a daily reality in prisons all over the world. This is understandable in the sense that short-term isolation can be a valuable disciplinary tool in prisons, but problematic since such practices can leave the isolated inmate very far from the sight and reach of justice. How can one ensure the rights of a citizen who is actually in a prison within a prison? Given this "quality" of solitary confinement, it is not surprising that the practice of isolating inmates carries with it a history of prisoner abuse. Even when practised according to law in democratic nations, the isolation of prisoners is a drastic measure. According to a criminological study of prison order, "the decision to segregate ... a long-term maximum-security prisoner" stands, "[w]ith the exception of the death penalty ... at perhaps the furthest point of the repertoire of sanctions and compulsions available to a liberal democratic state outside time of war".[13] This undoubtedly goes a long way towards explaining why isolation practices are not easily diminished. Politicians are often reluctant to cut back on state security measures, while prison authorities tend to hold on to their discretionary powers, as all authorities do. All these factors added up leaves us with a problematic area of prison policy. It is on the one hand difficult and most likely counterproductive completely to ban solitary confinement legally, while on the other hand it constitutes a remarkable demonstration of state power, which can easily lead to misuse and sometimes human rights violations. In studying the use and effects of solitary confinement, in other words, one finds oneself plummeting deep into a field of tension between the authority of the modern state and the integrity of the individual citizen. When dealing with prisons and human rights, solitary confinement is therefore a very important issue. It is also a very topical issue, not least in Scandinavia and the US, where its use has received intense human rights criticism, especially during the last couple of decades. This chapter will therefore trace the history, ideology and practice of solitary confinement in Denmark and the US, and aim to view these

10 Vivien Stern, *A Sin Against the Future: Imprisonment in the World*, Northeastern University Press, p. 194.

11 HM Chief Inspector of Prisons Anne Owers, speech given at LSE (London School of Economics) Thursday, 9 December 2004, p. 2. Downloaded from http://lse.ac.uk/Depts/human-rights/Documents/Rights%20behind%20bars.pdf (assessed 030106).

12 Solitary confinement is used in some psychiatric wards and hospitals (typically termed "seclusion"). Another, much less frequent use of solitary confinement can be found in connection with the isolation of people with dangerous and highly contagious diseases, who are detained (quarantined) upon arrival in a country.

13 Richard Sparks, Anthony E. Bottoms, and Will Hay, *Prisons and the Problem of Order*, 1996, p. 30.

findings in a human rights perspective.[14] Another, very topical threat to prisoners' rights in general will also be touched upon briefly: the "tough on crime" ideology and the current punitive turn in Western punishment, which has brought about a rise in the use of solitary confinement in the US.

Historically and institutionally, three different uses of solitary confinement will be identified and described:

- The adoption and subsequent abandonment of a large-scale practice of "rehabilitation through isolation" in prisons in several US states and in Denmark during the nineteenth and early twentieth centuries.
- The re-emergence of a large-scale use of solitary confinement in the US in connection with the rise of the so-called supermax prisons from the 1980s until today.
- The development of a "peculiarly Scandinavian" tradition of pre-trial solitary confinement as it took place in Denmark from the 1840s until today.[15]

It will be argued here that in both Denmark and several US states, the use of solitary confinement was embraced during the middle of the nineteenth century. But while the most severe isolation practices were generally abandoned relatively quickly in the US, the large-scale use of solitary confinement lingered on in Denmark into the twentieth century. Full-scale isolation of sentenced prisoners was finally abandoned in Denmark during the early 1930s, but pre-trial solitary confinement was still commonly used.

Following the Second World War – and apparently especially since the 1980s – the critique of solitary confinement became part of a human rights agenda. Indeed, the use of pre-trial isolation has declined significantly in Denmark during recent decades, partly due to human rights criticisms from international organizations. Still, in spite of medical and psychological expert advice, this particular practice has not been abandoned. Furthermore, the recent Danish penal debate and recent policy initiatives suggest that a new culture of control resting on punitive penal values might provoke a new rise in the use of solitary confinement in Dan-

---

14 Here, simply defined as the concept that human beings have inherent rights, which protect them from abuse as long as these rights are not transgressed. According to Donnelly, human rights "are, literally, the rights that one has because one is human" (Donnelly 2003, p. 7). Human rights are equal rights, inalienable rights and universal rights (Donnelly 2003, p. 10), and are not the same as legal rights (Donnelly 2003, p. 13). My use of the term "human rights" does not, in other words, refer directly (or solely) to any legal conventions or soft-law documents, unless I specifically refer to such material. I therefore generally use the term "human rights" as a broad category, which constitutes a perspective – or a discourse – which simply has the notion of equal, inalienable and universal human rights as its starting point, as opposed to a discourse which, for example, has state control and/or the incapacitation of individuals as its point of departure.

15 Malcolm Evans and Rod Morgan have called the pre-trial isolation of remand prisoners a "peculiarly Scandinavian phenomenon"; see Evans and Morgan, *Preventing Torture,* Clarendon Press, 1998, p. 247.

ish prisons. As will be shown, this has certainly been the case in several US states, where supermax prisons have "become political symbols of how 'tough' a jurisdiction has become".[16] Finally, the use of isolation practices has also experienced a revival in the current US war on terrorism, for example in connection with detention and interrogation at Guantanamo Bay and at facilities in Afghanistan.[17]

## 2 Rehabilitation Through Isolation: Solitary Confinement in the Nineteenth Century

From the 1770s to the 1850s, the ideology of *the modern penitentiary* (the modern prison system) established itself. With the construction of the so-called Auburn and Pennsylvania prison models in the 1820s, the aim of this modern penitentiary system became the rehabilitation of criminals through the use of isolation. The Auburn system (developed in the Auburn prison in New York State) permitted inmates to work together during the day, but under a regime of total silence. No communication was permitted. In Pennsylvania-model institutions (finally developed in Philadelphia in the "Cherry Hill" prison), there was no compromise with the ideal of isolation, and the prisoners spent all their time in the cell, where they also did their work. Here the inmate was supposed to turn his thoughts inward, to meet God, to repent his crimes and eventually to return to society as a morally cleansed Christian citizen.[18]

The ideology of the modern penitentiary, including the philosophy of rehabilitation through isolation, had an enormous impact all over the Western world. Numerous visitors from Europe and South America – official state delegations as well as other interested experts and curious celebrities – inspected American prisons during the 1830s, 1840s and 1850s, and the vast majority praised them as modern and impressive institutions. In the US the Auburn model became the most popular, but a number of Pennsylvania-model prisons were also constructed. The Europeans, on the other hand, favoured the Pennsylvania system and thus the most severe form of isolation. During the period between 1830 and the late nineteenth century, numerous prisons were therefore constructed all over the Western world based on

16 Roy D. King, 'The rise and rise of supermax: an American solution in search of a problem?', in *Punishment and Society* 1(2), 1999, p. 177. King quotes NIC (the National Institute of Corrections in the US).

17 Schlesinger, James R., Harold Brown, Tillie K. Fowler, Charles A. Homer, and James A. Blackwell. 2004. *Final Report of the Independent Panel to Review DoD Detention Operations*, Washington, DC: US Department of Defense 2004, p. 68; Karen Greenberg and Joshua Dratel (ed.), *The Torture Papers*, Cambridge University Press, 2005, p. 227.

18 See, for example, Michel Foucault, *Discipline and Punish*, Vintage Books 1995; Michael Ignatieff, *A Just Measure of Pain*, Macmillan 1978; Peter Scharff Smith, *Moralske hospitaler*, Forum 2003; and Peter Scharff Smith Smith, 'A Religious Technology of the Self: Rationality and Religion in the Rise of the Modern Penitentiary' in *Punishment and Society* no. 2, 2004 (A).

a system of social isolation, and hundreds of thousands of individuals were subjected to solitary confinement during the nineteenth century.[19]

The theory behind the modern penitentiary was in other words focused – at least in the official rhetoric – on both humanitarian principles and state-sponsored crime control. Seen from the perspective of today, one could say that, with the breakthrough of the modern penitentiary, social-control and human-rights perspectives fused on an ideological level. The new institutions were supposed to fight and reduce crime as well as rehabilitate criminals, and inmates were to receive proper hygienic and moral treatment without risking the kind of excessive corporal punishment which characterized pre-modern punishment. The large-scale use of solitary confinement was, in other words, (seemingly) an effort towards establishing not only a modern power technology, but also a humanitarian prison practice.

However, the reality in the modern penitentiaries did not live up to the theory and ideology behind them. It quickly became apparent that mental health problems were arising in the new penitentiaries, especially in the Pennsylvania-model prisons where isolation was enforced much more strictly. This was the case, for example, in the so-called "Cherry Hill" prison in Philadelphia, which was generally considered the "founding penitentiary" of the Pennsylvania model. During the initial operational years of this prison, the physician employed denied the existence of any serious health problems, but later in the 1830s reports about mental disorders materialized. However, such mental problems were often blamed on either the alleged pathological biology of imprisoned criminals or on the fact that many isolated prisoners masturbated. Still, many observers quickly established a clear connection between solitary confinement and the health of inmates. In fact all states which tried the Pennsylvania model, except Pennsylvania itself, ceased to use the system after only a few years.[20]

In Denmark solitary confinement was implemented on a large scale from 1859, when Vridsløselille Penitentiary opened based on the Pennsylvania system. During the early 1860s it became apparent that serious health problems had arisen in the prison. It quickly became normal procedure, for example, to transfer a number of the worst inmates (who became more or less uncontrollable) to insane asylums in different parts of the country, and the prison authorities fought a constant battle to avoid a general state of mental health chaos.[21] The first governor of Vridsløselille, Frederik Bruun, became a strong opponent of the regime of solitary confinement. Bruun concluded that prisoners in solitary confinement often fell into a state that resulted in "a total lack of energy and will power, in mental and physical laxity...

19 Smith 2004 (A). Concerning South America, see Ricardo Salvatore and Carlos Aguirre (ed.), *The Birth of the Penitentiary in Latin America*, University of Texas Press, 1996.

20 See Peter Scharff Smith, 'The Effects of Solitary Confinement on Prison Inmates', in Michael Tonry (ed.), *Crime and Justice*, University of Chicago Press 2006 (forthcoming).

21 Peter Scharff Smith, 'Isolation and Mental Illness in Vridsløselille 1859-1873: A New Perspective on the Breakthrough of the Modern Penitentiary', in *Scandinavian Journal of History* no. 1, 2004 (B).

which is either cured by means of fortifying medicine, a changed and improved diet, longer exercise spells or light work in the open air, or else gives way to depression and thence to higher degrees of mental disorder".[22]

To cut a long story short, the new isolation prisons produced severe problems wherever they were put into use. As one Dutch criminologist observed: "Again and again reports of insanity, suicide, and the complete alienation of prisoners from social life seriously discredited the new form of punishment."[23]

## 3 Abandoning Rehabilitation Through Isolation

From the 1860s especially, a sceptical attitude evolved towards the conception of "rehabilitation through isolation", and the ideology of the modern penitentiary faced a serious crisis. The founding nation of modern prison systems – the US – was among the first to abandon large-scale solitary confinement.[24] One reason was the substantial health problems related to isolating inmates. This was expressed, for example, by the US Supreme Court in 1890, in a statement describing how inmates were reacting to solitary confinement:

> A considerable number of prisoners fell, after even a short confinement, into a semi-fatuous condition, from which it was next to impossible to arouse them, and others became violently insane; others still, committed suicide; while those who stood the ordeal better were not generally reformed, and in most cases did not recover sufficient mental activity to be of any subsequent service to the community.[25]

Therefore, the Supreme Court continued, different isolation systems were tried out, but finally, "some 30 or 40 years ago [the 1850s and 1860s] the whole subject attracted the general public attention, and…solitary confinement was found to be too severe".[26]

Unsurprisingly the Pennsylvania model was therefore quickly abandoned in most US states and after 1858 only survived in Pennsylvania itself, where the system was legally abolished in 1913, though in reality it had ceased to exist long be-

22 Smith 2004 (B), p. 18.

23 Herman Franke, 'The Rise and Decline of Solitary Confinement', in *The British Journal of Criminology* 1992, p. 128.

24 According to Johnston, all US states that tried the Pennsylvania system abandoned this model after a few years, with the exception of Pennsylvania itself. Norman Johnston, *Forms of Constraint: A History of Prison Architecture*, University of Illinois Press 2000, p. 138. Johnston also writes: "Ironically, while Europe and, later, South America and Asia were building radial-plan prisons with cellular isolation, to be used at least in the initial phase of a sentence, the United States did not follow the example of Philadelphia's Eastern State Penitentiary [The Pennsylvania-system]", Johnston 2000, p. 147.

25 In re MEDLEY, 134 U.S. 160 (1890).

26 In re MEDLEY, 134 U.S. 160 (1890).

fore that.[27] Isolation was, of course, used throughout the nineteenth and twentieth centuries, not only in Pennsylvania-model institutions, but typically as short-term punishment in most prisons. But this was – and remains today in most prison systems – a relatively small-scale use of solitary confinement (compared to the scope of Pennsylvania-model isolation).[28]

The Pennsylvania model became much more popular in Europe and lingered on into the twentieth century in a number of countries – apparently especially in Holland, Belgium, Sweden, Norway and Denmark.[29] According to one observer, Vridsløselille penitentiary in Denmark was "one of the last prisons in the world" to give up the characteristics of the Pennsylvania system.[30] In Denmark the official belief up until the early 1930s was that prisoners could be reformed through the use of isolation.

Still, it is fair to say from an international viewpoint that from the 1860s onwards the Pennsylvania model had passed its heyday, and by the early 20th century the wave of large-scale solitary confinement had passed. As illustrated by the US Supreme Court decision of 1890, one could argue that the rights of the individual, as opposed to crime-control considerations, had gained the upper hand in evaluating the use of solitary confinement. As shown above, it was certainly presented in this manner when the damaging effects of solitary confinement were singled out as the obvious reason why this form of incarceration was uncivilized. As a result, the practice of states isolating their citizens gradually had to yield. In reality there were several reasons for the downfall of the philosophy of rehabilitation through isolation , but the adverse health effects were certainly one of them. So while economic issues, ideology, etc. had a hand in events, it still seems reasonable to conclude that a discourse which acknowledged basic human rights (other terms and labels were, of course, used at that time) in effect limited a state's social control options. As two prison psychiatrists explained in 1939, the Pennsylvania system was, with few exceptions, "no longer practiced by any civilized nation of the world".[31] Since

---

27 Harry Elmer Barnes and Negley K. Teeters, *New Horizons in Criminology*, 1960, p. 344.

28 In order to uphold order and discipline in a prison, a limited use of short-term solitary confinement might be necessary. Unfortunately isolation as an administrative and disciplinary tool inside prisons is often used solely at the discretion of the prison authorities without judicial intervention or proper regulations, and sometimes for long periods. In Denmark, for example, the prisoner Hans Enrico Nati, who had escaped from several prisons, was isolated altogether for more than four years and eight months; *see* Jacob Billing, *Springtur: Fem år i isolation*, Århus 2004.

29 Concerning prison reform and the use of solitary confinement in different countries, see, for example, Johnston 2000, especially Chapters 5, 6, and 7. Concerning developments in Scandinavia, see Smith 2003, p. 245. Concerning Holland, see Pieter Spierenburg, 'Four Centuries of Prison History', in *Institutions of Confinement*, edited by Norbert Finzsch and Robert Jütte, Cambridge University Press 1996, p. 30.

30 Johnston 2000, pp. 111 f.

31 Wilson, J. G., and M. J. Pescor *Problems in Prison Psychiatry*, Caldwell 1939, p. 25.

then, unfortunately, this attitude to the use of solitary confinement has changed to a significant extent.

## 4 The Rise of the Supermax in the US

While supermax prisons have clearly inherited elements from nineteenth-century penitentiaries, their more recent history is generally considered to begin with the October 1983 lockdown in Marion penitentiary in Illinois, following the killing of two prison guards in two different situations on the same day. This happened at a time when the US prison system had been struggling with rising prison violence for more than a decade.[32]

When the famous Alcatraz prison closed down in 1963, Marion penitentiary, which opened the following year, was to take over as a federal maximum security prison. But Marion did not open until 1964, and in the meantime the Federal Bureau of Prisons opted for a dispersion model, according to which so-called troublemakers were to be spread throughout the prison system. But problems with prison violence during the early 1970s brought the concentration model back, and troublemakers were sent to Marion. This was apparently difficult to handle, and in 1972 Marion Penitentiary opened a high-security unit intended for especially disruptive prisoners (among the inmates who were already identified as dangerous and difficult to manage). This in effect created an incarceration security level beyond the then maximum level-five prison. This was officially confirmed in 1979 when Marion became the first level-six "super-maximum security" prison.[33] But even this regime was to be superseded. What happened was that the October lockdown in 1983, after the simultaneous guard killings, was in fact never lifted. In other words, a lockdown situation – where inmates were confined to their cells without access to communal activities – came to constitute the normal regime, and solitary confinement became a reality for the inmates. The use of isolation as a tool against disruptive prisoners thus turned from an extraordinary measure into a routine one.

Thereafter the Marion lockdown regime (later termed "supermax") inspired correctional services in a large number of US states. By 1997 there were fifty-five supermax facilities in the US in thirty-four different states, and in 1998 around 20,000 inmates were imprisoned in supermax facilities, compared to fewer than fifty prisoners held in the very highest-security or close-supervision centers in England and Wales in 1999.[34] In 2004 there were more than sixty supermax prisons in the US.[35]

---

32 King 1999, pp. 165 et seq.

33 Pizarro, Jesenia, and Vanja M.K. Stenius, 'Supermax Prisons: Their Rise, Current Practices, and Effect on Inmates', *The Prison Journal* no. 2, 2004, p. 250.

34 King 1999, p. 164; Pizarro and Stenius 2004, p. 251.

35 Lorna Rhodes *Total Confinement: Madness and Reason in the Maximum Security Prison*, University of California Press 2004, p. 23.

## 5 Supermax Conditions

Officially supermax[36] prisons are

> free-standing facilities, or a distinct unit within a facility, that provides for the management and secure control of inmates who have been officially designated as exhibiting violent or seriously disruptive behavior while incarcerated. Such inmates have been determined to be a threat to safety and security in traditional high security facilities, and their behavior can be controlled only by separation, restricted movement, and limited direct access to staff and other inmates.[37]

In practice supermax conditions typically consist of solitary confinement for around 23 hours each day, in a barren environment which is under constant high-tech surveillance. Inmates are sometimes able to shout to each other but otherwise have no social contact, and most verbal communication with prison staff takes place through intercom systems.[38] Communication with the outside world is minimal. Visits and phone calls are few and far between and severely restricted, if allowed at all. So-called visits might take place only via video screens.[39] In fact, physical contact in a supermax may for a duration of several years "be limited to being touched through a security door by a correctional officer while being placed in restraints or having restraints removed".[40] These facilities typically claim to constitute a behaviour-modification regime, but in reality they have none or few programme activities (work, education, etc.). The few cases of education which do take place in some supermax prisons might themselves actually illustrate a lack of concern for human rights. In one supermax prison in the state of Washington, for example, isolation booths are used for education, which resembles nineteenth-century Pennsylvania-model methods. The inmates are isolated in small upright boxes so that solitary confinement can be maintained during classes.[41]

## 6 Health Problems and Dehumanizing Institutional Cultures

With the revival of large-scale solitary confinement in the US, the physical and psychological suffering from the era of the Pennsylvania-model prisons has returned with a vengeance. In studies of supermax facilities in the US, many adverse

36 Some use other terms to describe these facilities, such as for example "control units" or "special housing units" (SHU).

37 According to The National Institute of Corrections 1997, 'Supermax housing: a survey of current practice', p. 1.

38 Pizarro and Stenius 2004, p. 251.

39 Leena Kurki and Norval Morris 'The Purposes, Practices, and Problems of Supermax Prisons'. In *Crime and Justice: A Review of Research*, vol. 28, edited by Michael Tonry, University of Chicago Press 2001, p. 89.

40 Chase Riveland Supermax Prisons: Overview and General Considerations, National Institute of Corrections 1999, p. 11 (http://www.nicic.org/pubs/1999/014937.pdf).

41 Rhodes 2004, pp. 209 ff.

symptoms are reported with dramatic prevalence rates. In the so-called Pelican Bay SHU (special housing unit) in California, for example, the following list of symptoms were reported for between eighty-three and ninety-one per cent of the inmates, depending on the symptom: anxiety, headaches, lethargy, irrational anger, confused thought processes, social withdrawal, etc. Hallucinations and perceptual distortions were each suffered by more than forty per cent of the inmates studied.[42] Many other authors also report alarming rates of psychological problems and mental disease in supermax prisons.[43] Psychiatrist Terry Kupers has visited numerous control units, segregation units, etc. in the US, and concludes: "In all the supermaximum security units I have toured, between one-third and half of the prisoners suffer from a serious mental disorder."[44] It has to be remembered, of course, that a number of supermax and SHU prisoners are mentally ill on arrival (they are in that sense strictly speaking misplaced in the prison system). This group of mentally-ill prisoners will – like the healthy ones – generally experience a significant deterioration of their condition during their time in solitary confinement.[45]

When asked personally, inmates describe numerous symptoms. One supermax prisoner, for example, claimed that "[f]ew people can take this type of isolation", which was termed "psychological torture" by another. Others fear that prolonged solitary confinement "would make it harder for them to adjust to general-population imprisonment or life outside of prison".[46] The existence of this problem has been supported by other research into the effects of solitary confinement.[47]

Generally speaking, supermax prisons have been described producing "extreme states of mind".[48] Some of the relatively common incidents in these facilities reveal an institutional culture which certainly seems to justify that description. One example is the way that inmates often use their own faeces and urine as means of expressing themselves. As described by anthropologist Lorna Rhodes, who has interviewed several prisoners and prison guards in a supermax prison, it "is impossible to spend much time with prison workers without hearing about prisoners' defiant or deranged use of their body products".[49] It is apparently a characteristic of the condition of extreme isolation that inmates revert to "shit throwing" as their only weapon. Isolated and stripped of other tools, their bodies – in the form of their body waste – simply become the vehicle for their frustration and aggression. This practice also brings the history of solitary confinement to mind. In Vridsløse-

42 Craig Haney, 'Mental Health Issues in Long-Term Solitary and "Supermax" Confinement', in *Crime & Delinquency* no. 1, 2003, pp. 133 f.

43 See Smith 2006.

44 Terry Kupers, *Prison Madness*, Jossey-Bass Publishers 1999, p. xviii.

45 Kupers 1999. See also Jamie Fellner and Joanne Mariner, *Cold Storage: Super-Maximum Security Confinement in Indiana*, Human Rights Watch 1997, p. 35. See also Abramsky, Sasha, and Jamie Fellner, *Ill-Equipped: U.S. Prisons and Offenders with Mental Illness*, Human Rights Watch 2003, pp. 149 et seq.

46 Fellner and Mariner 1997, p. 32.

47 See Smith 2006.

48 Rhodes 2004, p. 29.

49 Rhodes 2004, p. 43. See also Kurki and Morris 2001, p. 98.

lille penitentiary in Denmark, which was constructed on the Pennsylvania model, the prison chaplain, for example, complained in his reports during the 1860s that inmates soiled their isolation boxes during Sunday services in the panoptic isolation prison church.[50]

Needless to say, the extreme supermax environment also creates several problems for the prison guards. Having faeces thrown in your face is just one example. As related by a prison guard: "Until you've stood there and had it dripping off your face you just don't know what it's like. I could tear down the door [to the cell] but all I get to do is write an infraction. It's tough. It's humiliating."[51] As illustrated by this quote, the dehumanizing quality of supermax confinement runs both ways and is very likely to create a framework that often motivates rather than restricts violence and a cynical culture.[52] The resulting atmosphere can breed severe guard brutality. One California court case concerning the Pelican Bay Supermax, for example, unravelled a disturbing misuse of force. Incidents of guard brutality included beatings and physical violence under various circumstances, "confinement of naked or partially dressed inmates in outdoor holding cages during inclement weather", excessive use of the so-called fetal restraint, etc.[53] In one particularly horrible incident, a mentally ill inmate was forced into a tub of scalding water where he suffered second- and third-degree burns. A nurse at the SHU infirmary where the incident took place testified that the inmate

> was in the bathtub with his hands cuffed behind his back, with an officer pushing down on his shoulder and holding his arms in place. Subsequently, another officer came into the nurse's station and made a call ... She overheard the officer say about Dortch [the inmate], who is African-American, that it 'looks like we're going to have a white boy before this is through, that his skin is so dirty and so rotten, it's all fallen off'.

The nurse then walked "over toward the tub and saw Dortch standing with his back to her. She testified that, from just below the buttocks down, his skin had peeled off and was hanging in large clumps around his legs, which had turned white with some redness. Even then, in a shocking show of indifference, the officers made no

50 Smith 2003, p. 263.

51 Rhodes 2004, p. 46.

52 According to Hans Toch, supermax treatment is "liable to enhance rather than reduce the violence of inmates"; Hans Toch, 'The future of supermax confinement', in *The Prison Journal* no. 3, 2001, p. 376, also p. 383.

53 *Madrid* v. *Gomez*, 889 F.Supp. 1146 (N.D. Cal. 1995). A fetal restraint (hog-tying) "involves handcuffing an inmate's hands at the front of his body, placing him in leg irons, and then drawing a chain between the handcuffs and legs until only a few inches separate the bound wrists and ankles". The massive number of incidents reported in this case took place in different parts of the Pelican Bay prison, which is made up of three different units, only one being (a very large) supermax, while one of the other units is a maximum security prison.

effort to seek any medical assistance or advice. Instead, it appeared to Kuroda [the nurse] that the officers were simply dressing Dortch to return him to his cell."[54]

That such events can take place in supermax settings will come as no surprise to those familiar with the extensive social-psychological research showing how dehumanizing environments and cultures can cause aggression.[55]

## 7 Supermax: An Irrational Reaction to a Misconceived Problem?

While bearing in mind that prison violence can be very difficult to handle, evidence suggests – as already illustrated – that supermax prisons constitute a serious threat to basic human rights. Supermax prisons also seem to be the result of an irrational overreaction to an exaggerated problem. These institutions are, at least officially, constructed to handle disruptive inmates and reduce prison violence. But it seems very unlikely that prisoners today are as vastly more disruptive than their counterparts twenty years ago as the dramatic rise of the supermax would suggest, which apparently no one has tried to prove through empirical studies anyway. Furthermore, existing research suggests that it is very problematic to reduce the problem of order in prisons to a question of the behaviour of individual inmates. Prison order is a complex issue, and it seems much more useful to focus on prison management and prison regimes in general than simply on specific inmates.[56] Creating a legitimate and moral prison regime is arguably a better way of handling problems of prison order.[57] This is indirectly confirmed by recent research, which, based on empirical evidence from facilities in three different US states, concludes that supermax prisons do not reduce violence in prison systems. In fact, "the effectiveness of supermax prisons as a mechanism to enhance prison safety remains largely speculative".[58] On the contrary, supermax prisons may in fact be "breeding grounds of violent recidivism", and inmates "may become 'the worst of the worst' because they have been dealt with as such".[59] In the words of a law professor and a senior researcher in the same field, there might be a case for a federal US supermax prison, but on a state level they "are a grave error in the sad tale of man's brutality to man".[60]

So why do supermax prisons exist? Since attempts to look for a rational penological reason appear to be fruitless, it seems more relevant to search for an ideological explanation. Seen in that light, Supermax prisons perhaps represent "a state

54 *Madrid* v. *Gomez* 889 F.Supp. 1146 (N.D. Cal. 1995).

55 See, for example, Stanley Milgram *Obedience to Authority*, Harper Torchbooks 1983; Craig Haney, Curtis Banks and Philip Zimbardo, 'Interpersonal Dynamics in a Simulated Prison', in *International Journal of Criminology and Enology* no. 1, 1973.

56 Kurki and Morris 2001, pp. 115 ff.

57 Sparks, Bottoms and Hay 1996.

58 Briggs, Chad S., Jody L. Sundt, and Thomas C. Castellano, 'The Effect of Supermaximum Security Prisons on Aggregate Levels of Institutional Violence', in *Criminology* 2003, p. 1371.

59 Toch 2001, p. 381.

60 Kurki and Morris 2001, p. 121.

of mind" and are not so much directed at the inmates and the prison system itself as at the public: supermax prisons have in that sense "become political symbols of how 'tough' a jurisdiction has become".[61]

## 8 The Ideological Context of the Supermax

The current trend in US penal policy is to be "tough on crime". Some prevailing initiatives include "three strikes and you're out" laws, so-called zero-tolerance policies, prison privatization, a revival of solitary confinement and mass imprisonment. Due to harsh and disproportionate laws and sentencing practices, the US prison population has simply exploded during the last decades, and it is now the largest in the world in both absolute and relative terms. This is by no means solely a right-wing phenomenon, and since Bill Clinton's presidency it has been hard to find a Democrat who could be termed "soft on crime". With no apparent interest in the possible effects on individuals and society at large, new laws and prison practices, which would have seemed highly inappropriate and downright unthinkable thirty or forty years ago, have been promoted at the state and federal levels during the last twenty years. These policies are based on punitive sentiments – or what the sociologist David Garland has called "a new pattern of cultural sensibilities" – which often do not rely on evidence or rational measures, but on the contrary "appear oddly archaic and downright antimodern".[62] As the criminologist Michael Tonry explains in his recent book, *Thinking about Crime*: "The United States has adopted criminal justice policies that reflective people should abhor and that informed observers from other Western countries do abhor."[63] It is in this ideological "tough on crime" context that the supermax has broken through, which explains why human rights-related criticisms of solitary confinement have had little impact so far.

Furthermore, this punitive ideology can easily support and fuse with the current security agenda inspired by the war on terrorism. The resulting political climate is not particularly favourable to a prisoners' rights agenda – to say the least – and has apparently already had an impact on the use of isolation practices in connection with interrogations of terrorist suspects.[64]

## 9 Supermax vs. Human Rights?

It is perhaps difficult to imagine a supermax regime without significant human rights problems since, "the structural tendencies for such prisons to abuse human

---

61 According to the National Institute of Corrections. Quoted from King 1999, p. 177.

62 David Garland, *The Culture of Control*, Oxford University Press 2001, p. 3 and 6.

63 Michael Tonry, *Thinking about Crime: Sense and Sensibility in American Penal Culture*, Oxford 2004, p. 195.

64 See, for example, *Salim Ahmed Hamdan* v. *Donald Rumsfeld* (US Supreme Court), Brief of *Amici Curiae* Human Rights First, p. 15, and 'Ending Secret Detentions', June 2004 (Human Rights First report), p. 11.

rights beyond necessary boundaries are ... extraordinary".[65] Accordingly, a huge list of criticisms directed against supermax confinement has been drawn up by Human Rights Watch (HRW), an organization which has contributed a significant share of the otherwise sparse research into supermax conditions. HRW has, for example, recommended that: (*a*) prisoners should not be isolated unless they are chronically violent and pose an extremely serious threat to prison safety; (*b*) all supermax confinement should be for the shortest possible time; (*c*) inmates should have meaningful appeal options; (*d*) cells should be much better equipped; (*e*) all inmates should have access to outdoor recreation; (*f*) facilities should include common areas; (*g*) inmates should be able to control the light in their cells; (*h*) supermax regimes should allow prisoners to maintain constructive lives, and should acknowledge their dignity and value as human beings; (*i*) inmates should be allowed out of their cells every day; (*j*) the longer isolation is upheld, the greater compensatory conditions are needed (increased programme activities etc.); (*k*) religious worship should be permitted; (*l*) more family contact should be allowed; (*m*) physical or verbal abuse by staff should be forbidden; (*n*) independent private groups should be able to investigate supermax conditions; and (*o*) the press, religious organizations and the like should have access to supermax prisons.[66]

It is obvious that several international human rights rules and convention articles could be breached if some of the above recommendations are not met. Article 18 of the International Covenant on Civil and Political Rights would, for example, be violated if religious worship were not allowed. Article 7 of the same convention, which prohibits torture as well as cruel, inhuman or degrading punishment, and Article 10, which calls for prisoners to be treated with humanity, could also be considered violated by typical supermax conditions.

Several paragraphs of the UN Standard Minimum Rules for the Treatment of Prisoners would also be violated by not complying with the above list.[67] According to number 11(a) of these prison rules, inmates should, for example, be able "to read or work by natural light"; supermax cells, by contrast, can be "almost devoid of natural light".[68] Furthermore, according to rule 21(1) inmates should "have at least one hour of suitable exercise in the open air daily if the weather permits"; conversely, prisoners in some supermax facilities are locked up in their cells twenty-four hours a day during weekends.[69] Seen in light of the extreme prevalence of mental illness in some supermax prisons, it is clear that rule 22(2) of the UN prison rules could

65 Franklin E. Zimring and Gordon Hawkins, 'Democracy and the Limits of Punishment: A Preface to Prisoners' Rights', in Michael Tonry (ed.), *The Future of Imprisonment*, Oxford University Press 2004, p. 169.

66 Human Rights Watch, 'Out of Sight: Super-Maximum Security Confinement in the United States', Vol. 12, no. 1, February 2000. See under 'II. Recommendations'.

67 Standard Minimum Rules for the Treatment of Prisoners. Adopted by the First United Nations Congress on the Prevention of Crime and the Treatment of Offenders, Geneva 1955. Approved by the Economic and Social Council in res. 663 C (XXIV) of 31 July 1957 and 2076 (LXII) of 13 May 1977.

68 Rhodes 2004, p. 21 (a description of a specific supermax control unit).

69 Rhodes 2004, n. 1 on p. 237.

also be considered violated, since this calls for "specialist treatment" and transfer to "specialized institutions" for sick inmates whose illness requires these services.[70] This is further specified in rule 82(1), which states that "persons who are found to be insane shall not be detained in prisons and arrangements shall be made to remove them to mental institutions as soon as possible."

Physical abuse of prisoners is, of course, an obvious source of human rights violations. The use of electrical stun shields, belts and guns in some supermax prisons has, for example, been a target of criticism. Amnesty International and other human rights organizations have attacked the use of such devices vigorously.[71] In 1999 Amnesty called for an immediate suspension of "the use of *all* electro-shock weapons" and described the so-called stun belt as "cruel, inhuman or degrading treatment or punishment as outlawed under international law".[72] The UN prison rules thus clearly state that "corporal punishment ... and all cruel, inhuman or degrading punishments shall be completely prohibited as punishments for disciplinary offences."[73] The stun belt certainly seems to live up to this definition. The belt is worn by a prisoner (considered to be dangerous) and can be set off by remote control, in which case it will deliver a 50,000-volt (three- to four-milliampere) shock lasting eight seconds. This causes temporary incapacitation followed by severe pain.[74] Supermax prisoners have described such use of electricity as "an attempt to reduce them to the status of animals".[75]

Not surprisingly, conditions like those in a typical supermax prison have in fact been described as constituting "inhuman treatment" – at least when measured according to the standards of the CPT (the European Committee for the Prevention of Torture).[76]

Serious criticism has also been raised by UN representatives interpreting the Convention Against Torture. In 1996 the UN Special Rapporteur on Torture stated that "[c]onditions at certain maximum security facilities [in the US] were said to result in the inhuman and degrading treatment of the inmates in those facilities",

---

70 Other paragraphs which may be violated include, for example, 37, 40, 42, 71(3), and 72(1). Paragraphs 59 and 77(1) are perhaps also violated, since supermax prisons typically do not run any treatment or educational programs.

71 Rhodes 2004, p. 91.

72 *United States of America: Cruelty in Control? The Stun Belt and other Electroshock Equipment in Law Enforcement*, Amnesty Report June 1999, AI index: AMR 51/54/99, pp. 2 f.

73 Standard Minimum Rules for the Treatment of Prisoners, paragraph 31. See also the European Prison Rules, rule 37.

74 *United States of America: Cruelty in Control? The Stun Belt and other Electroshock Equipment in Law Enforcement*, Amnesty report June 1999, AI index: AMR 51/54/99, p. 3.

75 Rhodes 2004, p. 91.

76 Kurki and Morris 2001, p. 115. See also CPT standards concerning punitive segregation, clear disciplinary procedures, and the principle of proportionality in Morgan and Evans 2001, pp. 117 et seq.

and in 2005 the Committee Against Torture "expressed concern over [t]he excessively harsh regime of the 'supermaximum' prisons".[77]

Unfortunately not only supermax conditions, but also the procedures for allocation to these facilities can be highly problematic. According to Hans Toch the basic application of supermax confinement "rests on arbitrariness papered over with a veneer of due process".[78] Prisoners are often sent to a supermax for something they might do and not for something they have done, and the whole process of allocation is strictly administrative and lacking transparency, not subject to judicial review or even to clear-cut laws. Supermax confinement is, in other words, a classical illustration of how state power can challenge due process considerations, a case of what Hans Toch has termed "the deprivation of fairness".[79]

Thus while the supermax and therefore also solitary confinement in present-day America can be (at least partly) explained through the rise of populist punitiveness and a "tough on crime" ideology favouring retribution and social exclusion, it is quite clear that a human rights discourse has had very limited impact in this area up until now. Seen in both legal and humanitarian perspectives a regression has taken place, which offers the contemporary American citizen less protection from the state in this area than was the case in the late nineteenth century. Prolonged solitary confinement is in itself no longer perceived as uncivilised by the state and its judges. Several US courts have criticised conditions in supermax prisons severely, but, although the constitutionality of supermax facilities remains unclear, long-term isolation as such has not been declared illegal.[80] One reason might be a "born-again conservative stance" among the US federal judiciary, since "courts have hesitated to tell prison administrators that conditions of confinement in their supermax or control units are constitutionally impermissible or unacceptable, even where judicial dicta reek of personal disapproval of such conditions".[81]

---

77 See the following UN documents: E/CN.4/1996/35. 9. January 1996 "Report of the Special Rapporteur, Mr. Nigel S. Rodley...", p. 39, and CAT/C/48/Add.3/Rev.1. 13 January 2006, "Consideration of reports submitted by state parties under article 19 of the convention; Second periodic reports of States parties due in 1999. UNITED STATES OF AMERICA, 6 May 2005", p. 44.

78 Toch 2001, p. 380.

79 Toch 2001, p. 380. See also Andrew Coyle, *A Human Rights Approach to Prison Management: Handbook for Prison Staff*, International Centre for Prison Studies 2002, pp. 76 ff.

80 See *Madrid* v. *Gomez* 1995; King 1999.

81 Hans Toch, 'Opening Pandora's Box: ameliorating the effects of long-term segregation conditions', in *Prison Service Journal*, Nov. 2002, p. 16. Still one can, of course, hope for improvements in the future. According to Toch, supermax settings "will have to undertake serious proactive ameliorative reforms" in order to "survive ongoing and future litigation" (Toch 2001, p. 376).

## 10 The Scandinavian Phenomenon of Solitary Pre-Trial Confinement

While the use of large-scale solitary confinement associated with the modern penitentiary (rehabilitation through isolation) was abandoned in the US and other countries during the latter half of the nineteenth century, the case was different in Scandinavia, Belgium and Holland. In Norway the ideology underlining the Pennsylvania model was confirmed in 1933 by prison regulations, and officially the system was not abolished until 1958.[82] In Sweden at the beginning of the twentieth century ninety per cent of all prisoners served their entire sentence in isolation, and solitary confinement was not abandoned until 1946.[83] In Denmark the Pennsylvania model (including panoptic isolation churches etc.) was used until the early 1930s.[84] In Belgium several elements of the Pennsylvania system continued to be used in some prisons until after World War II.[85] Finally, solitary confinement was used liberally in Holland throughout the first half of the twentieth century.[86]

It is interesting to note that this partly Scandinavian legacy from the early twentieth century is reflected in recent history. Denmark, Sweden, Norway and Iceland thus received criticism from the CPT during the 1990s for their use of pre-trial solitary confinement . Solitary confinement in remand prisons has simply been termed a peculiarly "Scandinavian phenomenon"[87], which contrasts with the traditional image of Scandinavian leniency in the area of penal policy.

## 11 Pre-Trial Solitary Confinement in Denmark: A Short History

Solitary confinement during pre-trial in Denmark was originally born out of the breakthrough of the ideology of the modern penitentiary. The Danish prison commission of 1840, which in 1842 presented a reform of the entire Danish prison system along the lines of the American prison models, was also engaged in a a reform of Danish jails. In 1846 this resulted in a new set of jail regulations, which prescribed solitary confinement during pre-trial. This initiative was based on both moral and crime-control considerations. It was thus clearly stated that (*a*) some remand prisoners could interfere with the investigation if they were not isolated, and (*b*) some would demoralise each other if they were incarcerated together.[88] The

82 Smith 2005.

83 Roddy Nilsson, 'The Swedish Prison System in Historical Perspective: A Story of Successful Failure?', in *Journal of Scandinavian Studies in Criminology and Crime Prevention* no. 4, 2003, p. 9; Roddy Nilsson, *En välbyggd maskin, en mardröm för själen*, Lunds University Press 1999, p. 443.

84 Smith 2003, p. 245.

85 Johnston 2000, p. 106.

86 Spierenburg 1996, p. 30.

87 Evans and Morgan 1998. The authors refer to the use of pre-trial solitary confinement as a "peculiarly Scandinavian phenomenon" (p. 247). See also the official reports from the CPT at: http://www.cpt.coe.int/en/

88 *Reglement for Arrestvæsenet i Danmark* 1846, sec. B (5). Isolation could be abandoned for health reasons, *see* sec. C(6).

initiative was, in other words, shaped by both the ideology of the modern penitentiary and the interests of police investigations.

By 1870 the 1846 reforms were so far advanced that the Danish jails could typically accommodate most or all detainees in solitary confinement, and isolation during pre-trial had become standard practice in Denmark.[89] This practice was confirmed by the 1916 law on the administration of justice, which focused on the need to protect police investigations, the moral argument of 1846 having disappeared.[90] Solitary confinement during pre-trial was now apparently only motivated by crime-control considerations. As late as the early 1970s, it was standard practice for remand prisoners to be subjected to solitary confinement when imprisoned – at least during the initial fourteen days.[91] From the late 1970s on, criticism of the Danish practice of pre-trial solitary confinement emerged on a mainly national basis.

## 12 Pre-Trial Solitary Confinement Conditions in Denmark

An isolation cell in a typical Danish remand prison is a barren environment of six to eight square meters, which contains a bed, a chair, a cupboard, a shelf and a sink.[92] Radio and TV can be allowed or disallowed according to circumstances and the wishes of the police. Isolated remand prisoners normally spend around twenty-three hours in their cell each day and are allowed out for two half-hour sessions in the exercise yard. This exercise takes place in isolation in a six-meter long, triangular space. Psychologically meaningful social contact is reduced to a minimum, and

89 According to *Beretning om Tilstanden i Landets samtlige Arresthuse efter de ved Justitsministeriets Cirkulære af 19 Mai 1870 fremkomne Oplysninger* [Report on the state of the national jails according to the information issued by the Ministry of Justice circular of 19 May 1870] by Frederik Bruun, *Kontoret for Fængselsvæsenet* [Department of Prisons] 1871, p. 2 et seq.

90 *Lov om retspleje* 1916, Chapter 72 § 784.

91 Erik Carlé, *Københavns fængsler i 100 år*, Justitsministeriet, Direktoratet for Kriminalforsorgen 1995, p. 264.

92 Seen from an isolated remand prisoner's perspective, the conditions in a typical cell in the 1990s were described as follows: "There are huge blobs of snot on the walls, which are filled with all kinds of stupid graffiti...and the floor is bare stone. There is an iron frame which you pull down from the wall – that is your bed. The ceiling is very high. The window is situated three and a half meters above the floor. You cannot look out unless you climb on top of your cupboard. But that is forbidden. You risk disciplinary punishment just by looking out. There is a tiny sink with cold water in the corner. A small, legless table is fastened to the wall, arranged together with a lamp and a chair. There are a set of sheets for the bed and a pillow and a disgusting blanket." Quoted from *Faklen*, no. 10, Winter 1999. Interview with Peter Lembcke, chairman of the criminal justice organization KRIM. Lembcke was isolated for almost a year. (Translated by the author.)

the existing stimuli are typically monotonous and occasional (being escorted to the toilet, the sound of slamming doors, etc.).[93]

Remand prisoners in isolation can request visits by a prison chaplain, a doctor or a psychologist, but only between twenty and forty per cent of the isolated inmates make this request. Often an inmate wishing to call a doctor or psychologist will have to wait one or two weeks for the actual visit, which can be crucial in a situation of acute mental stress. It is well known from research into the effects of solitary confinement that adverse health effects can set in quickly.[94] Furthermore, some remand prisons are not even able to arrange regular visits by a psychologist, and two-thirds of all isolated remand prisoners therefore lack this service.[95] Unfortunately the psychologist is likely to be the most relevant resource in this context. Some remand prisons claim that isolated inmates have altogether around three hours of contact with other people each day, while others report between one and two hours of contact.[96] The three-hour claim seems strange considering the isolation regimes being practised, but it is probably based on a very optimistic calculation of the number of times that inmates are escorted to the toilet, to the police station, to the court, to exercise areas in the yard, etc., and presumably includes the number of visits from the defence lawyer, family and friends. No claims have been made as to what this contact consists of, and it seems very unlikely that these hours contain a significant amount of meaningful social interaction. The contact that is presumably most important – visits from friends and relatives – are generally limited to a one-hour visit each week.[97]

The Danish solitary-confinement regime for remand prisoners is, in other words, very different from supermax conditions in a number of ways. The latter are

93 Ida Koch and Manfred Petersen, 'Isolation af varetægtsfængslede' i *Retspolitisk status*, 1988, pp. 72 et seq,; and CPT Visit Report, Denmark 2002, Section 19/44. For a critical review of recent law reforms concerning isolation in remand prisons, see Koch et al. 2003, pp. 321 et seq. See also '*Lov nr. 428 af 31. maj 2000*', including comments from politicians and organizations, *Strafferets- og Retsplejekontoret* [Office of Criminal Law and Procedure], Case no. 2000-730-0095, Doc. LSC20174. See also *Arbejdsgruppen vedr. varetægtsarrestanters 'ulovlige' kommunikation*, '*Arbejdsgruppens rapport* [Working Group Report]', January 2005.

94 Psychiatrist Henrik Steen Andersen concluded in an interview that "the reactions [to solitary confinement] often set in very quickly" according to Thelle, Hatla, and Anne-Marie Traeholt, 'Protection of Suspects' Rights versus Investigation Needs: The Use of Solitary Confinement in Denmark', in *How to Eradicate Torture: A Sino-Danish Joint research on the Prevention of Torture*, edited by Morten Kjærum, Xia Yong, Hatla Thelle, and Bixiaoqing, Social Sciences Documentation Publishing House 2003, p. 769.

95 See *Indstilling om enrumsanbringelse/udelukkelse fra fællesskab* [Position on solitary confinement/exclusion from social contact], *Arbejdsgruppen om enrum* [Working Group on Isolation], December 2001, p. 33. See also *Arbejdsgruppen vedr. varetægtsarrestanters 'ulovlige' kommunikation*, '*Arbejdsgruppens rapport* [Working Group Report]', January 2005.

96 Ibid., p. 31.

97 Ibid., p. 33.

generally based on a more high-tech form of surveillance, most likely requires less contact between staff and inmates, and allows for much more violent measures to be used against inmates in the form of stun belts, cell-extraction procedures, etc. Supermax prisons also seem to create a much more dehumanizing institutional culture. Still, both systems have a regime of solitary confinement at their core, which creates many similarities and accounts for an overlapping range of adverse health effects suffered by the inmates in both cases.

## 13 National Criticism and Debate

During the 1970s the Danish practice of isolation was "uncovered" after years of unquestioned use. Decades of heated debate started in 1977, apparently with the so-called Mexican case. A Mexican citizen was charged with espionage and was subjected to 139 days of solitary confinement from his arrest to his deportation to Mexico, without proper judicial intervention or involvement during his incarceration. The case caused a public outcry. Eighty-eight doctors, for example, complained to the Danish Minister of Justice about the Mexican's isolation.[98] Following this case, the use of solitary confinement in Danish prisons has been heatedly debated in the media time and time again.[99]

A number of specific cases created a focal point during the early years of the debate: for example, a couple of cases concerning the isolation of minors and a spy investigation case where a Danish–East German husband and wife were isolated for one year and half a year respectively. The main arguments revolved around the health effects of solitary confinement, the insufficient legal protection of isolated detainees, and the fear that solitary confinement might be used as psychological pressure by the police in order to provoke a confession. Many very different groups – lawyers, priests, doctors, prison inmates – criticised Denmark's use of pre-trial isolation, though the clear tendency was for state representatives, including ministers and various kinds of civil servant, to defend the Danish practice. Some went quite far in their defence, like a police commissioner, who remarked that "If solitary confinement is torture, then I am Little Red Riding Hood."[100] Defence attorney Erik Ninn-Hansen, who in 1980 stated that solitary confinement was often used "to squeeze out a confession", apparently changed his mind when he later became Denmark's Minister of Justice.[101] Although he could hardly have acquired a better

98 Koch, Ida E., and Manfred Petersen, 'Isolation af varetægtsfængslede', in *Retspolitisk Status: Festskrift i anledning af Dansk Retspolitisk Forenings 10 års jubilæum*, Jurist- og Økonomforbundets forlag 1988, p. 69.

99 During 1978 to 1979, for example, at least 64 articles were written about solitary confinement in the two national newspapers *Politiken* and *Information*.

100 Police Commissioner Volmer Nissen, quoted from the Danish newspaper *Information*, 8 January 1980.

101 Erik Ninn-Hansen, in an interview in the prominent Danish newspaper *Politiken*, 8 January 1980, translated by the author. Many other defence attorneys have explained the same thing: how pre-trial detention – and especially isolation – is in reality (sometimes or often) used as extortion; see, e.g., Petersen 1998, p. 34; Stagetorn, Merethe.

position from which to act on his earlier criticism, apparently no initiatives were taken specifically to root out the element of psychological pressure in the practice of pre-trial solitary confinement.

In 1979 the so-called Isolation Group was founded by a group of lawyers, prison chaplains, psychologists, etc. in order to put pressure on the government to reduce or abolish the use of pre-trial solitary confinement. Several of its members carried out studies and collected data which they claimed documented the damaging health effects of solitary confinement in Denmark. This work described adverse symptoms very much like the nineteenth-century literature and much like the American supermax–control unit studies, including confusion of thought processes, hallucinations, sleeplessness, anxiety, etc. Both acute and chronic symptoms of isolation were described.[102]

However, this research was considered inadequate by some observers, and in 1990 an official large-scale study was commissioned by the Ministry of Justice. In 1994 the result was published as a report on the effects of solitary confinement. Based on extensive empirical research involving 367 remand prisoners (including a control group), the study concluded that, compared with pre-trial detention without isolation, pre-trial detention in isolation involved strain and a risk of damaging the mental health of imprisoned individuals.[103] In 1997 this conclusion was strengthened and radicalised in a follow-up study, which simply recommended that, for both "medical and psychological" reasons, solitary confinement should not be used during the pre-trial period.[104]

All in all, since the late 1970s there has been ongoing internal Danish criticism of the health effects of solitary confinement on remand prisoners and, as will be explained below, reforms limiting, though not abolishing, this practice have been implemented. During spring 2004, the isolation of pre-trial detainees was once again debated in Danish media, but this time something interesting happened: the health effects were not the focus of the discussion, and the issue was instead very clearly influenced by the punitive "tough on crime" ideology described above. A very different debate and perspective on the use of isolation was the result. Under headlines such as "Isolation in Danish Prisons is an Illusion" and "Demands for Control in Prisons", the focus was placed on isolated remand prisoners' alleged abilities to communicate with the outside world, and politicians and police representatives called without hesitation for a stricter regime of solitary confinement.[105]

---

*Forsvarsadvokaten: Hverdag i retssale og fængsler*, Nørhaven 2003, pp. 38 et seq. Another Danish defense attorney stated the same in a radio interview recently: DR (*Danmarks Radio*) in the program '*Lige lovligt*', 6 May 2004.

102 See Smith 2006.

103 Andersen, Henrik Steen, Tommy Lillebæk, Dorte Sestoft, and Gorm Gabrielsen, *Isolationsundersøgelsen: Varetægtsfængsling og psykisk helbred*, Vol. 1-2, Schultz 1994.

104 Andersen, Henrik Steen, Tommy Lillebæk, and Dorte Sestoft, *Efterundersøgelsen: en opfølgningsundersøgelse af danske varetægtsarrestanter*, Schultz 1997.

105 Danish national newspaper *Jyllandsposten*, 23 March 2004 and 25 March 2004. See also Nicolai Scharling, 'Fri kommunikation: Arrestanter forpurrer efterforskning', 23 March 2004, on the homepage of the Danish Police, www.politiforbund.dk.

Within a matter of days after this story was brought up in the media, a working group consisting of representatives of the Danish prison service and the police was immediately formed. These representatives were of course well trained to discuss matters concerning criminal investigations and prison security – but no doctors, psychologists or other experts on the effects of solitary confinement were appointed to the group. In 2005 the working group produced a report, which suggested among other things the construction of a new isolation prison especially for the incarceration of remand prisoners under a regime of solitary confinement.[106]

The swift reaction by the authorities to these complaints – compared with the defensive, slowly moving and reluctant government responses to almost thirty years of hard criticism – suggest that the "tough on crime" ideology is high on the political agenda and can easily acquire precedence over due process and human rights considerations, even in a so-called penologically progressive country like Denmark.

## 14 International Human Rights Criticism, Standards, and Case Law Concerning Danish Practice

In 1980 and 1983 Amnesty International criticised the use of solitary confinement in Denmark, but international criticism grew stronger during the 1990s.[107] Two key actors were the CPT and the CAT (the UN Committee Against Torture). In 1997, for example, the CAT recommended to Denmark that "the use of solitary confinement be abolished, particularly during pre-trial detention, or at least that it should be strictly and specifically regulated by law (maximum duration etc.) and that judicial supervision should be introduced."[108] The CPT visited Denmark in 1990, 1996 and 2002, each time criticising issues concerning the use of solitary confinement during pre-trial. In 1990, for example, the CPT stated that solitary confinement should only be used in "exceptional circumstances", and in 1996 it called for an increase in meaningful social contact for isolated inmates; these statements were further elaborated in 2002. Issues relating to the length of imprisonment in isolation and the legal-judicial process for placing remand prisoners in solitary confinement have also been targeted, just to mention some of the central points among the many complaints raised by the CPT over the years concerning the Danish practice of pre-trial solitary confinement.[109]

Experts on prisons and human rights outside the CPT have reached similar conclusions. According to Andrew Coyle's handbook, *A Human Rights Approach to Prison Management*, solitary confinement "in a single cell with access to normal light and air…[where the inmate] can hear prisoners moving in adjacent areas" – in

106 *Arbejdsgruppen vedr. varetægtsarrestanters 'ulovlige' kommunikation*, '*Arbejdsgruppens rapport* [Working Group Report]', January 2005.

107 For a discussion of Amnesty's criticism, see Koch and Petersen 1988, p. 80.

108 Concluding observations of the Committee against Torture : Denmark. 01/05/97. A/52/44, para. 186.

109 The relevant reports are available at http://www.cpt.coe.int/en/hudoc-cpt.htm.

effect conditions similar to pre-trial isolation in Denmark – "should only be used in exceptional circumstances for short periods of time".[110] This is clearly not the case currently in Denmark (although things have certainly improved since the 1970s).

The approach to the issue of solitary confinement from the former European Commission of Human Rights and the current European Court of Human Rights (ECtHR) has so far been relatively low profile. The European Commission of Human Rights treated a number of complaints concerning solitary confinement, especially during pre-trial, prior to its abolition in 1999. The Commission did not accept the cases, and as late as 1999 the ECtHR supported this line by recalling "that Article 3 cannot be interpreted as generally prohibiting solitary confinement [a]lthough prolonged solitary confinement is undesirable, particularly where the prisoner is on remand ...".[111] Still, the European Commission of Human Rights and the CPT have both made it clear that the use of solitary confinement can amount to an Article 3 violation, depending on the specific circumstances concerning the case and the conditions of detention. In 1983, for example, the Commission explained how "complete sensory isolation coupled with total isolation, can destroy the personality and constitutes a form of treatment which cannot be justified by the requirements of security or any other reason".[112] The CPT has also described how solitary confinement "can amount to inhuman and degrading treatment".[113]

There are currently signs indicating that the ECtHR judges are disagreeing among themselves over whether or not to adopt a more restrictive line on this issue. In 2003 the court accepted a case concerning a former Danish remand prisoner who became paranoid psychotic during pre-trial isolation. The Danish citizen in question, a Mr Rohde, was arrested at Copenhagen airport in December 1994 and charged with drug trafficking, being sent directly from their into solitary confinement in Denmark's largest remand prison, where he spent almost a year while the police investigated the matter. In late November 1995 the Copenhagen City Court lifted the isolation after the accused had supplied the police and the court with a version of the story which they believed. At that point the detainee had difficulty leaving solitary confinement and stayed in voluntary isolation for two more weeks, after which he was transferred to communal prison detention. In May 1996 he was acquitted of the drug offences but convicted of tax fraud. It was later discovered that he had become insane (paranoid psychotic) during his stay in solitary confinement – a fact which both the Danish Supreme Court and the Danish Legal-Psychiatric Clinic, as well as the accused himself, agreed upon. A claim for compensation went through the entire Danish court system, and in the end the Danish Supreme Court offered some compensation but refused to define his treatment either as torture or as inhuman or degrading treatment. On 21 July 2005 the ECtHR passed

110 Coyle 2002, p. 81.

111 *Erdem* v. *Germany* 1999, quoted from Lorenzen et al., *Den Europæiske Menneskeretskonvention*, 2d edn., 2003, p. 117.

112 *Kröcher* v. *Switzerland* (1983). Quoted from Coyle 2002, p. 81.

113 Morgan and Evans, *Combating torture in Europe* 2001, p. 118.

judgment against Mr Rohde, though three out of seven judges dissented and found that Denmark had breached Article 3 of the convention.[114]

Another recent ECtHR case also indicates that the treatment of cases concerning solitary confinement is currently causing disagreement in the court. The case concerns the famous terrorist Ilich Ramirez Sanchez, better known as "Carlos the Jackal", who was sentenced to life imprisonment in 1997 for murdering three police officers in 1975. Sanchez spent eight years and two months in solitary confinement, from his detention in 1994 until his transfer to Saint-Maur Prison in 2002. The reason for maintaining his isolation was "his dangerousness, the need to maintain order and safety in the prison and the likelihood that he might seek to escape". Sanchez was also medically examined to determine whether or not he was considered fit for solitary confinement. Sanchez's cell measured 6.84 square meters and he left it only for a two-hour walk each day. He only received visits from his lawyers, twice-weekly visits by a doctor, and a monthly visit by a cleric. There was no contact with other prisoners or prison officers. In October 2002 Sanchez was taken out of solitary confinement but was returned to an isolation regime following a prison transfer in March 2004.[115] The judges ruled by four votes to three that there had been no violation of Article 3 concerning torture or inhuman or degrading treatment. The court "acknowledged that the applicant's detention had posed serious difficulties for the French authorities and understood that they had considered it necessary to take extraordinary security measures to detain a man who, at the time in question, was viewed as the most dangerous terrorist in the world". The court also pointed out that Sanchez had had "very frequent visits from his 58 lawyers, including his current representative, who had visited him more than 640 times over a period of four years and ten months". But even in the case of the allegedly "most dangerous terrorist in the world", who had had relatively frequent visits during his stay in isolation, three judges dissented. Furthermore, the *Sanchez v. France* case has now been referred to the Courts' Grand Chamber.

## 15 Reforms and Developments in Practice from the 1970s until Today

The first major law reforms since 1916 concerning the use of pre-trial solitary confinement in Denmark were introduced in 1978 as a response to the sudden and extensive rise in criticisms. Solitary confinement of remand prisoners now became subject to judicial review and was no longer decided exclusively by the police. Still, according to the law, the police simply had to invoke "the reason for the detention in remand" as a reason why the detained individual should be isolated.[116] In effect, if the police argued that the accused might interfere with the ongoing investigation,

114 *Rohde* v. *Denmark*, app. no. 69332/01, ECtHR 21 July 2005.

115 *Ramirez Sanchez* v. *France*, app. no. 59450/00, Press release issued by the Registrar 27 January 2005.

116 Lov nr. 234 af 8. Juni 1978, § 770, stk. 3.

solitary confinement would normally be granted. Therefore, on average 43% of all remand prisoners were isolated during the period from 1979 to 1982.[117]

New law revisions came into force in 1984, clearly stating that isolation could be used in order to keep the detainee from interfering with the ongoing investigation. A proportionality principle was also introduced, according to which the possible length of the period of isolation was connected to the severity of the charges. Remand prisoners could not be isolated for more than eight weeks unless the charges against them could result in imprisonment for six years or more. This is perhaps a problematic principle: the question is, how can pain be applied and graduated according to a possibly non-existent offence?[118] Nevertheless the intention was once again to reduce the use of solitary confinement. This happened to a certain degree. In 1984, 31.4% of all remand prisoners were isolated, compared to 21.5% in 1990. Still, this was a very significant proportion, involving more than 1,000 imprisonments in isolation, and, as explained above, national and international criticism continued throughout the 1990s.

Following the 1997 Danish expert recommendation to abolish the use of pre-trial isolation from a medical and psychological viewpoint, a new law was introduced in 2000. This time the principle of proportionality was further elaborated and tied not only to the seriousness of the charge, but also to the detainee's mental and physical health. A so-called maximum limit of three months was introduced – "so-called", since according to the law it was still possible to isolate individuals for an unlimited period of time when special circumstances required this. It was (and is) still possible to isolate children under the age of eighteen.[119]

During the late 1990s, prior to the 2000 law (possibly inspired by the international criticisms and the Danish reports on the health effects of isolation), there was a significant decline in the use of pre-trial isolation. In 1995, 20.1% of all remand prisoners were isolated compared to 10.4% in 1999.[120] This decline continued on a smaller scale into the new millennium, but was reversed especially during 2004. In 2001 9.5% of all remand prisoners were isolated compared to 9.8% in 2004, and the total number of pre-trial detentions in solitary confinement had gone up from 553 in 2001 to 580 in 2004. It was also a stated purpose of the 2000 law to reduce the length of individual isolations. Despite this, the average length of a stay in pre-trial solitary confinement rose from 28 days in 2000 to 36 days in 2004.[121] Due to this serious rise in the average length of a stay in pre-trial solitary confinement, the ac-

117 *Betænkning om Isolation af varetægtsarrestanter*, Betænkning nr. 975, 1983, p. 88.

118 Koch and Petersen 2003, p. 320.

119 Koch and Petersen 2003, pp. 321 et seq.

120 See *Rigsadvokaten informerer*, no. 21/2003, appendix C.2 (statistics from the Director of Public Prosecutions), *Rigsadvokaten informerer*, no. 42/2004 including an attached '*redegørelse* [summary]'; *Statistik om Isolationsfængsling*, Justitsministeriets Forskningsenhed, maj 2004 (statistics on the use of pre-trial solitary confinement from the Ministry of Justice Department of Research, May 2004).

121 *Arbejdsgruppen vedr. varetægtsarrestanters "ulovlige" kommunikation*, '*Arbejdsgruppens rapport* [Working Group Report]', January 2005, p. 51; *Rigsadvokaten informerer* no. 40/2005, bilag B.2.

tual number of days spent in such conditions has risen significantly. In 2000 a total of 17,366 days were spent by remand prisoners in pre-trial isolation, compared to 20,880 days in 2004.[122] Seen from this perspective, the 2000 law revisions, whose primary function was to reduce the use and length of solitary confinement, seem to have been a failure.

Still, the last thirty years has seen a certain response from the Danish authorities, and, compared to the original situation in the 1970s, a significant decline in the use of pre-trial solitary confinement. But the Danish state has always been very reluctant to acknowledge any problems officially, and solitary confinement is still not used just in exceptional circumstances as recommended by the CPT. Altogether one must conclude that Denmark's willingness to uphold a practice which doctors and psychologists recommend abolishing and its reluctance to meet international recommendations reveal qualities which run counter to the Danish (and Scandinavian) self-image of humanitarian leniency and decency in all areas of state and society.

## 16 Conclusion

> *"The international instruments make clear that solitary confinement is not an appropriate punishment other than in the most exceptional circumstances; whenever possible its use should be avoided and steps should be taken to abolish it".*[123] (Professor of Prison Studies Andrew Coyle)
>
> *The "use and prolongation of solitary confinement should be 'resorted to only in exceptional circumstances'" and prisoners subject to such restrictions for an extended period should be "guaranteed appropriate human contact"*[124] (Rod Morgan and Malcolm D. Evans, referring to the CPT standards).

The history of solitary confinement illustrates how states sometimes give a priority to the interests of crime control over human rights and due process. This is not surprising. The apparently recent retreat away from human rights considerations in this area – especially in the US – is perhaps more surprising, especially when seen in a historical perspective. While the issue of the health of prisoners (and thus arguments concerning some of their basic human rights) clearly helped provoke a gradual decline in the use of solitary confinement during the latter half of the nineteenth century, these considerations are clearly not given the same weight by decision-makers in the contemporary USA. Human rights-oriented criticism has had more, though still only limited success in Denmark, and the basic issue, namely that several hundred individuals are isolated during pre-trial each year, has

122 Calculations are based on *Rigsadvokaten informerer* no. 40/2005, bilag B.2; *Arbejdsgruppen vedr. varetægtsarrestanters "ulovlige" kommunikation*, '*Arbejdsgruppens rapport* [Working Group Report]', January 2005, p. 51.

123 Coyle 2002, p. 80.

124 Rod Morgan and Malcolm D. Evans, *Protecting Prisoners* 1999, p. 55 et seq.

not been solved in a satisfactory manner from a human rights point of view. Decision-makers in Denmark have simply refused to follow medical and psychological advice calling for the abandonment of isolation during pre-trial.

In recent decades, solitary confinement has also found an ally in a new punitive ideology, which runs contrary to the due process–human rights approach, but which in some ways also departs from the crime control approach. The "tough on crime" discourse rests more on new "sensibilities" and populism than on a modern crime-control rationale. Punitive policies are apparently adopted primarily to satisfy, or create, public sentiments of justice, and crime-control issues become almost irrelevant. Authorities make no attempt to identify an evidence-based framework for their isolation policies, and do not seem overly worried when research proves these policies to be ineffective or downright destructive, or "even" extremely costly. This seems to be the case especially with the rise of the supermax in the US, but it also has relevance in the case of Denmark, where the evidence indicates that the use of solitary confinement during pre-trial is primarily a product of tradition and history, not a rational, evidence-based practice.

In both the US and Denmark, in other words, solitary confinement is taking place on a relatively large scale, and is not thoroughly based on rational penal considerations. Whether tradition, local penal culture, issues of crime control or a punitive "tough on crime" ideology constitutes the main motive behind the use of isolation, human rights considerations have clearly taken a back seat, especially in the US. Historically speaking, on the other hand, the use of, and problems with, solitary confinement was dealt with much more effectively in the US in the nineteenth century than in Denmark, where serious reforms had to wait until the 1930s (for sentenced prisoners) and the 1970s (for remand prisoners). Seen from a human rights perspective and in an international context, the late nineteenth-century attitude towards solitary confinement as expressed by the US Supreme Court seems to constitute an enlightened high point, while the current US attitude perhaps represents an all-time low. While the phrase that we have to "learn a lesson from history" might be a cliché, it certainly rings exceptionally true when it comes to the issue and history of solitary confinement.

# 11. The Right to a Nationality and the European Convention on Human Rights

*Eva Ersbøll*

## 1 Nationality and Human Rights

The Universal Declaration of Human Rights (1948) provides that everyone has the right to a nationality. However, this right was not included in the European Convention on Human Rights (1950) nor in any of the protocols to the Convention. This omission cannot be explained by the right to a nationality being an unimportant right – quite the contrary.

Legally, nationality is an expression of a particularly close bond between a person and a state. With the status of a national of a state, in principle the individual obtains full rights in that state, while in international relations the individual may count on its protection. The right to a nationality is thus of great importance to the individual. However, it is also of great importance to a state to be able to decide alone who shall be its nationals. Therefore states have been reluctant to assume international obligations in this particular field.

Even so, the contracting parties to the European Convention on Human Rights (ECHR) have agreed to restrict their powers under general international law to the extent and within the limits of the obligations they have assumed under the Convention. Although the right to a nationality is not itself protected by the Convention, one might ask whether a refusal of the right could – in certain special circumstances and quite independently – violate another right already covered by the Convention.

In this chapter I examine whether and, if so, to what extent the ECHR may be applied in matters of nationality. First, some comments will be made on the importance of the right to a nationality. Secondly, the international and regional, that is European, rules on nationality will be briefly reviewed. Finally, the question of the applicability of the ECHR in matters of nationality will be considered.

*S. Lagoutte, H-O. Sano and P. Scharff Smith (eds.),* Human Rights in Turmoil, *pp. 249-270.*
 *ISBN 90 04 15432 9.*

## 2 The Importance of Nationality

Reading the work of Hannah Arendt (1906–1975), we obtain an insight into the importance of nationality. In Arendt's work *The Origins of Totalitarianism* from 1950, she analyses the problem of statelessness in Europe after World War I, her description leaving no doubt as to the necessity of ensuring the right to a nationality.[1]

The background to Arendt's analysis is the dissolution of the two multinational states of pre-war Europe, Russia and Austria-Hungary, and the stateless people and minorities who suddenly lost rights that had been thought of and even defined as inalienable, namely the Rights of Man or human rights. Stateless persons had no government to represent and protect them, and denationalisation became a powerful weapon of the totalitarian politics.[2] At that time mass denationalisation was something new and unforeseen, presupposing a totalitarian state structure. Arendt talks of a "totalitarian infection", pointing out that there was "hardly a country left on the Continent that did not pass between the two wars some new legislation which, even if it did not use this right extensively, was always phrased to allow for getting rid of a great number of its inhabitants at any opportune moment".[3]

In Nazi Germany there was no reluctance to use denaturalisation and denationalisation towards the Jews, and adjacent countries were not immediately prepared to help the Jewish refugees. The "inalienable human rights" proved to be unenforceable, even in countries whose constitutions were based upon them, whenever people who were no longer the nationals of any sovereign state appeared. According to Arendt, stateless persons were convinced that their loss of national rights was identical with a loss of human rights. First, they suffered the loss of their homes, and then government protection, which did not imply just the loss of their legal status in their own country, but in all countries. Arendt writes about the importance of possessing a nationality:

> We became aware of the existence of a right to have rights (and that means to live in a framework where one is judged by one's actions and opinions) and a right to belong to some kind of organised community, only when millions of people emerged who had lost and could not regain these rights because of the new global political situation.[4]

She concludes that only with a completely organised humanity could the loss of home and political status become identical with expulsion from humanity altogether.

1 Hannah Arendt, *The Origins of Totalitarianism*, 1951.
2 Ibid., p. 267.
3 Ibid., p. 208.
4 Ibid., p. 294.

## 3 International Law on Nationality

When in 1924 the League of Nations decided actively to promote the development of international law, and a committee of experts was convened to prepare a provisional list of the subjects of international law "the regulation of which by international agreement would seem to be most desirable and realisable at the present moment", nationality was included only after some hesitation due to the general perception that most questions of nationality raised political considerations.[5] However, the Hague Codification Conference of 1930 succeeded in producing a Convention on Nationality, The Hague Convention on Certain Questions relating to the Conflict of Nationality Laws.[6]

The first Article of the Convention codifies the generally accepted principle that "(i)t is for each State to determine under its own law who are its nationals." The importance of the Convention appears from the second paragraph of the Article, according to which a state's nationality law shall be recognized by other states (only) "in so far as it is consistent with international conventions, international custom, and the principles of law generally recognised with regard to nationality". This introductory Article reflects the agreement that, under international law, the power of a state to confer its nationality is not unlimited.[7] However, in general each state has the power to decide who shall be its nationals, as in Article 2 of the Convention, according to which "any question as to whether a person possesses the nationality of a particular State shall be determined in accordance with the law of that State."[8]

After World War II, the international community decided that it would never again experience the disregard and contempt for human rights which it had witnessed in the preceding years (see also the preamble of the Universal Declaration of Human Rights (UDHR)). It was recognised that nationality has human rights aspects, and the following provisions were included in Article 15:

> Everyone has the right to a nationality.
> No one shall be arbitrarily deprived of his nationality nor denied the right to change his nationality.

When the UN's Third Committee discussed the wording of the provision, opinions varied on both the use and the understanding of the term "arbitrarily". It was, how-

5 See Shabtai Rosenne, *League of Nations, Committee of Experts for the Progressive Codification of International Law*, 1925-1928, Volume 1, Minutes (1972), pp. 28-9.

6 *Convention on Certain Questions relating to the Conflict of Nationality Laws*, signed at The Hague, 12 April 1930. League of Nations Treaty Series, Vol. 179, p. 89.

7 See Ian Brownlie, *Principles of Public International Law*, Sixth Edition (2003), p. 377, stating that, despite its limitations, Article 1 remains a useful authority for the view that international law sets limits to the power of a state to confer nationality.

8 Article 2 should be read in conjunction with Article 1 in such a way that there is a presumption that national law is in accordance with international law.

ever, the predominant perception that not only illegal decisions but also unreasonable and unjust legislation could be covered by the term.[9]

The idea was that the rights of Universal Declaration should be transformed into binding human rights treaty provisions, and that a special convention should be adopted in order to solve the problem of statelessness. But work on these issues made slow progress. Not until 1961 did states reach agreement on the adoption of the Convention on the Reduction of Statelessness, and not until 1966 did they adopt the International Covenant on Civil and Political Rights (ICCPR). The complexity of the problems concerning nationality meant that none of the Conventions contain provisions similar to those of Article 15 of the Universal Declaration, although Article 24 (3) of the ICCPR states that every child has the right to acquire a nationality, and a similar provision has been included in the UN Convention on the Rights of the Child (1989), Article 7.

## 4 European Law on Nationality

Although the ECHR does not contain any provision on the right to a nationality, the Council of Europe has dealt with issues relating to nationality for over thirty years and adopted a number of conventions and recommendations within this field. In 1988 the Council of Europe's Committee of Experts for the Development of Human Rights started examining the question of the right to a nationality as a human right and considering the possibility of inserting such a right into the ECHR as an additional protocol to the Convention.[10]

The examination indicated a prevailing trend in international human rights development in the area of nationality and common grounds for agreement among European countries, but states were not disposed to adopt an additional protocol to the ECHR on the right to a nationality; in particular, they did not seem to be ready to submit themselves to the supervision of the European Court of Human Rights within this field.[11] The need for European standards concerning nationality was, however, agreed upon, and in 1992 an expert committee on nationality initiated a feasibility study for a new, comprehensive convention on nationality, on

9 UN Official Records 1948, pp. 348, cf. A/C. 3/SR 123 Gaor C 3 summary records of the hundred and twenty-third meeting.

10 See Johannes M. M. Chan, 'The Right to a Nationality as a Human Right: The Current Trend Towards Recognition' in *Human Rights Law Journal* (1991), Vol. 12, p. 7.

11 See Chan (1991), p. 9; Horst Schade, 'The Draft Convention on Nationality', in *Austrian Journal of Public and International Law* (1995) 49, pp. 99-103; Eva Ersbøll, 'Retten til at have rettigheder', in Kjærum, Slavensky and Vedsted-Hansen (eds), *Grundloven og menneskerettigheder i et dansk og europæisk perspektiv* (1997), p. 193.

which basis a draft text was prepared.[12] As a result, the European Convention on Nationality (ECN) was adopted in 1997.[13]

The Convention repeats the generally recognised principles of law regarding nationality. Thus, it states that matters of nationality are generally considered to be within the domestic jurisdiction of each state, and that a state's law shall be accepted by other states in so far as it is consistent with "international conventions, customary international law, and the principles of law generally recognised with regard to nationality". Furthermore, the Convention contains general principles on which the more detailed rules on the acquisition and loss of nationality are to be based, such as the right to a nationality, as first stated in Article 15 of the UDHR, and the obligation to avoid statelessness, which it refers to as a part of customary international law; the prohibition against arbitrary deprivation of nationality and the principle of non-discrimination are also included in the Convention. More specific rules on the acquisition and loss of nationality are contained in the Convention's chapter III, and in other chapters the Convention deals with procedures relating to the acquisition and loss of nationality, multiple nationality and military obligations in cases of multiple nationality and issues of nationality arising from state succession. The Convention's weakness is the lack of any supervisory machinery for it.[14]

## 5 The Relevance of the European Convention on Human Rights in Matters of Nationality

The major strength of the ECHR is its effective enforcement machinery.[15] However, the Convention organs only have powers to handle complaints about violations of the ECHR and its Protocols, as in Article 19 of the ECHR, and cannot control compliance with other human rights standards.[16] Nevertheless, as already mentioned, the ECHR may be of some relevance to matters related to nationality questions, as in (also) the introduction to the explanatory report to the European Convention on Nationality (ECN), paragraph 16, which states the following:

12 See Margaret Killerby, 'Steps taken by the Council of Europe to Promote the Modernisation of the Nationality Laws of European States', in Síofra O'Leary and Teija Tiilikainen (eds), *Citizenship and Nationality Status in the New Europe* (1998), p. 21.

13 *The European Convention on Nationality* (ETS No. 166) was adopted on 6 November 1997 and made available for signature by both Council of Europe member states and non-member states. The Convention entered into force on 1 March 2000, and as of 23 January 2006 it has been ratified by fourteen states, including Denmark, which ratified it on 24 July 2002; cf. Order no. 17 of 12 June 2003 (the Danish Law Gazette C).

14 Apart from preparing draft treaties, recommendations and other legal documents, the Committee of Experts on Nationality has been a forum for the exchange of information among states on issues on nationality.

15 However, the Court has come under pressure due to the very large number of complaints.

16 See e.g. the case of *Yelena Fedorova et autres contre la Lettonie*, app. no. 69405/01, ECtHR 9 October 2003.

> Even if the ECHR and its protocols do not, except for Article 3 of Protocol No. 4 (prohibitions on the expulsion of nationals), contain provisions directly addressing matters relating to nationality, certain provisions may apply also to matters related to nationality questions.

In a note, reference is made to a number of judgments from the European Court of Human Rights dealing mainly with the right of non-nationals to stay in a host country where they have resided for many years with their families; reference is also made to "the important opinion of the European Commission of Human Rights in the case of the East African Asians, 14 December 1973". The text lists the most important ECHR articles that may apply to matters related to nationality, but it is not quite clear how the provisions listed may be applied in nationality questions. While such questions may arise in a number of different areas, in general it is important to distinguish between on the one hand questions on the rights of nationals (citizenship rights), and on the other hand questions on the right to a nationality. In the first case we are dealing with the rights and benefits of nationals versus non-nationals, in the latter with the criteria for the acquisition and loss of nationality.

Questions regarding the rights of nationals are often raised by non-nationals who wish to obtain equal rights with nationals, normally in relation to residence rights, especially in cases concerning deportation. Aliens are protected against collective expulsion under Article 4 of Protocol No. 4 to the ECHR, but they do not enjoy the same general protection against expulsion as nationals do. However, under certain circumstances, deportation of a non-national may constitute a violation of the ECHR, particularly Articles 3 and 8.[17] Furthermore, nationals and fully integrated non-nationals may be in comparable situations, in which case expelled non-nationals may claim that a deportation makes them victims of discrimination on the grounds of nationality, contrary to Article 14 taken together with Article 8. There is ample case law from the Convention organs concerning the rights of nationals and non-nationals, which is mainly what the explanatory report to ECN refers to, but normally in such cases questions concerning the right to a nationality as such will not arise.

Such questions may, however, arise if a state does not recognise that a person has (a right to) its nationality and thus treats that person as an alien. If the Convention organs are to examine whether the consequences of such a denial of nationality may raise an issue under the ECHR, it presupposes that they (also) examine and assess the state's decision on (the right to) nationality. The question whether and, if so, to which extent the ECHR allows such an examination and assessment in respect of the right to a nationality will be dealt with below.[18]

---

17 See also the explanatory report to the ECN.

18 The general question as to when a distinction *based on* nationality is to be regarded as objectively justified or discriminatory according to Article 14 of the ECHR is thus outside of the scope of this article. It should, however, be noted that the European Court of Human Rights has stated that very strong reasons would have to be put forward before it could regard a difference in treatment based exclusively on the ground of nationality

## 6 The Strasbourg Case Law Concerning Nationality

As mentioned above, the explanatory report to the ECN lists the most important provisions of the ECHR in relation to nationality questions. Below, case law from the Convention organs dealing with nationality issues pursuant to these provisions will be examined.

### *6.1 P 4-3 on the Right of Nationals to Stay in their own Country*

The only provision in the ECHR and its additional protocols which explicitly concerns nationals is, as also mentioned above, Article 3 of Protocol No. 4 to the ECHR (P4-3), which reads as follows:

> 1. No one shall be expelled, by means either of an individual or of a collective measure, from the territory of the State of which he is a national.
> 2. No one shall be deprived of the right to enter the territory of the State of which he is a national.

According to the terms of the provision, its scope *ratione personae* is "nationals". In this respect it differs from the similar provision in ICCPR, Article 12 (4), according to which "(n)o one shall be arbitrarily deprived of the right to enter his own country". The UN Human Rights Committee has maintained that Article 12 (4) comprises both nationals and certain other categories of individuals with special ties or claims in relation to a given country.[19] This raises the question of whether the European Court of Human Rights might interpret the term "national" in P4-3 as encompassing more that formal technical nationality and thus give it an autono-

---

as compatible with the ECHR; see e.g. *Gaygusuz v. Austria*, app. no. 17371/90, ECtHR 16 September 1996.

19 See e.g. *Steward v. Canada*, 01/11/1996, and *CCPR General Comment No. 27: Freedom of movement (Art. 12), 02/11/99*, according to which persons covered by Article 12 (4) can be identified through an interpretation of "his own country": The scope of "his own country" is broader than the concept "country of his nationality" and covers, at the very least, an individual who, because of his or her special ties to or claims in relation to a given country, cannot be considered a mere alien. As examples of persons covered by the provision are mentioned nationals who have been stripped of their nationality in violation of international law, as well as individuals whose country of nationality has been incorporated in or transferred to another national entity, whose nationality has been denied them; other persons may also be covered, including stateless persons arbitrarily deprived of the right to acquire the nationality of the country of such residence. The reference to the concept of "arbitrariness" is intended to emphasise that it applies to all state actions, legislative, administrative and judicial; it guarantees that even interference provided for by law should be in accordance with the provisions, aims and objectives of the Covenant and should, in any event, be reasonable in the particular circumstances. A state party must not, by stripping a person of nationality or by expelling an individual to a third country, arbitrarily prevent this person from returning to his or her own country.

mous Convention meaning closer to the term "his own country" used in Article 12 (4) of the ICCPR. Harris et al.[20] and Mole[21] have both argued that this could be the case.

The European Court of Human Rights had an opportunity to attach an autonomous Convention meaning to the term "national" in the *Slivenko* case, in which the Court was asked to decide whether the expulsion of a Russian military officer's wife and daughter from Latvia violated P4-3.[22] The wife had moved to Latvia together with her parents when she was one month old, and the daughter had been born in Latvia. In reality, both mother and daughter had lived all their lives in Latvia, and they had both been citizens of the Latvian SSR (Soviet Socialist Republic) until Latvia regained its independence in 1991. Thereafter they were considered "ex-USSR citizens" or "non-citizens"; later they were forced to leave Latvia pursuant to the Latvian-Russian treaty on the withdrawal of Russian troops. Before the European Court of Human Rights, the mother and the daughter alleged that their removal from Latvia violated P4-3, as Latvia was their motherland; they had not lived in or had citizenship of any other country than Latvia, and they were therefore to be regarded as Latvian "nationals" within the meaning of P4-3. For its part, the Latvian government contended that "nationality" within the meaning of P4-3 is governed exclusively by the norms of domestic law, and that the state is accordingly entitled to determine whether or not a person is its national. The Court observed that P4-3 secures an absolute and unconditional freedom from expulsion of a national but then added the following:

> However, the Court considers that for the purpose of Article 3 of Protocol No. 4 the applicants' "nationality" must be determined, in principle, by reference to the national law. A "right to nationality" similar to that in Article 15 of the Universal Declaration of Human Rights is not guaranteed by the Convention or its protocols, although an arbitrary denial of nationality may under certain circumstances amount to an interference with the rights under Article 8 of the Convention (see, *mutatis mutandis*, *Karassev and Family v. Finland* ...). / Latvian legislation makes no distinction between the notions "citizenship" and "nationality", and it is undisputed that the first and the third applicants have not been Latvian citizens at any time after 27 June 1997, that is the date of the entry into force of the Convention with regard to Latvia. Nor is there any indication that the first and the third applicants have been arbitrarily denied Latvian citizen-

20 D. J. Harris, M. O'Boyle and C. Warbrick, *Law of the European Convention on Human Rights* (1995), p. 563, where it is stated that "the term presumably has an autonomous Convention meaning that would permit the Strasbourg authorities to take into account the limited controls to which general international law subjects states when granting or withdrawing nationality".

21 Nuala Mole, 'Multiple Nationality and the European Convention on Human Rights in Europe', in the report on the 2nd European conference on nationality: *Challenges to national and international law on nationality at the beginning at the new millennium* (Strasbourg, 8 and 9 October 2001), p. 142.

22 *Tatjana Slivenko and Others v. Latvia*, app. no. 48321/99, ECtHR 23 January 2002.

> ship. / It follows that the first and the third applicants cannot be regarded as Latvian "nationals" within the meaning of Article 3 of Protocol No. 4 to the Convention ...[23]

Thus, the Court did not agree with the view of the applicants that they should be regarded as "nationals" in the sense of P4-3. Nor, however, did the Court support the view of the Latvian government that it is "exclusively" up to the national legislature to determine whether or not a person is its national. Instead the Court stated that the question of a person's nationality "in principle" must be determined with reference to the national law. In accordance with the guiding principle of international law as codified in The Hague Convention of 1930 and the ECN of 1997, it must thus be assumed that national law does not violate international law (cf. above, sections 3 and 4).[24] The Court referred to its view in the *Karassev* case (see below), that an arbitrary denial of nationality may under certain circumstances constitute a violation of Article 8 of the ECHR, but in the specific case the complaint relating to the applicants' removal from Latvia was not incompatible with the absolute prohibition of expulsion of nationals stipulated in P4-3, *as* it was undisputed that the applicants had not been Latvian nationals at any time after the ECHR had entered into force in Latvia, and *as* there was no indication that they had arbitrarily been denied Latvian nationality. However, the Court's conclusion that the applicants could not therefore be considered nationals in the sense of P4-3 seems to imply that a given indication of arbitrary denial of nationality may raise questions pursuant not only to Article 8 but also to P4-3.[25]

Furthermore, it is conceivable that a denial of nationality may raise questions pursuant to P4-3 if the purpose of the denial is to evade the prohibition against expulsion of nationals. The committee which drafted the Fourth Protocol to the ECHR contemplated inserting a provision to the effect that "a State would be forbidden to deprive a national of his nationality for the purpose of expelling him".[26] Although the principle which inspired the proposal was approved by the committee, the majority of experts thought it inadvisable to try and tackle the delicate question of the legitimacy of measures depriving individuals of nationality.[27] However, it should not be necessary either to have an explicit prohibition against

23 Ibid., § 77-79.

24 By way of comparison, it may be mentioned that, although it is stated in the EU *Declaration on Nationality of a Member State* that the question of whether an individual possesses the nationality of a Member State "will be settled solely by reference to the national law of the Member State concerned" (see the Final Act to the Maastricht Treaty (1992)), the European Court of Justice has declared, e.g. in Case C-369/90, ECR 1992 I-4239, *Mario Vicente Micheletti and others and Delegación del Gobierno en Cantabria* (ECJ 7 July 1992), that it is for each member State, having due regard to Community law, to lay down the conditions for the acquisition and loss of nationality.

25 In this particular case, there was no information that the applicants had applied for Latvian nationality, which would probably also have been refused on the grounds that they were close family members of a Russian military officer.

26 See *Explanatory Report to Protocol No 4* (ETS No. 46), paragraph 23.

27 Ibid.

a state resorting to *ad hoc* denationalisation to avoid the particular international obligations which apply to the state in relation to its nationals. If it can be proved that the purpose of a withdrawal or a refusal of nationality is to evade an obligation as stated in P4-3, it seems likely that the European Court of Human Rights would consider this a violation of the provision.[28] In a case from 1969, *X against Germany*, the Court examined whether there was such causal connection between the denial of nationality and expulsion.[29] The applicant had been born in Sarajevo and had grown up with a German family, by whom he claimed to be adopted, which, however, proved (formally) not to be the case. The family had lived in the Sudetenland both before and after this became Czech territory, and later moved to Germany. When the applicant moved to Germany, he was an adult; after some years he was expelled due to repeated criminal activity. Before the European Commission of Human Rights, he claimed that the expulsion violated P 4-3 as he should be regarded as a German subject (or at least a stateless person). The Commission found that the risk of expulsion was a consequence of the German authorities' refusal to grant the applicant nationality; this raised the question of whether there was a relationship of cause and effect between the refusal to grant the applicant German nationality and his expulsion from Germany such that it could form the basis of a presumption that the refusal had had the sole purpose of making the expulsion possible. However, under the particular circumstances of the case, the Commission did not find any reason to conclude that the German authorities had denied the applicant nationality with the sole purpose of expelling him.

Summing up, it may be argued that, if an individual complains to the European Court of Human Rights that he or she has been expelled from a state contrary to P4-3, the Court will have to consider the question of whether the applicant can be regarded as a national on the basis of that state's internal legislation, including the question of whether the applicant has arbitrarily been denied or deprived of the state's nationality.[30] If it is established that the applicant is a national, expulsion will constitute a violation of P4-3. If denial or deprivation has taken place arbitrar-

28 See also Nuala Mole (2001), p. 138, with references.

29 *X contre la République Fédérale d'Allemagne*, app. no. 3745/68, ECtHR 15 December 1969.

30 See also *Yelena Fedorova et autres contra la Lettonie*, 09/10/2003. The applicant was a stateless woman who had lived in Latvia since she was nine years old. She spent three years out of Latvia after getting married, and when she returned to Latvia with her small child after a divorce, she was expelled. The European Court of Human Rights stated that, under certain circumstances, a denial of nationality could constitute a violation of the rights according to Article 8. However, the applicant had not had Latvian nationality at any time, and there were no indications of an arbitrary refusal of Latvian nationality. As to the question of the application of P4-3, the Court recalled that this provision applies to "nationals" only, and that the term "national" is defined, in principle, "par un renvoi au droit interne"; since the applicant could not be regarded as a Latvian national, her complaint was incompatible *ratione personae* with the ECHR and declared inadmissible.

ily with the purpose of making expulsion possible, this may likewise constitute a violation of P4-3.

### 6.2 Article 3 on the Prohibition against Torture, Inhuman or Degrading Treatment

The provision in P4-3, mentioned above, is not phrased as a right but as a prohibition against deprivation of the right of a national to enter his own state. Thus, the right of entry is assumed to be an existing right, which corresponds to the fact that the right to settle and reside in the territory of the state of nationality is considered "(o)ne of the functions inherent in the concept of nationality".[31] All the same, not all member countries of the Council of Europe have ratified P4 and thus committed themselves to respect Article 3 of the Protocol, and therefore it is noteworthy that the European Commission of Human Rights has established that, under certain circumstances, Article 3 of the Convention may protect nationals who wish to enter the state of which they are nationals, cf. the case of *East African Asians v. the United Kingdom*.[32]

The applicants in this case were of Asian descent and resident in Kenya and Uganda, like many Asians had been for centuries, but especially since the period of the British colonisation of East Africa from the latter half of the nineteenth century. When East African countries gained independence at the beginning of the 1960s, only those residents who had been born in East Africa and had a parent also born there automatically became nationals of the country where they resided. Others had a right for two years to opt for nationality. Later, when the so-called "Africanisation" policy was introduced, those who had not become nationals of the country where they resided experienced increasing difficulties by way of restrictions etc. The applicants belonged to the category of Asians who had not become the nationals of an East African country, but who had retained their status as citizens of United Kingdom and Colonies (or in six cases, British protected persons) and were therefore given the right to claim a British passport and to be exempted from British immigration control imposed in 1962. The policies of "Africanization" resulted in a considerable increase in the number of East African Asians entering Britain for permanent settlement (between 1965 and 1967, the number increased from 6,150 to 13,600 and during the first two months of 1968 the number was 12,800). In 1968, this lead to an amendment to the Immigrants Act, whereby more East African Asians, including the applicants, became subject to immigration control.[33]

---

31 P. Weis, *Nationality and Statelessness in International Law* (1979), p. 45.

32 *East African Asians v. United Kingdom*, 14 December 1973, D.R. 78-A, September 1994.

33 The change of the Immigration Act in 1968 implied that "citizens of the United Kingdom and Colonies" were only exempt from immigration control if they or at least one of their parents or their grandparents were born in the UK or had been naturalised there or acquired British nationality by adoption or registration in the UK (ibid., paragraph 32).

Having been refused admission into the UK, the applicants submitted before the European Commission of Human Rights that, by refusing to admit them to the UK or to allow them to stay there permanently, the UK reduced them to the status of second-class citizens; they claimed that this degradation was based on their colour or race, and amounted to "degrading treatment" in the sense of Article 3. The Commission agreed that discrimination based on race could, under certain circumstances, amount to degrading treatment within the meaning of Article 3, and that discrimination in the present cases would be considered under Article 3 and not under Article 14.[34] Since P4-3 had not been ratified by the UK and no right to enter the territory of the state of which a person is a national as such is otherwise guaranteed by the ECHR, the Commission thus implicitly accepted that the refusal of a right which is not itself protected by the ECHR may nevertheless under certain circumstances violate another right already included in the Convention. The Commission referred to its case law concerning the right of asylum and the right of an alien not to be expelled. Although neither of these rights is guaranteed by the ECHR, the Commission had found that the contracting state parties had agreed to restrict the free exercise of their power under general international law, including the power to control the entry and exit of aliens, to the extent and within the limits of the obligations which they had assumed under the Convention. The Commission found that the considerations concerning the position of aliens "apply, *mutatis mutandis*, to the present applications brought by citizens".[35]

Defining the subject to be examined, the Commission noted that "(i)t follows that in the present case, the Commission is not being called upon to consider the rights of entry or residence as such, but that it is being invited to examine the different question whether the decisions complained of amount to 'degrading treatment' in the sense of Article 3".[36] Defining the elements to be considered, the Commission observed that it was not faced with the general question whether racial discrimination in immigration control constitutes as such degrading treatment, but rather whether the legislation that the UK had applied in the case of the applicants discriminated against them on the basis of their race or colour, and, if this was the case, whether the application of the legislation in the special circumstances of the cases constituted degrading treatment. Among the special circumstances, the Commission singled out the fact that the cases concerned persons who were not aliens, but "were and remained citizens of the United Kingdom and Colonies, and that as such, although they had the same duties as other citizens, under the 1968 Act they no longer had the same right of entry". Their continued residence in East Africa had become illegal, and, being refused entry by the only state of which they were nationals – the UK – they had nowhere else to go.[37]

34 Ibid., paragraph 180.

35 Ibid., paragraphs 184–187.

36 Ibid., paragraph 187.

37 Ibid., paragraph 191. Another special circumstance was a "pledge" of free entry, which the UK should have given to the citizens of the UK and Colonies in East Africa.

The Commission found it established that the 1968 Act had racial motives and that it covered a racial group. When the Bill was introduced in Parliament, it was clear that it was directed against the Asian citizens of the UK and Colonies in East Africa, especially those in Kenya.[38] The Commission found that the government had admitted its racial motives, since the Home Secretary had stated, "the origin of this Bill lies ... in a considered judgement of the best way to achieve the idea of a multi-racial society".[39] The government had also declared that the objective of the Act was to promote "racial harmony". On this basis, the Commission concluded that the 1968 Act discriminated against citizens of the UK and Colonies in East Africa who were of Asian origin on grounds of their colour or race. The discriminatory provisions of the 1968 Act had also to be seen in the context of other laws and regulations in the field of citizenship which gave preference to "white people". Furthermore, the Commission pointed out a number of circumstances that were bound to have created the expectation among the East African Asians that their British nationality would guarantee them entry into and residence in the UK in the future. As to the relevance of the persons concerned being citizens of the UK and Colonies with the same rights as other citizens, the Commission added:

> They were thus, as submitted by the applicants, reduced to the status of second-class citizens.[40]

The Commission was of the opinion that the increasingly difficult situation for the Asians in East Africa was foreseeable in 1968, and even though the hardship of the applicants was not directly caused by the UK, by its actions the UK had exposed the applicants to the possibility of this occurring.

On this basis the Commission concluded that the differential treatment of a group of persons on the basis of race may be capable of constituting degrading treatment while differential treatment on some other ground would raise no such question. The racial discrimination to which the applicants had been publicly subjected by the application of the 1968 Act was found to constitute an interference with their human dignity which amounted to degrading treatment in the sense of Article 3 of the ECHR.[41]

The Convention organs have referred to the case of the *East African Asians* in several other cases concerning nationality issues, e.g. the cases *Slepcik* and *Zeibeck* concerning the acquisition and loss of nationality respectively. In the *Slepcik* case concerning Roma gypsies, who wanted to acquire Czech nationality after the dissolution of the Czechoslovak Federal Republic, the Commission took into account the possibility "that in the particular circumstances of the case the impossibility

38 Ibid., paragraph 199. The Commission referred to a statement by the former Secretary of State for the Colonies, indicating that the main purpose was to exclude that "most of the 200,000 Asians in East Africa would continue to be free to come here at will".

39 Ibid., paragraph 200.

40 Ibid., paragraph 205.

41 Ibid., paragraph 208.

for the applicants to acquire Czech citizenship was capable of raising issues under Article 3 and 14".[42] In the *Zeibek* case concerning Greek nationals of Turkish descent, who had lost their Greek nationality upon leaving Greece, the Commission recalled that differential treatment of a group of persons on the basis of race might be capable of constituting degrading treatment prohibited under Article 3 of the Convention.[43]

To conclude: if a refusal by a state to admit its nationals to its territory (or to stay there permanently) is based on race or ethnicity, the refusal may constitute an interference with the human dignity of the persons concerned amounting to degrading treatment in the sense of Article 3 of the ECHR. The *East African Asians* case may be seen as one concerning "citizens' rights", i.e. the right to enter and reside in the country of nationality; but since this right is generally accepted as one of the functions inherent in the concept of nationality, and since the state's duty of admission is generally accepted as an inherent duty of states resulting from the concept of nationality,[44] it can be argued that in reality the case is just as much a case about the right to a (full) nationality, or – to put it differently – the right not to be treated as "a second-class citizen" on the ground of race or ethnicity. Consequently, it may be assumed that a denial or withdrawal of nationality on the ground of race or ethnicity, according to the circumstances, may also constitute degrading treatment under Article 3.

When discrimination arises in a case concerning the right to a nationality, it may be of importance that the Convention's Article 3 can be applied, since the right to a nationality is not guaranteed by the ECHR or its protocols, and the Convention's non-discrimination guarantee in Article 14 has no free-standing status, being merely accessory to the other substantive guarantees of the Convention; thus, it can only be invoked in association with one of these rights (see below). And Protocol No. 12 to the ECHR, which sets out a general prohibition of discrimination, has only recently entered into force and only 13 states have ratified it so far.

It is also of importance whether Article 3 can be applied in cases of discrimination on other grounds than race and ethnicity. The European Commission of Human Rights has stressed that it may constitute a special form of affront to human dignity publicly to single out a group of persons for differential treatment because of race. It could, however, be argued that other kinds of discriminatory treatment might also violate human dignity; in the literature, references have been made to discrimination against children born out of wedlock and sexual discrimination, and it has been found to be "(a)rguable that discrimination on any of these grounds, all of which concern personal characteristics, is degrading contrary to Article 3".[45]

---

42 *Slepcik v. the Netherlands and the Czech Republic*, app. no. 30913/96, ECtHR 2 September 1996.

43 *Zeibek v. Greece*, app. no. 34372/97, ECtHR 21 May 1997.

44 See Weis (1979), pp. 45, 47.

45 See Harris, O'Boyle and Warbrick (1995), p. 83.

### 6.3 *Article 6 on the Right to a Fair Trial*

In the explanatory report to ECN, Article 6 of the ECHR is mentioned among the important provisions concerning the right to nationality. In the Convention organs' case law, however, it is established that Article 6 (1) applies exclusively to proceedings dealing with the determination of civil rights and obligations or of any criminal charge, and that proceedings concerning a person's nationality do not determine either civil rights or a criminal charge, and that therefore Article 6 of the ECHR does not apply in cases concerning the right to a nationality.

In 1972, the European Commission on Human Rights declared a complaint about a violation of Article 6 of the ECHR in connection with deprivation of nationality inadmissible.[46] The applicant was an Austrian national by birth, but in 1971 the Austrian authorities declared that he had lost his Austrian nationality according to Austrian nationality law because in 1948 he had acquired British nationality by naturalisation. He was informed that there was no remedy against the decision. Subsequently he complained to the European Commission on Human Rights that he had been deprived of his Austrian nationality without even a fair hearing, and accordingly he alleged a violation of Article 6 (1) of the EHRC on the part of Austria.

The Commission stated that Article 6 was exclusively applicable to proceedings dealing with the determination of civil rights and obligations or a criminal charge. Concerning the applicability of the provisions of Article 6 (1) in the case of the applicant, the Commission stated:

> Accordingly, they do not apply to the above proceedings instituted by the applicant since they clearly did not determine a criminal charge brought against him and his civil rights and obligations were not involved as it is a prerogative of the State to regulate citizenship and the relevant rules constitute public law. The proceedings in question, therefore, were of a public law nature.

The reasons for not considering the applicant's civil rights involved in the proceedings dealing with nationality questions seem to be both *that* the regulation of acquisition and loss of nationality is a prerogative of the state and *that* Article 6 (1) is not applicable since the relevant rules (therefore) constitute public law. The latter view is debatable. In France for instance during one century, the categorisation of nationality rules was strongly debated by courts and by scholars: was it part of public or private law? To resolve the problem, starting in 1927, an autonomous Code de la Nationalité was adopted, but in 1993, a reform reintegrated nationality into the Civil Code, where it used to be from 1803 – 1927.[47] In any case, both views may reflect a traditional conception of law, which to a certain extent is changing. It is now

46 *X against Austria*, app. no. 5212/71, ECtHR 5 October 1972.

47 Patrick Weil and Alexis Spire, 'France', in Rainer Bauböck, Eva Ersbøll, Kees Groenendijk and Harald Waldrauch (eds.): *Acquisition and Loss of Nationality, Policies and Trends in 15 European States* (forthcoming 2006).

generally recognised that state discretion in the field of nationality must take into account international law and in particular the fundamental rights of individuals. Furthermore, over time the Convention organs have applied the term "civil rights" to a broader extent than just private law, and recent jurisprudence, by which more and more rights and obligations have been brought within the scope of Article 6, is not easy to explain in terms of any distinction between private and public law that is found in European national law.[48]

Nevertheless, in several recent decisions, the Strasbourg organs have maintained that proceedings concerning a person's right to a nationality do not determine his or her "civil rights".[49] This view has been maintained, even when applicants have pointed out that the consequences of their loss of nationality have been that they cannot work, travel, drive a car or get married.[50] However, in the *Karassev* case, discussed below, in which the determination of the question of nationality was not beyond doubt, the Commission avoided the argument that the regulation of nationality is the prerogative of the state, and instead stated:

> Even assuming that the applicant Pasi Karessev could arguable claim a "right" to Finnish citizenship, the Commission cannot find that the right was "civil", given that it was not, as such, of a pecuniary or otherwise of a private law character. [...] The Commission reaches the same conclusion as regards any "obligation" which might have been determined by the citizenship proceedings.[51]

The condition in Article 6, that the applicant must have a right according to national law, may very well be fulfilled in cases relating to nationality, among other things because states may have undertaken international obligations to recognise in their internal law that certain groups of persons shall acquire their nationality. It seems that the crucial point is the perception of the Convention organs that the right to a nationality "as such" is not a "civil right" in the sense of Article 6 (1), as in the *Karassev* case.[52] It does not seem to matter that (the possession of) nationality has legal consequences of a pecuniary or otherwise private law character, conse-

48 Harris, O'Boyle and Warbrick (1995), p.175.

49 See e.g. *S v. Switzerland*, app. no. 13325/87, ECtHR 15 December 1988, concerning a divorced Egyptian national whose wife (after the divorce) had been recognised as a Swiss National and whose son had been included in the act of recognition (whereby the son acquired dual nationality). The father, who according to Egyptian Islamic law had parental custody, complained under Article 6 (1) of the ECHR that in the proceedings the Swiss authorities had not heard him personally.

50 See *Zeibek v. Greece*, app. no. 34372/97, ECtHR 21 May 1997, concerning the revocation of Greek nationality of persons of non-Greek stock (*allogenis*) who had left Greece "with no intention to return". On the same subject, see *Galip contre la Grèce*, No 17309/90, 30/08/1994.

51 *Karassev and Family v. Finland*, app. no. 31414/96, ECtHR 14 April 1998.

52 As it is in the sense of the UN Convention on the Elimination of All Forms of Racial Discrimination (1965), which in Article 5 (1) prohibits racial discrimination in the enjoyment of (d) "other civil rights, in particular" (iii) "the right to nationality".

quences that are most obvious in cases of expulsion, to which only aliens may be subjected. The fact that expulsion or exclusion may have major repercussions on the excluded person's private or family life or his prospects of employment is recognised by the European Court of Human Rights in the *Maaouia* case.[53] However, neither in this leading case on expulsion did this suffice to bring the proceedings within the scope of civil rights as protected by Article 6 (1) of the Convention.[54] But here, the main argument for not applying Article 6 was that the provisions of the Convention must be construed in the light of the entire Convention system, including the Protocols, and that the adoption of Protocol No. 7 (P-7) to the ECHR, which contains procedural guarantees applicable to the expulsion of aliens, showed (in the majority of the Court's opinion) that states were aware that Article 6 did not apply to procedures for the expulsion of aliens; the understanding was that by adopting the Protocol states clearly intimated their intention not to include proceedings for the expulsion of aliens within the scope of Article 6 (1) of the ECHR. For several reasons two judges (Loucaides and Traja) disagreed with this finding. In a dissenting opinion they claimed that, according to the Vienna Convention on the Law of Treaties, Article 31, the word "civil" in Article 6 (1) should be interpreted in the context in which it appears and in the light of the object and purpose of the Article. Using this approach, they believed that the word "civil" had the meaning "non-criminal"; once the word "criminal charge" had been used, another term intended to cover the rest of the adjudicative procedures would have to be found, and "civil" seemed appropriate to achieve the purpose of covering all other legal rights of a non-criminal nature. They considered it evident that the object and purpose of Article 6 (1) was to ensure, through judicial guarantees, a fair administration of justice to any person in the assertion or determination of his legal rights and obligations, and that an independent judicial form of control was especially required for the protection of the individual against the powerful authorities of the state.

As mentioned above, there has been a general trend towards the European Court of Human Rights extending the application of the terms "civil rights and obligations" to matters that do not ordinarily belong to the sphere of private law. Among others, the Court has held that a dispute between an applicant and a public authority concerning the grant of a licence was a determination of a civil right, and applying a teleological interpretation, as argued for in the dissenting opinion in the *Maaouia* case, there seems to be strong arguments not to exclude nationality issues from the scope of Article 6 (1). In this connection, it should be noted that the trend in European nationality law is towards the expansion of nationality entitlements,[55] and that nationality may be considered "the right to have rights" (see above, section 2).

---

53 *Maaouia v. France*, app. no. 39652/98, ECtHR 5 October 2000.

54 Ibid., paragraph 38.

55 For further details, see Randall Hansen and Patrick Weil (eds.), *Towards a European Nationality: Citizenship, Immigration and Nationality Law in the EU*, p. 6 (on the rights of second-generation migrants). See also Bauböck et al. (2006 forthcoming).

### 6.4 Article 8 on the Right to Respect for Private and Family Life

The above-mentioned *Karassev* case counts among the leading cases dealing with the question of whether a denial of nationality may raise an issue under Article 8 of the ECHR.[56] The applicant was born in Finland on 16 December 1992 of parents who had been born in the former Soviet Union and were nationals of that country. They arrived in Finland in 1991 and applied for asylum, but their request was rejected, and the Finnish Ministry of the Interior ordered their expulsion to the Russian Federation. The family appealed to the Supreme Administrative Court, which referred the matter back to the Ministry for renewed consideration, since the expulsion order had not concerned the applicant. Subsequently, the applicant asked to be granted Finnish nationality by application, but this request was refused, as the Ministry of the Interior considered both the applicant and his parents to be nationals of the Russian Federation; the parents had arrived in Finland on a tourist visa, and at the time when the Russian Citizenship Act entered into force in February 1992, they were not permanent residents in Finland, but in the Russian Federation. Therefore they had become Russian nationals, and the applicant had consequently obtained Russian nationality at birth according to the descent principle. In 1996, however, the Russian Embassy in Finland certified that the applicant's parents were not Russian nationals. On this basis, the applicant withdrew his request for Finnish nationality by application, and instead he requested the Finnish President to confirm that he had received Finnish nationality *ex lege* at birth pursuant to the Finnish nationality law, according to which a child born in Finland receives Finnish nationality at birth if it does not at that time receive the nationality of any other country. Before the European Court of Human Rights, the applicant complained about the Finnish authorities' procrastination in regularising his residence in Finland and the resulting effects on his entitlement to various benefits, claiming that he should have been considered a Finnish national by birth, and invoking Articles 8 and 14 of the ECHR in his support. The Court noted that, although a right to a nationality as such is not guaranteed by the ECHR and its protocols, it did not "exclude that an arbitrarily denial of a citizenship might in certain circumstances raise an issue under Article 8 of the Convention because of the impact of such denial on the private life of the individual".[57] Therefore, the Court found it necessary to examine whether the Finnish decisions "disclose such arbitrariness or have such consequences as might raise issues under Article 8 of the Convention".[58] The Court found that the

56 *Andrei Karassev and family v. Finland*, app. no. 31414/96, ECtHR 12 January 1999.

57 In the *Slivenko* case (app. no. 48321/99, ECtHR 23 January 2002, paragraph 77), the European Court of Human Rights (referring to the *Karassev* case) stated more directly: "an arbitrary denial of nationality may under certain circumstances amount to an interference with the rights under Article 8 of the Convention". See also *Aleksandr Kolosovskiy contre la Lettonie*, app. no. 50183/99, ECtHR 29 January 2004.

58 The Court referred among others to the case of *Kafkasli contre la Turquie*, app. no. 21106/92, ECtHR 22 May 1995 and 18 February 1998, concerning a person of Georgian origin who had been deprived of his Turkish nationality because of espionage and had been excluded from regaining it for forty years. He complained of a violation of the

statement from the Russian Embassy supported the applicant's contention that the Finnish authorities' interpretation of the Russian Citizenship Act was not correct, but a later opinion from a specialist body, the Russian Citizenship Commission – although not without ambiguity – did not seem to be in contradiction with the way in which the Finnish authorities had interpreted the Russian Citizenship Act. For that reason the Court concluded that the decision of the Finnish authorities was not arbitrary in a manner that could raise issues under Article 8 of the EHRC. As to the consequences of the denial to recognise the applicant as a Finnish national, the Court noted that he was not threatened with expulsion from Finland, neither alone nor together with his parents, who had residence permits etc., which could also be issued to the applicant at their request; the applicant also enjoyed social benefits and the like in Finland. Against this background, the Court did not find that the consequences of the refusal to recognise the applicant as a Finnish national, taken separately or in combination with the refusal itself, could be considered sufficiently serious to raise an issue under Article 8.

Summing up, the European Court of Human Rights has in principle proved willing to examine whether a denial of nationality is arbitrary in such a way that it raises an issue under Article 8 of the ECHR. In dealing with a complaint about a denial of nationality, the Court may thus (under certain circumstances) examine *whether* the denial of nationality is arbitrary in a way that could raise issues under Article 8, and *whether* the consequences of the denial can be considered sufficiently serious to raise an issue under Article 8.[59]

### 6.5 Article 14 on the Enjoyment of the Convention Rights and Freedoms without Discrimination on any Ground

It is well known that Article 14 on the prohibition against discrimination complements the other substantive provisions of the Convention and the Protocols. Article 14 has no independent existence; although its application does not necessarily presuppose a breach of the substantive provisions, there can be no room for its

right to respect for his private life as a result of certain restrictions due to his statelessness and of the refusal of his request for restoration of his Turkish nationality. The European Commission on Human Rights admitted that the case did raise serious factual and legal issues under Article 8, which had to be decided through a full hearing of the case on its merits (22/05/1995). In hearing the case on its merits, however, the Commission did not find that there had been a violation of Article 8 (18/02/1998; Council of Ministers Resolution DH (98) 19).

59 In the *Slivenko* case (admissibility decision 23/01/02; cf. above), the European Court of Human Rights did not find any indication that the applicant had been arbitrarily denied nationality. However, the Court declared the applicants' complaint under Article 8 concerning their removal from Latvia admissible, and a Grand Chamber found that the Latvian authorities had overstepped their margin of appreciation and that they had failed to strike a fair balance between the legitimate aim of protection of national security and the interest of the protection of the applicant's rights under Article 8; accordingly there had been a violation of Article 8 (judgment 09/10/2003).

application unless the facts at issue fall within the ambit of one or more of these provisions.[60] Thus, the Convention organs can only handle a complaint about discrimination in nationality matters pursuant to Article 14 if the decision on nationality raises an issue under one (or more) of the substantive rights of the ECHR.

In 1984, the European Commission on Human Rights found that the right to acquire a particular nationality is neither covered by, or sufficiently related to, any provision of the ECHR, and therefore it rejected a complaint that Dutch nationality law was discriminatory on the grounds of sex as being incompatible *ratione materiae* with the ECHR, as in the case of *K. and W. v/the Netherlands*.[61] One of the applicants was a British national from Hong Kong, who was expelled from the Netherlands because he had been found guilty of dealing in heroin. The applicant and his wife, a Dutch national, had lived together since 1979, and they married in 1983, while the applicant was in prison. Before the European Commission on Human Rights, the applicant complained that the Act on Dutch Citizenship was discriminatory, as a woman married to a Dutch man would be able to obtain Dutch nationality simply by writing a letter expressing this wish to the mayor of the municipality, thus rendering expulsion impossible. For him, however, as a man married to a Dutch woman, this possibility did not exist, and this constituted in his opinion a violation of Article 14 in conjunction with Article 8 of the Convention. The Commission recalled that Article 14 only prohibits discrimination with respect to the enjoyment of the rights and freedoms set forth in the Convention, and although the applicant had invoked Article 8 of the Convention, read in conjunction with Article 14, the Commission found that "the right to acquire a particular nationality is neither covered by, nor sufficiently related to, this or any other provision of the Convention".

It seems that the view of the Commission should be interpreted in the light of the facts of the case and the state of international law of that time. The applicant had not been married to a Dutch national or applied for Dutch nationality before he had been sentenced to imprisonment, and it was not unusual at that time for the contracting state parties' nationality law not yet to have introduced the concept of equality between spouses.[62] In the *Karassev* case mentioned above, the applicant had invoked Article 8 as well as Article 14 of the ECHR, and the Court did not exclude the possibility that arbitrary denial of nationality might under certain circumstances raise an issue under Article 8. However, leaving open the question of whether the complaint fell within the ambit of Article 8 so as to make Article 14 applicable, the Court found no substantiation for the applicants' allegation that

60 See *Abdulaziz, Cabales and Balkandali v. The United Kingdom*, app. no. 9214/80; 9473/81 and 9474/81, ECtHR 28 May 1985, paragraph 71.

61 See *Family K. and W. v/the Netherlands*, No 11278/84, 01/07/1985, D.R. 43, October 1985, p. 216.

62 See *Council of Europe recommendation 1081 (1988) on problems of nationality in mixed marriages*, paragraph 9, where it states that "the law on nationality has been substantially amended in many member states in recent years, particularly for the purpose of introducing the concept of equality between spouses".

the decisions on his right to Finnish nationality were based on the ethnic and/or national background of the his parents. The examination of the Court of this complaint therefore did not disclose any appearance of a violation of the rights of the ECHR, but – to sum up – the Court did not exclude the applicability of Article 14 (in conjunction with Article 8).

### 6.6 P 12 on the Prohibition of Discrimination on any Ground

On 1 April 2005, Protocol No. 12 to the ECHR entered into force. The Protocol's Article 1 (P12-1) provides a general non-discrimination clause and thereby affords a broader scope of protection than Article 14, insofar as it covers all situations where a person might be discriminated against by a public authority.[63] As mentioned above, the Protocol has only been ratified by 13 states, and there is not any case law from the European Court of Human Rights yet. However, in states which have ratified the Protocol, claims that rejection of nationality violates the principle of non-discrimination will in principle fall within the scope of the protocol; its non-discrimination provision is comparable to the ICCPR's Article 26, and it is worth mentioning that the UN Human Rights Committee has declared that such claims fall within the scope of Article 26.[64]

## 7 Concluding Remarks

It appears from the practice of the European Commission on Human Rights and the European Court of Human Rights that even though the right to a nationality is not as such guaranteed by the ECHR, a complaint about an arbitrary denial or deprivation of nationality may, according to the circumstances, raise an issue under the Convention. The examination of decisions on (the right to) nationality must take its point of departure in the internal nationality legislation of the states concerned. So far, only one case on nationality has been declared admissible (the case concerning the *East African Asians*), but in several cases the Convention organs have taken the opportunity to declare that an arbitrary denial or withdrawal of nationality may raise an issue under the ECHR.

In so far as the right to nationality can be considered "the right to have rights",[65] this legal situation should occasion no surprise. Traditionally states have granted their nationals more and better rights than non-nationals, and to a certain extent it is still generally accepted that nationality forms a legal criterion for differential treatment. To that extent, a non-national cannot complain for being treated differ-

63 Luzius Wildhaber, 'Protection against Discrimination under the European Convention on Human Rights – A Second-Class guarantee?', in Ineta Ziemele (ed.), *Baltic Yearbook of International Law*, Volume 2, 2002, pp.71-82.

64 Communication 1136/2002, *Vjatseslav Borzov v. Estonia*, views of 26 July 2004.

65 Not only Hannah Arendt (see above, section 2), but also Earl Warren, Chief Justice of the US Supreme Court, has applied this characterisation; cf. *Perez v. Brownell*, 356 U.S. 44, 1958 and *Trop v. Dulles*, 356 U.S.86, 1958.

ently from a national. But if a person complains that the state has arbitrarily refused to recognise him or her as a national, and a certain differential treatment is based on his or her status as a non-national (decided by an arbitrary refusal to recognise his or her right to a nationality), this may raise an issue under the Convention, not only in the situations described above, but in all situations where the Articles of the ECHR allow states to treat nationals and non-nationals differently.

Thus, this may happen within the sphere of the rights to freedom of expression, freedom of association and freedom of assembly, since Article 16 of the Convention allows the contracting state parties to impose restrictions on the political activities of non-nationals in respect of these freedoms (Article 16 in conjunction with Articles 10, 11 and 14). Likewise it may happen with regard to electoral rights (cf. P1-3): if, for instance, an applicant complains that a state has arbitrarily refused to recognise him as a national and has consequently refused to grant him voting rights contrary to P1-3, an examination of whether there has been a violation of P1-3 makes it necessary for the Court to examine whether the decision on the applicant's nationality discloses such arbitrariness, and whether it has such consequences as might raise an issue under P1-3. The question as to whether the decision concerning (the right to) nationality was arbitrary will be dealt with primarily on the basis of the relevant internal nationality law. Furthermore, it is to be expected that the Court will allow the state a rather wide "margin of appreciation", since the right for a state to determine under its own law who are its nationals is an essential element of its sovereignty. Nevertheless, the ECHR may acquire increased importance in nationality matters in the future. Around the world, denationalisation and arbitrary and discriminatory conditions for obtaining nationality are becoming growing problems.[66] In Europe, many persons are "stateless", especially in some of the states which became independent after the dissolution of the former Soviet Union and ex-Yugoslavia. However, the possible scope of the ECHR concerning the right to a nationality may, judged by the Convention organs' case-law, depend on whether the applicants have actively made any efforts to be recognised as nationals of the state concerned.[67] The concept of nationality was explored by the International Court of Justice in the famous *Nottebohm* case, which defined "nationality" as "a legal bond having as its basis a social fact of attachment, a genuine connection of existence, interests and sentiments, together with the existence of reciprocal rights and duties".[68] It may be in the light of this interplay that the Court will consider the question whether a decision on the right to a nationality discloses such arbitrariness or has such consequences as might raise issues under the ECHR.

66 See e.g. Open Society Justice Initiative, *Racial Discrimination and the Rights of Non-Citizens*, Submission of the Open Society Justice Initiative to the UN Committee on the Elimination of Racial Discrimination on the occasion of its 64th session, February 2004, and *Prevention of Discrimination, The rights of non-citizens*, Final Report of the Special Rapporteur, Mr David Weissbrodt, E/CN.4/Sub.2/2003/23.

67 With the proviso that the legislation does not unreasonably obstruct the acquisition of nationality.

68 *Nottebohm Case*, ICJ Reports 1955, p. 23.

# 12. Reflections of a Former Judge of the European Court of Human Rights

*Isi Foighel**

Courts of Law are all too often housed in solemn buildings with cold marble floors and roofs propped up by stern, indomitable columns. Grand staircases extend to the upper floors and, where there are windows, they are opaque. "Herein resides the most serious business", these buildings declare. Here dwells the power of the state and its justice. From these halls it shall be decreed who will go free, who will be incarcerated, who shall be wealthy and who will be forced into bankruptcy.

The European Court of Human Rights in Strasbourg has an entirely different feel. The building in which it is housed is made of steel and glass – indeed; there is so much glass that the edifice is all but transparent. To those who pass by, stop to stare or enter into its main hallway, this building too tells a story, the story of human rights, in other words, the rights and freedoms belonging to every human being and which no single ruler or parliament shall ever be able to rescind. In the façade of this building there is a pride and perhaps even a tinge of exhibitionism. It is the opposite of Kafka's castle. Everything about it invites the onlooker to peer in, learn, imitate the way the best minds go about maintaining human rights and defending them, and making eye contact with judges who are at the same time *looking out* at them and at the real world, never forgetting the people to whom they are committed and whom they serve.

## 1 The Case of the "Green Jackets"

It was in 1994, at this beautiful location in Strasbourg, that the case of *Jersild versus Denmark* was tried.[1] When the case came to the court, many observers were

---

* This chapter is partly based on the author's lecture of the 18 March 2005 on the occasion of University of Copenhagen's celebration of his more than fifty years' membership of the Faculty of Law. The article was published in Danish by Christian Ejlers, Publishers, in their annual *Katalogårbog 2005*.

1 *Jersild v. Denmark*, app. no. 15890/89, ECtHR 23 September 1994. For an in-depth analysis of this case, see Lene Johannesen, *New limits: a legal comment on a case about*

*S. Lagoutte, H-O. Sano and P. Scharff Smith (eds.),* Human Rights in Turmoil, *pp. 271-283.*
 ISBN *90 04 15432 9.*

shocked to discover that Denmark was being accused of violating a journalist's freedom of expression. Even worse, the State of Denmark was later found guilty of violating the European Convention on Human Rights. The judgment gave rise to some very difficult questions. Should the European Convention on Human Rights supersede the Danish penal code; should the European Court of Human Rights overrule a judgment by the Danish Supreme Court? This discussion is still very much alive, but before we can understand the issues being debated, we must obtain a firm grasp of the background to this case.

Back in 1985, when Denmark had only a single TV station, DR (Danish Broadcasting), on Sunday evenings it would air a news programme called *The Sunday Journal*. Each week a significant proportion of the Danish population would gather in front of their television sets to watch various talking heads interact with real world issues. One such Sunday the journalist Jens Olaf Jersild was featured interviewing several "Green Jackets", that is young people who were dressed in "cast off" green military jackets and who made a point of living on the fringes of society. Jersild's interlocutors resided in the slummier areas of Copenhagen, and avoided work. More perniciously, these young people had founded what they referred to as a new Nazi Party.

Editors of *The Sunday Journal* thought it would be of interest to the Danish public to hear the Green Jackets' views concerning foreigners living in Denmark. Jersild was given free reign to broadcast uncensored interviews. For the first time in the history of Danish television, the public was confronted with examples of the worst kind of race hatred. In expressing their views, the Green Jackets employed prurient and racy language.

After the eight-minute broadcast was over, the Bishop of Aalborg apparently filed a complaint with the Danish police against the Green Jackets, the *Journal*'s editor, Lasse Jensen, and Jersild himself. All three parties were subsequently found guilty of violating the provision of the Danish Penal Code on propounding and disseminating offensive and insulting racist language.[2] The Green Jackets and Lasse Jensen did not appeal against the verdict, but Jersild brought his case to the Danish Supreme Court (*Højesteret*).

What came before the Court was a complex problem. On the one hand, section 266 B of the Danish Penal Code had definitely been violated. On the other hand, Article 10 of the European Convention on Human Rights, which also formed a part of Danish Law, guaranteed Jersild's right to freedom of expression. The Supreme Court had to strike a balance between these two rules.

---

*freedom of expression and hate speech*, Copenhagen, The Danish Centre for Human Rights, 1996.

2 Section 266 B of the Penal Code states that: "Any person who, publicly or with the intention of disseminating it to a wide circle of people, makes a statement, or other communication, threatening, insulting or degrading a group of persons on account of their race, colour, national or ethnic origin or belief shall be liable to a fine or to simple detention or to imprisonment for a term not exceeding two years".

The Supreme Court declared that freedom of expression is a fundamental freedom and deserves the strongest possible protection. The great majority of the judges (all but one) found that in this case, freedom of expression had been used by a journalist to publicize totally trivial statements made by persons to whom no one would attach any importance. But these statements had apparently caused offence to thousands of Danish citizens.

After weighing the arguments, the Court decided that it was more important to protect the thousands of citizens than to defend a single journalist. Finally, therefore, Jersild was sentenced to a 1000 DKK fine.[3]

But Jersild did not drop the case and instead summoned the state of Denmark to the European Court of Human Rights in Strasbourg.[4] Denmark lost. Contrary to Denmark's own Supreme Court, the Strasbourg Court found that the right to freedom of speech was more important than the rights of citizens who felt violated by what they considered its excessive use.

I confess that at the time I was astonished by the verdict. My own sense was that, because none of the judges of the European Court of Human Rights had any knowledge of the Danish language and perhaps had never even been to Denmark, they ought to have allowed Denmark to have its way. After all, was the European Court of Human Rights really in a better position to evaluate the effects of a Danish television broadcast on Danish society than the Danish Supreme Court itself?

Later, however, I had an opportunity to discuss the question with one of the judges who had taken part in the case, who came from Eastern Europe.– He explained what had probably been the decisive factors for the Court. From the Court's point of view, he told me, the most important thing at the time was to protect the rights and freedoms granted recently to the newly liberated countries in Eastern Europe. For several decades, journalists living under Communist rule were heavily censured and unable to inform their publics of the many heinous crimes their governments were committing. Nor did the international community have access to the crimes being concealed by these regimes. But for Russian, Polish, Czech and Ukrainian journalists, conditions had recently improved. In those early days, reporters had obtained a level of freedom which was in some regions comparable to those prevailing in the free world. But the situation was still very uncertain. A wrong decision or move here or there, and all the new-found freedoms might fall by the wayside.

For its part, the European Court of Human Rights has remained committed to upholding the position that it took in *Jersild versus Denmark*. It is also important to underscore another aspect of that case: once one understands the Court's argu-

3 For a description of the proceedings before the Danish Courts, see Johannesen, op. cit., pp. 6-9.

4 According to the rules of procedure of the Court, the national judge shall take part in all cases against his own country. At the time of the case I was the Chairman of the Board of Governors of Danish Radio and Television, therefore I had to declare myself not impartial and took no part in the case.

ments, one also grasps how the European Convention on Human Rights evolves in step with the development of society. Human Rights are simply never static.

## 2 The Case of Pedal-Ove

The evolution of the European Court's interpretation of freedom of expression is interesting. From the beginning,[5] the Court maintained that freedom of expression was a fundamental human right that needed to be preserved, even though particular expressions may be hurtful, shocking or provocative. The European Court of Human Rights also made important distinctions between reportage and evaluations, and between facts and values.[6] Further down the line, the Court maintained that protecting freedom of expression is a matter of protecting not only the right to put forward statements of substance, but also the right to express substance in a particular form.[7] In several cases,[8] the Court has accepted that, in order to gain public attention, a journalist may have to employ hyperbole and be provocative. Indeed, when it comes to political talk and debates that are of public interest,[9] there are very few constraints upon freedom of speech. It was not until 1997 that the Court established certain constraints upon freedom of expression. In instances when the Court found that a journalist had made a value judgement without having proper supporting evidence, the Court argued that he or she might not be protected by the principle of freedom of expression. The Court has also held that journalists who insist upon protection of their right to freedom of expression must be prepared to live up to the press's highest ethical codes, which would include, for example, commitment to thorough research practices and to the kind of reporting that is undertaken in good faith rather than in accordance with a hidden agenda of its own.

Constraints upon the right to freedom of expression came to light in the case of two journalists, Pedersen and Baadsgaard, who, while employed by Danish Broadcasting (DR), took legal proceedings against Denmark.[10]

The case concerned "Pedal-Ove", who was found guilty of murdering his wife in 1982 by the High Court of Western Danmark (*Vestre Landsret*). Pedal-Ove received a prison sentence of seven years. Pedersen and Baadsgaard produced two TV programmes shown in 1990 and in 1991, in which they seriously questioned the proof that the Danish court brought against Pedal-Ove. After the first programme, and presumably because of it, Pedal-Ove was declared innocent by the Special

5 *Handyside v. The United Kingdom*, app. no. 5493/72, ECtHR 7 December 1976 and *Sunday Times v. United Kingdom*, app. no. 6538/74, ECtHR 26 April 1979.

6 *Lingens v. Austria*, app. no. 9815/82, ECtHR 8 July 1986.

7 *Oberschlick v. Austria*, app. no. 11662/85, ECtHR 23 May 1991.

8 *Prager and Oberschlick v. Austria*, app. no. 15974/90, ECtHR 26 April 1995 and *Wingrove v. The United Kingdom*, app. no. 17419/90, ECtHR 25 November 1996.

9 See, in Danish, Jens Elo Rytter in *Europæisk Retskultur – på Dansk* (2004) pp. 187,196ff.

10 *Pedersen and Baadsgaard v. Denmark*, app. no. 49017/99, ECtHR 17 December 2004.

Court of revision (*Den Særlige Klageret*) and received a substantial sum in compensation. The second program was called "The Police's Blind Eye" and was broadcast after Pedal-Ove had been set free. In this programme, the Police Commissioner was accused of wilfully suppressing a testimony that, had it appeared before the court, would have made the case for Pedal Ove's innocence. Neither the Court nor the Defence Attorney had been informed by the police of this testimony.

The Police Commissioner, who had found the testimony in question untrustworthy and therefore irrelevant to his case, accused the two journalists of defamation and brought the case to the Danish Supreme Court. The Supreme Court found the journalists guilty. Although the Court emphasised that the journalists had actually been defending the public interest, it argued that it was neither necessary nor fair to make such a coarse personal and unsubstantiated attack on the Police Commissioner.[11]

The journalists brought the case to the European Court of Human Rights in Strasbourg, alleging that, through the judgment of its Supreme Court, Denmark had violated their freedom of expression. Denmark was found not guilty. In passing its judgement in *Pedersen and Baadsgaard versus Denmark*, the European Court of Human Rights emphasised the difference between the present case and the *Jersild* case. In *Jersild versus Denmark*, the Court found that the journalist had done nothing more than report the views of the "Green Jackets". In the case of *Pedersen and Baadsgaard versus Denmark*, the situation was different: their programme did not confine itself to reportage. In fact, except for the two journalists, no one had accused the Police Commissioner of suppressing the witness's testimony. It was the opinion of the journalists alone that the prosecution had committed a serious crime, and it was only because of them that the accusation had been spread throughout the country. The Court further laid down that, although these journalists may have believed that they were acting in the public interest, it still remained incumbent upon them to conform to the profession's highest ethical standards, which, in the Court's view, they had not done.

## 3 The Judicial Revolution

*Jersild versus Denmark* and *Pedersen and Baadsgaard versus Denmark*, like other judgments laid down by the European Court of Human Rights, are examples of the most significant judicial revolution that has taken place over the past four hundred years. What has this revolution consisted of? In order to grasp it, one must first understand that, since the beginning of the seventeenth century, when the system of International Law was first established, a feature of this branch of the law was that it did not regulate relations between a government and its own citizens: these were all internal affairs or what have been called "reserved domains". Without violating international law, any government could treat its citizens as it wished, which is to say, within the limits of the country's national law or constitution. No other country could interfere.

11 Supreme Court's judgment of 28 October 1998.

In 1948, when the United Nations General Assembly adopted the Universal Declaration on Human Rights, a dramatic change occurred. Clearly, this declaration was neither a convention nor a pledge. As an agreement it was non-binding, and its content was rather vague. Nonetheless, this declaration is the most important document in the development of human rights, if only because, for the first time in human history, the human rights of the individual became an international issue.

Certainly human rights have been rather well understood for hundreds of years, for example, in the English Magna Charta of 1219, the French Revolution of 1789, the American Declaration of Independence of 1776 and the Danish Rights and Freedoms set out in the Constitution of 1849. And yet, until the UN declaration, human rights were national rights, rights that any nation could change and abolish at will. Then came the United Nations Universal Declaration, which made it possible for one country to protest against the violation of human rights in another country. It also became possible to judge a country's behaviour towards its own citizens in an international forum. Very soon human rights became regulated through binding international conventions.

For Europe the Universal Declaration had special significance. In connection with the creation of the Council of Europe, in 1950 European states ratified the European Convention on Human Rights. Unlike the UN Declaration, this was a legally binding document. At the same time the European Court of Human Rights was created and was given the power and authority to handle complaints from individuals against their own government. This sort of document had never been seen before in the history of mankind.

As a young teacher of law at the University of Copenhagen, I was delighted that we Europeans were witnessing this extraordinary development within the international system of law. Shortly afterwards, I met my teacher, Professor Max Sørensen, who had been the Danish government's representative during the drawing up of the European Convention on Human Rights. I therefore had an opportunity to congratulate him for having participated in the establishment of a European human rights system. He looked at me for a long time and then responded with amazing patience. "Don't be naïve, Foighel", he said; "this Court will never function. No government will accept being dragged before an international court by its own citizens." Painstakingly, Professor Sørensen explained that the rules had been made so as to allow compromises – friendly settlements – before cases ever came before the Court. There was no talk of jurisprudence here, my teacher said, only of politics. The only reason that governments had agreed to establish this court in the first place had to do with the end of the Second World War and their wish to enhance the importance of the individual now as opposed to the grandeur of the state.

It must be admitted that in the first fifteen years of the Court's existence, Professor Sørensen was proved right: not a single case came before the European Court of Human Rights. However, in 1998, the last year in which I acted as a Judge at the Court, we handed down 700 judgments. By 2005, there were 75,000 cases waiting to be heard. During this time span, the Court expanded to include judges from the central and east European countries. There are now 45 judges at the Court representing 45 member states of the Council of Europe.

## 4 Is the Court a Political Instrument?

In course of time, freedom of expression, as articulated in the cases mentioned above, has been formulated ever more precisely. All these cases are examples of the dynamic interpretation of the European Convention on Human Rights. The European Court of Human Rights interprets each right in accordance with various trends, together with legal and social developments in Europe.

Critics of this trend have insisted that this is home-made law – standard setting – by judges who lack any democratic legitimacy, as they are not elected by the citizens of Europe. These new standards go further, it has been argued, than what the original state parties could have expected from the European Convention on Human Rights when it was ratified in 1950.

This criticism cannot be substantiated. It was the state parties themselves who designed the European Court of Human Rights and gave it the authority to interpret each single article. The fact that this interpretation follows legal trends and developments in European states does not mean that the Court is creating laws according to an agenda of its own. Judges form or recant judgements according to the trends manifested in society. In this way, the Court mirrors political developments, which are constantly changing.

Nevertheless, critics have argued that this dynamic interpretation gives the Court the means to create new rules without respecting national parliaments, whose task it is to change the law if developments make this necessary. This criticism does not recognize that what takes place in the European Court of Human Rights is something else entirely, as illustrated by the following example.

In 1989, in a case brought by a transsexual against the United Kingdom,[12] the European Court of Human Rights decided that a man who had undergone a male to female sex-change operation did not have the right to marry another man or to have a new birth certificate which gave his gender as female. The Court ascertained that in his case there had been no violation of the woman's right to private life. In 2002, in a similar case,[13] the Court established that a transsexual who had undergone a similar operation had the very same rights that had been refused a decade earlier.

What had happened in the meantime? Before deciding on these cases, the European Court of Human Rights investigated carefully judgments and practices in the member states of the Council of Europe. In 1989, there was a wide difference of opinion in these countries concerning the rights of transsexuals. As there was no consensus, it could not be established that the English practice was wrong. In 2002, a similar investigation of member states' legislation and practices showed that, both generally and in their judicial decisions, member states had acquired a

12 *Cossey v. The United Kingdom*, app. no. 10843/84, ECtHR 27 September 1990.

13 *Christine Goodwin v. the United Kingdom*, app. no. 28957/95, ECtHR 11 July 2002.

more liberal understanding of sexual minorities. In other words, there was a new trend in Europe that naturally had to be reflected in the Court's judgments.

This dynamic interpretation is never understood by the judges to mean that they have the liberty to "invent" or create new rules –quite the opposite: The judges are obliged to make the Court's decisions follow judicial developments in Europe generally. As the Court has stated many times, the European Convention of Human Rights is a living instrument that both follows and reflects judicial developments in the member states of the Council of Europe.

In interpreting the national judicial evolution the European Court of Human Rights may be mistaken, but this is not the same as saying that the judges are politicising their judgements.

## 5 Can the Court Limit Human Rights?

When the Court itself admits that its interpretations of the provisions of the European Convention on Human Rights are influenced by domestic legislative and judicial developments, one can also ask whether this holds true if domestic legislation and practice develop in a restrictive or inhumane direction. This is not a theoretical question. In recent years, there has been a more or less general tendency in the growth of racism, hatred of foreigners and anti-Semitism in Europe. At the same time, terrorism has spread throughout European capitals. Governments are therefore sometimes inclined to think that issues of security should take priority over the protection of human rights.

If Europe evolves into a fascist continent in which the individual is worthless, there will of course no longer be a European Convention on Human Rights or a European Court of Human Rights. But such a revolution may come about gradually. In every country, a situation or a condition in a specific area can evolve in such a way that it is incompatible with the principle of respect for the individual. Obvious examples are laws concerning foreigners and measures to combat terrorist activity. It is evident that changes in these areas will influence the Court's decisions because the judges themselves are not unaffected by turbulence in society. Nevertheless, it is essential to emphasise that, even in such areas, the Convention is, of course, still binding. Furthermore, there is good reason to believe that the European culture and ethos of democracy – that is, the normative foundation of the European Convention on Human Rights – will not vanish but will always form the starting point for the Court's interpretations.

Still, recent practice has shown that the Court feels that it has the right to curtail certain rights because of society's evolution, and especially because of the increasing threats of terrorism. This problem, for example, arose in a case concerning the situation in Northern Ireland.[14]

Early one morning the British police in Ireland arrested a Mrs Murray and brought her to the police station for questioning. She was accused of active participation in the IRA, a banned organization. She was held because she had visited

14 *Murray v. The United Kingdom*, app. no. 14310/88, ECtHR 28 October 1994.

her brother in USA, who had been arrested for illegally collecting money for the purchase of munitions and also for smuggling weapons. During the hearing she answered all the questions by giving her name and date of birth. She insisted upon doing this throughout the four hours of interrogation with different interrogators. The police had to release her without being able to press charges against her.

Mrs Murray brought her case against the United Kingdom before the European Court of Human Rights, claiming that her imprisonment was groundless and in conflict with the European Convention on Human Rights, Article 5, which protects individual freedom. The UK government asserted that imprisonment was reasonable because seemingly valid information about her criminal behaviour existed. This evidence could not be shown in Court because it came from an anonymous informer whose identity could not be disclosed for security reasons.

The European Court of Human Rights was in a serious dilemma. On the one hand, it was the Court's accepted jurisprudence that the legality of a detention necessitated at least some objective factors which could indicate a reasonable or probable suspicion.

On the other hand, the detention was related to the fight against terrorism, in which secret informers were relevant tools. To disclose their identity would be fatal.

The Court solved this problem by underlining that in this case the detention, seen as a means of combating terror, had not lasted more than four hours. Such a short period of time could be accepted even by an innocent person, being the price that every citizen must pay in order to be able to live in a society where the authorities' attempts to fight terrorism. However, it is difficult to predict how far the Court will be ready to go in this direction. So far the ugly threat of terrorism has influenced the European Court of Human Rights without compromising human rights. It therefore mirrors the new standards that have evolved in society.

## 6 The Enormous Case Load

An enormous number of cases have for some years been pending before the European Court of Human Rights. The load is growing by some 45,000 new cases each year and is giving cause for concern. The Court is trying to reduce the problem on its own. One method is to pass sentences which intend to be directly applicable to many persons in similar situations. This is something new. In principle the Court normally has direct influence only on a specific case and on those directly involved in it.

This new method was tried for the first time in the case of *Broniowski versus Poland.* This concerns more than 100,000 Poles who were forced to leave Polish territory during the Second World War, when their property was turned over to the Soviet Union. At the time, it was decided that the Polish state should compensate its citizens for the land. In the years after the War, this policy was transformed into laws which were never enforced. Broniowski, who had inherited land that had been taken from him and his family, took his case to the European Court of Human Rights in order to claim restitution.

The European Court of Human Rights concluded that Broniowski's property rights had been violated. At the same time, the Court found that nearly 80,000 individuals were in the same situation and would be able to bring a case before the Court. Before deciding on the amount of compensation that was due to Broniowski, the Court requested that the Polish government take all relevant steps in order to insure that the 80,000 individuals concerned received fair compensation. A compromise was made, and the case was deleted from the Court's docket.[15]

Cases such as this show that, when there are major problems in domestic systems, the European Court of Human Rights system is inadequate. With the Broniowski judgement, the Court has found a means of minimizing the number of cases while still insuring protection for the rights of the persons concerned.

## 7 Minor Cases

The European Court of Human Rights has been criticized for hearing mostly minor cases that in reality are far removed from what are understood as genuine human rights violations. It is true that the Court has been interested in cases that, by Danish standards, for example, are of no major importance or consequence. However, it is a bit lopsided to insist, as has been done, that the Court uses its extensive powers in ignorance to judge a parking case or a refusal to identify oneself to a bus company or to the police. If there are cases in these categories (parking problems or similar petty affairs), the problems actually examined by the Court are much more important. One case concerned the right of the state to punish parking offences with imprisonment without due process of law. Another case concerning a refusal to disclose one's identity to a bus company dealt with the question of whether the state had the right to deprive an individual of his or her personal freedom for the price of a bus ticket. Naturally it is legitimate to insist that these were trivial or banal matters, but the violations of the principles involved were not at all trivial.

In some situations, it is really very difficult to decide how much importance an apparently trivial case may have for the protection of the fundamental rights of a individual.

Some years ago, I was a judge in the case of *Burghartz versus Switzerland.*[16] A Swiss citizen wished to use his wife's maiden surname as a family name. The Swiss authorities refused, and the case was brought before the European Court of Human Rights. The applicant asserted that this was a question of sex discrimination. Since the wife had the right to take his surname, the fact that he did not have the right to take hers involved discrimination.

Spontaneously, before the case was heard, I said to my Hungarian colleague that I thought it was a waste of time for nine judges to make a decision on such a triviality as a case concerning a family name. "Just the opposite", said my colleague; "Names can be very important. In Slovakia, there is a minority of 800,000 people of Hungarian extraction. Slovakia has decided that these people

15 *Broniowski v. Poland*, app. no. 31443/96, ECtHR 28 September 2005.

16 *Burghartz v. Switzerland*, app. no. 16213/90, ECtHR 22 Februar 1994.

shall not marry unless they have a Slovakian name. In other words, the Slovakian government controls the use of names to discriminate against these people by taking their national identity and violating their freedoms." He further drew my attention to the fact that in Central Europe Jewish populations had been ridiculed and made fun of for years by giving them animal names such as Hirsch, Fuchs, Vogel (Foighel) or Fisch. The poorest and most wretched of them had been given names such as Gold, Silver, Bernstein, Einstein, Diamant, etc.

A peculiar example of this (mis)use of names to ridicule a particular group of people is found in the history of Copenhagen. When in 1833 the Jewish community wanted to build a synagogue, the City of Copenhagen gave them a piece of land in a street called "Garbage Street" (*Skidenstræde*). After the synagogue had been built, the representatives of the Jewish community complained about the street name, which the city authorities then changed to "Crystal Street" (*Krystalgade*)!

As these examples show, laws governing names are not always harmless. In the case of *Burghartz*, the Court ruled in favour of the applicant and thus countermanded the state's right to allocate names. The Court undoubtly did Europe a service. Violations of people's personal integrity and self-esteem can have many aspects.

## 8 Communist Versus Western European Law

Investigating more closely the statistics concerning the case load of the European Court of Human Rights, one finds that more than half the cases come from Central and East European countries, above all from Russia.

This is partly because dictatorships in these countries looked down on their own people for more than sixty to eighty years in a manner which is far from the respect for the individual traditionally found in Western Europe. In the former communist regimes, the individual simply did not count. The average citizen had few or no rights, and from an administrative point of view he was next to worthless. All the powers of the state were vested in the Party, and there was no rule of law in the democratic sense. According to the usual socialist ideology, the Administration was an arm of the Party, and Party decisions could not be controlled, judged or circumvented by the courts. Perhaps the communist regime culture lives on to some extent in Russia and elsewhere because complaints against the use of force, failure to give permission and the misuse of free judgements are still not always handled satisfactorily. Such cases are now being brought in great numbers before the European Court of Human Rights, which represents the individual's only chance to be heard and to have his case judged by a neutral body.

Some years ago, for example, a brother and his sister inherited a house in which the brother lived on the first floor while his sister had an apartment on the second floor. The brother denied his sister access to his floor where the electrical fuses were located. This had the effect that she had to live without electricity for several months. The police refused to assist her, and she could not bring this administrative rejection before a court of law. Eventually she brought the case to the European Court of Human Rights instead.

It is obvious that there are thousands of such cases. This was not envisaged in the European Convention on Human Rights, and it has given the Court a somewhat poor reputation as a Court for small, supposedly insignificant cases. However, the problem is diminishing and is slowly being solved.

## 9 The Court and the National Legislator

When the judgments of the European Court of Human Rights come under pressure, as often happens when a state is found guilty of violating the Convention on Human Rights, it is often claimed that the Court's dynamic interpretation is preventing national politicians from taking a political position on questions which really are political. However, this is not the case.

The Court does not advise on how the law of a particular member state should evolve. In cases where a country's legislation or administration is judged by the Court to be against the European Convention on Human Rights, the problem that is thereby revealed can only be resolved by the national legislative body concerned.

The case against Denmark for delaying the payment of damages to haemophiliacs is a case in point.[17] Some Danish haemophiliacs received contaminated blood some years ago and opened a case in the Danish High Court to obtain compensation. The case lasted for seven years! Subsequently, the European Court of Human Rights judged that duration of seven years was not reasonable. This judgment then had to be implemented by the Danish legislature, whose reaction was praiseworthy in that it secured a more effective Danish administration of justice. In this respect, though, the last word still belonged to the national legislature.

It is true that the European Convention on Human Rights curtails democratic governments' and parliaments' competences and thus limits the power of these organs to make rules which reflect, in all circumstances, the internal political situation. However, it is generally accepted that every international treaty curtails a nation's freedom of action. When it is claimed that the European Court of Human Rights should not decide questions that are within the remit of elected parliaments, this shows that the European Human Rights system has not been understood. It is precisely the curtailment of a government's or political majority's ability to treat a person at will and possibly in violation of human rights which is the real purpose of human rights law, its *raison d'être*. This cannot be a threat to democratic society, only of assistance.

## 10 More than Fifty Years

Trying to evaluate the effects of the European Convention on Human Rights over more than the past fifty years, I must admit that it has influenced some areas and not others. The world has become more insecure and is fearful of terrorism and other disturbances. But when one looks at freedom of expression, one can be satisfied that more than 400 million people during this time have had obtained freedoms

17 *A. and others v. Denmark*, app. no. 20826/92, ECtHR 8 February 1996.

they did not have before. And when we look too at the many other discussions that have taken place, we find that human rights as they are practised today are playing an increasing role in the international discourse. There is little doubt that countries today are often judged according to their position in observing human rights.

One function of the Danish Institute for Human Rights is to promote human rights. Every year, the Institute invites ninety Chinese jurists to visit Denmark to observe how a small democracy has organized its judicial system. In October 2002, I had the opportunity to tell a group of Chinese prosecutors about a dramatic situation that had taken place just a week before in Copenhagen. A famous politician from Chechnia, called Sakajev, had come to Denmark to participate in a privately arranged conference. The government of Russia quickly heard about it and insisted that the Danish government extradite Sakajev to Russia to be tried for terrorism in Chechnia.

It was a complex situation. At the time Denmark held the Chair of the European Union, and, in this role, had to conduct complicated and vital negotiations with Russia concerning the enclave of Kaliningrad. In this connection, the then newly elected President of Russia, Vladimir Putin, had been invited to Copenhagen for discussions with the Danish Prime Minister, and also to have dinner with Her Majesty the Queen. After investigating the Russian political charges against Sakajev, the Danish government announced that it could not deliver him to Russia. Putin at once cancelled his visit to Copenhagen, after which the vital negotiations, which were Denmark's responsibility, had little chance of success.

I asked the Chinese jurists if they thought Denmark had handled the situation correctly. One of the female prosecutors ventured to say, "I do not know all the details so I cannot judge the specific case. But from what you have told us, I wish to express my astonishment and admiration that a little country is ready to risk so much because of its respect for human rights". Her very moving response said a great deal about Denmark, but also about the Chinese society from which she came.

The Idea of Human Rights must continue to be ready to conquer new areas.

## About the Contributors

**John P. Cerone** is professor and director of the Center for International Law & Policy at the New England School of Law, where he teaches Public International Law, Human Rights Law, International Criminal Law, and related courses. Prior to joining the New England faculty in 2004, he was Executive Director of the War Crimes Research Office at American University Washington College of Law, where he served as a legal adviser to various international criminal courts and tribunals. As a practicing international lawyer, he has worked for a number of different inter-governmental and non-governmental organizations, including the United Nations, the Organization for Security and Cooperation in Europe, the International Secretariat of Amnesty International, and the International Crisis Group, under the auspices of which he has had extensive field experience in conflict and post-conflict environments, such as Afghanistan, Kosovo, Sierra Leone, and East Timor. He has also been awarded research fellowships to pursue his scholarly activities at the Max Planck Institute for Comparative Public Law and International Law and the Danish Institute for Human Rights.
jcerone@faculty.nesl.edu

**Eva Ersbøll** is researcher at the Danish Institute for Human Rights. She is a lawyer and formerly a legal assistant to the Danish Parliamentary Ombudsman and an analyst to the Commissioner of the Council of the Baltic Sea States on Democratic Institutions and Human Rights, inclusive the Rights of Persons belonging to Minorities. Eva Ersbøll has published on a number of topics, including human rights of persons suffering from senile dementia, non-discrimination and nationality. Her current main research focuses on Danish nationality law and nationality law in Europe.
eer@humanrights.dk

**Isi Foighel**, professor, dr.jur. (University of Copenhagen), former judge at the European Court of Human Rights. Senior Researcher at the Danish Institute of Human Rights. Has been Visiting Professor at Harvard, Berkeley and Tel-Aviv universities. Has lectured on Human Rights in the Baltic States, China, Ukraine, Georgia, Armenia and Uganda etc. Books and articles on International Law, Taxation Law and Human Rights.
ifo@humanrights.dk

**Peter Vedel Kessing**, Ph.D. Candidate, Faculty of Law, Copenhagen University and the Danish Institute for Human Rights. Working on a project on terrorism and human rights with a specific focus on the right to freedom for torture and arbitrary detention. The project is analyzing the contemporary challenges to the international prohibition against torture in times of peace and in times of armed conflict. Peter Vedel Kessing has been working with international cooperation on prevention of torture and other forms of ill-treatment for several years and has been publishing articles on torture and the relationship with counter-terrorism measures.
Peter.Vedel.Kessing@Jur.ku.dk; pvk@humanrights.dk.

**Morten Kjærum**, Master of Law; Executive Director, the Danish Institute for Human Rights (DIHR) and Co-director, the Danish Centre for International Studies and Human
Rights; President of the International Coordination Committee for National Human Rights Institutions. Since 2002: Member of the UN Committee on the Elimination of Racial Discrimination (CERD). From 1986 till today, Morten Kjærum has written more than 50 titles on issues related to a number of human rights issues and in particular refugee law and the prohibition against racial discrimination.
mok@humanrights.dk.

**Stéphanie Lagoutte**, Doctor in Law from the University of Paris I, Panthéon-Sorbonne and Ph.D. from University of Aarhus, Denmark is a Legal Researcher at the Danish Institute for Human Rights, Copenhagen, Denmark. Stéphanie Lagoutte has been publishing articles about the right to respect for family life, the reform of the European Court of Human Rights, freedom of religion, and fair trial. She is the editor of a report on the response to Protocol 12 in the Nordic countries. She is currently working on a research project concerning the proceduralisation of the jurisprudence of the European Court of Human Rights. Her fields of interest and teaching are i.a. International and regional protection of human rights, European Court of Human Rights, freedom of religion, right to respect for family life, family law, and foreigners law.
sla@humanrights.dk

**Èva Maria Lassen** holds a Ph.D. in history and is a Senior Research Fellow at the Danish Institute for Human Rights. Previous positions include fellowships at Lucy Cavendish College and Gonville and Caius College, University of Cambridge. Her research interests include the history of human rights; the relationship between modern human rights and religious traditions; the Holocaust and the emergence of international human rights law; Jewish contributions to the development of international human rights law; Christian values and human rights; women's rights and religious traditions; religious freedom and Islam. She has written extensively on these subjects. She is E.MA Director, the European Master's Degree in Human Rights and Democratisation, and a member of the Executive Committee of the Master's Programme. She is a member of several national and international com-

mittees, amongst them the ODIHR Panel of Experts on Freedom of Religion or Belief (OSCE).
eva@humanrights.dk.

**Helle Malmvig** is a Senior Research Fellow at the Danish Institute for International Studies (since 2003). She holds a Ph.D. in International Relation from University of Copenhagen, an MSc in Political Science from University of Copenhagen, and an MSc with distinction in International Relations of the Middle East, SOAS, University of London. She has published on a number of topics, including state sovereignty and humanitarian interventions, the concept of the state in International Relations, and Western foreign and security policies in the Middle East. Her new book on state sovereignty and intervention is published by Routledge "New International Relations Series" in 2006.
hma@diis.dk

**Hans-Otto Sano**, Ph..D. Economic history, MA history with a specialization in development studies. Research Director at the Danish Institute for Human Rights since 2002. Hans-Otto Sano is an expert on human rights and development. He has coordinated a joint Nordic research project on good governance and has written several articles on these subjects. His current research focuses on three topics: rights-based development, global governance, and human rights indicators. Action research is conducted in cooperation with DanChurchAid on the value added and constraints of rights-based approaches, research on human rights indicators is undertaken as part of a cooperation with the World Bank. The article of the book is part of the author's project on global governance which also comprises research on human rights in foreign policy.
hos@humanrights.dk

**Peter Scharff Smith**, Ph.D. in History, MA in Social sciences and History. Peter began his research project on the history and effects of solitary confinement in 2003 as a Visiting Fellow at the University of Cambridge. He is currently a Senior Researcher at the Danish Institute for Human Rights. Peter Scharff Smith has published numerous books and articles on prisons, prison history and human rights, as well as historical works on fascism, communism and the Nazi war of extermination at the Eastern front during WWII. He is also a regular contributor to the public debate on prisons, penal issues and human rights. His most recent work deals with diverse subjects such as solitary confinement, children of imprisoned parents, detention and interrogation practices in the war on terror, and inmate treatment and rehabilitation programs in prisons.
pss@humanrights.dk

**Sten Schaumburg-Müller**, Ph.D. and Candidate in law, Bachelor in philosophy, has been working as private lawyer in Denmark and for two years as legal advisor to a Zambian women's rights organization. He is presently attached to the Department of Jurisprudence at Aarhus University with teaching and research in mass media law, general jurisprudence and international legal issues including human rights, law and development, and the relationship between local law and human rights. For 5 years a board member of Danish Association for International Cooperation (Mellemfolkeligt Samvirke) and presently a board member of the Danish Institute of Human Rights. ssm@jura.au.dk

**Hatla Thelle**, Ph.D in history, MA in Chinese Studies, is a senior researcher at the Danish Institute for Human Rights since 1997. Hatla Thelle has done research on social security reform in China and social policy in Asia and published articles on implementation of human rights in different social and cultural settings. She is a programme manager of the China programmes at the Danish Institute of Human Rights dealing especially with human rights and social and criminal justice in China. Her current research project deals with establishment of a legal aid system in China in collaboration with Nordic scholars working on implementation of law at the local level.
hth@humanrights.dk

# Index

# International Studies in Human Rights

1. Bertrand G. Ramcharan: *Humanitarian Good Offices in International Law*. The Good Offices of the United Nations Secretary General in the Field of Human Rights. 1983 ISBN 90-247-2805-3
2. Bertrand G. Ramcharan: *International Law and Fact-Finding in the Field of Human Rights*. 1983 ISBN 90-247-3042-2
3. Bertrand G. Ramcharan: *The Right to Life in International Law*. 1985 ISBN 90-247-3074-0
4. Katarina Tomaševski and Philip Alston: *Right to Food*. 1984 ISBN 90-247-3087-2
5. Arie Bloed, Pieter van Dijk: *Essays on Human Rights in the Helsinki Process*. 1985 ISBN 90-247-3211-5
6. K. Tornudd: *Finland and the International Norms of Human Rights*. 1986 ISBN 90-247-3257-3
7. Berth Verstappen and Hans Thoolen: *Human Rights Missions. A Study of the Fact-Finding Practice of Non-Governmental Organizations*. 1986 ISBN 90-247-3364-2
8. Hurst Hannum: *The Right to Leave and Return in International Law and Practice*. 1987 ISBN 90-247-3445-2
9. H. Danelius and Herman Burgers: The United Nations Convention Against Torture. *A Handbook on the Convention Against Torture and Other Cruel, Inhuman or Degrading Treatment or Punishment*. 1988 ISBN 90-247-3609-9
10. David A. Martin: *The New Asylum Seekers: Refugee Law in the 1980's*. The Ninth Sokol Colloquium on International Law. 1988 ISBN 90-247-3730-3
11. Cecilia Medina: *The Battle of Human Rights. Gross, Systematic Violations and the Inter-American System*. 1988 ISBN 90-247-3687-0
12. Claus Gulmann, Lars Adam Rehof: *Human Rights in Domestic Law and Development*. Assistance Policies of the Nordic Countries. 1989 ISBN 90-247-3743-5
13. Bertrand G. Ramcharan: *The Concept and Present Status of the International Protection of Human Rights. Forty Years After the Universal Declaration*. 1989 ISBN 90-247-3759-1
14. Angela D. Byre: *International Human Rights Law in the Commonwealth Caribbean*. 1991 ISBN 90-247-3785-0
15. Natan Lerner: *Group Rights and Discrimination in International Law*. 1990 ISBN 0-79230-853-0
16. Shimon Shetreet: *Free Speech and National Security*. 1991 ISBN 0-79231-030-6
17. Geoff Gilbert: *Aspects of Extradition Law*. 1991 ISBN 0-79231-162-0

18. Philip E. Veerman: *The Rights of the Child and the Changing Image of Childhood.* 1992 ISBN 0-79231-250-3
19. Mireille Delmas-Marty: *The European Convention for the Protection of Human Rights.* International Protection versus National Restrictions. 1992 ISBN 0-79231-283-X
20. Arie Bloed and Pieter van Dijk: *The Human Dimension of the Helsinki Process.* The Vienna Follow-up Meeting and its Aftermath. 1991 ISBN 0-79231-337-2
21. Lyal S. Sunga: *Individual Responsibility in International Law for Serious Human Rights Violations.* 1992 ISBN 0-79231-453-0
22. Dinah Shelton and Stanislaw J. Frankowski: *Preventive Detention.* A Comparative and International Law Perspective. 1992 ISBN 0-79231-465-4
23. Michael Freeman and Philip E. Veerman: *Ideologies of Children's Rights.* 1992 ISBN 0-79231-800-5
24. Stephanos Stavros: *The Guarantees for Accused Persons Under Article 6 of the European Convention on Human Rights.* An Analysis of the Application of the Convention and a Comparison with Other Instruments. 1993 ISBN 0-79231-897-8
25. Allan Rosas, Diane Goodman and Jan Helgesen: *Strength of Diversity.* Human Rights and Pluralist Democracy. 1992 ISBN 0-79231-987-7
26. Andrew Clapham and Kees Waaldijk: *Homosexuality: A European Community Issue.* Essays on Lesbian and Gay Rights in European Law and Policy. 1993 ISBN 0-79232-038-7
28. Howard Charles Yourow: *The Margin of Appreciation Doctrine in the Dynamics of European Human Rights Jurisprudence.* 1995 ISBN 0-79233-338-1
29. Lars Adam Rehof: *Guide to the Travaux Préparatoires of the United Nations Convention on the Elimination of all Forms of Discrimination against Women.* 1993. ISBN 0-79232-222-3
30. Allan Rosas, Arie Bloed, Liselotte Leicht and Manfred Nowak: *Monitoring Human Rights in Europe.* Comparing International Procedures and Mechanisms. 1993 ISBN 0-79232-383-1
31. Andrew Harding and John Hatchard: *Preventive Detention and Security Law: A Comparative Survey.* 1993 ISBN 0-79232-432-3
32. Yves Beigbeder: *International Monitoring of Plebiscites, Referenda and National Elections.* Self-Determination and Transition to Democracy. 1994 ISBN 0-79232-563-X
33. Thomas David Jones: *Human Rights: Group Defamation, Freedom of Expression and the Law of Nations.* 1997 ISBN 90-411-0265-5
34. David M. Beatty: *Human Rights and Judicial Review: A Comparative Perspective.* 1994 ISBN 0-79232-968-6
35. Geraldine Van Bueren: *The International Law on the Rights of the Child.* 1995 ISBN 0-79232-687-3
36. Tom Zwart: *The Admissibility of Human Rights Petitions.* The Case Law of the European Commission of Human Rights and the Human Rights Committee. 1994 ISBN 0-79233-146-X
37. Helene Lambert: Seeking Asylum. Comparative Law and Practice in Selected European Countries. 1995 ISBN 0-79233-152-4
38. E. Lijnzaad: *Reservations to UN-Human Rights Treaties.* Ratify and Ruin? 1994 ISBN 0-7923-3256-3

39. L.G. Loucaides: *Essays on the Developing Law of Human Rights*. 1995 ISBN 0-7923-3276-8
40. T. Degener and Y. Koster-Dreese (eds.): *Human Rights and Disabled Persons*. Essays and Relevant Human Rights Instruments. 1995 ISBN 0-7923-3298-9
41. J.-M. Henckaerts: *Mass Expulsion in Modern International Union and Human Rights*. 1995 ISBN 90-411-0072-5
42. N.A. Neuwahl and A. Rosas (eds.): *The European Union and Human Rights*. 1995 ISBN 90-411-0124-1
43. H. Hey: *Gross Human Rights Violations: A Search for Causes*. A Study of Guatemala and Costa Rica. 1995 ISBN 90-411-0146-2
44. B.G. Tahzib: *Freedom of Religion or Belief*. Ensuring Effective International Legal Protection. 1996 ISBN 90-411-0159-4
45. F. de Varennes: *Language, Minorities and Human Rights*. 1996 ISBN 90-411-0206-X
46. J. Raikka (ed.): *Do We Need Minority Rights?* Conceptual Issues. 1996 ISBN 90-411-0309-0
47. J. Brohmer: *State Immunity and the Violation of Human Rights*. 1997 ISBN 90-411-0322-8
48. C.A. Gearty (ed.): *European Civil Liberties and the European Convention on Human Rights*. A Comparative Study. 1997 ISBN 90-411-0253-1
49. B. Conforti and F. Francioni (eds.): *Enforcing International Human Rights in Domestic Courts*. 1997 ISBN 90-411-0393-7
50. A. Spiliopoulou Akermark: *Justifications of Minority Protection in International Law*. 1997 ISBN 90-411-0424-0
51. A. Boulesbaa: *The U.N. Convention on Torture and the Prospects for Enforcement*. 1997 ISBN 90-411-0457-7
52. S. Bowen (ed.): *Human Rights, Self-Determination and Political Change in the Occupied Palestinian Territories*. 1997 ISBN 90-411-0502-6
53. M. O'Flaherty and G. Gisvold (eds.): *Post-War Protection of Human Rights in Bosnia and Herzegovina*. 1998 ISBN 90-411-1020-8
54. A.-L. Svensson-McCarthy: *The International Law of Human Rights and States of Exception*. With Special Reference to the *Travaux Préparatoires* and the Case-Law of the International Monitoring Organs. 1998 ISBN 90-411-1021-6
55. G. Gilbert: *Transnational Fugitive Offenders in International Law*. Extradition and Other Mechanisms. 1998 ISBN 90-411-1040-2
56. M. Jones and L.A. Basser Marks (eds.): *Disability, Divers-ability and Legal Change*. 1998 ISBN 90-411-1086-0
57. T. Barkhuysen, M.L. van Emmerik and RH.P.H.M.C. van Kempen (eds.): *The Execution of Strasbourg and Geneva Human Rights Decisions in the National Legal Order*. 1999 ISBN 90-411-1152-2
58. S. Coliver, P. Hoffman, J. Fitzpatrick and S. Bowen (eds.): *Secrecy and Liberty: National Security, Freedom of Expression and Access to Information*. 1999 ISBN 90-411-1191-3
59. W.S. Heinz and H. Fruhling: *Determinants of Gross Human Rights Violations by State and State-Sponsored Actors in Brazil, Uruguay, Chile, and Argentina*. 1960-1990. 1999 ISBN 90-411-1202-2
60. M. Kirilova Eriksson: *Reproductive Freedom*. In the Context of International Human Rights and Humanitarian Law. 1999 ISBN 90-411-1249-9

61. M.B. Eryilmaz: *Arrest and Detention Powers in English and Turkish Law and Practice in the Light of the European Convention on Human Rights.* 1999 ISBN 90-411-1269-3
62. K. Henrard: *Devising and Adequate System of Minority Protection.* Individual Human Rights, Minority Rights and the Right to Self-Determination. 2000 ISBN 90-411-1359-2
63. K. Tomasevski: *Responding to Human Rights Violations.* 1946-1999. 2000 ISBN 90-411-1368-1
64. L.-V.N. Tran: *Human Rights and Federalism.* A Comparative Study on Freedom, Democracy and Cultural Diversity. 2000 ISBN 90-411-1492-0
65. C. Tiburcio: *The Human Rights of Aliens under International and Comparative Law.* 2001 ISBN 90-411-1550-1
66. E. Brems: *Human Rights: Universality and Diversity.* 2001 ISBN 90-411-1618-4
67. C. Bourloyannis-Vrailas and L.-A. Sicilianos: *The Prevention of Human Rights Violations.* 2001 ISBN 90-411-1672-9
68. G. Ulrich and K. Hastrup: *Discrimination and Toleration.* New Perspectives. 2001 ISBN 90-411-1711-3
69. V.O. Orlu Nmehielle: *African Human Rights System.* Its Laws, Practice and Institutions. 2001 ISBN 90-411-1731-8
70. B.G. Ramcharan: Human Rights and Human Security. 2002 ISBN 90-411-818-7
71. B.G. Ramcharan: The United Nations High Commissioner for Human Rights. The Challenges of International Protection. 2002 ISBN 90-411-1832-2
72. C. Breen: *The Standard of the Best Interests of the Child.* A Western Tradition in International and Comparative Law. 2002 ISBN 90-411-1851-9
73. M. Katayanagi: *Human Rights Functions of United Nations Peacekeeping Operations.* 2002 ISBN 90-411-1910-8
74. O.M. Arnadottir: *Equality and Non-Discrimination under the European Convention on Human Rights.* 2002 ISBN 90-411-1912-4
75. B.G. Ramcharan: *The Security Council and the Protection of Human Rights.* 2002 ISBN 90-411-1878-0
76. E. Fierro: *The EU's Approach to Human Rights Conditionality in Practice.* 2002 ISBN 90-411-1936-1
77. Natan Lerner: *Group Rights and Discrimination in International Law.* Second Edition. 2002 ISBN 90-411-1982-5
78. S. Leckie (ed.): *National Perspectives on Housing Rights.* 2003 ISBN 90-411-2013-0
79. L.C. Reif: *The Ombudsman, Good Governance and the International Human Rights System.* 2004 ISBN 90-04-13903-6
80. Mary Dowell-Jones: *Contextualising the International Covenant on Economic, Social and Cultural Rights: Assessing the Economic Deficit.* 2004 ISBN 90-04-13908-7
81 Li-ann Thio: *Managing Babel: The International Legal Protection of Minorities in the Twentieth Century.* 2005 ISBN 90-04-14198-7
82. Klaus Dieter Beiter: *The Protection of the Right to Education by International Law: Including a Systematic Analysis of Article 13 of the International Covenant on Economic, Social and Cultural Rights.* 2005 ISBN 90-04-14704-7
83. Janneke Gerards: *Judicial Review in Equal Treatment Cases.* 2005 ISBN 90-04-14379-3

84. Virginia A. Leary and Daniel Warner (eds.): *Social Issues, Globalisation and International Institutions: Labour Rights and the EU, ILO, OECD and WTO.* 2006
ISBN-90-04-14579-6

85. J.K.M. Gevers, E.H. Hondius and J.H. Hubben (eds.) *Health Law, Human Rights and the Biomedicine Convention: Essays in Honour of Henriette Roscam Abbing*, 2005
ISBN 90 04 14822 1

86. Claire Breen, *Age Discrimination and Children's Rights*, 2005 ISBN 90 04 14827 2

87. B.G.Ramcharan, *Human Rights Protection in the Field*, 2005 ISBN 90 04 14847 7

88. Geoff Gilbert, *Responding to International Crime*, Second Edition, 2006
ISBN 90 04 15276 8

89. Tom Obokata, *Trafficking of Human Beings from a Human Rights Perspective: Towards a Holistic Approach*, 2006 ISBN 90 04 15405 1

90. Peter Bartlett, Oliver Lewis and Oliver Thorold, Mental Disability and the European Convention on Human Rights, 2006, ISBN 90 04 15423 X

91. Ronald Craig, Systemic Discrimination in Employment and Ethnic Equality, 2006,
ISBN 90 04 15462 0

92. Stéphanie Lagoutte, Hans-Otto Sano and Peter Scharff Smith (eds.), *Human Rights in Turmoil*, 2007 ISBN 90 04 15432 9

This series is designed to shed light on current legal and political aspects of process and organization in the field of human rights

MARTINUS NIJHOFF PUBLISHERS – LEIDEN • BOSTON